The Digital Twin Handbook

Other related titles:

You may also like

- PBTE109 | Ahmadi | Digital Twins for 6G: Fundamental theory, technology and applications | 2024
- PBHE046 | Dhanaraj | Digital Twin Technologies for Healthcare 4.0 | 2022
- PBCE132 | Leong | Human–Machine Collaboration and Interaction for Smart Manufacturing | 2022
- PBPC057 | Alazab | AIoT Technologies and Applications for Smart Environments | 2022
- PBCE096 | Zeadally | Cyber-Physical System Design with Sensor Networking Technologies | 2016

We also publish a wide range of books on the following topics:
Computing and Networks
Control, Robotics and Sensors
Electrical Regulations
Electromagnetics and Radar
Energy Engineering
Healthcare Technologies
History and Management of Technology
IET Codes and Guidance
Materials, Circuits and Devices
Model Forms
Nanomaterials and Nanotechnologies
Optics, Photonics and Lasers
Production, Design and Manufacturing
Security
Telecommunications
Transportation

All books are available in print via https://shop.theiet.org or as eBooks via our Digital Library https://digital-library.theiet.org.

IET Computing 071

The Digital Twin Handbook

Challenges, opportunities and future research directions

Edited by
Dhaval Thakker, Zeeshan Pervez and
Bhupesh Kumar Mishra

The Institution of Engineering and Technology

About the IET

This book is published by the Institution of Engineering and Technology (The IET).

We inspire, inform and influence the global engineering community to engineer a better world. As a diverse home across engineering and technology, we share knowledge that helps make better sense of the world, to accelerate innovation and solve the global challenges that matter.

The IET is a not-for-profit organisation. The surplus we make from our books is used to support activities and products for the engineering community and promote the positive role of science, engineering and technology in the world. This includes education resources and outreach, scholarships and awards, events and courses, publications, professional development and mentoring, and advocacy to governments.

To discover more about the IET please visit https://www.theiet.org/.

About IET books

The IET publishes books across many engineering and technology disciplines. Our authors and editors offer fresh perspectives from universities and industry. Within our subject areas, we have several book series steered by editorial boards made up of leading subject experts.

We peer review each book at the proposal stage to ensure the quality and relevance of our publications.

Get involved

If you are interested in becoming an author, editor, series advisor, or peer reviewer please visit https://www.theiet.org/publishing/publishing-with-iet-books/ or contact author_support@theiet.org.

Discovering our electronic content

All of our books are available online via the IET's Digital Library. Our Digital Library is the home of technical documents, eBooks, conference publications, real-life case studies and journal articles. To find out more, please visit https://digital-library.theiet.org.

In collaboration with the United Nations and the International Publishers Association, the IET is a Signatory member of the SDG Publishers Compact. The Compact aims to accelerate progress to achieve the Sustainable Development Goals (SDGs) by 2030. Signatories aspire to develop sustainable practices and act as champions of the SDGs during the Decade of Action (2020–30), publishing books and journals that will help inform, develop, and inspire action in that direction.

In line with our sustainable goals, our UK printing partner has FSC accreditation, which is reducing our environmental impact to the planet. We use a print-on-demand model to further reduce our carbon footprint.

Published by The Institution of Engineering and Technology, London, United Kingdom

The Institution of Engineering and Technology (the "**Publisher**") is registered as a Charity in England & Wales (no. 211014) and Scotland (no. SC038698).

First published: 2025

The Institution of Engineering and Technology
Futures Place,
Kings Way,
Stevenage Herts,
SG1 2UA,
United Kingdom

www.theiet.org

British Library Cataloguing in Publication Data

A catalogue record for this product is available from the British Library

ISBN 978-1-83953-898-8 (hardback)

ISBN 978-1-83953-899-5 (PDF)

Typeset in India by MPS Limited

Cover image credit: lupengyu/Moment via Getty Images

Contents

Preface **xiii**
About the editors **xv**

1 Understanding digital twins as a digital counterpart of physical systems **1**
Bhupesh Kumar Mishra, Dhaval Thakker and Zeehan Pervez
1.1 Introduction 2
1.1.1 Historical journey of digital twins 2
1.1.2 Digit twins: taxonomy 3
1.1.3 Characteristics of digital twin 7
1.2 Who, why and when should use digital twins 8
1.3 How should we define digital twin model 11
1.4 Challenges of digital twin and future scope 13
References 14

2 Towards a maturity model for digital twins **23**
Alexander Rossmann and Yusuf Bozkurt
2.1 Introduction 23
2.2 Theoretical foundation 25
2.2.1 Digital twins 25
2.2.2 Maturity models 32
2.2.3 Digital twins and maturity 35
2.3 Maturity model 41
2.4 Measurement model 47
2.5 Discussion 53
References 55

3 Digital twins: towards future smartness **61**
Rajan Kadel, Krishna Paudel, Ramesh Shrestha and Samar Shailendra
3.1 Introduction 61
3.2 Digital twins: enablers 64
3.2.1 Data collection 64
3.2.2 Data processing 68
3.2.3 Data presentation 72
3.3 Security by design, not as overlay 77

3.4 Sustainability, innovation and lifestyle 79
3.4.1 Sustainability 79
3.4.2 Innovation 80
3.4.3 Lifestyle 80
3.5 Towards future smartness 81
References 82

4 Digital twins for citizen engagement 91
Andrew S. Wilson and Adrian Walker
4.1 Introduction 91
4.2 SCORE—the foundations for virtual Bradford 92
4.3 Data-driven decision-making: Bradford's digital strategy 95
4.4 Approaches to citizen engagement 97
4.4.1 Government-backed initiatives 97
4.4.2 Humanities-led place-based research and the UN Sustainable Development Goals 99
4.4.3 Social and health-based contexts 102
4.5 Conclusion 102
References 103

5 Digital twins and smart cities solutions 107
Asad Khattak, Muhammad Ali Raza, Hayat Ullah, Naila Tabassum and Muhammad Zubair Asghar
5.1 Introduction 107
5.2 Smart cities features based on digital twins 108
5.2.1 Feedback-driven urban planning 108
5.2.2 Dynamic resource optimization 109
5.2.3 Resilience and risk management 109
5.2.4 Citizen-centric services 110
5.3 Digital twin applications in smart cities 110
5.3.1 Smart cities management brain 110
5.3.2 Transportation and traffic management 112
5.3.3 Public epidemic services in smart cities 115
5.3.4 Flood monitoring and emergency response services 117
5.3.5 Efficient energy management and longevity 118
5.3.6 Intelligent infrastructure and asset maintenance 120
5.4 Challenges and opportunities 121
5.4.1 Concerns about data security and privacy 121
5.4.2 Integration of a variety of systems and technologies 122
5.4.3 Intelligent infrastructure and asset maintenance 122
5.5 Prospects for the future and emerging trends in digital twins and smart cities 123
5.5.1 Digital twin technology in urban management and planning 123
5.6 Conclusion 124
5.6.1 Technology limitations 124

5.6.2 The future of technology with recent advances 125
References 125

6 Blockchain for digital twins to empower smart city 129
Ravi Chandra Koirala, Sujan Sharma, Santiago Matalonga and Keshav Dahal
6.1 Introduction 130
6.1.1 Smart city and the global urbanisation trend 130
6.1.2 The role of digital twins in creating people-centred smart city 131
6.1.3 The potential of digital twin technologies in smart city development 131
6.1.4 The enhancing impact of blockchain in empowering smart city 132
6.1.5 Objectives and scope of this chapter 133
6.2 Digital twins and smart city 133
6.2.1 Understanding the concept of digital twin 133
6.2.2 Virtual simulations and result prediction 134
6.2.3 Situational control and the connected metaverse 135
6.2.4 The role of DT in smart city development 135
6.3 Blockchain technology for smart city 137
6.3.1 Overview of blockchain technology 137
6.3.2 Enhanced traceability and transparency in smart city 137
6.3.3 Improved connectivity and efficient service management 138
6.3.4 Establishing a foundation for secure and efficient smart city operations 138
6.4 Integrating blockchain and DT in smart city development 139
6.4.1 Blockchain-enabled trust in digital twin smart city applications 139
6.4.2 The potential benefits of combining blockchain and DT 140
6.4.3 Challenges and considerations in implementation 141
6.5 Characteristics and technologies of a blockchain-enabled digital twin city 142
6.5.1 The key characteristics of a blockchain-enabled smart city 142
6.5.2 Technological infrastructure for a DT city 144
6.5.3 Real-world application scenarios 145
6.6 Case studies and examples 147
6.6.1 Successful implementation of blockchain and DT in smart city 148
6.6.2 Lessons learned from real-world deployments 155
6.6.3 Potential for scaling and expanding the model 156
6.7 Proposing a new model 157
6.7.1 Layers of the proposed model 157
6.7.2 Key features of the model 158

6.7.3 Benefits of the model 160
6.7.4 Implementation pathway 161
6.8 Summary and future directions 161
6.8.1 Recap 161
6.8.2 The implications for future smart city development 162
6.8.3 Closing remarks and the way forward 163
References 163

7 Emerging technologies for securing digital twins 171
Raman Singh and Bhisham Sharma
7.1 Introduction 171
7.2 Security threats in digital twin 173
7.2.1 Data breaches 174
7.2.2 Cyberattacks 175
7.2.3 Other security threats 176
7.3 Application of blockchain for securing the digital twins 177
7.4 Application of artificial intelligence for securing the digital twins 181
7.5 Application of quantum encryption for securing the digital twins 183
7.6 Conclusions and future research directions 184
References 185

8 Digital twin technology in Industry 4.0: revolutionising quality control in intelligent manufacturing 189
Tahir Mahmood
8.1 Introduction 190
8.2 Digital transformation products 191
8.3 Digital twin and its five dimensions 192
8.3.1 Physical objects 193
8.3.2 Virtual models 193
8.3.3 Digital twin database 194
8.3.4 Service 194
8.3.5 Connections 194
8.4 Information required for digital twin development 194
8.5 The digital twin implementation layers 195
8.5.1 Layer 1: digital virtualisation 195
8.5.2 Layer 2: digital twin synchronisation 196
8.5.3 Layer 3: modelling and simulation 196
8.5.4 Layer 4: federated digital twin 196
8.5.5 Layer 5: intelligent digital twin services 196
8.6 Role of digital twin in Industry 4.0 principles 197
8.6.1 Technical assistance 197
8.6.2 Decentralised decision-making 197
8.6.3 Interconnection/connectivity 197

8.6.4 Information transparency 197
8.6.5 Intelligence and awareness 197
8.6.6 Knowledge 198
8.6.7 Interoperability 198
8.7 Connection of quality control, Industry 4.0 and digital twin 198
8.7.1 A real-time monitoring framework 198
8.7.2 Quality measures in a digital twin 200
8.7.3 Existing quality control studies using digital twin 202
8.8 Summary and concluding remarks 202
References 208

9 The role of digital twins in realising circular economy in the era of Industry 4.0 and Industry 5.0 213
Julius Sechang Mboli
9.1 Introduction 214
9.1.1 Overview of Industry 4.0 and Industry 5.0 214
9.1.2 Introduction to circular economy 215
9.1.3 Introduction to digital twins 215
9.2 Digital twins in Industry 4.0 216
9.2.1 Key components and technologies 216
9.2.2 Applications and use cases 218
9.2.3 Benefits and challenges 219
9.3 DTs in Industry 5.0 and the circular economy 220
9.3.1 Human-centric and sustainable approach 220
9.3.2 Customisation, personalisation and circularity 221
9.3.3 Ethical and environmental considerations 222
9.4 Case studies and industry examples 223
9.5 Future directions and trends 224
9.5.1 Evolution of digital twin technology 224
9.5.2 Digital twin integration with Industry 5.0 technologies 226
9.5.3 Challenges and opportunities 228
9.6 Conclusion 230
References 231

10 Digital twins services architectural design: practical implementation 237
Gayan Dihantha Kuruppu Kuruppu Appuhamilage, Maqbool Hussain, Wajahat Ali Khan, Ben Anderson and Asad Masood Khattak
10.1 Overview 238
10.1.1 What are digital twin services? 238
10.1.2 What is digital twin architecture? 239
10.1.3 What are the different architectures? 243
10.1.4 What are the challenges? 247
10.2 Digital twin platforms 249
10.2.1 What are the limitations? 249

10.2.2 What are the advantages? 250
10.2.3 How to select a digital twin platform? 251
10.2.4 Types of digital twin platforms 253
10.3 Discussion and conclusion 266
References 267

11 Digital twins services implementation: Azure cloud **273**
Gayan Dihantha Kuruppu Kuruppu Appuhamilage, Maqbool Hussain, Wajahat Ali Khan and Asad Masood Khattak
11.1 Overview 274
11.2 Development environment 275
11.2.1 The Azure subscription Studio 2022 on your personal computer 275
11.2.2 Sign in to Azure from Visual Studio 276
11.3 Digital twin models 276
11.3.1 Schemas 277
11.3.2 Meta classes 288
11.3.3 JSON-LD DTDL models 295
11.4 Azure services 295
11.4.1 Control plane APIs 296
11.4.2 Data plane APIs 301
11.5 Discussion and conclusion 313
References 314

Conclusion: the future of digital twins and their transformative impact 315
C.1 Digital twin maturity and implementation frameworks 315
C.2 Understanding digital twin limitations and challenges 316
C.3 Advancements in DT security and emerging technologies 317
C.4 The role of digital twins in future technological advancements 317
C.5 The future of digital twins: research, policy and industry collaboration 318

Index **321**

Preface

The integration of advanced digital technologies is transforming, revolutionising and redefining urban environments, industries and the way organisations manage resources, optimise operations and engage with digital processes. Digital twins (DTs) are among the most transformative revolutions in recent years that come with the concept of virtual representations of physical objects, systems or processes that empower real-time monitoring, predictive analytics and informed decision-making. The concept of DT has evolved beyond its initial conceptualisation into an integral component of digital-era technological ecosystems. DTs serve as bridges between the physical and digital worlds, enabling digital-physical integration through a continuous exchange of data and process. Despite extensive research and promising applications, DTs still face challenges, including conceptual clarity, maturity models and interoperability frameworks for large-scale implementation. DTs have a profound impact across multiple sectors, with applications covering urban planning, manufacturing, cybersecurity, sustainability and smart city development, discussed in Chapters 1, 2, 3 and 5 of the book. These chapters discuss how DT can be useful by integrating real-time monitoring, predictive analytics and optimisation and how DTs can offer to organisations, researchers, citizens and governments as a valuable tool for improving operational efficiency.

Whether applied in urban planning, healthcare, manufacturing or environmental sustainability, DT technology has the potential to redefine global operations, optimise decision-making and support future-proof innovations. Beyond industrial applications, DTs also play a pivotal role in smart cities and citizen engagement, enabling real-time observation and control of various operations and processes, including energy consumption and response, transportation systems and infrastructure management. Chapter 4 explores Virtual Bradford (a metropolitan city in northern England), an open-access DT model that facilitates data-driven urban planning, citizen engagement and environmental sustainability. By leveraging 3D geospatial technologies and interactive platforms, DT redefine urban governance, transforming decision-making processes and increasing accessibility for citizens. Whilst DT technologies open new prospects, they also present privacy and security challenges. The integration of AI-based intelligent infrastructure, smart city applications and cloud-based DT solutions raises concerns about cybersecurity threats, unauthorised access and system vulnerabilities. To showcase the integration of emerging technology to DT, Chapter 6 presents how blockchain and DTs can be integrated in smart cities to bring a fundamental shift in urban planning and service delivery. This book additionally dedicates Chapter 7 to exploring security frameworks and emerging technologies such as blockchain and AI-powered models to protect sensitive data and strengthen DTs' environments.

As businesses are shifting towards Industry 5.0, where human-centric approaches complement automation, DT facilitate more personalised, adaptable and sustainable industrial environments. Chapters 8 and 9 of this book highlight the growing adoption of DT technology in manufacturing and Industry 4.0 and 5.0, where organisations rely on Internet of Things (IoT), artificial intelligence (AI), cloud computing and big data to enhance automation, production efficiency and quality control. Through intelligent data handling, DTs optimise and improve predictive maintenance strategies, supply chains, and enhance system adaptability. Furthermore, different chapters of this book also incorporate ethical concerns accompanying DT adoption, including data privacy, surveillance risks and potential biases in decision-making algorithms, arguing that organisations must steer these considerations responsibly to ensure that DT applications align with industry standards, regulations and best practices. Moreover, DT technology is continuously progressing, and its extensive adoption requires collaboration among industry, academia and governments. Therefore, standardisation remains a critical challenge, with interoperability concerns preventing seamless DT integration across different platforms and industries. Chapters 10 and 11 additionally examine various commercial platforms, open-source and custom-built DT solutions, highlighting their capabilities, advantages and limitations. Special attention is given to Microsoft Azure's DT services, providing insight into their architecture, implementation strategies and real-world applications.

In a nutshell, through this book, we explore the next frontiers of digital-physical integration, intelligent automation and sustainable development. DTs will continue to shape industries and societies in reflective ways. This book serves as a comprehensive exploration of DT's technology, its applications across various domains and the challenges that must be addressed to achieve and utilise its full potential. This book also investigates the essential challenges in defining DT models, digital transformation, cultural transformation and bridging the skills gap. Whilst digital transformation focuses on replicating physical systems in digital environments, cultural transformation looks after confidence in data-driven technologies. Besides, bridging the skills gap ensures that organisations can effectively develop, deploy and utilise DT within various industries and applications.

To put it concisely, this book provides a holistic outline of DT technology, bridging the gap between theoretical research, practical applications and future aspirations. Furthermore, this book also emphasises how organisations can leverage DTs to drive innovation and enhance digital transformation by highlighting technical challenges and refining security measures. In summary, this book provides the DT strengths and challenges to readers, academics, technology professionals, industry professionals and policymakers to embark on a rational journey through the evolving landscape of DT innovation.

About the editors

Dhaval Thakker is professor of artificial intelligence (AI) and Internet of Things (IoT) and is currently at the University of Hull, UK. He also acts as the University's Turing academic lead. He leads the Responsible AI Research Group, which focuses on safe, fair, and explainable AI solutions for high-stakes domains such as healthcare, law, defence, and energy. Since 2018, Professor Thakker has contributed to projects with a total awarded value of £12.8M. He has fostered extensive national and international collaborations, resulting in collaborative funding applications and culminating in impactful research. His interdisciplinary research interests and expertise offer a balanced focus on advancing AI, with particular attention to generative AI and the applications of IoT technologies. Through his research, he aims to enhance AI's contribution to societal benefit under the 'AI for Social Good' initiative, embodying a commitment to developing AI technologies that prioritise explainability, safety and fairness. His work is applied in regulated sectors such as law, defence, manufacturing, sustainability and healthcare. He actively publishes in leading high-impact journals such as the *Semantic Web Journal*, *Elsevier Journal of Engineering Applications of Artificial Intelligence* and *Transactions on Emerging Telecommunications Technologies*. His research has received multiple best paper awards, including at the 10th IEEE Conference on IoT, Big Data and AI for a Smart and Safe Future (2019) and the 12th European Semantic Web Conference (2015). He regularly serves as a reviewer for the Engineering and Physical Sciences Research Council (EPSRC) and the Natural Environment Research Council (NERC).

Zeeshan Pervez is director of the Centre for Cyber Resilience and Artificial Intelligence (CYBRAI), and professor of cybersecurity at the University of Wolverhampton, UK. He is a senior member of IEEE, an ACM distinguished speaker, a senior fellow of the Higher Education Academy (UK), SPRITE+ expert fellow and a full member of the EPSRC Peer Review College (UK). He has a strong track record of successfully completing research, industry and capacity-building projects funded by Innovate UK, the Scottish Funding Council, Scottish Innovation Centres, the European Commission, Erasmus+, Microsoft Research and international research institutes. He has over 18 years of research and industry experience in addressing technological and societal challenges and in designing and developing enterprise-ready solutions. His areas of expertise include cybersecurity, applied ML/AI, Internet of Things, edge computing and data analytics. The application areas of his research include, but are not limited to, cyber resilience, digital twins, industry 4.0, smart cities, predictive maintenance, facilities management and healthcare. He is regularly invited by national and international research and academic institutes to deliver talks on topics ranging from cyber resilience of critical infrastructure, AI-driven cybersecurity and digital twin-enabled city planning to name a few. He has successfully supervised to completion 29 postdoctoral fellows and postgraduate research/taught and undergraduate students (as lead and co-supervisor). He has served as a TPC member of over 100 conferences and as a regular reviewer for more than 30 IEEE Transactions, Elsevier, and Springer journals. He has chaired or evaluated over 40 doctoral exams for UK and international higher education institutes. He is serving as an external examiner to several UK higher education institutes for their computing programme boards – postgraduate, undergraduate and international provisions. He has led the development, validation and delivery of postgraduate programmes, namely MSc Information & Network Security and MSc Advanced Computing (big data and IoT).

Bhupesh Kumar Mishra is lecturer in AI and data science at the Centre of Excellence for Data Science, Artificial Intelligence and Modelling (DAIM), University of Hull, UK, where he leads interdisciplinary initiatives across healthcare, industrial optimisation, and environmental sustainability. With over 7 years of experience in academic research, strategic project guidance and industry collaboration, he integrates advanced AI algorithms, machine learning techniques, large language models and complex systems modelling to address real-world challenges through ethical, scalable solutions. Dr Mishra's contributions include securing competitive funding from bodies such as UKRI and the British Academy, supporting transformative research into responsible healthcare systems, climate-resilient infrastructure and data-informed decision-making. He supervises a broad cohort of doctoral and postgraduate students working in areas such as healthcare analytics, smart cities and AI for social good, fostering innovation across academic and applied domains. With over 30 publications in high-impact journals and conferences, several recognised with best paper awards, he has also been actively engaged in peer review and serves on organising committees for leading international venues. He also supports CPD initiatives through AI course development and contributes to research networks advancing inclusive, explainable technologies. His research vision is rooted in interdisciplinary rigour and societal relevance and promotes dialogue between academic analysis and industry application, ensuring that emerging technologies align with ethical frameworks and respond meaningfully to pressing global challenges.

Chapter 1

Understanding digital twins as a digital counterpart of physical systems

Bhupesh Kumar Mishra[1], Dhaval Thakker[2] and Zeeshan Pervez[3]

Abstract

Digital twins (DTs) are virtual copies of physical objects, processes or systems that enable real-time monitoring, analysis, optimisation and modelling. DTs can enhance resource utilisation, improve productivity and contribute across diverse industries and domains. Defining a DT model involves addressing three key challenges: digital transformation, cultural transformation and bridging the skills gap. Digital transformation replicates physical systems digitally, while cultural transformation fosters trust in data-driven approaches. Bridging the skills gap equips organisations to effectively develop and utilise DTS. Despite their transformative potential, implementing DTs involves challenges and considerations that require careful navigation, as these abstract representations cannot fully replicate all physical system intricacies and overconfidence in their accuracy may lead to overlooked flaws during real-world applications. Privacy concerns emerge with data collection for DT deployment, risks of surveillance and system privacy. Similarly, DTs may also face challenges such as high costs, ethical concerns and the need for accurate, real-time data integration. In addition, DTs' can be vulnerable to risks like cyberattacks and data breaches due to reliance on interconnected digital systems. However, a systematic DT implementation process that includes setting objectives, collecting reliable data, developing virtual models, iterative testing, deploying validated models and monitoring performance can minimise these risks. Besides, user training can ensure knowledge gaps and facilitate improvement. As a futuristic DTs scope, it requires collaboration among academia, governments and industries to establish standardised approaches addressing interoperability, privacy and technological barriers for widespread DT adoption. By overcoming these challenges, DTs have the potential to redefine operational strategies, foster innovation and deliver sustainable, smart solutions across various domains.

Keywords: Digital twins; taxonomy; manufacturing; urban planning; healthcare

[1]Centre of Excellence for Data Science and Artificial Intelligence Modelling, University of Hull, UK
[2]School of Computer Science and Engineering, University of Hull, UK
[3]School of Engineering, Computing, and Mathematical Sciences, University of Wolverhampton, UK

1.1 Introduction

Digital twins (DT) are virtual digital representations that precisely replicate objects, systems or processes that exist in real time [1]. These virtual representations enable real-time monitoring, analysing, evaluating and optimising the performance, efficiency, security and reliability of their real-world equivalents. DTs can represent digital objects and are often used to link the physical and digital worlds. In principle, DTs serve as a connecting bridge between the physical and digital states, offering an interactive and comprehensive digital representation that enables data exchange models, algorithms and simulations to their real-world equivalent with corresponding features and behaviour [2]. In other words, the DTs as a concept adopt advanced real-time monitoring, data analytics and simulation to provide valuable insights into the performance and presentation of physical objects and systems.

DTs are attracting interest from practitioners and scholars from different sectors and businesses, as this technology provides accurate virtual interpretations of objects, data and simulations of operational processes [3]. A significant advantage of DTs is their capability to predict systems' behaviours and potential issues [4]. Through continuous monitoring and data analysis, DTs enable organisations to optimise their processes and resource utilisation, productivity enhancement, efficiency improvement and cost savings. By leveraging real-time data and predictive modelling techniques, DTs can forecast maintenance needs, reduce downtime and extend the lifespan of systems. To put it in another way, by mirroring their real-world equivalents, DTs offer a better understanding of systems and the workings of components and facilitate enhanced management and analysis.

Over the years, DTs have shown great promising potential across different application areas. However, they come with challenges and issues such as data collection and quality, data security and integration complexity [5]. There has been an enhancement in DTs' technologies, nonetheless, barriers to the adoption of DT to existing infrastructure cannot be overlooked, which often comes in the form of technology adoption, lack of skilled people and culture [6]. In addition, it is true that DTs are evolving at a fast pace evolving concept which creating additional challenges in bringing a widely accepted DT reference framework [4]. Despite noticeable progress and efforts, there is a need to understand the DT and implementation gaps for the prevalent adoption of the DT basic concept and technology. Understanding the strengths and promises of DTs, why and when DT technology is needed and how and what the industry can adopt so that DT can help deliver sustainable and smart infrastructure assets is crucial.

1.1.1 Historical journey of digital twins

The idea of twinning an operating physical system with a functional duplication has evolved over many years. The enhancements in digital technologies have initiated opportunities to extract data, gain understanding and achieve wider and extended situational awareness of a physical system's performance [7]. This brings the concept of DT technology and transforms the horizon of industries and systems through its ability to create comprehensive virtual replicas of physical systems. However, the formal ideas of DT have been around since the early 2000s when Grieves first gave the DT terminology in a 2003 presentation and later documented it in a white paper [8]. The National Aeronautical Space Administration (NASA) published a paper in 2012 entitled 'The Digital Twin Paradigm for Future NASA and U.S. Air Force Vehicles', defining Digital Twins as: 'A Digital Twin is an integrated multiphysics, multiscale, probabilistic simulation of an as-built vehicle or system that uses the best available physical models, sensor updates, fleet history, etc., to mirror the life of its corresponding flying twin' [9].

1.1.2 Digit twins: taxonomy

In the context of DTs, taxonomy defines the structured classification of any system that facilitates organising and outlining different elements, definitions and concepts associated with DTs [10]. DT taxonomy for the systematic representation, which provides a framework for understanding and categorising the different aspects of DTs, making it easier to study and apply them in various fields [11]. By creating a taxonomy, practitioners and researchers can better analyse and compare various DT ideas and hence develop a deeper understanding and deliver effective implementation. A taxonomy of DTs, as visualised in Figure 1.1, typically includes the following dimensions:

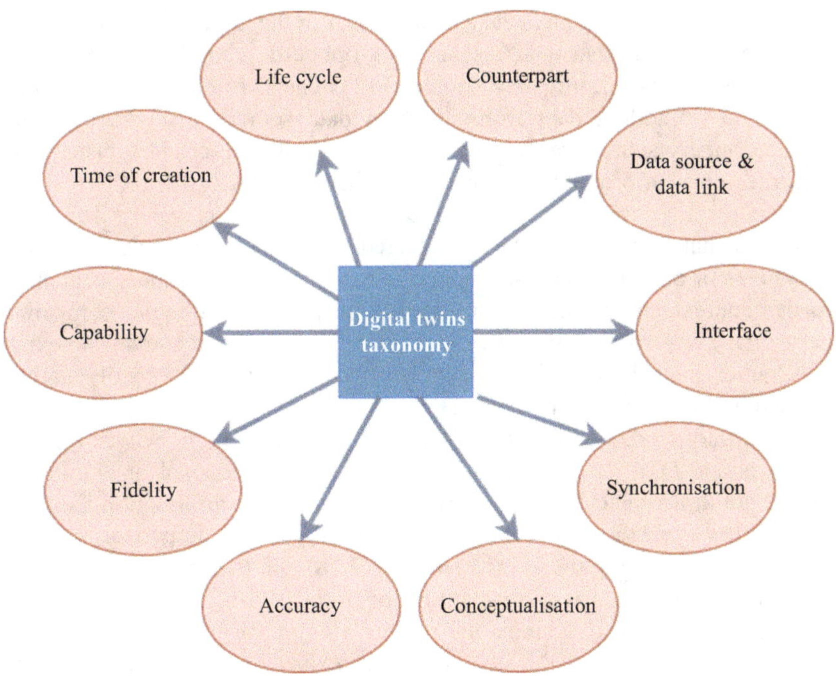

Figure 1.1 Taxonomy of digital twins with different dimensions

1.1.2.1 Counterpart

In the context of DTs, the term 'counterpart' refers to the physical resource the DT corresponds to. This could be anything that anyone wants to replicate in a digital realm, ranging from a piece of machinery, a building, an entire industrial process or even a human body in the context of healthcare. More often, physical objects are prone to faults and failures, which have a major impact on the physical systems. One of the primary reasons for creating the digital counterparts of such physical objects is to monitor the status of the physical infrastructure, such as machinery performance, urban planning, water distribution, electric transmission networks and many other systems [12]. The digital counterparts are tied with the physical systems by close system communication and data links with components such as sensors, actuators and information-processing units, where the digital counterparts interact with the physical environment through physical communication devices such as dashboards and screens, allowing alternative ways to investigate the physical systems. In this completely closed system, the counterpart systems continuously get updated from the physical system [13].

1.1.2.2 Data sources and data links

Data source is an important component of DTs as it provides the ability to gather, store and represent all relevant data of real-world counterparts. Data link provides the interface for the DT system through an API (application programming interface) gateway to access the physical system [14]. For the DTs implementation, data are collected from various sources such as onboard product systems, internal enterprise systems and third-party sources [15]. The DTs database is frequently supplemented by adding data from different data sources that can be primary sources, secondary sources or tertiary (third-party) data sources [16]. The primary data sources provide original and raw data collected directly from the real-world counterpart for a specific purpose. On the other hand, the secondary data sources provide data that have already been collected, processed and made available by other systems or organisations. Secondary data supports their primary context with a broader context and is often more accessible and cost-effective compared to primary data. The tertiary data sources are third-party data that come from external sources rather than directly from their system. This data is typically gathered, aggregated and sold by external entities.

The taxonomy data link establishes the communication between physical counterparts and DTs [10]. The link can be either unidirectional or bidirectional, where the unidirectional data link depicts the automatic information flow commencing either from the physical system to the digital counterpart or vice versa, and never changes during the DTs' lifetime [17,18]. On the other hand, data links are established in such a way that automatic information flows between digital counterparts and physical systems as well as vice versa [19,20]. Data links are mutually exclusive, making DT acquire either a one- or bi-directional data link, which makes the dimension mutually exclusive.

1.1.2.3 Interface

An interface in DTs defines gateways that can be used to access the data from different sources or systems. The interface also provides the required information or features of the implemented DT system, making the physical system available and accessible [14]. In the DTs system, there can be different interfaces, such as user-to-twin system interface, twin-to-object interface and twin object-to-twin object interface, for data flow and information communication [21]. Interfaces are designed to establish different types of interactions, such as communication among twin objects and between twin objects and physical devices, however, the interface design depends on the application type and need. The interface system also holistically provides observability and controllability so that the DT systems can optimise operational settings based on system components and characteristics such as systems' preferences and behaviours, real-time data [22].

1.1.2.4 Synchronisation

Synchronisation is the process of updating the DTs with their corresponding physical systems or objects [23]. Synchronisations imply updates of the simulation models to uncover how to operate DT applications most efficiently and effectively. Synchronisation may become challenging as many DTs are dynamic and frequent updates are required for the digital counterparts as per the changes in their physical systems [13]. Synchronisation ensures the accuracy of the digital systems, allows them to reflect any changes in the physical system timely manner and mirrors the internal behaviour of the physical systems. With DTs, synchronisation is crucial to keep the states of digital counterparts consistent with those of their physical systems, as the DT represents the virtual replica of physical systems [24]. Therefore, synchronisation is essential to keep the DTs coordinated with the physical system, otherwise, it can lead to incorrect outcomes and catastrophic results.

1.1.2.5 Conceptualisation

Conceptualisation describes the relationship between the DT system and its corresponding physical system using models and data [25]. A conceptual DT model aims to support the description of the physical system without discussion of particular tools or technologies for achieving DTs. The conceptual description labels the different roles and the relationships of behavioural components on a conceptual level. The conceptualisation of a DT provides augmented analysis and decision support, along with a more individualised focus on specific cases that gives a balance between precision and personalisation [26]. Conceptualisation is important while realising the DTs as they can be wrongly manipulated, understood and implemented [27]. Therefore, it is crucial to critically analyse any underlying assumptions along with potential ambiguities while conceptualising DTs.

1.1.2.6 Accuracy

Accuracy is an essential component in realising the DTs as concerned with the quality of the system on how accurately the digital representation of the physical object is expressed and also determines the DT system's effectiveness in practical implementations [28]. If the DT model fails to depict the physical system, further modification to the digital counterpart is essential to make sure the DT model accurately represents the physical system [29]. In other words, the accuracy of the DT system refers to the degree to which the DT model can replicate the properties, prediction and performance of the physical system under different specifications. By simulating the physical system properties and performance in the form of a DT model under different specifications, the accuracy of the model can be verified and validated, and any inconsistencies can be dealt with. Besides, it is also important to note that the complexity of the model has a direct impact on the accuracy of the DT model. In general, the more complex the DT models are, the more challenging it is to achieve higher accuracy [30].

1.1.2.7 Fidelity

Fidelity is defined as the degree to which a DT model simulates the actual physical system states and behaviour in a measurable way [31]. Fidelity is the measure of how closely a virtual representation matches the real world. Fidelity, along with accuracy, is a measure of DT model performance and part of DT model verification and validation [32]. Fidelity measures ensure the effectiveness of DT Systems in achieving identical behaviour to the physical system [33]. Fidelity measuring in a DT system is important as it brings the worthiness of defining the DT systems at the minimum essential level of fidelity and hence optimises the computational costs.

1.1.2.8 Capability

Capability in DT refers to the ability of a digital counterpart to monitor, simulate and optimise the performance of a physical object, system or process using real-time data. DT progression and the feasibility of replicating the physical system's functionality are often referred to in terms of 'capability' [34]. Different types of DT systems bring different capabilities depending on the primary functionality of the physical system and the purpose of digital replication. Capability levels are correlated with the types of DT, whether predictive, informative, autonomous or focused on optimisation, combined with real-time modelling and big data to enable domain-specific services [4]. Combining the digitalisation capabilities with rational features and functionalities of the physical system, the DT application gains a higher efficiency in its impact on the DT system [35].

1.1.2.9 Time of creation

The time of creation of DT systems separates into three appearances, determining the sequential order in which the respective parts of the DT emerge [11]. In other words, time of creation refers to whether the DT is developed before, after or in parallel (developed with the simultaneous creation of both the physical and DT systems). Developing a DT system before the physical system can be highly favourable, especially for complex projects [36]. This allows for detailed simulations and analysis to identify potential issues and optimise the design before the physical system can be realised. This also reduces and facilitates remote monitoring and control, improves predictive maintenance, costs and risks, and enables customisation. Moreover, having DT before the physical system provides the training environments that allow users to interact with the system and learn about the system without causing any damage or harm to the physical system [37].

Developing a DT system after the physical system is beneficial when the system's requirements are well-understood and straightforward [38]. This approach can be beneficial for less complex or smaller-scale projects. Additionally, when rapid prototyping and iterative physical testing are preferred, a physical system allows direct observation of performance [39,40]. In such cases, a DT can be created after a stable physical system to enhance monitoring, maintenance and optimisation. Developing a physical system and its DTs in parallel is beneficial in scenarios where real-time feedback and iterative improvements are vital [41]. This approach allows simultaneous implementation and testing of both physical and DT prototypes. This integrated approach augments system flexibility and encourages a seamless system transition to the final product.

1.1.2.10 Life cycle

The life cycle of DT begins with the planning, design, monitoring and update stages, where a digital counterpart representation of a physical system or object is created using data from different sources such as databases, historical data, sensors or Internet of Things (IoT) devices [42]. The life cycle helps to understand the system and to identify possible design issues. During the planning and design, functionalities and features of physical systems are collected with the virtual realisation of those functionalities and features in the digital counterparts [43]. Once the DT system is operational, the DT collects data to observe performance. In the monitoring and update phase, DT operations along with physical systems are continuously monitored to observe any changes in the system and hence the corresponding update to the systems [44]. Throughout the asset's life cycle, DTs remain dynamic, evolving to provide continuous value through better decision-making and performance optimisation [45].

1.1.3 Characteristics of digital twin

Characteristics of DTs depend on the simulation capabilities of the physical systems' features as data collection, storage, communication, environment, functionalities, analysis and closed-loop feedback [46]. Broadly, DTs are characteristically divided into the following two categories:

(i) **Dynamic**: Dynamic DTs focus on real-time updates and analysis, maintain dynamic information, support system operation and activities, and contribute to the functional environment [47]. The dynamic DTs should have the ability to learn and update the features and functional status of the physical system from multiple data sources [48]. A dynamic DT aims to integrate heterogeneous physical system properties and data supporting intelligent and dynamic operational management. The dynamic DT needs to adopt dynamic capabilities to react to system-changing aspects efficiently [49]. A dynamic DT links multi-stakeholder teams and improves mutual collaboration by providing a feasible solution that can be adopted to build real-time connectivity between physical systems with digital counterparts. A dynamic DT is commonly applied during the product and production design stage to simulate, monitor, analyse and control the system which often requires high computing and data processing capacity [50].

(ii) **Self-evolving**: Self-evolving or adaptive DTs continuously learn and adapt autonomously, which not only use real-time data but also learn from it over time and improve their accuracy and performance without human intervention [51]. The adaptive DT should have the ability to constantly monitor its outcome against the expected performance, and hence the ability to adjust its control mechanism to make sure desired goals are achieved [52]. Such a control adjustment ability of the DT system to continuously measure the system's deviation from regular operating settings and hence apply the appropriate adaptation in the system to bring back the DT operations to normal operating Settings. This self-evolving DT system requires continuous monitoring and analysis of the system data, functional output, system state and behaviour along with the environment to gather decisive information to control the system's deviation from normal operating settings.

1.2 Who, why and when should use digital twins

In the realm of the advanced technological era, DTs are contributing to managing digital infrastructures and services. As it has been discussed, DTs are virtual replicas of physical objects, systems or processes that provide real-time data and insights and also the virtual platform for planners, administrators and decision-makers to replicate diverse scenarios [53]. DTs facilitate the decision-makers and planners for the development conditions of public facilities by enabling more effective resource allocation [54]. DTs are a supporting tool for maintenance planners as they offer insights into the usage patterns using data analytics, generate maintenance scheduling and overall planning [55]. DTs enhance the efficiency of planning and operational maintenance by providing real-time visibility into the actions and activities. Moreover, DT technology allows better planning, pre-emptive maintenance and assurance of safer infrastructure with functional diversity. And so, DTs are essential to achieve a dynamic and accurate representation of physical systems to digital counterparts with real-time monitoring, simulation and optimisation.

Regardless of the systems, DTs have primarily been used for broader purposes. Firstly, DTs enhance **predictive maintenance** [32,56–59]. By continuously analysing real-time data gathered predominantly using sensors, DTs bring the capacity to identify patterns and predict potential faults before they appear. This proactive preparedness reduces interruptions, increases the lifespan of machinery, and hence optimises maintenance costs. Secondly, DTs enhance **decision-making** [60–64]. They provide real-time insights and alternative circumstances through simulations, helping decision-makers to plan strategies. DTs create the informed-decision-making opportunity that helps with additional confidence to decision-makers on implementing any decisions. Lastly, DTs contribute to **sustainability** [65–69]. By optimising resource use and helping organisations achieve their sustainability goals. DTs are uniquely placed to overcome sustainability challenges with learnt action plans towards achieving sustainability goals.

The usability of DTs makes them suitable for implementation into wider application domains to maximise benefits from the strength of DT systems and features. Following, but not limited to, are the application areas where DTs have been applied and proven their suitability for enhancing application performances, optimising resource utilisation, improving decision-making and driving innovation in operational processes. In **urban planning** [70,71], DTs can simulate numerous digital counterparts (scenarios) to optimise infrastructure maintenance and development with amended resource allocation and efficient operations. DTs also help not only to plan the existing urban areas but also to the future urbanisation and city planning. They facilitate better urban route planning, supply management, risk mitigation, energy supply and other resources. Urban planners can employ DTs to simulate traffic patterns, test new transport routes, along with assessing the risk and impact of environmental factors and hence make data-driven decisions to improve city management. DTs are crucial in **businesses and industries** as they enable to simulate and prediction of the behaviour of their critical assets, leading to improved efficiency, safety and decision-making [72,73]. For example, in manufacturing [74,75], DTS can help in identifying potential issues before they occur, a set of integrated virtual information to actual physical systems with operational details. Additionally, they can optimise energy usage and promote sustainability by providing data-driven insights into resource consumption [76,77]. They also help in simulating energy profiles and provide energy management plans by identifying inefficient and malfunctioning components. In the **healthcare** [78–80], DTs benefit through the creation of data-driven patient-specific simulations for diagnosis and treatment planning for different health conditions. The potential to use DTs to assist in personalised medicine, surgical circumstances and the expansion of new medicines and therapies is ultimately improving health services.

In agriculture [81–83], DTs can simulate different agriculture and farming-related conditions to minimise resource consumption and fertiliser use and hence maximise yields. DTs provide a synchronised real-time virtual representation of agriculture data, processes or the environment through digitised counterparts, modelling and simulation, and they provide useful insight for all domains of agriculture. Besides, DTs also help in virtual experimentation to inform controlling agriculture practices. **In engineering** [84–86], DTs are used to design and test systems and services and optimise the product. In other words, the DT technology allows for pre-emptive prediction, maintenance and better planning, safeguarding engineering design and models remain safe and functional. Doing so, DTs enable engineers to execute virtual prototyping of the physical system with corresponding digital counterparts. This allows for reducing the dependency on designing the physical prototypes and accelerating the design and development process. For example, the automotive industry has benefited from the use of DTs for vehicle design, testing, analysis and maintenance [87,88]. When it comes to

manufacturing engineering [74,75,89], DTs enable companies to optimise production lines, predict equipment failures and improve product designs, leading to substantial cost savings and efficiency enhancements. However, the adoption of DT in engineering and manufacturing also requires reliable sensors, data infrastructure and skilled manpower. In general, DTs help manufacturers to forecast and address any potential issues and hence apply appropriate changes to the smooth running of the systems, optimise the performance and hence the overall operation.

Besides these areas of application, DT has also been used in other domains. In **supply chains and logistics** [90–92], DTs can simulate and analyse supply chain operations, identifying bottlenecks and inefficiencies. This helps businesses streamline their logistics, improve delivery times and reduce operational costs. The DTs facilitate companies to develop predictive metrics, diagnostic estimates and physical resource descriptions for their logistics system optimisation. They enhanced overall logistics operational efficiency by providing real-time data analytics and understanding. With the supply chain optimisation, the company's business by DT has direct benefits towards **improving customer and client engagement** [93,94]. DT system provides customers with specified and described details on any services or products, which eventually enhance the customer's and clients' experience and satisfaction. DT has shown the potential to accelerate data-driven and value-added in cooperative business practices that significantly enhance customer relationships. This includes the customisation and responsiveness of services with efficiency, enabling the DT to go beyond optimising the operational processes. DT's application can be further explored in the domain of **customisation and personalisation of products** [95–97] where DTs allow industries to prepare or design customised solutions as per clients' needs by simulating numerous scenarios and configurations. In addition, DTs have the potential for mass production and specific product analysis, which leads to products that better meet the specific group of customers.

In **energy systems** [98–100], DTs facilitate monitoring energy consumption data and analysing to understand the patterns. It also helps to optimise the energy distribution by identifying the areas where energy can be saved. Furthermore, this contributes to sustainability and cost savings by analysing the impact of the implementation of newer technology, capacity expansions and predictive maintenance. Moreover, DTs have shown their implication for **enhancing safety and risk management** [101,102]. The high operational risk industries, such as construction and manufacturing, DT can simulate potential risks and safety measures. This helps in building safer working environments and reduces the risk factors. For example, **in fire risk management** [103], the DT system can simulate building-specific fire scenarios such as fire emergence and recognition, intensity of fire and impacted areas. With these simulations, fire risk management can be better planned by sharing safety information, exit routes and safe zones. Similarly, for **automobile safety** [104], DTs can simulate the risk by collecting a wide range of automobile data, such as manufacturing data, internal and external environment, different operational properties and services data, along with driver perception data, external systems and services. With analytics, DT can make automated risk management decisions and hence recommend safety measures.

1.3 How should we define digital twin model

While DTs provide numerous benefits across different applications, it is important to understand how this can be implemented. DT implementation in any organisation comprehends three core challenges to be addressed: **digital transformation**, **cultural transformation** and **bridging the skill gap** [6]. Digital transformation [6,105,106] is the must-need action where the physical systems, objects or environments are virtually replicated. Digital transformation is the broader method of applying different technologies to understand how any system or organisations operate. DTs replicate the physical objects to their corresponding digital counterparts as a part of digital transformation. In general, digital transformation is the process of applying technologies that fundamentally mimic the functional operation of any physical system or business to bring an understanding of how the system or business operates. The next action to realise the DTs in any organisation is cultural transformation [107], where digital replicas can be trusted as physical objects or systems. For example, DTs in healthcare can create a virtual patient where the diagnosis and treatment are based on simulated environments. How and up to what level the simulated scenarios, data, and results can be utilised requires a cultural transformation of decision-making from the physical system to digital data-driven decision-making. DT integration into the existing system requires a strategic adjustment in organisational working culture and decision-making mindset, with a priority [108]. Without a systematic integration, DT implementation may face challenges. Another challenge to implementing DTs is bridging the skills gap, as the right skills are needed to perform the tasks effectively [109]. The skills gap in implementing DTs in any organisation can also impact the acceptance of the DTs application [6].

Having addressed the three key challenges discussed above, DTs can be effectively implemented to achieve operational efficiency, improved decision-making and sustainable long-term outcomes across various industries. Steps presented in Figure 1.2 are the summarised key steps to using DTs, based on the recent applications reviewed for this chapter.

1. **Objectives setting**: This step is the starting point of DT implementation, which identifies the goals of the application, clearly outlining what is aimed to achieve as the outcome. The objective can be data analytics with a hypothesis, improvement in operational efficiency, predictive maintenance, cost minimisation or system optimisation. To define the precise objective, experts, stakeholders or problem owners' involvement is important as they bring the knowledge to complete the objective. Their engagement in defining the objective also ensures that DT addresses the right problems as per the organisation or system's needs. During this phase, key performance measures such as cost saving, accuracy in prediction or optimisation in functional components are also set to align with objectives and the organisation's working nature.
2. **Data collection:** In this phase, data sources are identified that can be primary, secondary or tertiary through databases, historical facts, warehouses, real-time

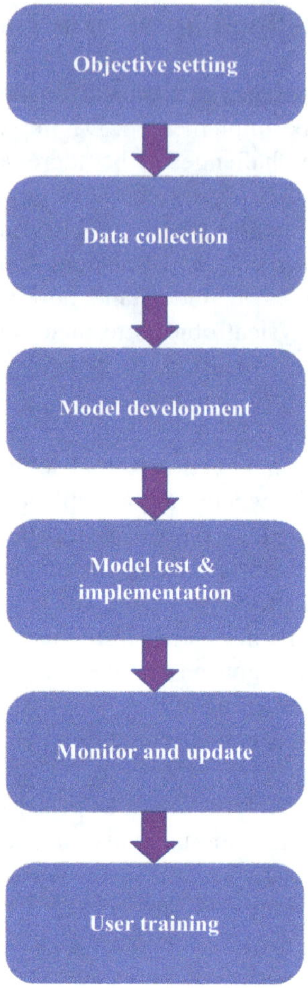

Figure 1.2 Key steps of designing digital twins

monitoring systems, sensors or IoT devices. While identifying the data source, only problem-specific data sources, covering all aspects of physical objects or systems, need to be linked and integrated into the DT system. While collecting the data, ensuring the quality of data is another factor that needs to be taken care of so that accurate, reliable and complete data are collected while maintaining data integrity. Data collection can be continuous or periodic, based on the nature of the application.

3. **Model development**: After having the data, a virtual model is the next step of DT implementation. For model development, simulation, 3D modelling or analytical algorithms can be applied to replicate the digital counterpart's physical system or object characteristics, function and performance. The model development also covers the design and implementation of performance

measures such as monitoring data, prediction values or operational values plots. In general, model development is an iterative process to reflect all the assets of physical systems or objects to achieve accurate and calibrated replicas.

4. **Model test and implement**: In the next step, the digital model gets tested, reflecting different sets of performance measures criteria. Test results get analysed and used as feedback to upgrade and improve the model. Testing is also an iterative process that has been applied along with model development. As a part of testing, verification and validation are applied by comparing the actual system and virtual system data and operations to confirm the DT model functioning. After the validation and verification, DT models get deployed or integrated into the existing system or environment with minimal disruption.
5. **Monitor and update**: In this step, the deployed DT modes are continuously monitored by analysing the outcome against the set performance measures. Monitoring is applied to make sure the system is performing as per the need and has relevance and reliability. During the model operation, a regular update is frequently checked with the data source, data and system characteristics to reflect any potential changes in the physical system or objects.
6. **User training**: This step is applied depending on the existing skill set at the organisation to bridge the skillset gap. As a part of user training, comprehensive training materials are developed, and the training sessions are organised for stakeholders and users. The training materials and session cover the complete overview of the DT application with a description of capabilities and limitations. The training sessions can bring additional advantages as they can provide real-user feedback to the system and highlight any updates and changes the DT system may go through.

1.4 Challenges of digital twin and future scope

While DTs hold great promise, it is important to comprehend their limitations and potential drawbacks, which can vary with domains and applications. DTs are similar and very close to the physical system in their characteristics and functionality, yet the digital counterparts are mainly abstract representations of the physical system, which may ignore some features and functionality [110]. For example, in the domain of product development and testing, DT can speed up innovation by facilitating rapid design iteration and testing under various specifications. Still, there is a potential consequence to this confidence in virtual replications. The risk lies in the assumption that DT counterparts can perfectly replicate physical models, which is not always the case; therefore, inferring the DT model parameters every so often fails to compensate [111]. Overconfidence in the accuracy and extensiveness of DT might lead to ignoring or missing flaws or issues that only become evident during real-world physical system implementation.

If the DT limitations are not adequately accounted for, it can result in loss of time and cost and eventually failures of the system. For example, smart cities and urban planning have benefited from DTs through efficient resource allocation.

However, the deployment of DT in the urban context raises worries about privacy and surveillance, since for urban DT applications, extensive data collection is essential to create a precise digital counterpart of city infrastructure that can put residents' privacy at risk [112]. The integration of DT can also face challenges such as interoperability among different systems, continuous and accurate data and feature updates. Furthermore, the dependence on technology to direct city advancement might lead to a digital divide, where only cities with advanced technological capacity can implement complex DT systems [113]. In similar ways, the healthcare sector also benefited from DTs by creating simulated models to monitor and analyse patients' health conditions and personalised treatment plans and to anticipate the results, making the healthcare operation more effective. Nevertheless, the implementation of DTs in healthcare is puzzling because of the need for large amounts of on-time and accurate data, higher implementation costs, a skilled workforce, ethical concerns with data privacy and the complexity of integrating DT technology with existing medical systems [114]. In manufacturing and industrial operations, the DT brings its usability with real-time monitoring and predictive capacities and enhances overall efficiency. However, the dependence on digital counterparts also brings the risk of data breaches and cyberattacks [115]. The more dependent and interconnected a system becomes on DTs, the more susceptible it is to external risks.

From a futuristic perspective, overcoming these challenges requires more collaboration between academia, government and industry to develop regulated and standard approaches so that DTs will be acceptable to the wider domain without much hassle. The future success of DT will depend on how effectively these challenges are addressed and how the technology progresses to meet the needs of diverse domains.

References

[1] Javaid M, Haleem A, and Suman R. Digital twin applications toward Industry 4.0: a review. *Cognitive Robotics*. 2023;3:71–92.

[2] Ding H, Seenivasan L, Killeen BD, Cho SM, and Unberath M. Digital twins as a unifying framework for surgical data science: the enabling role of geometric scene understanding. *Artificial Intelligence Surgery*. 2024;4(3):109–38.

[3] Attaran M, and Celik BG. Digital twin: benefits, use cases, challenges, and opportunities. *Decision Analytics Journal*. 2023;6:100165.

[4] Sharma A, Kosasih E, Zhang J, Brintrup A, and Calinescu A. Digital twins: state of the art theory and practice, challenges, and open research questions. *Journal of Industrial Information Integration*. 2022;30:100383.

[5] Lv Z, and Xie S. Artificial intelligence in the digital twins: state of the art, challenges, and future research topics. *Digital Twin*. 2022;1:12.

[6] Broo DG, and Schooling J. Digital twins in infrastructure: definitions, current practices, challenges and strategies. *International Journal of Construction Management*. 2023;23(7):1254–63.

[7] Boyes H, and Watson T. Digital twins: an analysis framework and open issues. *Computers in Industry*. 2022;143:103763.

[8] Fuller A, Fan Z, Day C, and Barlow C. Digital twin: enabling technologies, challenges and open research. *IEEE Access*. 2020;8:108952–71.

[9] Glaessgen E, and Stargel D, editors. The digital twin paradigm for future NASA and U.S. Air Force vehicles. *53rd AIAA/ASME/ASCE/AHS/ASC Structures, Structural Dynamics and Materials Conference*; 2012.

[10] Van der Valk H, Haße H, Möller F, Arbter M, Henning J-L, and Otto B, editors. A taxonomy of digital twins. *Americas Conference on Information Systems*; 2020.

[11] van der Valk H, Haße H, Möller F, and Otto B. Archetypes of digital twins. *Business & Information Systems Engineering*. 2022;64(3):375–91.

[12] Tomko M, and Winter S. Beyond digital twins – a commentary. *Environment and Planning B: Urban Analytics and City Science*. 2019;46(2):395–9.

[13] Jiang Y, Yin S, Li K, Luo H, and Kaynak O. Industrial applications of digital twins. *Philosophical Transactions of the Royal Society A*. 2021;379 (2207):20200360.

[14] Ala-Laurinaho R, Autiosalo J, Nikander A, Mattila J, and Tammi K. Data link for the creation of digital twins. *IEEE Access*. 2020;8:228675–84.

[15] Minerva R, Lee GM, and Crespi N. Digital twin in the IoT context: a survey on technical features, scenarios, and architectural models. *Proceedings of the IEEE*. 2020;108(10):1785–824.

[16] Damjanovic-Behrendt V, and Behrendt W. An open source approach to the design and implementation of digital twins for smart manufacturing. *International Journal of Computer Integrated Manufacturing*. 2019;32(4–5):366–84.

[17] Bakliwal K, Dhada MH, Palau AS, Parlikad AK, and Lad BK. A multi agent system architecture to implement collaborative learning for social industrial assets. *IFAC-PapersOnLine*. 2018;51(11):1237–42.

[18] Schultenkämper S, Bäumer FS, Bellgrau B, Lee YS, and Geierhos M. From digital tracks to digital twins: On the path to cross-platform profile linking. In: Sales TP, de Kinderen S, Proper HA, Pufahl L, Karastoyanova D, and van Sinderen M (eds.), *Enterprise Design, Operations, and Computing. EDOC 2023 Workshops*. Cham: Springer; 2024.

[19] Tao F, Cheng J, Qi Q, Zhang M, Zhang H, and Sui F. Digital twin-driven product design, manufacturing and service with big data. *The International Journal of Advanced Manufacturing Technology*. 2018;94:3563–76.

[20] Eneyew DD, Capretz MA, and Bitsuamlak GT. Toward smart-building digital twins: BIM and IoT data integration. *IEEE Access*. 2022;10:130487–506.

[21] Khan LU, Han Z, Saad W, Hossain E, Guizani M, and Hong CS. Digital twin of wireless systems: overview, taxonomy, challenges, and opportunities. *IEEE Communications Surveys & Tutorials*. 2022;24(4):2230–54.

[22] Lee KS, Lee J-J, Aucremanne C, Shah I, and Ghahramani A. Towards democratization of digital twins: design principles for transformation into a human-building interface. *Building and Environment*. 2023;244:110771.

[23] Tan B, and Matta A. The digital twin synchronization problem: framework, formulations, and analysis. *IISE Transactions*. 2024;56(6):652–65.
[24] Akbarian F, Fitzgerald E, and Kihl M. Synchronization in digital twins for industrial control systems. arXiv preprint arXiv:200603447. 2020.
[25] Eramo R, Bordeleau F, Combemale B, van Den Brand M, Wimmer M, and Wortmann A. Conceptualizing digital twins. *IEEE Software*. 2021;39(2):39–46.
[26] Kaul R, Ossai C, Forkan ARM, *et al*. The role of AI for developing digital twins in healthcare: the case of cancer care. *Wiley Interdisciplinary Reviews: Data Mining and Knowledge Discovery*. 2023;13(1):e1480.
[27] Korenhof P, Blok V, and Kloppenburg S. Steering representations—towards a critical understanding of digital twins. *Philosophy & Technology*. 2021;34:1751–73.
[28] Lu R, Rausch C, Bolpagni M, Brilakis I, and Haas CT. Geometric accuracy of digital twins for structural health monitoring. In: Oyguc R, and Tahmasebinia F (eds.), *Structural Integrity and Failure*. London: IntechOpen; 2020.
[29] Tao F, Xiao B, Qi Q, Cheng J, and Ji P. Digital twin modeling. *Journal of Manufacturing Systems*. 2022;64:372–89.
[30] Srinivas Timmapuram SG, and Shahela VK. Exploring the performance and accuracy of digital twin models. *International Research Journal of Engineering and Technology (IRJET)* 2023;10(5):517–22.
[31] Gross DC. Report from the fidelity implementation study group. *Fall Simulation Interoperability Workshop Papers*; 1999.
[32] You Y, Chen C, Hu F, Liu Y, and Ji Z. Advances of digital twins for predictive maintenance. *Procedia Computer Science*. 2022;200:1471–80.
[33] Muñoz P, Wimmer M, Troya J, and Vallecill A. Measuring the fidelity of a physical and a digital twin using trace alignments. *IEEE Transactions on Software Engineering*. 2024;50(12):3122–3145.
[34] Metcalfe B, Boshuizen HC, Bulens J, and Koehorst JJ. Digital twin maturity levels: a theoretical framework for defining capabilities and goals in the life and environmental sciences. *F1000Research*. 2023; 12:961.
[35] Popescu D, Dragomir M, Popescu S, and Dragomir D. Building better digital twins for production systems by incorporating environmental related functions—literature analysis and determining alternatives. *Applied Sciences*. 2022;12(17):8657.
[36] Grieves M, and Vickers J. Digital twin: mitigating unpredictable, undesirable emergent behavior in complex systems. In: Kahlen J, Flumerfelt S, and Alves A (eds), *Transdisciplinary Perspectives on Complex Systems*. Cham: Springer; 2017, pp. 85–113.
[37] Bucchiarone A. Gamification and virtual reality for digital twin learning and training: architecture and challenges. *Virtual Reality & Intelligent Hardware*. 2022;4(6):471–86.
[38] Zhang L, Zhou L, and Horn BK. Building a right digital twin with model engineering. *Journal of Manufacturing Systems*. 2021;59:151–64.

[39] Huang S, Wang G, Lei D, and Yan Y. Toward digital validation for rapid product development based on digital twin: a framework. *The International Journal of Advanced Manufacturing Technology*. 2022;119:2509–2523.

[40] Kalantari S, Pourjabar S, Xu TB, and Kan J. Developing and user-testing a 'Digital Twins' prototyping tool for architectural design. *Automation in Construction*. 2022;135:104140.

[41] Nocetti DFG, and Fleming PJ. *Parallel processing in digital control*. Berlin: Springer Science & Business Media; 2012.

[42] Zhao J, Xiong X, and Chen Y. Design and application of a network planning system based on digital twin network. *IEEE Journal of Radio Frequency Identification*. 2022;6:900–4.

[43] Segovia M, and Garcia-Alfaro J. Design, modeling and implementation of digital twins. *Sensors*. 2022;22(14):5396.

[44] Rodríguez F, Chicaiza WD, Sánchez A, and Escaño JM. Updating digital twins: methodology for data accuracy quality control using machine learning techniques. *Computers in Industry*. 2023;151:103958.

[45] Edington L, Dervilis N, Abdessalem AB, and Wagg D. A time-evolving digital twin tool for engineering dynamics applications. *Mechanical Systems and Signal Processing*. 2023;188:109971.

[46] Flores-García E, Kim G-Y, Yang J, Wiktorsson M, and Do Noh S, editors. Analyzing the characteristics of digital twin and discrete event simulation in cyber physical systems. *IFIP International Conference on Advances in Production Management Systems*; 2020: Springer.

[47] Qiuchen Lu V, Parlikad AK, Woodall P, Ranasinghe GD, and Heaton J, editors. Developing a dynamic digital twin at a building level: using Cambridge campus as case study. *International Conference on Smart Infrastructure and Construction 2019 (ICSIC) Driving Data-Informed Decision-Making*; 2019: ICE Publishing.

[48] Lu Q, Xie X, Parlikad AK, Schooling JM, and Konstantinou E. Moving from building information models to digital twins for operation and maintenance. *Proceedings of the Institution of Civil Engineers-Smart Infrastructure and Construction. 2020*;174(2):46–56.

[49] Witschel D, Döhla A, Kaiser M, Voigt K-I, and Pfletschinger T. Riding on the wave of digitization: insights how and under what settings dynamic capabilities facilitate digital-driven business model change. *Journal of Business Economics*. 2019;89(8):1023–95.

[50] Hämäläinen M. Urban development with dynamic digital twins in Helsinki city. *IET Smart Cities*. 2021;3(4):201–10.

[51] Zhang N. *Digital twins and intelligence: a symbiotic framework*. University of Birmingham; 2024.

[52] Ogunsakin R, Mehandjiev N, and Marin CA. Towards adaptive digital twins architecture. *Computers in Industry*. 2023;149:103920.

[53] Correia JB, Abel M, and Becker K. Data management in digital twins: a systematic literature review. *Knowledge and Information Systems*. 2023;65 (8):3165–96.

[54] Grieves M. Intelligent digital twins and the development and management of complex systems. *Digital Twin*. 2022;2:8.

[55] Errandonea I, Beltrán S, and Arrizabalaga S. Digital twin for maintenance: a literature review. *Computers in Industry*. 2020;123:103316.

[56] van Dinter R, Tekinerdogan B, and Catal C. Predictive maintenance using digital twins: a systematic literature review. *Information and Software Technology*. 2022;151:107008.

[57] Liu Z, Meyendorf N, and Mrad N, editors. The role of data fusion in predictive maintenance using digital twin. *AIP Conference Proceedings*; 2018: AIP Publishing.

[58] Chen C, Fu H, Zheng Y, Tao F, and Liu Y. The advance of digital twin for predictive maintenance: the role and function of machine learning. *Journal of Manufacturing Systems*. 2023;71:581–94.

[59] Singh APA, and Gameti N. Leveraging digital twins for predictive maintenance: techniques, challenges, and application. *IJSART*. 2024;10(09):118–28.

[60] Kuehn W. Digital twins for decision making in complex production and logistic enterprises. *International Journal of Design & Nature and Ecodynamics*. 2018;13(3):260–71.

[61] Villalonga A, Negri E, Biscardo G, *et al.* A decision-making framework for dynamic scheduling of cyber-physical production systems based on digital twins. *Annual Reviews in Control*. 2021;51:357–73.

[62] Granacher J, Nguyen T-V, Castro-Amoedo R, and Maréchal F. Overcoming decision paralysis—A digital twin for decision making in energy system design. *Applied Energy*. 2022;306:117954.

[63] West S, Stoll O, Meierhofer J, and Züst S. Digital twin providing new opportunities for value co-creation through supporting decision-making. *Applied Sciences*. 2021;11(9):3750.

[64] Chaplin JC, Martinez-Arellano G, and Mazzoleni A. Digital twins and intelligent decision making. In: Chaplin J, Pagano C, and Fort S (eds.), *Digital Manufacturing for SMEs: An Introduction*. 2020, pp. 159–86.

[65] Tzachor A, Sabri S, Richards CE, Rajabifard A, and Acuto M. Potential and limitations of digital twins to achieve the sustainable development goals. *Nature Sustainability*. 2022;5(10):822–9.

[66] Purcell W, Neubauer T, and Mallinger K. Digital twins in agriculture: challenges and opportunities for environmental sustainability. *Current Opinion in Environmental Sustainability*. 2023;61:101252.

[67] Rojek I, Mikołajewski D, and Dostatni E. Digital twins in product lifecycle for sustainability in manufacturing and maintenance. *Applied Sciences*. 2020;11(1):31.

[68] Pater J, and Stadnicka D. Towards digital twins development and implementation to support sustainability: systematic literature review. *Management and Production Engineering Review*. 2021;13(3):63–73.

[69] He B, and Bai K-J. Digital twin-based sustainable intelligent manufacturing: a review. *Advances in Manufacturing*. 2021;9(1):1–21.

[70] Dembski F, Wössner U, Letzgus M, Ruddat M, and Yamu C. Urban digital twins for smart cities and citizens: the case study of Herrenberg, Germany. *Sustainability*. 2020;12(6):2307.

[71] Schrotter G, and Hürzeler C. The digital twin of the city of Zurich for urban planning. *PFG–Journal of Photogrammetry, Remote Sensing and Geoinformation Science*. 2020;88(1):99–112.

[72] Kukushkin K, Ryabov Y, and Borovkov A. Digital twins: a systematic literature review based on data analysis and topic modeling. *Data*. 2022;7 (12):173.

[73] Wilking F, Schleich B, and Wartzack S. Digital twins-definitions, classes and business scenarios for different industry sectors. *Proceedings of the Design Society*. 2021;1:1293–302.

[74] Kritzinger W, Karner M, Traar G, Henjes J, and Sihn W. Digital twin in manufacturing: a categorical literature review and classification. *Ifac-PapersOnline*. 2018;51(11):1016–22.

[75] Onaji I, Tiwari D, Soulatiantork P, Song B, and Tiwari A. Digital twin in manufacturing: conceptual framework and case studies. *International Journal of Computer Integrated Manufacturing*. 2022;35(8):831–58.

[76] Teng SY, Touš M, Leong WD, How BS, Lam HL, and Máša V. Recent advances on industrial data-driven energy savings: digital twins and infrastructures. *Renewable and Sustainable Energy Reviews*. 2021;135:110208.

[77] Bortolini R, Rodrigues R, Alavi H, Vecchia LFD, and Forcada N. Digital twins' applications for building energy efficiency: a review. *Energies*. 2022;15(19):7002.

[78] Turab M, and Jamil S. A comprehensive survey of digital twins in healthcare in the era of metaverse. *BioMedInformatics*. 2023;3(3):563–84.

[79] De Benedictis A, Mazzocca N, Somma A, and Strigaro C. Digital twins in healthcare: an architectural proposal and its application in a social distancing case study. *IEEE Journal of Biomedical and Health Informatics*. 2022; 27(10):5143–54.

[80] Kamel Boulos MN, and Zhang P. Digital twins: from personalised medicine to precision public health. *Journal of Personalized Medicine*. 2021;11 (8):745.

[81] Pylianidis C, Osinga S, and Athanasiadis IN. Introducing digital twins to agriculture. *Computers and Electronics in Agriculture*. 2021;184:105942.

[82] Purcell W, and Neubauer T. Digital twins in agriculture: a state-of-the-art review. *Smart Agricultural Technology*. 2023;3:100094.

[83] Cesco S, Sambo P, Borin M, Basso B, Orzes G, and Mazzetto F. Smart agriculture and digital twins: applications and challenges in a vision of sustainability. *European Journal of Agronomy*. 2023;146:126809.

[84] Wagg D, Worden K, Barthorpe R, and Gardner P. Digital twins: state-of-the-art and future directions for modeling and simulation in engineering dynamics applications. *ASCE-ASME Journal of Risk and Uncertainty in Engineering Systems, Part B: Mechanical Engineering*. 2020;6(3):030901.

[85] Al-Sehrawy R, and Kumar B, editors. Digital twins in architecture, engineering, construction and operations. A brief review and analysis. *Proceedings of the 18th International Conference on Computing in Civil and Building Engineering: ICCCBE 2020*; 2021: Springer.
[86] Jiang F, Ma L, Broyd T, and Chen K. Digital twin and its implementations in the civil engineering sector. *Automation in Construction*. 2021; 130:103838.
[87] Piromalis D, and Kantaros A. Digital twins in the automotive industry: the road toward physical-digital convergence. *Applied System Innovation*. 2022;5(4):65.
[88] Biesinger F, Kraß B, and Weyrich M, editors. A survey on the necessity for a digital twin of production in the automotive industry. *2019 23rd International Conference on Mechatronics Technology (ICMT)*; 2019: IEEE.
[89] Kholopov V, Antonov S, Kurnasov E, and Kashirskaya E. Digital twins in manufacturing. *Russian Engineering Research*. 2019;39:1014–20.
[90] Le TV, and Fan R. Digital twins for logistics and supply chain systems: literature review, conceptual framework, research potential, and practical challenges. *Computers & Industrial Engineering*. 2024;187:109768.
[91] Moshood TD, Nawanir G, Sorooshian S, and Okfalisa O. Digital twins driven supply chain visibility within logistics: a new paradigm for future logistics. *Applied System Innovation*. 2021;4(2):29.
[92] Guo D, and Mantravadi S. The role of digital twins in lean supply chain management: review and research directions. *International Journal of Production Research*. 2025;63(5):1851–1872.
[93] Augustine P. The industry use cases for the digital twin idea. *Advances in Computers*. 2020;117:79–105.
[94] Zarco CG, editor. Digital twin and services: a theoretical development framework. *2024 IEEE Technology and Engineering Management Society (TEMSCON LATAM)*; 2024: IEEE.
[95] Stavropoulos P, and Mourtzis D. Digital twins in Industry 4.0. In: Mourtzis D (ed.), *Design and Operation of Production Networks for Mass Personalization in the Era of Cloud Technology*. Amsterdam: Elsevier; 2022. p. 277–316.
[96] Aheleroff S, Zhong RY, and Xu X. A digital twin reference for mass personalization in industry 4.0. *Procedia CIRP*. 2020;93:228–33.
[97] Mourtzis D, Angelopoulos J, and Panopoulos N. Personalized PSS design optimization based on digital twin and extended reality. *Procedia CIRP*. 2022;109:389–94.
[98] You M, Wang Q, Sun H, Castro I, and Jiang J. Digital twins based day-ahead integrated energy system scheduling under load and renewable energy uncertainties. *Applied Energy*. 2022;305:117899.
[99] Kabir MR, Halder D, and Ray S. Digital twins for IoT-driven energy systems: a survey. *IEEE Access*. 2024;12:177123–177143.
[100] Palensky P, Cvetkovic M, Gusain D, and Joseph A. Digital twins and their use in future power systems. *Digital Twin*. 2022;1:4.

[101] Virando GE, Lee B, Kee S-H, and Yee J-J. Digital twin simulation and implementation in safety risk management process. *IEEE Access*. 2024; 12:195671–195695.

[102] Agnusdei GP, Elia V, and Gnoni MG. A classification proposal of digital twin applications in the safety domain. *Computers & Industrial Engineering*. 2021;154:107137.

[103] Kim Y-J, Kim H, Ha B, and Kim W-T. Advanced fire emergency management based on potential fire risk assessment with informative digital twins. *Automation in Construction*. 2024;167:105722.

[104] Almeaibed S, Al-Rubaye S, Tsourdos A, and Avdelidis NP. Digital twin analysis to promote safety and security in autonomous vehicles. *IEEE Communications Standards Magazine*. 2021;5(1):40–6.

[105] Saunila M, Holopainen M, Nasiri M, Ukko J, and Rantala T. Digital transformation with digital twins-distinct mechanisms of enabling and controlling uses. *Technology Analysis & Strategic Management*. 2024;36(6):1323–36.

[106] Rahmani R, Jesus C, and Lopes SI. Implementations of digital transformation and digital twins: exploring the factory of the future. *Processes*. 2024;12(4):787.

[107] Oliveira PP. Digital twin development for airport management. *Journal of Airport Management*. 2020;14(3):246–59.

[108] Kober C, Medina FG, Benfer M, Wulfsberg JP, Martinez V, and Lanza G. Digital twin stakeholder communication: characteristics, challenges, and best practices. *Computers in Industry*. 2024;161:104135.

[109] Plummer D, Kearney S, Monagle A, *et al*. Skills and competency framework: Supporting the development and adoption of the Information Management Framework (IMF) and the National Digital Twin. 2021. https://www.cdbb.cam.ac.uk/files/010321cdbb_skills_capability_framework_vfinal.pdf.

[110] Batty M. Digital twins. *Environment and Planning B: Urban Analytics and City Science*. 2018;45(5):817–20.

[111] Arcones DA, Weiser M, Koutsourelakis S, and Unger JF. Model bias identification for Bayesian calibration of stochastic digital twins of bridges. *Applied Stochastic Models in Business and Industry*. 2025;41(3):e2897.

[112] Ramu SP, Boopalan P, Pham Q-V, *et al*. Federated learning enabled digital twins for smart cities: concepts, recent advances, and future directions. *Sustainable Cities and Society*. 2022;79:103663.

[113] Wang D, Zhou T, and Wang M. Information and communication technology (ICT), digital divide and urbanization: evidence from Chinese cities. *Technology in Society*. 2021;64:101516.

[114] Abd Elaziz M, Al-qaness MA, Dahou A, *et al*. Digital twins in healthcare: Applications, technologies, simulations, and future trends. *Wiley Interdisciplinary Reviews: Data Mining and Knowledge Discovery*. 2024;14(6): e1559.

[115] Mustofa R, Rafiquzzaman M, and Hossain NUI. Analyzing the impact of cyber-attacks on the performance of digital twin-based industrial organizations. *Journal of Industrial Information Integration*. 2024;41:100633.

Chapter 2
Towards a maturity model for digital twins

Alexander Rossmann[1] and Yusuf Bozkurt[1,2]

Abstract

The concept of digital twins is receiving increasing attention in research and management practice. Mentioned initially in 2003 by Michael Grieves, digital twins pave the way for cyber-physical integration and serve as a bridge between the physical and cyber worlds. Despite extensive research, there still needs to be a clear conceptualisation for digital twins. In addition to the conceptualisation of digital twins, another research gap relates to the development and implementation of measurement models for the degree of maturity of the implementation of digital twins. Such measurement models address whether a digital twin exists and which components must be implemented to implement digital twins effectively. Based on a comprehensive literature review, this research presents a holistic artefact for conceptualising maturity, grounded in the nine layers of the reference architecture of digital twins. Insights from maturity research are combined with this modelling, resulting in a practically applicable measurement model for digital twins with 72 items. This has extensive implications for further research and business practice. The present research's limitations and the need for additional research on the maturity of digital twins are discussed in conclusion.

Keywords: Digital twins; digital maturity; digital capabilities

2.1 Introduction

The concept of digital twins (DTs) is receiving increasing attention in both research and management practice [1,2]. Initially introduced by Michael Grieves in 2003 [3], DTs represent a transformative approach that facilitates cyber-physical integration, bridging the gap between the physical and digital realms. Conceptualised initially for application in manufacturing, the scope of DTs has since expanded to encompass a variety of domains, including smart cities [4], healthcare [5], management [6] and psychology [7]. This expansion underscores DTs' versatility and broad applicability as a technology.

[1]Herman Hollerith Centre, Faculty of Informatics, Reutlingen University, Germany
[2]Department of Computing, Engineering and Physical Sciences, University of the West of Scotland, UK

Since their inception, DTs have evolved into a pivotal strategic technology trend, drawing significant scholarly interest. A comprehensive search of academic databases reveals a marked increase in research on DTs. Before 2017, the number of academic publications addressing DTs was limited, often restricted to annual single-digit figures. However, post-2017, there has been an exponential rise in the volume of scholarly articles dedicated to this topic, reflecting a growing recognition of the potential of DTs to revolutionise various sectors [8].

The rapid proliferation of DTs in academic literature mirrors their increasing adoption in practical applications. In smart cities, DTs optimise urban planning and infrastructure management [4]. In healthcare, they offer innovative solutions for patient monitoring and personalised medicine [5]. In management, DTs enhance decision-making processes and operational efficiency management [6]. Furthermore, in psychology, they provide novel tools for behavioural analysis and mental health interventions [7].

Therefore, since its introduction in 2003, the concept of DTs has demonstrated substantial growth in both academic and practical contexts [8]. The exponential increase in related research and the expansion of their application domains highlight the significance of DTs as a transformative technology poised to drive future innovations across multiple fields. Continued exploration and development of DTs are imperative for unlocking their full potential and addressing emerging challenges in an increasingly digitalised world.

Despite extensive research, a clear conceptualisation of the term digital twin still needs to be done. Furthermore, different reference models are available for implementing DTs [9]. More or less consistent examples of the concept can be found in corporate practice [1]. There is agreement that implementing a DTs comprises the following components: *Physical entities*, which include vehicles, components, products, machines, streets, parking lots, buildings or other physical objects [10]. Data generation strategies require identifying the physical entities for digital twinning and the relevant data to be generated – a *network and connectivity* component covering data acquisition and transmission as crucial elements for real-time information flow. *Data storage* and processing as heterogeneous data sources and domain knowledge gathered from application processes must be integrated into operational databases. *Data integration* as data needs to be interpreted and prepared. *Data models*, *algorithms*, *virtual entities* and *virtual twins*. Machine learning (ML) and data-processing tools provide multiple solutions ranging from analytics to automation, giving the DTs decision-aiding capabilities via enabling tools. *Micro-services* and the *deployment of data models* in real-life processes [11]. Moreover, as DTs affect real-life processes, security is a major cross-architectural issue in designing twinning concepts. Finally, another component pertains to the generation of *business models*. This layer is essential because DTs only make sense if they drive business innovations and lead to compelling customer experience and business models [9].

Beyond the conceptualisation of DT, another research gap exists in developing and implementing measurement models for the maturity level of DT implementation [12]. Such measurement models are essential to determine the current degree of implementation of a DT and to derive possible pathways for further improvement [12]. Finally, such measurement models also address whether a DT exists and which components must be implemented to implement a DT concept effectively.

Concerning this research gap, this paper addresses the following research questions: (1) How is a DT conceptually defined? (2) Which dimensions are essential for determining the maturity level of a DT? (3) How can the maturity of a DT be measured?

To answer these questions, a mixed-method approach based on the design science research framework is implemented [13]. The fundamental objective of this research is to develop an applicable framework for determining the maturity of DTs. To this end, a multi-level and systematic literature review (SLR) is conducted in focal areas of (1) DTs and (2) maturity models, as well as the combination of these two research areas. Finally, an artefact in the form of a conceptual model and measurement model for determining the maturity level of DTs is derived from the literature review and operationalised in the form of a questionnaire. Furthermore, a guideline for evaluating the measurement model is presented.

2.2 Theoretical foundation

The chapter on theoretical foundations deals with the conceptualisation of DTs, the design of digital maturity models and measuring their maturity.

2.2.1 Digital twins

The theoretical foundations for the conceptualisation of DTs are highly dynamic. The research on DTs has grown significantly, particularly in recent years [9]. Grieves's initial description [3] defines a DT as a virtual representation of a physical product. Later, Grieves expands on this definition by describing DTs as consisting of three components: a physical product, a virtual representation of that product and bidirectional data connections that feed data from the physical product to the virtual representation and back. Scholars have also provided evidence that DTs not only deal with physical products but apply to any connection and bidirectional exchange between a virtual and physical entity [11,14,15].

Multiple reviews on the topic of DTs are present in current research. A meta-review of existing SLRs for DTs leads to a deeper conceptualisation, a description of current application areas and a reference architecture for DTs [9]. Such a deep foundation is also essential for developing measurement models for the maturity level for DT, as otherwise, it remains to be seen which dimensions are required to determine a maturity level and which items can be used to measure them.

The *conceptualisation of DTs* has become a pivotal topic of multiple scholarly reviews, driven by their diverse applications across various domains. Early literature primarily emphasised the role of DTs in smart manufacturing, physical production and product lifecycle management [11]. Consequently, these initial conceptualisations incorporated domain-specific attributes into defining a DT. However, with the expanding application of DTs across numerous fields, a generalised conceptualisation lacking domain-specific characteristics is necessitated [9].

A comprehensive synthesis of various reviews leads to a mutual understanding that a DT can be defined as a cyber-physical system comprising physical and virtual (digital) components [9]. As Michael Grieves initially posited, DTs bridge the physical and cyber worlds [3]. The bidirectional data flow between a physical entity and its digital counterpart, achieving full integration, is recognised as a fundamental characteristic of DTs. This bidirectional integration implies that a DT is not merely a static representation of a physical object but involves dynamic interaction and synchronisation between the physical and digital components [3,11,14,15].

This dynamic interaction encompasses several critical properties, including data models, connectivity, accuracy and synchronisation. The data models must accurately reflect the physical object, while robust connectivity ensures seamless data exchange. Accuracy is paramount to maintaining the digital representation's fidelity, and synchronisation guarantees that the physical and digital parts are consistently aligned. Moreover, developing a DT is purpose-driven and aimed at achieving specific benefits. The actual value of a DT emerges when the processing of real-world data within the digital component generates actionable insights and delivers corresponding services to the physical component [8,16].

Furthermore, this evolving conceptualisation suggests that specific applications within artificial intelligence (AI), such as ML algorithms, should be considered integral to the constitution of a DT. These AI-driven applications enhance DTs' capability to analyse vast amounts of data, predict outcomes and optimise processes, significantly augmenting their functionality and utility [17].

The conceptualisation of DTs has transitioned from domain-specific definitions to a more generalised and inclusive understanding [9]. This broader conceptualisation recognises the essential properties and dynamic interactions that define a DT, highlighting its role as a transformative technology [18]. The integration of AI and the focus on achieving tangible benefits underscore the significance of DTs in driving innovation and efficiency across multiple domains. Continued research and development are essential to refine this concept further and fully exploit its potential in an increasingly digitalised world. Based on the defined properties, the concept of a DT is defined as follows:

> *Digital twins need to be conceptualised as cyber-physical systems, with an interactive relationship between the physical and digital parts, purpose, data connectivity in both directions, corresponding data models, task-specific levels of model accuracy and data synchronisation procedures, embedded AI in the digital part of the twin, and dedicated services in the physical part.* - [9]

The general conceptualisation of DTs is highly beneficial for various *application areas*. Initially conceived for manufacturing, DTs have progressively permeated numerous domains, including smart cities [4], healthcare [5], management [6] and psychology [7]. This broad applicability demonstrates that the essence of DTs is not confined to any specific domain; instead, digital twinning is a versatile framework facilitating applications across multiple sectors. Central to this framework is the focus on bidirectional interactions between physical and digital entities [3,11,14,15].

Such a generalised conceptualisation is well-documented in SLRs, where researchers have developed diverse approaches to DTs [9]. For instance, in smart manufacturing, DTs have been implemented to enhance cyber-physical production systems, emphasising service-oriented architectures within extended production environments [14]. DTs have also been applied to provide stakeholder-specific services throughout the product life cycle, illustrating their utility in marketing and sales contexts [19].

A meta-review underscores the systematic expansion of the DT concept into various domains [9]. The ongoing research and practical implementations suggest that the proliferation of DTs is poised to continue, driven by the promise of diverse and impactful applications. For example, DTs facilitate urban planning and infrastructure management in smart cities [4]. In healthcare, they enable personalised medicine and advanced patient monitoring [5]. In management, DTs optimise operational efficiency and decision-making processes [20], while in psychology, they offer innovative tools for behavioural analysis and mental health interventions [7].

The evolving generalisation of DTs underscores their transformative potential across multiple fields. The documented evidence from various SLRs highlights DTs' adaptability and expansive utility, suggesting a continued trajectory of growth and innovation [9]. Future research should focus on refining these applications and exploring new domains, ensuring that the full potential of DTs is realised in an increasingly digitalised world.

Relevant sub-concepts for a general *reference architecture for DTs* are present in multiple SLRs. Rathore *et al.* provide a holistic approach for a general reference architecture for DTs with multiple layers [17]. The layers constitute a hierarchical order and include multiple forward and backwards interactions. Furthermore, distinguishing between layers supports defining properties and relevant technologies per layer. Essential components for such an architecture are also presented in [11]. Table 2.1 gives an overview of a nine-layer architecture and corresponding properties based on [9].

The bottom layer of a DT architecture comprises various *physical entities*, encompassing vehicles, components, products, machines, streets, parking lots, buildings and other tangible objects. The defining characteristic of these entities is their existence in the real world [10]. To provide a comprehensive and universally applicable framework, we adopt the term 'physical entity' to refer to any real-world object, irrespective of whether it has been integrated into a DT system. This terminology aligns with current literature, ensuring consistency and clarity in the discourse. When a physical entity is incorporated into a DT, it is called a 'physical twin' [10]. This distinction is crucial for accurately describing the stages of DT implementation. A physical entity becomes a physical twin once it is digitally replicated, facilitating real-time data exchange and interaction between the physical and digital realms [10,11,15,17,18,21]. This differentiation not only aids in precise communication but also underscores the progressive nature of DT development. These terms enhance our understanding and discussion of DT architectures,

Table 2.1 Reference architecture for digital twins

Layer	Properties	Sources
Business model, Business processes	Value propositions, revenue streams, cost structure, purpose	[10,11,15,17, 19,20,24]
System security, Data privacy	Security, privacy, risks, abuse, encryption, authorisation	[20]
Deployment, components, micro-services	Micro-services, deployment, loose coupling, interfaces, applications	[11,17,19,24,25]
Data models, algorithms, virtual entity, virtual twin	Data models, algorithms, ML, decision rules	[8,10,11,14, 16–18,20,21]
Data preparation, data representation	Semantics, ontologies, data labels, fidelity, twinning accuracy	[8,10,11,14, 16–18,21]
Data storage, data integration	Databases, synchronisation, big-data processing	[8,10,11,14, 16–18,21]
Network, connectivity	Network architecture, data exchange protocols, middleware platforms, streaming	[8,10,11,14, 16–18,21]
Data generation	Parameters, types of data, fidelity, accuracy	[8,10,11,14,15, 17,18,21]
Physical entities, physical twin	Physical existence, objects	[10,11,15,17, 18,21]

promoting a clear conceptual framework. By distinguishing between physical entities and physical twins, we can better address the complexities of creating and managing DTs. This approach ensures that the discourse remains structured and coherent, providing a solid foundation for further research and application in DT technology. Consequently, this refined terminology is instrumental in advancing the study and implementation of DTs across various domains.

The second layer of DT architecture encompasses various strategies for *data generation*, which are pivotal for the accurate and effective functioning of DTs [11]. This layer necessitates the identification of physical entities to be digitally twinned, as well as the determination of relevant parameters for data generation. Parameters refer to the types of data and the specific information that can be derived from these data points. Common technologies employed for data generation include sensors and log files, which are instrumental in capturing real-time data from physical entities [10]. A critical aspect of this layer is fidelity, which is defined by the number of parameters captured, their accuracy, and the level of abstraction involved in transferring data between the virtual and physical twins. Fidelity is essential for ensuring the DT accurately reflects the physical entity. High fidelity implies a comprehensive mirroring of physical characteristics and functionalities, whereas lower fidelity may involve twinning only specific critical components of the physical entity. The concept of fidelity also encompasses the required precision for digital twinning. It determines whether the DT will represent a minor aspect of the physical entity or provide a full-scale replication [22,23]. This precision is crucial for various applications, as it influences the effectiveness and utility of the DT in real-world scenarios. Thus, the second layer of DT architecture focuses on robust data generation strategies and the concept of fidelity. Accurate data generation and appropriate fidelity levels are vital for creating functional and reliable DTs, enhancing their applicability across diverse domains [8,10,11,14,15,17,18,21]. This structured approach ensures that DTs can effectively support decision-making processes and operational efficiencies in various sectors.

The third layer of the DT reference architecture encompasses *network and connectivity* components, which are critical for ensuring seamless data acquisition and transmission. This layer is fundamental for maintaining real-time information flow and robust connectivity. It includes designing and implementing network architectures, data exchange protocols and middleware platforms that facilitate efficient information exchange and stream processing. Network architecture within this layer involves the integration of various communication protocols, which are essential rule sets enabling machine-to-machine connectivity between communicating entities. These protocols ensure reliable and secure data transmission across the network. Additionally, the connectivity infrastructure utilised in DTs, such as Wi-Fi, Bluetooth, ZigBee and mobile radio communication, is covered under this layer [8,10,11,14,16–18,21]. These technologies provide the necessary framework for consistent and high-speed connectivity, enabling the effective functioning of DTs. The third layer's focus on network and connectivity is pivotal for achieving the real-time, bi-directional data flow required for DTs' accurate and efficient operation. This layer's robust infrastructure ensures that DTs can support complex and dynamic applications across various domains.

The DT reference architecture's fourth layer encompasses *data storage* and *processing*. This layer is critical for managing various application processes' vast and heterogeneous data sources. Effective integration of this diverse data is essential for creating a cohesive and functional DT system. To achieve this, operational database systems and integrated data lakes are utilised. These systems facilitate the seamless amalgamation of data from multiple sources, ensuring that all relevant information is accessible and usable. The data storage component focuses on the efficient and secure storage of large volumes of data. In contrast, data integration ensures that disparate data types and formats are harmonised into a unified framework. Big-data processing capabilities are also a vital aspect of this layer, enabling the analysis and extraction of valuable insights from the integrated data [11]. This comprehensive data management approach supports DTs' robust functionality, allowing for advanced analytics and informed decision-making. The fourth layer's focus on data storage and processing is essential for harnessing the full potential of DT technology [8,10,11,14], [16–18,21]. By ensuring efficient data management, this layer provides a solid foundation for the advanced capabilities of DTs across various applications.

The fifth layer of the DT reference architecture is dedicated to interpreting and preparing *integrated data*. This involves utilising advanced knowledge representation tools to create DTs, with ontologies being a prominent choice. Ontologies are particularly favoured due to their ability to address integration and domain-specific modelling challenges and facilitate the reuse and sharing of knowledge across different systems [11]. The fifth layer employs knowledge representation languages such as the W3C Web Ontology Language and knowledge management models like the Resource Description Framework to achieve a knowledge-based system. These foundational tools provide the necessary structure for creating and managing DTs. They enable the semantic integration of sensor data, which is crucial for developing comprehensive taxonomies, ontologies, data formats and standards. Semantic integration ensures that data from various sources can be harmonised and interpreted coherently. This is essential for maintaining the accuracy and reliability of DTs and enhancing their ability to support complex decision-making processes. By leveraging these advanced tools and methodologies, the fifth layer facilitates the creation of robust and versatile DTs that can effectively model and manage the intricacies of real-world systems [8,10,11,14,16–18,21].

The sixth layer of the DT reference architecture is critical, encompassing *data models*, *algorithms*, *virtual entities* and *twins*. This layer leverages ML and AI to enhance the functionality and efficacy of DTs. ML and AI tools offer a wide range of solutions, from advanced analytics to automation, thereby significantly augmenting the decision-making capabilities of DTs [11]. At the core of this layer are sophisticated data models and algorithms designed to process and analyse vast amounts of data in real-time. These models facilitate the creation of virtual entities that mirror their physical counterparts with high fidelity. The integration of ML algorithms enables these virtual entities' continuous learning and adaptation based on new data inputs, ensuring that the DTs remain accurate and up-to-date. AI-driven data-processing tools are pivotal in this layer by providing robust analytics capabilities. These tools can identify patterns, predict outcomes and generate insights for informed decision-making. For instance, predictive maintenance algorithms can forecast equipment failures before they occur, allowing for proactive interventions. Similarly, optimisation algorithms can enhance operational efficiencies by recommending adjustments based on real-time data. The application of ML and AI within the DT framework also facilitates automation. Automated processes driven by AI can manage routine tasks, freeing up human resources for more strategic activities. Moreover, the decision-making capabilities provided by these tools empower organisations to make data-driven decisions with greater accuracy and confidence [20]. AI is indispensable for the advanced functionality of DTs. By incorporating intelligent data models, adaptive algorithms and powerful analytics tools, this layer ensures that DTs can effectively simulate, predict and optimise real-world processes, driving innovation and efficiency across various domains [8,10,11,14,16–18,20,21].

The seventh layer of the DT reference architecture focuses on microservices and the deployment of data models in real-life processes [11,17,19,24]. Microservices represent a modern software development approach characterised by loosely coupled services. This architectural style allows applications to be built as a suite of relatively small, consistent, isolated and autonomous services, each performing specific tasks [25]. The microservices architecture provides several advantages, including increased flexibility, scalability and ease of maintenance, which are critical for the effective implementation and operation of DTs. In the context of DTs, microservices facilitate the seamless integration and deployment of data models into real-world processes. By leveraging microservices, different components of a DT can be developed, deployed and scaled independently. This modular approach enhances the robustness and agility of DT systems, enabling them to adapt to changing requirements and environments efficiently. Microservice architectures are applicable across various domains. In the realm of smart production, for instance, the Reference Architectural Model Industry 4.0 (RAMI 4.0) provides a comprehensive framework that includes layers and microservices tailored for production systems [26]. RAMI 4.0 facilitates the monitoring and tracing of shop-floor assets, enabling automated conflict resolution and performance enhancement through decision-aiding support and control mechanisms. By employing microservices, DTs can achieve higher operational efficiency and effectiveness. This architectural style supports the dynamic interaction between physical and digital entities, ensuring that DTs can provide real-time insights and facilitate informed decision-making. Deploying data models via microservices thus represents a critical enabler for the practical application and success of DT technologies across diverse industrial and commercial settings.

The eighth layer of the DT reference architecture addresses *system security and data privacy*, both critical concerns given the impact of DTs on real-life processes. Security is a paramount, cross-architectural issue in designing twinning concepts due to integrating sensitive data, particularly in stakeholder-related services such as after-sales support, product customisation and content personalisation. As a result, data privacy has emerged as a significant consideration in DT implementations. Privacy-preserving approaches in DTs are generally classified into cryptographic and noncryptographic. Cryptographic approaches encompass encryption schemes and cryptographic primitives, ensuring data protection through secure encoding. On the other hand, noncryptographic approaches involve policy-based authorisation infrastructures that control access to sensitive information based on predefined policies and rules [20]. A robust reference architecture for DTs must incorporate properties that detect and mitigate security and privacy concerns. This involves implementing mechanisms to identify potential breaches and associated risks, thereby minimising the exposure of DTs to security threats. Adequate security and privacy measures are essential for maintaining the integrity and trustworthiness of DT systems, ensuring that they can safely and reliably support various applications across different domains.

The ninth layer of the DT reference architecture focuses on generating *business models*, a critical aspect for realising the full potential of DTs. This layer emphasises that the actual value of DTs lies in their ability to drive business innovations and enhance customer experiences, ultimately leading to compelling and sustainable business models [10,11,15,17,19,20,24]. Despite the increasing interest in DTs across various application areas, their adoption remains predominantly within the manufacturing industry. However, even within this sector, there has been limited scholarly attention to the business model implications of DTs [27,28]. DTs aim to enhance customer experience by enabling the creation of better-suited products and services. By leveraging real-time data and advanced analytics, DTs facilitate the development of high-quality products tailored to customer needs, thereby improving customer satisfaction. Additionally, DTs can expand the customer base by providing new market access opportunities and fostering co-creation initiatives with customers. These initiatives enable businesses to engage customers in development, leading to innovative products and services that better meet market demands. Furthermore, DTs drive the development of new products, services and value propositions by enabling continuous feedback loops and iterative improvements. This iterative process allows companies to refine their offerings based on real-world performance data and customer feedback. The ability to rapidly adapt to changing market conditions and customer preferences is a significant advantage, positioning businesses to remain competitive in dynamic environments. By integrating DTs into their operations, companies can develop more effective products and services, achieve higher customer satisfaction and create sustainable value propositions. This layer highlights the necessity of considering business model implications to fully exploit the potential of DT technology across various industries.

In summary, the twinning process begins with collecting data from the physical entities or using already-collected data in the virtual twin (using computer-aided software or simulations). The data are subject to analysis and decision-making, in which statistical and probabilistic approaches or mathematical models are employed to develop the DTs. Various big-data processing tools that allow parallel processing on multiple nodes may be employed throughout the process. The overall data flow for developing purpose-driven DTs begins with creating a data model. After the data model is developed and tested, data from physical and virtual twins deploy specific services to achieve the given organisational objectives such as design optimisation, dynamic process planning or content customisation [17].

The presented architecture shows common ground with existing frameworks for specific domains; for example, the open systems interconnection model consists of seven layers (physical, data link, network, transport, session, presentation and application) and paves the way for layered network architectures with the use of abstraction layers. A clear definition of DTs and the presentation of a reference architecture is also essential for determining the maturity level. Maturity models must refer to all the critical components of DT and reflect the state of development. Therefore, the reference model shown in Table 2.1 forms the starting point for recording the maturity level in different components of DTs.

2.2.2 Maturity models

Another theoretical basis of this chapter relates to the state of research on maturity models. The rise of digital technologies has become an essential driver for change in multiple industries. Digital technologies affect all firm levels, including business model frameworks, customer interfaces, customer experience and internal processes [18]. Therefore, firms must develop digital capabilities to manage the transformation process successfully [2,19]. Prior research assumes that developing specific digital capabilities leads to higher digital maturity [2]. Moreover, the degree of digital maturity can impact corporate performance. However, measurement frameworks for digital maturity are rare in scholarly work. The following section discusses available digital maturity measurement models and their applicability to DTs.

The term 'digital maturity' receives particular attention in [29]. Westerman *et al.* [29] prove that firms with higher digital maturity earn superior corporate performance. This research stream separates the concept of digital maturity into digital capabilities (e.g., strategy, technological expertise, business models, customer experience) and leadership capabilities (e.g., governance, change management, culture). Firms with mature digital capabilities and weak leadership capabilities are called *Fashionistas*, while firms with mature leadership capabilities and weak digital capabilities are called *Conservatives*. Corresponding to [29], firms must develop both capability dimensions to achieve *digital mastery*. Firms that do so show superior corporate performance, measured by indicators such as revenue per employee, earnings before interest and taxes, and product margins. Management practice has heavily adopted Westerman *et al.*'s [29] model. Multiple consultancy companies have developed a corresponding framework to measure digital maturity, including KPMG,[1] McKinsey,[2] and Boston Consulting Group.[3] Capgemini Consulting disseminates corresponding measurement models to estimate its clients' digital maturity [30]. Thus, many corporate transformation projects have been inspired by frameworks and models for digital maturity.

As such, it is of significant interest to evaluate whether the practical discussion around digital maturity and the implementation of corresponding measurement models are supported by research. Rossmann's highly cited literature review [12] includes 25 search results for relevant maturity and measurement models [31–55]. Based on a comprehensive analysis of this work, a general maturity model for implementing digital technologies with eight dimensions was developed: (1) strategy (explicit, cross-functional, transformative, evaluated), (2) leadership (commitment, style, role, leadership adoption), (3) business model (customer value, innovation, digitalisation, co-creation), (4) operating model (agility, integration, resources, cooperation), (5) people (expertise, learning, employee adoption, specialisation), (6) culture (transparency, dynamic, empowerment, attitude toward change), (7) governance (coordination, alignment, measurability, target orientation) and (8) technology (data, interaction, automation, workplace). This led to an eight-factor structure in conceptualising digital maturity with 32 items. Table 2.2 displays the complete item formulation for each capability dimension.

Of course, whether and how general measurement models for digital maturity can be used specifically for the context of DTs is still being determined. Therefore, specific models for measuring the maturity of DTs are discussed below. The findings from the reference architecture and maturity models can then be integrated into a new maturity model for DTs.

[1]https://assets.kpmg.com/content/dam/kpmg/pdf/2016/04/ch-digital-readiness-assessment-en.pdf.
[2]http://www.mckinsey.com/solutions/digital-quotient.
[3]http://www.bcg.com/de-de/capabilities/technology-digital/digital-acceleration-index.aspx

Table 2.2 Dimensions and items for the measurement of digital maturity

#	Capability	Items
1	Strategic capability	Our firm has implemented a digital strategy. The digital strategy of our firm is documented and communicated. The digital strategy of our firm has a significant influence on existing business and operating models. The digital strategy is being continuously evaluated and adapted.
2	Leadership capability	Our executives support the implementation of the digital strategy. The digital strategy is only implemented in individual functional areas (inverse). The culture of leadership in our firm is based on transparency, cooperation and decentralised decision- making processes. The digital strategy of our firm has an influence on the task and role profiles of executives.
3	Market capability	Digital products and services are embedded in our business interfaces and business processes and create a perceptible impact on customer experience. There is a direct added value created by the progressive digitisation of products and services of our firm (e.g., cost reductions, increased productivity, better customer experience, customer differentiation). Digital products and services have a large impact on the overall performance of our firm. Our firm is creating significant sales volume via digital channels.
4	Operational capability	There are sufficient resources (time, people, budget) available to implement the digital strategy within our firm. We established a strong cross-functional cooperation and co-creation with stakeholders throughout our value chain. Digital and physical processes are fully integrated by holistic process models. The impetus of our digital strategy is leading to innovations in operations.
5	People and expertise capability	Within our firm, there are sufficient experts on digital core issues. Within our firm, further education opportunities for digital core topics are available. Within our firm, comprehensive measures to strengthen digital literacy development are implemented. Within our firm, new job profiles have been created for employees with expertise in digital core topics.
6	Cultural capability	Decisions within our firm are transparent to our own employees. Digitisation has an impact on the decision-making agility of our firm. In day-to-day business, employees and executives exchange information about the digital transformation of our firm. Continuous change is part of our corporate culture.

(Continues)

Table 2.2 (*Continued*)

#	Capability	Items
7	Governance capability	Guidelines for the use of digital technologies are communicated and used by employees. Our firm implements a holistic management model for the digital strategy and corresponding key metrics. The key metrics for the digital strategy are fully integrated into controlling. The corporate strategy and the digital strategy are intensively networked and complement each other.
8	Technology capability	Our firm uses large amounts of data to optimise strategies, processes and products. Within our firm, we use tools for digital modelling, automation and control of business processes. Our firm has implemented enterprise-wide digital workplace concepts. Digital platforms are used for day-to-day collaboration. Digital technologies are the mainspring for the further development of products and services.

2.2.3 Digital twins and maturity

Several research approaches have recently focused on the relationship between DTs and maturity models. This section discusses these approaches. The focus is on examining relevant literature and related work, paying particular attention to the dimensions and items identified within DT maturity models and the methodologies used to collect and analyse data in these maturity models.

In reviewing related works, the focus was not exclusively on the peer-reviewed academic literature, often called *white literature*. Instead, a broader analysis horizon was adopted, and the so-called *grey literature* was also included. This approach, known as a multivocal literature review [56], provides a more comprehensive and multifaceted view of the research field. Multivocal literature reviews greatly benefit researchers and practitioners, offering a comprehensive summary of the current state of the art and practical applications [56]. This is particularly important in the DTs field, which is a highly relevant topic in both industry and academia. Industry players, such as consulting companies and technology providers [57–60], are intensively addressing the topic and publishing relevant material online or in practice-relevant magazines. These sources do not fall into the peer-reviewed category but contribute significantly to the understanding and development of DTs.

Figure 2.1 illustrates the procedural approach applied to identify relevant work. In the grey literature section, a systematic search was conducted using the search term 'Digital Twin Maturity Model' on Google. We carefully analysed the first five pages of search results by scrolling through the titles of the websites and,

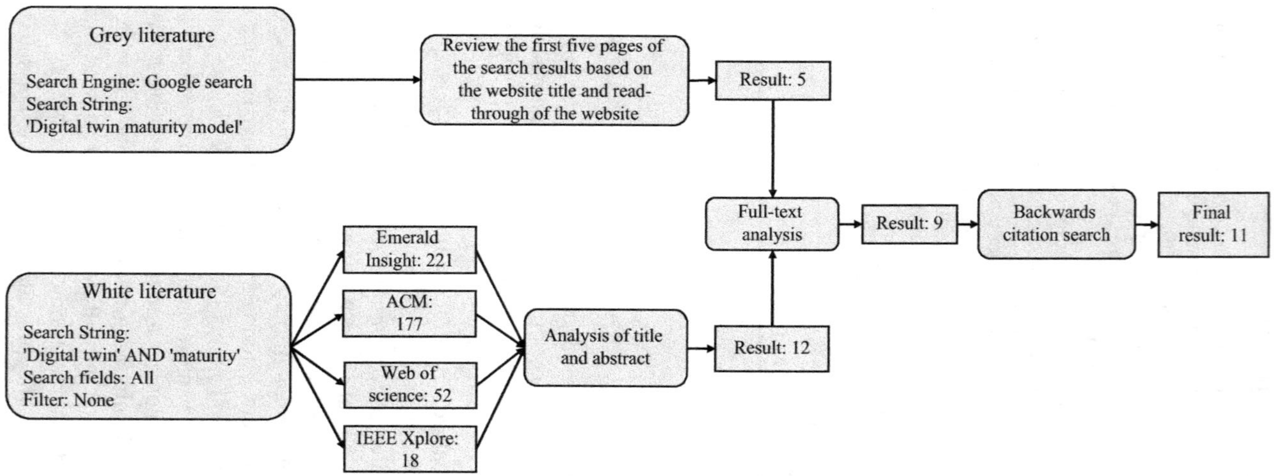

Figure 2.1 Related work search process

for articles that seemed relevant, reading through the website at a raw level. This process resulted in five promising articles included in the set for later full-text analysis. In parallel, the white literature was searched using the same search term in the four scientific databases/search engines: Emerald Insight, ACM, Web of Science and IEEE Xplore. The results' titles and abstracts were read, leading to twelve promising articles to be analysed in a full-text analysis. The full-text analysis of seventeen potentially relevant articles led to nine relevant articles. Two relevant articles were identified by applying backwards citation, resulting in eleven relevant articles. These articles are listed in Table 2.3 and summarised by their primary contribution to the concept of DT maturity models, which lists the items of the presented maturity models.

Table 2.3 Related work on 'Digital Twin Maturity Models'

Source	Contribution to the DT maturity model research, dimensions and items of the maturity levels
[61]	A maturity model for DTs is presented, in which the communication between the DT and the physical object and the degree of standardisation in the modelling of the exchanged data and data sources are taken as maturity criteria. Both aspects are presented in a 4×5 matrix, which enables a simultaneous consideration of five communication and four standardisation levels. The communication levels are defined as follows: C1) Representative: no communication between the physical and the virtual object. C2) Simulator: unidirectional communication between the physical and the virtual object. C3) Monitor: the physical object is monitored by visualising sensor data. C4) Smart monitor: extended monitoring is made possible by linking and enriching the data received. C5) Digital twin: bidirectional communication is available in which interaction with the virtual model directly impacts the physical object. The standardisation levels are evaluated as follows: S1) Hands-on: no standardisation; the information model is proprietary. S2) Basic model: an information model enables data exchange. S3) Twin of twins: a standardised information model can link different DTs. S4) World model: full integration into ecosystems can be achieved by standardised components.
[62]	Presents a ten-dimensional maturity model for implementing DTs in the commercial aerospace industry. The dimensions and their respective levels are defined as follows: D1) Analytical capability: monitoring, diagnosis, prediction, prescription D2) Frequency of model update: weeks, days, hours, minutes D3) Frequency of data collection: demand-based, flight history data, in-flight data, real-time D4) Modelling scope: parts, subsystems, complete product, product environment D5) Decision implementation: no consideration of DT data, human in the loop, hybrid, automated connection

(Continues)

Table 2.3 (*Continued*)

Source	Contribution to the DT maturity model research, dimensions and items of the maturity levels
	D6) Life cycle integration: one-stage, two-stage, three-stage, full integration D7) Degree of customisation: as-maintained, as-operated, as-built, as-manufactured D8) Affected company level: process, product, business model D9) Accessibility of operational data: access in process, restricted access, full access, sole ownership D10) Stage of implementation: Conceptual, development, deployment, deployed
[63]	Presents a maturity model for DTs in asset management. Based on the Gemini principles, the model provides a structured overview of the development and implementation of DTs. It consists of three primary dimensions: purpose, trust and function, and nine sub-categories: (1) purpose, (2) value creation, (3) public good, (4) function, (5) federation, (6) development, (7) trust, (8) openness and (9) detailed by 27 rubrics. In addition, six maturity levels are listed to represent the level of the system: (0) unaware, (1) identifiable, (2) aware, (3) communicative, (4) interactive and (5) instructive and intelligent.
[65]	Presents four maturity levels of DTs in the context of real-time analysis: First level: data transparency is achieved in a consistent real-time database through continuous data collection during the execution of individual work steps. Second level: transparency extends across several production steps and requires a consistent real-time database that includes data from dependent production steps. Third level: real-time data transparency encompasses all product aspects of a physical object. Virtualisation is holistic and does not only include isolated elements. Fourth level: real-time data transparency spans product lifecycles and covers all aspects of physical objects, including changes over time. All levels are considered based on three dimensions: continuity and consistency of real-time data, analytical capabilities of the organisation for real-time validation and quality assessment, and stakeholder integration.
[66]	Describes the 'Digital Twin 8-Dimension Model', a structured approach to planning DTs. Each dimension has three or four levels, and a higher level does not strictly represent a refinement but a different realisation space. The model is not a maturity model but a tool to support the individual business context situations of the specific DT. Dimensions: (1) Integration breadth, (2) connection mode, (3) update frequency, (4) cyber-physical systems (CPS) intelligence, (5) simulation capabilities, (6) digital model richness, (7) human interaction and (8) product lifecycle
[67]	Examines the concept of DTs in the context of ports. The aim is to cope with the increasing growth in freight transport while improving the ecological footprint. Five successive levels of maturity are outlined: 1) Replication of assets: creating and maintaining digital records representing the system's physical components. 2) Connection: connecting models capable of capturing events in the real world.

(*Continues*)

Table 2.3 (Continued)

Source	Contribution to the DT maturity model research, dimensions and items of the maturity levels
	3) Synchronisation: static and dynamic data integration to enable real-time situational awareness. 4) Interaction: two-way communication and control commands remotely. 5) Automation: the DT makes autonomous decisions based on real-time and historical data, enabling complete remote control.
[68]	Describes six maturity elements for DTs in building context as a 'maturity spectrum': E0 – reality capture (for existing physical assets): captures accurate, as-built records of the assets' geometric structure or system design. E1 – 2D map/system or 3D model (object-based): as an entry point for new assets and is updated after the design process. E2 – linked to persistent (static) data, metadata and BIM level 2: links E1 to persistent data sets such as design information, material specifications, inspection reports and asset management information. E3 – enrichment with real-time (dynamic) data: captures and displays real-time operational data from sensors and the IoT E4 – two-way integration and interaction: physical state can be changed by the DT but requires additional sensors and mechanisation E5 – autonomous operation and maintenance: a vision of the future where the DT becomes autonomous and can correct anomalies without human interaction.
[69]	Describes five maturity levels of DT solutions. Level 0: data silos without standardisation. Level 1: company-wide information models and APIs for DTs. Level 2: correlations between models in DTs. Level 3: integration of advanced models such as ML and simulations. Stage 4: multiple models for complex use cases, e.g., to predict the remaining service life of an engine.
[70]	Deals with DTs from an urban perspective, considering people, governance and technology as driving forces. A four-stage maturity model is presented with the stages: 1) Strategy stage (awareness): a city develops the political and financial basis for implementing DTs. 2) Experimental twins (explorative): DTs are created for specific use cases to test predictive modelling and interoperability. 3) Insightful twins (predictive): cities use DTs to predict policy impacts and make informed decisions. 4) Intelligent twins (future ready): AI-enabled twins tackle policy challenges in real-time and create a more resilient and sustainable future.
[71]	The maturity model aims to support organisations in evaluating software solutions, provides a framework for a DT strategy and creates a roadmap for developing a DT. The model is presented in a matrix structure with features and capabilities on the axes: • Features (read from bottom to top): spatial representation, static parametric data, streaming sensor data, historical event data, analytical capabilities and AI, entity control capability • Capabilities (read from left to right): digital model, digital image, DT

(Continues)

Table 2.3 (Continued)

Source	Contribution to the DT maturity model research, dimensions and items of the maturity levels
	The features at the bottom left represent early implementations, while those at the top right are implemented later in the evolution.
[64]	Present a method for the comprehensive assessment of DTs. Potential functions and features are considered at different stages of development. The maturity model evaluates DTs based on seven categories with a total of 31 characteristics.: (1) Context, (2) data, (3) computing capacity, (4) modelling, (5) integration, (6) control, (7) human–machine interface This method allows an application-specific evaluation and shows possibilities for improving DTs for specific applications.

The related work provides self-assessment methods in which participants are asked to assess their maturity level subjectively. To illustrate the results, these are often presented in visual form. An example is [61], using a 4×5 matrix where participants can tick the box corresponding to their self-perception. However, there is no standardised data collection. In [62], a similar method asks participants to rate their perceived maturity level for each dimension and visualises the results in a network diagram. Only two maturity models use mathematical approaches to calculate the DT maturity level, such as [63], which uses a questionnaire with rating grids and a 5-point Likert scale. The results are analysed mathematically and displayed in a three-dimensional coordinate system. The maturity model described in [64] relies on systematic self-assessment by the user using a points system. Each category has an individual rating scale. The overall result is calculated using a weighted mathematical formula to determine the maturity level of the DT. Despite the various approaches, most related work lacks a systematic method for quantifying the maturity level. Instead, only the presentation and description of maturity levels are presented without explaining how the maturity model should be applied [65–71]. This results in a research gap in the systematic recording and qualification of the maturity level, especially regarding the possibility of recording and measuring the maturity level comparably, for example, by implementing a standardised questionnaire. In addition, existing studies have limitations in the lack of transparency regarding the origin and basis of the proposed maturity models [61,68,70,71]. The results of the 11 most influential papers are summarised in Table 2.3.

The results from the literature analysis largely confirm the dimensions and components of the reference architecture from Table 2.1. However, most studies also lack an operationalisation of the maturity model in the form of an applicable measurement model. Therefore, the following design process refers to the design of an artefact for (1) integrating the findings from reference and maturity models and (2) implementing a maturity model for DTs as an applicable measurement model.

2.3 Maturity model

The following subchapter integrates the findings from previous chapters into a conceptual artefact for an integrated maturity model for DTs. The model is based on the construct working definition and the reference architecture for DTs presented in the theoretical foundation. In addition, maturity dimensions and concrete indicators for measuring the maturity of DTs are derived. As a result, this leads to a conceptual reference model for systematically measuring the maturity level of DTs.

It can be assumed that each dimension of the reference model also determines the maturity level of a DT. Therefore, the nine dimensions of the reference architecture from Table 2.1 are also used as core dimensions of the maturity model. In addition, the maturity level in each dimension is determined by questions that general maturity models induce. For example, the sub-area of the reference architecture for *business models* can be addressed whether specific strategies for business models of DTs exist, whether the enterprise leadership supports this, whether a suitable review of the business models from the perspective of the market and the internal business processes has taken place, whether well-founded governance structures and human resources are available for implementation, etc. In this way, relevant questions about the maturity level can be defined at each architecture level of the DT. An overview of the logic generated in this way can be found in Table 2.4.

Accordingly, the conceptual model shown in Table 2.4 provides the basis for a holistic assessment of the maturity level of DTs across all relevant architectural levels and in all relevant sub-dimensions of the digital maturity level. When applied in the corporate context, this allows both maturity assessments of a DT as a whole and at individual architectural levels to be recorded. This also forms a basis for the formulation of suitable measurement models.

Table 2.4 A conceptual maturity model for digital twins

Layer of reference architecture/ maturity dimensions	Operationalisation of the maturity dimension	Description
1. Business model	Strategy	Deals with the development, testing and further development of strategies for a DT's business models
	Leadership	Deals with the management of organisational units related to the organisational embedding of a DT
	Market	Deals with markets and customers for the use of DT's products and services
	Operations	Deals with internal processes and operating procedures for the organisational operation of a DT

(Continues)

Table 2.4 (Continued)

Layer of reference architecture/ maturity dimensions	Operationalisation of the maturity dimension	Description
	People	Addresses the relevant people, roles, expertise and competencies for the successful implementation of a business model for DT
	Culture	Addresses the corporate culture required for the successful operation of a business model with a DT
	Governance	Deals with the management of KPIs, operating parameters, interfaces and the general communication processes relating to the business model of DTs and the organisational environment
	Technology	Deals with the fundamental technologies required for the implementation of a DT from a business model perspective
2. System security	Strategy	Deals with the development, testing and further development of strategies to ensure the system security and data privacy of DTs
	Leadership	Deals with the management of the development and operation of a DT from the perspective of system security and data privacy
	Market	Deals with the collection and implementation of system security and data privacy requirements from the perspective of external markets and DT's customers
	Operations	Deals with the recording and implementation of system security and data privacy requirements from the perspective of the relevant operating models for DT
	People	Addresses the relevant people, roles, expertise and competencies for ensuring system security and data privacy in the context of DTs
	Culture	Addresses the corporate culture required to ensure system security and data privacy
	Governance	Deals with control models and indicators in relation to ensuring the system security and data privacy of DTs
	Technology	Addresses the degree to which appropriate technologies are used to ensure system security and data privacy
3. Deployment	Strategy	Deals with the development, testing and further development of strategies for deployment as well as ensuring architectures for general DT deployability

(Continues)

Table 2.4 (*Continued*)

Layer of reference architecture/ maturity dimensions	Operationalisation of the maturity dimension	Description
	Leadership	Deals with the management of the development and operation of a DT in relation to the deployment of individual components and the general promotion of deployability
	Market	Deals with the collection and implementation of requirements for deployments of individual components and relevant interfaces from the perspective of external markets and DT customers
	Operations	Deals with the collection and implementation of requirements for deployments of individual components and relevant interfaces from the perspective of the DT's internal operating model
	People	Deals with the relevant people, roles, expertise and competencies for implementing the deployment of individual components of the DT and increasing deployability in general
	Culture	Deals with the corporate culture that is favourable for the deployment of different components of a DT and the general increase in deployability
	Governance	Deals with control models, KPIs and indicators for the deployment of individual components of a DT and for the general increase in deployability
	Technology	Addresses the degree to which appropriate technologies are used to simplify and integrate the deployment of DT components and generally promote deployability
4. Data models & algorithms	Strategy	Deals with the development, testing and further development of data models, algorithms, ML approaches and other forms of AI in DTs
	Leadership	Deals with the management of the development and operation of a DT with regard to the use of ML approaches and AI in general
	Market	Deals with the development and implementation of requirements for data models, algorithms and AI from the perspective of DT's external markets and customers
	Operations	Deals with the development and implementation of requirements for data models, algorithms and AI from the perspective of the DTs operating model

(Continues)

Table 2.4 (Continued)

Layer of reference architecture/ maturity dimensions	Operationalisation of the maturity dimension	Description
	People	Addresses the relevant people, roles, expertise and competencies for the development and implementation of relevant data models, AI and ML approaches
	Culture	Addresses the corporate culture that supports the application of data models, automation through AI and the application of ML
	Governance	Deals with control models, KPIs and evaluation metrics for the development and implementation of data models, algorithms and ML approaches in the context of a DT
	Technology	Deals with the use and suitability of the technologies used for the application of data models, AI approaches, ML models and their integration into DTs
5. Data preparation & data representation	Strategy	Deals with the development, testing and further development of data structures, procedures for data preparation and data representation in organisational environments
	Leadership	Deals with the management of the development and operation of a DT in relation to the definition and application of data preparation and data representation approaches
	Market	Deals with the development and implementation of requirements for data, data formats, data preparation and data representation from the perspective of DT's external markets and customers
	Operations	Deals with the development and implementation of requirements for data, data formats, data preparation and data representation from the perspective of the DT operating model
	People	Addresses the relevant people, roles, expertise and competencies for the definition and selection of appropriate data, data formats and the implementation of approaches to data preparation and data representation
	Culture	Addresses the organisational culture required for effective data definition, data availability and effective approaches to data preparation and data representation
	Governance	Deals with control models and indicators for the definition of data as well as the selection and application of suitable methods of data preparation and data representation

(Continues)

Table 2.4 (*Continued*)

Layer of reference architecture/ maturity dimensions	Operationalisation of the maturity dimension	Description
	Technology	Addresses the degree of use of appropriate technologies for data preparation and data representation
6. Data storage	Strategy	Deals with the development, testing and further development of data storage strategies
	Leadership	Deals with the management of the development and operation of a DT in relation to the appropriate storage of data
	Market	Deals with the development and implementation of data storage requirements from the perspective of external markets and DT's customers
	Operations	Deals with the development and implementation of data storage requirements from the perspective of the DT's operating model
	People	Addresses the relevant people, roles, expertise and competencies for defining and selecting appropriate approaches to data storage
	Culture	Addresses the corporate culture that is conducive to effective data storage solutions
	Governance	Deals with control models and KPIs for the selection and implementation of data storage approaches
	Technology	Addresses the degree to which appropriate technologies are used for data storage
7. Networks & connectivity	Strategy	Deals with the development, testing and further development of strategies for implementing networks and ensuring connectivity between different components of the DT and its environment
	Leadership	Deals with the management of the development and operation of a DT in terms of ensuring high- performance networks and ensuring connectivity between the components of a DT
	Market	Deals with the development and implementation of network and connectivity requirements from the perspective of DT's external markets and customers
	Operations	Deals with the development and implementation of network and connectivity requirements from the perspective of the DT operating model

(Continues)

Table 2.4 (Continued)

Layer of reference architecture/ maturity dimensions	Operationalisation of the maturity dimension	Description
	People	Addresses the relevant people, roles, expertise and competencies to ensure sufficient resources in terms of networks and connectivity
	Culture	Addresses the corporate culture that is conducive to building high-performance networks and connectivity standards
	Governance	Deals with control models for the selection and implementation of technologies for networking and the promotion of connectivity
	Technology	Deals with the degree to which appropriate technologies are used for the development and implementation of networks and the promotion of connectivity
8. Data generation	Strategy	Deals with the development, testing and further development of strategies for the definition and implementation of approaches to data generation
	Leadership	Deals with the management of the development and operation of a DT in relation to the implementation of data generation approaches
	Market	Deals with the development and implementation of requirements for the definition of relevant data and data sources as well as for data generation in general from the perspective of DTs markets and customers
	Operations	Deals with the development and implementation of requirements for the definition of relevant data and data sources as well as for data generation in general from the perspective of the DT operating model
	People	Addresses the relevant people, roles, expertise and competencies for defining appropriate data and implementing appropriate approaches to data generation
	Culture	Addresses the organisational culture that is conducive to data generation and effective approaches to data generation
	Governance	Deals with management models and KPIs for the development and implementation of data generation approaches
	Technology	Deals with the extent to which appropriate technologies are used to define suitable data and implement effective approaches for data generation

(Continues)

Table 2.4 (Continued)

Layer of reference architecture/ maturity dimensions	Operationalisation of the maturity dimension	Description
9. Physical entities	Strategy	Deals with the development, testing and further development of strategies for defining the relevant physical objects of a DT, including the associated sensors and actuators
	Leadership	Deals with the management of the development and operation of a DT in relation to the definition and inclusion of physical objects and the associated sensors and actuators
	Market	Deals with the definition of relevant objects including the associated sensors and actuators from the perspective of relevant markets and DT customers
	Operations	Deals with the definition of relevant objects including the associated sensors and actuators from the perspective of the DT's operating model
	People	Deals with the relevant people, roles, expertise and skills for selecting suitable objects for DT, including the associated sensors and actuators
	Culture	Addresses the corporate culture that is conducive to comprehensive and effective connection of physical objects to DTs
	Governance	Deals with control models and indicators for selecting suitable objects for DTs, including the associated sensors and actuators
	Technology	Deals with the extent to which appropriate technologies are used to augment physical objects with suitable sensors and actuators

2.4 Measurement model

The conceptual foundations for maturity measurement in the form of measurement dimensions and indicators are supplemented by an operationally applicable assessment tool [9]. The data for evaluating the maturity level of a DT is rarely available in objective form. Therefore, it is not possible to draw on data from the actual operation of a DT. As with other maturity models, survey-based measurement models are appropriate. These can be linked directly to the conceptual model from Table 2.4 and lead to a standardised survey for recording the digital maturity level from different perspectives. The survey can be used to gather indications of the maturity level of individual sub-dimensions of a DT as well as the overall maturity level of a DT initiative. Therefore, the measurement model's conceptual basis is based on the nine architectural dimensions and eight maturity levels of the conceptual model. This results in a total of 72 items for measuring the maturity level of a DT. Based on a complete survey, (1) both the maturity level of each architecture level and (2) the holistic maturity level for each facet of the digital maturity level can be determined. An initial design for implementing a corresponding questionnaire can be found in Table 2.5.

Of course, it must be taken into account that the items presented here are only to be understood as an initial design draft. However, based on the presented foundation, common and accepted methods of scale development can be applied. In evaluating the artefact, an empirical investigation of relevant implementations of a DT in business practice is recommended. Given an empirical survey with an appropriate sample, psychometric properties of the maturity model, such as convergent validity, discriminant validity and reliability, can be measured using Likert scales.

Table 2.5 Items for the measurement of DTs maturity

#	Layer	Dimension	Item
1	1. Business model	S	We have a transparent, tested and implemented strategy for a business model in the context of our DT
2		L	Our leadership supports the implementation of a business model as part of the development of a DT
3		M	In the markets relevant to us, customers demand products and services that are made possible by our DT
4		O	The internal processes and operating procedures for the effective operation of the DT are fully implemented in our company
5		P	We have sufficient employees with suitable expertise and skills for the operation and further development of business models in the context of DTs
6		C	Our corporate culture supports the implementation of business models associated with the operation of a DT
7		G	We have implemented effective governance models, KPIs and indicators for managing the business models in the context of DT
8		T	We have the necessary technologies for the successful operation of business models in the context of DTs
9	2. System security	S	We have a transparent and tested strategy to ensure system security and data privacy in the context of our DT

(Continues)

Table 2.5 (*Continued*)

#	Layer	Dimension	Item
10		L	Our leadership supports the implementation of measures to promote system security and data privacy in the context of our DT
11		M	We have a complete understanding of the requirements of our markets and customers regarding system security and data privacy in the context of our DT
12		O	We have a comprehensive understanding of the requirements from the perspective of our internal processes and procedures concerning system security and data privacy in the context of our DT
13		P	Within our company, there are sufficient employees with extensive expertise and competence to ensure system security and data privacy in the context of our DT
14		C	Our corporate culture supports the assurance of system security and data privacy in the context of our DT
15		G	We have implemented comprehensive control models, KPIs and indicators for the governance of system security and data privacy in the context of our DT
16		T	We use appropriate technologies to ensure system security and data privacy in the implementation of our DT
17	3. Deployment	S	We have a transparent and tested strategy for the deployment of individual components of our DT and the overall promotion of deployability
18		L	Our leadership supports the measures for the implementation of the deployment of individual components of our DT and the general promotion of deployability
19		M	We have a complete understanding of the requirements of our markets and customers regarding the deployment of individual components of our DT and the overall promotion of deployability
20		O	We have a comprehensive understanding of the requirements of our internal processes and procedures concerning the deployment of individual components of our DT and the general promotion of deployability
21		P	We have sufficient employees with the appropriate expertise and competence to implement the deployment of individual components of our DT and to generally promote deployability
22		C	Our corporate culture supports the deployment of individual components of our DT and fosters overall deployability

(Continues)

Table 2.5 (Continued)

#	Layer	Dimension	Item
23		G	We have implemented comprehensive control models, KPIs and indicators for the governance of the deployment of individual components of our DT and the overall promotion of deployability
24		T	We use appropriate technologies for the deployment of individual components of our DT and the general promotion of deployability
25	4. Data models & algorithms	S	We have a transparent and tested strategy for integrating data models, AI and ML into our DT
26		L	Our leadership supports the application of data models, AI and ML in our DT
27		M	We have a comprehensive understanding of the requirements of our markets and customers with regard to the integration of data models, AI and ML in our DT
28		O	We have a comprehensive understanding of the requirements of our internal processes and workflows with regard to the integration of data models, AI and ML in our DT
29		P	We have sufficient staff with the appropriate expertise and competence to integrate data models, AI and ML into our DT
30		C	Our corporate culture supports the integration of data models, AI and ML in our DT
31		G	We have implemented comprehensive control models, KPIs and indicators for the governance of integrating data models, AI and ML in our DT
32		T	We use appropriate technologies to support the integration of data models, AI and ML in our DT
33	5. Data preparation & representation	S	We have a transparent and tested strategy for developing data structures and implementing approaches to data preparation and data representation in our DT
34		L	Our leadership supports initiatives for the development of data structures and the implementation of approaches to data preparation and data representation in our DT
35		M	We have a comprehensive understanding of the requirements of our markets and customers regarding the development of data structures and the implementation of approaches to data preparation and data representation in our DT
36		O	We have a complete understanding of the requirements of our internal processes and workflows regarding the development of data structures and the implementation of approaches to data preparation and data representation in our DT

(Continues)

Table 2.5 (Continued)

#	Layer	Dimension	Item
37		P	Within our company, there are sufficient employees with extensive expertise in the development of data structures and the implementation of approaches to data preparation and data representation in DTs
38		C	Our corporate culture supports the development of data structures and the implementation of approaches to data preparation and data representation in DTs
39		G	We have established comprehensive control models, KPIs and metrics for governing the development of data structures and the implementation of approaches to data preparation and data representation in DTs
40		T	We have the appropriate technologies for the development of data structures and the implementation of approaches to data preparation and data representation in DTs
41	6. Data storage	S	We have a transparent and tested strategy for the setup and utilisation of data storage in DTs
42		L	Our leadership supports initiatives for the setup and utilisation of data storage in DTs
43		M	We have a comprehensive understanding of the requirements of our markets and customers regarding the setup and utilisation of data storage in DTs
44		O	We have a complete understanding of the requirements of our internal processes and workflows regarding the setup and utilisation of data storage in DTs
45		P	Within our company, there are sufficient employees with relevant expertise and competence to implement measures for the setup and utilisation of data storage in DTs
46		C	Our corporate culture supports measures for the setup and utilisation of data storage in DTs
47		G	We have established comprehensive control models, KPIs and indicators for governing the measures related to the setup and utilisation of data storage in DTs
48		T	We have the appropriate technologies to implement measures for the setup and utilisation of data storage in DTs
49	7. Network & connectivity	S	We have a transparent and tested strategy for the development and operation of networks and ensuring connectivity in the context of our DT
50		L	Our leadership supports initiatives for the development and operation of networks and ensuring connectivity in DTs

(Continues)

Table 2.5 (Continued)

#	Layer	Dimension	Item
51		M	We have a comprehensive understanding of the requirements of our markets and customers regarding the development and operation of networks and ensuring connectivity in DTs
52		O	We have a complete understanding of the requirements of our internal processes and workflows regarding the development and operation of networks and ensuring connectivity in DTs
53		P	Within our company, there are sufficient employees with relevant expertise and competence for the development and operation of networks and ensuring connectivity in DTs
54		C	Our corporate culture supports the development and operation of networks and ensuring connectivity in DTs
55		G	We have established comprehensive control models, KPIs and indicators for the development and operation of networks and ensuring connectivity in DTs
56		T	We have the appropriate technologies for the development and operation of networks and ensuring connectivity in DTs
57	8. Data generation	S	We have a transparent and tested strategy for defining and implementing approaches to data generation in the context of our DT
58		L	Our leadership supports initiatives for defining and implementing approaches to data generation in DTs
59		M	We have a comprehensive understanding of the requirements of our markets and customers for defining and implementing approaches to data generation in DTs
60		O	We have a complete understanding of the requirements of our internal processes and workflows for defining and implementing approaches to data generation in DTs
61		P	Within our company, there are sufficient employees with relevant expertise and competence for defining and implementing approaches to data generation in DTs
62		C	Our corporate culture supports the definition and implementation of approaches to data generation in DTs
63		G	We have established comprehensive control models, KPIs and indicators for defining and implementing approaches to data generation in DTs

(Continues)

Table 2.5 (*Continued*)

#	Layer	Dimension	Item
64		T	We have the appropriate technologies for defining and implementing approaches to data generation in DTs
65	9. Physical entities	S	We have a transparent and tested strategy for defining relevant physical objects for our DT, including the associated sensors and actuators
66		L	Our leadership supports initiatives for defining relevant physical objects for our DT, including the associated sensors and actuators
67		M	We have a comprehensive understanding of the requirements of our markets and customers regarding the definition of relevant physical objects for our DT, including the associated sensors and actuators
68		O	We have a complete understanding of the requirements of our internal processes and workflows regarding the definition of relevant physical objects for our DT, including the associated sensors and actuators
69		P	Within our company, there are sufficient employees with relevant expertise and competence regarding the definition of relevant physical objects for our DT, including the associated sensors and actuators
70		C	Our corporate culture supports the definition of relevant physical objects for DTs, including the associated sensors and actuators
71		G	We have established comprehensive control models, KPIs and indicators for defining relevant physical objects for DTs, including the associated sensors and actuators
72		T	We have the appropriate technologies for defining relevant physical objects for DTs, including the associated sensors and actuators

2.5 Discussion

This section deals with the theoretical and practical implications, limitations of the present research and possible pathways for further research projects.

The present work contains a variety of theoretical implications. This research aims to conceptualise the construct of DT maturity and corresponding measurement models. We systematically reviewed related research and empirical studies to develop a well-grounded conceptual definition and measurement model for the digital maturity of DTs. As a result, we present a novel model for the conceptualisation of the digital maturity of DTs with nine dimensions: business model, system security, deployment, data models & algorithms, data preparation & data representation, data storage, networks & connectivity, data generation, and physical entities. Thus, the maturity level can be linked to the architectural levels of a DT [9]. First of all, this concept allows a discussion and measurement of the maturity level of a DT at the individual relevant levels, which are decisive for the development of a corresponding solution. In addition, the operationalisation of the maturity level per dimension is deepened by theoretical work from the field of general maturity models [12]. This allows specific maturity operationalisations per core dimension (e.g., about the business model of DTs) to be presented in eight further sub-dimensions: strategy, leadership, market, operations, people, culture, governance and technology. This is the first holistic maturity model for DTs in all relevant architectural dimensions and with complete implementation via a comprehensively presented maturity index. Among other things, this makes it clear that implementing DTs in companies is not only associated with technological challenges. Other issues are also essential about the digital maturity level. For example, DTs must also support the implementation of new business models, ensure system security and data protection, integrate AI and define suitable data formats. The main theoretical contribution of this paper lies in developing and presenting a holistic and comprehensive modelling for the maturity level of DTs, which can also be used very easily in business practice.

Practitioners can immediately adopt the measurement framework and use the defined metrics to evaluate the current state of their efforts and progress in DTs. One possible implementation of the maturity model is to record and discuss a DT's digital maturity level using standardised surveys. In full mode, the maturity model presented offers a questionnaire with nine dimensions, eight operationalisations for the maturity level and a total of 72 items. In an ideal scenario, the digital maturity level is captured using a sample from the perspective of various stakeholders. The results can be used, among other things, to measure and visualise the maturity level for each of the nine core dimensions. However, measuring different operationalisations of digital maturity (e.g., strategic maturity) across all nine core dimensions is also possible. If implementing the entire measurement model proves too cumbersome, individual items from the model can be applied and used for specific assessments. In any case, the measurement of digital maturity, as with all other maturity models, should only serve as a starting point for discussions within the management team. However, based on the measurement model, it is straightforward to establish a common language. Optimisation options and differing perspectives become clear. This marks the first time a comprehensive and directly applicable measurement model for the digital maturity of DTs has been available in this form.

As with any research, there are various limitations to consider regarding this study. A significant limitation concerns the lack of empirical validation for the conceptual and proposed measurement models. While the foundations for developing the maturity model have already been extensively tested in specific areas [9,12], the overall model presented here requires further evaluation through business practice. In the context of the design science research approach, this refers to evaluating the given artefact. This could, for instance, relate to applying the measurement model and the psychometric validation of the proposed scales and items using multiple case studies.

Further research can take various directions. The proposed maturity model and the associated measurement model require empirical validation through different implementations of a DT. This could also include examining how the presented artefacts can be applied to various forms of a DT. Moreover, the maturity model presented here can be compared with other available approaches in the research field and appropriately extended [61,62,71]. Continued empirical validation may reveal a need to deepen specific maturity dimensions. Additionally, engagement with business practice may indicate whether additional dimensions need to be added to capture the maturity of a DT fully.

In summary, it can be stated that this research presents, for the first time, a holistic concept and an associated measurement model for the maturity of a DT. This offers extensive implications for both theory and practice. Thus, the discussion surrounding the application of DTs, the assessment of their maturity and the derivation of concrete action steps for the further development of DTs is set to gain further momentum.

References

[1] A. Fuller, Z. Fan, C. Day, and C. Barlow, 'Digital twin: Enabling technologies, challenges and open research,' *IEEE Access*, vol. 8, pp. 108952–108971, 2020, doi:10.1109/ACCESS.2020.2998358.

[2] F. Tao and M. Zhang, 'Digital twin shop-floor: A new shop-floor paradigm towards smart manufacturing,' *IEEE Access*, vol. 5, pp. 20418–20427, 2017, doi:10.1109/ACCESS.2017.2756069.

[3] M. Grieves, '*Digital Twin: Manufacturing Excellence through Virtual Factory Replication*,' Florida Institute of Technology, Melbourne, 2014.

[4] N. Mohammadi and J. E. Taylor, 'Smart City Digital Twins,' in *2017 IEEE Symposium Series on Computational Intelligence (SSCI)*, 2017, pp. 1–5. doi:10.1109/SSCI.2017.8285439.

[5] Y. Liu, L. Zhang, Y. Yang, L. Zhou, L. Ren, and F. Wang, 'A novel cloud-based framework for the elderly healthcare services using digital twin,' *IEEE Access*, vol. 7, pp. 49088–49101, 2019, doi:10.1109/ACCESS.2019.2909828.

[6] R. Parmar, A. Leiponen, and L. D. W. Thomas, 'Building an organizational digital twin,' *Business Horizons*, vol. 63, no. 6, pp. 725–736, 2020.

[7] A. Gaggioli, 'Digital twins: An emerging paradigm in cyberpsychology research?,' *Cyberpsychology, Behavior, and Social Networking*, vol. 21, no. 7, pp. 468–469, 2018.

[8] H. van der Valk, H. Haße, F. Möller, M. Arbter, J.-L. Henning, and B. Otto, 'A Taxonomy of Digital Twins,' in *Proceedings of the 26th Americas Conference on Information Systems*, 2020, pp. 1–10.

[9] A. Rossmann and D. Hertweck, 'Digital Twins: A Meta-Review on Their Conceptualization, Application, and Reference Architecture,' in *Hawaii International Conference on System Sciences*, 2022.

[10] D. Jones, C. Snider, A. Nassehi, J. Yon, and B. Hicks, 'Characterising the digital twin: A systematic literature review,' *CIRP Journal of Manufacturing Science and Technology*, vol. 29, pp. 36–52, 2020.

[11] K. Y. H. Lim, P. Zheng, and C.-H. Chen, 'A state-of-the-art survey of digital twin: Techniques, engineering product lifecycle management and business innovation perspectives,' *Journal of Intelligent Manufacturing*, vol. 31, pp. 1–25, 2019.

[12] A. Rossmann, 'Digital Maturity: Conceptualization and Measurement Model,' in *39th International Conference on Information Systems*, San Francisco, 2018. [Online]. Available: https://assets.kpmg.com/content/dam/kpmg/pdf/2016/04/ch-digital-readiness-assessment-en.pdf.

[13] A. Hevner, S. March, J. Park, and S. Ram, 'Design science in information systems research,' *MIS Quarterly*, vol. 28, no. 1, p. 75, 2004.

[14] X. Wu, V. Goepp, and A. Siadat, 'Concept and engineering development of cyber physical production systems: A systematic literature review,' *International Journal of Advanced Manufacturing Technology*, vol. 111, no. 1–2, pp. 243–261, 2020, doi:10.1007/s00170-020-06110-2.

[15] H. Zhang, L. Ma, J. Sun, H. Lin, and M. Thürer, 'Digital twin in services and industrial product service systems: Review and analysis,' *Procedia CIRP*, vol. 83, pp. 57–60, 2019.

[16] C. H. dos Santos, J. A. B. Montevechi, J. A. de Queiroz, R. de Carvalho Miranda, and F. Leal, 'Decision support in productive processes through DES and ABS in the digital twin era: A systematic literature review,' vol. 60, pp. 2662–2681, 2022, doi:10.1080/00207543.2021.1898691.

[17] M. M. Rathore, S. A. Shah, D. Shukla, E. Bentafat, and S. Bakiras, 'The role of AI, machine learning, and big data in digital twinning: A systematic literature review, challenges, and opportunities,' *IEEE Access*, vol. 9, pp. 32030–32052, 2021.

[18] W. Kritzinger, M. Karner, G. Traar, J. Henjes, and W. Sihn, 'Digital Twin in manufacturing: A categorical literature review and classification,' *IFAC-PapersOnLine*, vol. 51, no. 11, pp. 1016–1022, 2018.

[19] T. Y. Melesse, V. Di Pasquale, and S. Riemma, 'Digital twin models in industrial operations: A systematic literature review,' *Procedia Manufacturing*, vol. 42, pp. 267–272, 2020.

[20] M. Perno, L. Hvam, and A. Haug, 'Enablers and Barriers to the Implementation of Digital Twins in the Process Industry: A Systematic Literature Review,' in *2020 IEEE International Conference on Industrial Engineering and Engineering Management (IEEM)*, 2020, pp. 959–964. doi:10.1109/IEEM45057.2020.9309745.

[21] T. Catarci, D. Firmani, F. Leotta, F. Mandreoli, M. Mecella, and F. Sapio, 'A Conceptual Architecture and Model for Smart Manufacturing Relying on Service-Based Digital Twins,' in *2019 IEEE International Conference on Web Services (ICWS)*, 2019, pp. 229–236. doi:10.1109/ICWS.2019.00047.

[22] R. Soderberg, K. Warmefjord, J. S. Carlson, and L. Lindkvist, 'Toward a Digital Twin for real-time geometry assurance in individualized production,'

CIRP Annals of Technology, vol. 66, no. 1, pp. 137–140, 2017, doi:10.1016/j.cirp.2017.04.038.

[23] B. A. Talkhestani, N. Jazdi, W. Schloegl, and M. Weyrich, 'Consistency check to synchronize the Digital Twin of manufacturing automation based on anchor points,' *Procedia CIRP*, vol. 72, pp. 159–164, 2018, doi:10.1016/j.procir.2018.03.166.

[24] M. R. Enders and N. Hoßbach, '*Dimensions of digital twin applications: A literature review*,' *AMCIS 2019 Proceedings*, 2019. Available: https://aisel.aisnet.org/amcis2019/org_transformation_is/org_transformation_is/20.

[25] J. Thönes, 'Microservices,' *IEEE Software*, vol. 32, no. 1, p. 116, 2015.

[26] A. Rojko, 'Industry 4.0 concept: Background and overview,' *International Journal of Interactive Mobile Technologies*, vol. 11, no. 5, pp. 77–90, 2017.

[27] F. Adrodegari, N. Saccani, C. Kowalkowski, and J. Vilo, 'PSS business model conceptualization and application,' *Production Planning & Control*, vol. 28, no. 15, pp. 1251–1263, 2017.

[28] M. Ghobakhloo, 'The future of manufacturing industry: A strategic roadmap toward Industry 4.0,' *Journal of Manufacturing Technology Management*, vol. 29, no. 6, pp. 910–936, 2018.

[29] G. Westerman, D. Bonnet, and A. McAfee, *Leading Digital: Turning Technology into Business Transformation*. Brighton, MA: Harvard Business Review Press, 2014.

[30] Capgemini Consulting, 'Digital Transformation Benchmark – 2012 Emergence of the Digital Utility.' Accessed: Aug. 14, 2024. [Online]. Available: https://www.capgemini.com/wp-content/uploads/2017/07/digital_transformation_benchmark_2012.pdf

[31] A. Anand, R. Sharma, and T. Coltman, 'Four steps to realizing business value from digital data streams,' *MIS Quarterly Executive*, vol. 15, no. 4, pp. 259–277, 2016.

[32] K. N. Andersen, R. Medaglia, R. Vatrapu, H. Z. Henriksen, and R. Gauld, 'The forgotten promise of E-government maturity: Assessing responsiveness in the digital public sector,' *Government Information Quarterly*, vol. 28, no. 4, pp. 439–445, 2011, [Online]. Available: http://doi.org/10.0.3.248/j.giq.2010.12.006

[33] I. Balaban, N. B. Redjep, and M. K. Calopa, 'The analysis of digital maturity of schools in Croatia,' *International Journal of Emerging Technologies in Learning*, vol. 13, no. 6, pp. 4–15, 2018, [Online]. Available: https://doi.org/10.3991/ijet.v13i06.7844

[34] S. Burke, 'HPE launches interactive digital marketing maturity assessment tool,' *CRN*, vol. 1375, pp. 18–19, 2018.

[35] D. Chaffey, 'Applying organisational capability models to assess the maturity of digital-marketing governance,' *Journal of Marketing Management*, vol. 26, no. 3–4, pp. 187–196, 2010, [Online]. Available: http://doi.org/10.0.4.56/02672571003612192

[36] J. Chen, 'Digitization to gain momentum: German companies leading digital maturity,' *Chemical Week*, vol. 179, no. 15, pp. 22–24, 2017.

[37] Y. K. Dwivedi, V. Weerakkody, and M. Janssen, 'Moving towards maturity: Challenges to successful E-government implementation and diffusion,' *Data Base for Advanced in Information Systems*, vol. 42, no. 4, pp. 11–22, 2011.

[38] O. Gonzalez-Rojas, D. Correal, and M. Camargo, 'ICT capabilities for supporting collaborative work on business processes within the digital content industry,' *Computers in Industry*, vol. 80, pp. 16–29, 2016, [Online]. Available: https://doi.org/10.1016/j.compind.2016.04.004

[39] P. Gottschalk, 'Maturity levels for interoperability in digital government,' *Government Information Quarterly*, vol. 26, no. 1, pp. 75–81, 2009, [Online]. Available: http://doi.org/10.0.3.248/j.giq.2008.03.003

[40] A. Heberle, W. Lowe, A. Gustafsson, and O. Vorrei, 'Digitalization canvas – towards identifying digitalization use cases and projects,' *Journal of Universal Computer Science*, vol. 23, no. 11, pp. 1070–1097, 2017.

[41] E. A. Isaev, N. L. Korovkina, and M. S. Tabakova, 'Evaluation of the readiness of a Company's IT department for digital business transformation,' *Business Informatics*, vol. 44, no. 2, pp. 55–64, 2018, [Online]. Available: https://doi.org/10.17323/1998-0663.2018.2.55.64

[42] E. H. A. Hanaei and A. Rashid, 'DF-C2M2: A Capability Maturity Model for Digital Forensics Organisations,' in *2014 IEEE Security and Privacy Workshops*, 2014, pp. 57–60. [Online]. Available: https://doi.org/10.1109/SPW.2014.17

[43] V. Đurek, N. Kadoic, and N. B. Reep, 'Assessing the Digital Maturity Level of Higher Education Institutions,' in *2018 41st International Convention on Information and Communication Technology, Electronics and Microelectronics (MIPRO)*, 2018, pp. 671–676. [Online]. Available: https://doi.org/10.23919/MIPRO.2018.8400126

[44] G. C. Kane, D. Palmer, A. N. Phillips, D. Kiron, and N. Buckley, 'Achieving digital maturity,' *MIT Sloan Management Review*, vol. 59, no. 1, pp. 1–29, 2017.

[45] M. Kerrigan, 'A capability maturity model for digital investigations,' *Digital Investigation*, vol. 10, no. 1, pp. 19–33, 2013, [Online]. Available: https://doi.org/10.1016/j.diin.2013.02.005

[46] E. Maemura, N. Moles, and C. Becker, 'Organizational assessment frameworks for digital preservation: A literature review and mapping,' *Journal of the Association for Information Science and Technology*, vol. 68, no. 7, pp. 1619–1637, 2017, [Online]. Available: https://doi.org/10.1002/asi.23807

[47] T. Mettler and R. Pinto, 'Evolutionary paths and influencing factors towards digital maturity: An analysis of the status quo in Swiss hospitals,' *Technological Forecasting and Social Change*, vol. 133, pp. 104–117, 2018, [Online]. Available: https://doi.org/10.1016/j.techfore.2018.03.009

[48] E. P. Morais, J. A. Pires, and R. Gonçalves, 'Suitability of E-business maturity models for digital economy,' in *6th Iberian Conference on Information Systems and Technologies (CISTI 2011)*, 2011, pp. 1–4.

[49] C. Perakslis, 'Digital maturity: Perceiving the digital-panopticon [last word],' *IEEE Technology & Society Magazine*, vol. 36, no. 4, p. 88, 2017.

[50] A. A. Pflaum and P. Gölzer, 'The IoT and digital transformation: Toward the data-driven enterprise,' *IEEE Pervasive Computing*, vol. 17, no. 1, pp. 87–91, 2018, [Online]. Available: https://doi.org/10.1109/MPRV.2018.011591066

[51] S. Poruban, 'Achieving digital maturity,' *Oil & Gas Journal*, vol. 115, no. 7, p. 14, 2017.

[52] J. Seitz and A. Burosch, 'Digital Value Creation,' in *2018 IEEE International Conference on Engineering, Technology and Innovation (ICE/ITMC)*, 2018, pp. 1–5. [Online]. Available: https://doi.org/10.1109/ICE.2018.8436380

[53] A. Tarhan, O. Turetken, and H. A. Reijers, 'Business process maturity models: A systematic literature review,' *Information and Software Technology*, vol. 75, pp. 122–134, 2016, [Online]. Available: https://doi.org/10.1016/j.infsof.2016.01.010

[54] O. Valdez-de-Leon, 'A digital maturity model for telecommunications service providers,' *Technology Innovation Management Review*, vol. 6, no. 8, pp. 19–32, 2016.

[55] E. Whelan, J. Anderson, B. van den Hooff, and B. Donnellan, 'How IT and the rest of the business can innovate together,' *Communications of the Association for Information Systems*, vol. 36, p. 261, 2015.

[56] V. Garousi, M. Felderer, and M. V. Mäntylä, 'Guidelines for including grey literature and conducting multivocal literature reviews in software engineering,' *Information and Software Technology*, vol. 106, pp. 101–121, 2017, doi: 10.1016/j.infsof.2018.09.006.

[57] Bosch, 'Digital Twins | Bosch Connected Industry.' Accessed: Mar. 21, 2024. [Online]. Available: https://www.bosch-connected-industry.com/de/en/iiot-insights/digital-twins

[58] IBM, 'What Is a Digital Twin? | IBM.' Accessed: Mar. 21, 2024. [Online]. Available: https://www.ibm.com/topics/what-is-a-digital-twin

[59] Amazon, 'Digital Twin IoT – AWS IoT TwinMaker – AWS.' Accessed: Mar. 21, 2024. [Online]. Available: https://aws.amazon.com/iot-twinmaker/?nc1=h_ls

[60] PTC, 'What is Digital Twin and why is it important? | PTC.' Accessed: Mar. 21, 2024. [Online]. Available: https://www.ptc.com/en/industry-insights/digital-twin

[61] U. Weber and H. Grosser, 'Digital Twins: Leading the Way to Tomorrow's Ecosystems,' 2019. Accessed: Jul. 14, 2023. [Online]. Available: https://www.detecon.com/drupal/sites/default/files/2021-03/ST_DigitalTwins_V1_EN_251119.pdf

[62] F. G. Medina, A. W. Umpierrez, V. Martinez, and H. Fromm, 'A Maturity Model for Digital Twin Implementations in the Commercial Aerospace OEM Industry,' in *Proceedings of the 2021 10th International Conference on Industrial Technology and Management, ICITM 2021*, Institute of Electrical and Electronics Engineers Inc., Mar. 2021, pp. 149–156. doi: 10.1109/ICITM52822.2021.00034.

[63] L. Chen, X. Xie, Q. Lu, A. K. Parlikad, M. Pitt, and J. Yang, 'Gemini principles-based digital twin maturity model for asset management,'

Sustainability (Switzerland), vol. 13, no. 15, p. 8224, 2021, doi: 10.3390/su13158224.

[64] J. F. Uhlenkamp, J. B. Hauge, E. Broda, M. Lutjen, M. Freitag, and K. D. Thoben, 'Digital twins: A maturity model for their classification and evaluation,' *IEEE Access*, vol. 10, pp. 69605–69635, 2022, doi: 10.1109/ACCESS.2022.3186353.

[65] P. Stahmann, A. Krüger, and B. Rieger, 'Digital twins for real-time data analysis in Industrie 4.0: Pathways to maturity,' in *Proceedings of the 2nd International Conference on Innovative Intelligent Industrial Production and Logistics, IN4PL 2021*, SciTePress, 2021, pp. 123–130. doi: 10.5220/0010688700003062.

[66] R. Stark and T. Damerau, 'Digital Twin,' in L. Laperrière, and G. Reinhart (eds.), *CIRP Encyclopedia of Production Engineering*, Berlin, Heidelberg: Springer, 2019, pp. 1–8. doi: 10.1007/978-3-642-35950-7_16870-1.

[67] R. Klar, A. Fredriksson, and V. Angelakis, 'Assessing the Maturity of Digital Twinning Solutions for Ports,' in *IEEE Annual Conference on Pervasive Computing and Communications Workshops and Other Affiliated Events*, Jun. 2023, pp. 552–557. doi: 10.1109/percomworkshops56833.2023.10150378.

[68] S. Evans, C. Savian, A. Burns, and C. Cooper, *Digital Twins for the Built Environment*. London, UK: Institution of Engineering and Technology (IET), 2019.

[69] S. Malakuti, 'Emerging Technical Debt in Digital Twin Systems,' in *2021 26th IEEE International Conference on Emerging Technologies and Factory Automation, ETFA*, Institute of Electrical and Electronics Engineers Inc., Sep. 2021, pp. 1–4. doi: 10.1109/ETFA45728.2021.9613538.

[70] P. Kogut, 'DUET's Digital Twin Maturity Model Supports Cities in Their Digital Transformation.' Accessed: Jul. 14, 2023. [Online]. Available: https://www.digitalurbantwins.com/post/duet-s-digital-twin-maturity-model-supports-cities-in-their-digital-transformation

[71] S. Yates, 'Model, Shadow, or Twin: The Digital Twin Maturity Model.' Accessed: Jul. 14, 2023. [Online]. Available: https://woolpert.com/news/blogs/model-shadow-or-twin-the-digital-twin-maturity-model/

Chapter 3

Digital twins: towards future smartness

Rajan Kadel[1]*, Krishna Paudel*[1]*, Ramesh Shrestha*[2] *and Samar Shailendra*[1]

Abstract

Digital twin (DT) technology is an advanced concept replicating physical systems in a virtual environment, enabling enhanced monitoring and optimisation. The implementation of DT relies on three core domains: data collection, data processing and data presentation. Emerging technologies such as the Internet of Things, robotics, and drones form the foundation of data collection. Big data, cloud computing and artificial intelligence drive intelligent data processing. Reality technologies and holographic communications provide immersive visualisation of DT outputs. These technologies must be developed with security-by-design principles to foster consumer trust and confidence. Moreover, achieving true 'smartness' in DT requires a holistic approach that integrates environmental sustainability, global economic considerations and user experience throughout the design, development and implementation process.

Keywords: Digital twin; design security; emerging technologies; environmental sustainability; global economics; smartness; user experience

3.1 Introduction

Digital twin (DT) technology is emerging as a cornerstone for achieving future smartness in society. By mirroring physical entities in the digital realm, DTs enable transformative changes across the economy, environment and human experience [1]. This chapter explores the integration of advanced technologies to enable DTs and delves into the critical role of these technologies in effectuating smartness to achieve an improved quality of life, attain happiness and maintain sustainable undertakings encompassing more transformative and socio-technical design.

According to the Cambridge online dictionary, 'Smartness is the quality of being intelligent, or able to think quickly or intelligently in difficult situations', and *Intelligent* means being able to learn and understand things quickly and easily. The

[1]School of Information Technology and Engineering, Melbourne Institute of Technology, Australia
[2]Avant Garde Solutions Pvt. Ltd., Kathmandu, Nepal

best example of a smart system is the *Human* itself [2]. This traditional definition of smartness may not capture the notion of modern use in contemporary discourses, as smartness can depend on the context and can have various dimensions. If this plain vanilla definition of smartness is used, then many devices and systems otherwise considered smart do not qualify as smart anymore [3], necessitating a more elaborate and comprehensive definition.

While there is no consensus in the literature on the general definition of smartness, specific contexts offer their definitions. Regarding smart cities, Albino *et al.* [4] define smartness as the utilisation of information technology in hard and soft domains in an integrated manner such that it contributes to the improvement of citizens' living quality. Buildings, the environment and infrastructure are included in the hard domain, while education, culture and innovation are included in the soft domain of the urban environment. Similarly, Mukti *et al.* [5] defines smartness as the utilisation of information technology in a holistic manner to improve the urban quality of life.

A broader discussion and definition of smartness can be found in [6] as

> *'In general smartness is usually associated with some digital technology or environment, but it should be understood in a much broader sense that it is a way of knowledge and representation of the whole world so that action can be done in and upon that world. And this depends upon new practices, technologies, and devices, including Artificial Intelligence (AI) and Machine Learning (ML)'.*

Similarly, smartness is defined by Alter [3] as:

> *'Purposefully designed entity X is smart to the extent to which it performs and controls functions that attempt to produce useful results through activities that apply automated capabilities and other physical, informational, technical, and intellectual resources for processing information, interpreting information, and/or learning from information that may or may not be specified by its designers'.*

This definition emphasises the importance of useful results achieved with automated capabilities and resources for processing, interpreting information and learning for improvement of the result. It can be inferred from the above definitions that information processing is a key task for which data is required. Data collection, termed as sensing by Alter [3] requires a comprehensive understanding of the current situation or environment. Technologies for data collection or sensing, followed by storage and transmission, are at the forefront of the required technologies for smartness. AI, ML, big data analytics and associated technologies are core technologies for smartness without which no meaningful and thoroughly reasoned decision can be made utilising the huge data at hand. For the result to be useful, it should be presented to the users, and technologies that make this possible (technologies for presentation, user interaction and feedback) are equally important. We can list the above-mentioned technologies as the core technologies and any other technologies that support these functions can be termed as auxiliary technologies. However, the list does not end there, as smartness may necessitate application-specific technologies too. This grouping of technologies into three domains is rudimentary or coarse, as there can be overlapping between them.

Figure 3.1 illustrates the smartness triquetra inside a context triangle. As discussed previously, we can broadly classify these technologies into three domains: data collection (collection, transport, storage), data processing (data preparation, data analytics, knowledge discovery and decision-making) and data presentation (decision or result presentation, user participation and interaction, evaluation and feedback). Moreover, the essence of smartness should not be technology-driven but focused on improving security design and user experience or satisfaction through quality of life improvement and offering sustainable solutions considering the environment and economy. The degree of the merit of the contribution of these technologies towards future smartness depends upon the context these technologies are used, and the mere use of the technology does not guarantee smartness, but the result of the use of technology determines its contribution. This trait of smartness is represented in Figure 3.1 as the context of smartness. We propose that sustainability is the foundation for this context which has environmental as well as economic aspects. The economic aspect pushes for innovation, whereas the environmental aspect guides our lifestyle and our economic and governance activities to maintain and protect the world for us and our future to attain a human experience that is better, more fulfilling and satisfying. We believe this is the correct approach towards smartness, and this resonates with the socio-technical system design paradigm [7] as well. A DT which serves as a dynamic, real-time virtual replica of a physical entity, can provide an accurate and continuously updated model with its real-world counterpart and is able to solve real life problems in real time, contributing

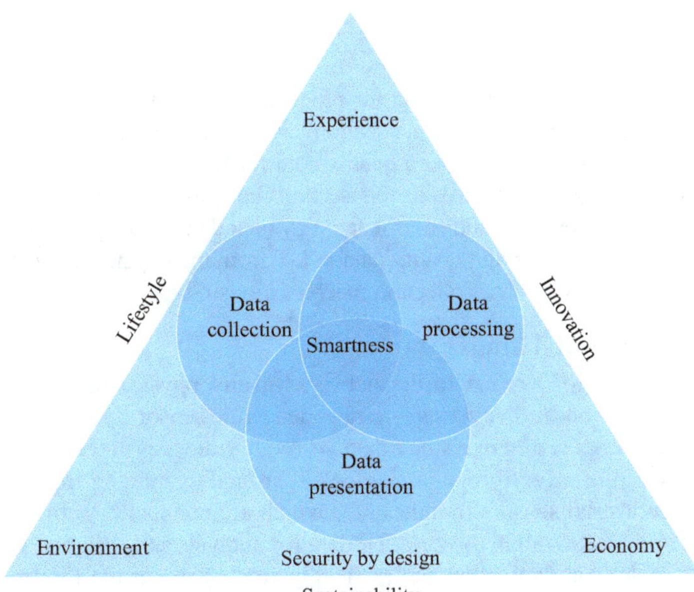

Figure 3.1 Smartness triquetra inside context triangle

as a primary enabler for intelligent systems. These virtual models acts as active, cognitive entity capable of generating insights, making predictions, providing proactive decision-making, significantly influencing future processes and applications – the key attributes essential for achieving true smartness.

Smartness with Digital Twin (DT)

The concept of *Smartness* spans three main domains: data collection, data processing and data presentation. Rather than being solely driven by technological advancement, the focus of these aspects should prioritise enhancing user experience and satisfaction with the aid of technology such as Digital Twin (DT). DTs have the potential to improve quality of life and provide sustainable solutions that takes into account environmental and economic considerations to enhance user experience.

3.2 Digital twins: enablers

This section provides an overview of the foundational platform technologies for future smart systems to enable DTs, structured around the three domains: data collection, data processing and data presentation. It highlights the role of technologies such as sensors and drones in data collection; AI, Cloud and analytics in data processing; and immersive visualisation using AR/VR and holograms for data representation and smart user experience.

3.2.1 Data collection

Data is an integral component of smartness and there is a need for efficient methods to collect, prepare, store and transmit data for processing. Quality data is one of the prerequisites for quality decisions. In this section, we discuss key technologies for data collection and data preparation to feed quality data for further analysis and processing. Data collection is the primary task in this section, but this domain of smartness also encompasses data governance and control and may include data pre-processing in many cases. The need of real-time and quality data in DT from the physical systems can only be achieved by the proper data collection mechanism using various technologies.

3.2.1.1 Internet of Things

Internet of Things (IoT) refers to the network of any physical objects – devices, vehicles, buildings and other items – embedded with sensors, software and other technologies to connect and exchange data with other devices and systems over the Internet. This implies everything that we look at around us ranging from desktops to mobiles and industrial sensors to light bulbs which are connected to the Internet are IoT devices and are essentially generating data for analysis and insights. We decided to have IoT under data collection as the 'Things' of IoT are at the forefront as they sense the information without human intervention and connected actuators can carry out tasks without processing. IoT is significant because it enables a vast array of applications that improve efficiency, convenience and quality of life. By integrating everyday objects with the internet, IoT facilitates real-time data collection and analysis, leading to smarter decisions and automation of tasks. Especially, the modern world is driven by the data and insights drawn from it. The latest wave of Generative AI (GenAI) and the drive for artificial general intelligence (AGI) is not possible without a large amount of data which is captured through IoT devices.

IoT presents numerous opportunities across various sectors. In healthcare, IoT devices such as wearable fitness trackers and remote monitoring systems provide real-time health data, enabling proactive healthcare and personalised treatment plans. In smart homes, IoT-enabled devices like smart thermostats, lighting systems and security cameras enhance comfort, energy efficiency and safety. In manufacturing, often referred to as Industry 4.0, IoT helps optimise production processes through predictive maintenance, real-time monitoring and automation, leading to increased efficiency and reduced downtime. In agriculture, IoT applications in precision farming allow farmers to monitor soil moisture, weather conditions and crop health, optimising resource use and improving yields. In transportation, IoT in logistics and transportation improves fleet management, reduces fuel consumption and enhances route planning through real-time tracking and data analytics. Therefore, IoT plays a significant roles in DTs by providing real-time data collection from the physical environment, seamless connectivity between the physical and digital system which is crucial for an enhanced decision-making process [8–10].

The vast number of interconnected heterogeneous devices over the Internet poses significant challenges in terms of architecture, quality of service, security and privacy. With the advent of AI, ensuring data security and protecting user privacy is one of the foremost challenges. IoT devices can be vulnerable to cyber-attacks, leading to data breaches and unauthorised access. Interoperability is another challenge, as the lack of standardisation among IoT devices from different manufacturers has resulted in compatibility issues, seamless integration and operation. Moreover, the management and analysis of the massive amounts of data generated by IoT devices require robust infrastructure and sophisticated analytics tools, which can be resource-intensive and complex to implement.

3.2.1.2 Robotics

Robotics is an interdisciplinary field that combines engineering and computer science to create, design and operate robots that are machines capable of replicating or substituting human actions which are especially well-suited for increasing task efficiency. It is the study and design of systems that combine mechanical and electrical components with computer brains, drawing on fields such as mechanical engineering, electrical engineering and computer science [11].

Robots have various opportunities across various industries, where they can be applied to do a variety of tasks such as moving materials, putting pieces together and checking things. It is more concerned with repetitive and often risky jobs, which increases safety and puts greater emphasis on creative parts of manufacturing. The application of Robotics is also increasing in the healthcare sector to assist doctors during surgery. They can perform precise movements and tasks during surgeries. The

Vinici System, a robot that performed prostate surgery in the United States in 2008, is a good example of how robots are advancing the world's intelligence [12]. In addition, they are utilised to improve imaging (such as Magnetic Resonance Imaging (MRI) and Three-Dimensional (3D) ultrasound). Robots play a crucial role in collecting data where installing sensors by humans is not feasible due to safety, security and accessibility issues. Moreover, Robots have made contributions to the military and armed forces, where they can be employed to dispose of bombs, carry supplies to soldiers in remote locations and explore unfamiliar territories. Today, this sector utilises robots to execute rescue operations and examine dangerous scenarios. The application of robotics has assisted in the study of space, contributing to the discovery of other planets and providing maintenance of equipment on International Space Stations. The advancement of the robotics industry has resulted in the creation of a human-like robot, with Sophia being an example. Therefore, robotics plays a significant roles in DTs by providing real-time physical interaction data from the physical environment, acts as a simulation and experimental platforms for testing scenarios before real-world implementation to ensure safety and accuracy, and also assisting on task automation on DT-generated insights [13–15].

The robotics business has numerous challenges, including high development costs, complex software structures and the demand for energy-efficient solutions [16,17]. Furthermore, they face difficulties in adapting to new technologies, properly integrating AI, hiring talented workers and exploring creative business opportunities through innovative applications [18]. In conclusion, Robots are an excellent example of automation driving the globe towards smartness, from vehicle manufacturing to helping doctors during surgery. Robotics is all about developing smart machines that can perform activities similar to humans, making our jobs easier and safer in a variety of industries.

3.2.1.3 Drones

A drone is an automated flying device that can be operated and controlled remotely which works with sensors and Global Positioning System (GPS) and thus extends the functionality of IoT as a data collection system. Drone technology also combines with IoT and an IoT-Drone is created where all types of data collection, transfer, mining, real-time monitoring and control result in improved efficiency [19]. Drone links to the IoT components like Cloud, Analytics and AI which allows for data collection, job automation and decision-making.

With increasing population and food demand, traditional farming practices need to be replaced by automated technology such as drones to improve agricultural efficiency and output [20]. The use of IoT drones in agriculture has made it possible to combine real-time crop monitoring with ML and Convolutional Neural Networks for crop disease detection and data analysis [19]. These drones also have multidimensional cameras, which are used for mapping and monitoring fields, automatic pesticide application by spraying, analysis of soil, crop condition examinations, planting, controlling livestock, crop spraying, weather monitoring, growth monitoring and GPS tracking, all of which help to improve agricultural efficiency and reduce chemical use. Drones are also being utilised to transport items, particularly in the final stage of the delivery process known as 'last-mile delivery', which is the most expensive aspect of distribution logistics [21]. Companies like Amazon and DHL are integrating them into their delivery operations to reduce delays in traffic, noise and pollution in cities. While drones have constraints in weight and taking-off duration when compared with traditional vehicles, they can assist in reducing delivery time, costs and environmental effects. Drones are also widely used in the field of medicine, where they are utilised for recording accidents, providing medical services, assessing patients in disasters, conducting secure and search missions, and assisting with remote telemedicine and patient care at home [22]. They can transport and deliver all kinds of medical materials, non-biological and biological, and include samples from the laboratory, blood, transplantation material, medicine, pharmaceuticals and medical devices. Furthermore, It can help doctors cut their time for diagnosis and treatment, transport an organ for transplant, help provide visuals during cardiopulmonary resuscitation and help study disease control, for instance, COVID-19. Moreover, IoT drones help rescuers to identify human beings in risky environments like when a building collapses and fires, among others [19]. Drones are expected to enable applications to improve the quality of life in smart cities [23]. Drones play a significant part in smart cities because they enable surveillance, improve communication systems, support sustainable aerial services, improve information sharing and delivery, and facilitate smart sensing applications within smart city environments.

Drone technology includes a variety of challenges including security defects, privacy concerns, regulatory compliance and the requirement for effective cybersecurity solutions to successfully manage risk [24]. It also involves complicated frameworks, payload constraints, infrastructure needs, data analysis difficulties and compliance with aviation rules [18]. In conclusion, drones are crucial for making things smarter. They work with IoT to help share data and make better choices and this leads to smart solutions. In agriculture, drones help with operations, using resources well and encouraging environmentally friendly practices. Therefore, drones plays a significant roles in DTs in data gathering from hard-to-reach areas, airspace management including autonomous drones and safety critical missions including emergency responses [25–27].

Data collection: powering the heart of DTs

Sensing the current state of the environment and responding accordingly is a form of smartness which can be termed as primitive smartness whereas collecting a large quantity of data, analysing or processing those data and making thorough decision entails smartness in 21*st* century and the future. Hence, real-time sensing or data collection is a fundamental prerequisite for smart DTs.

3.2.2 Data processing

Data processing is at the heart of smartness because it helps to make the precise and accurate decision and it can be stated without any loss of generality that *Better the quality of decision, higher the degree of smartness*. Data processing can start from data preparation and may extend to post-processing in many cases. The need of real-time processing capability using various technologies is the key for a successful implementation of DTs. In this section, we highlight key data processing and associated technologies and how they help us achieve smartness or make smart decisions in DTs.

3.2.2.1 Big data technologies

Big data refers to the vast volume, velocity and variety of data generated from various sources such as social media, IoT/sensors and user devices. According to Bernard Marr survey [28], 2.5 quintillion bytes of data are generated every day. According to the data growth projections as shown in Figure 3.2, the numbers are growing exponentially and are expected to reach 181 zettabytes of new data every day by 2025. Traditional data processing systems are unable to manage and analyse such huge data and data growth. The importance of big data lies in its ability to represent, store and analyse this huge data to reveal hidden relationships, trends and insights that can spur creativity and decision-making in a variety of industries leading to a smarter society and the ecosystem.

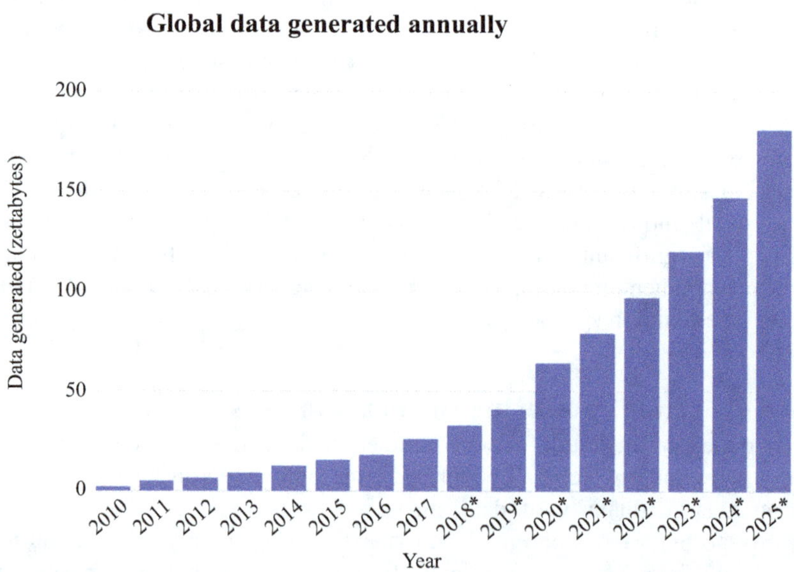

Figure 3.2 Annual data growth over internet [29]

In today's digital era, businesses use big data to learn consumer behaviour, extract industry trends and bring operational effectiveness through ML and analytics. For example, in healthcare, analysing patient data can lead to better outcomes through fast detection and treatment plans [30]. While in e-commerce, the customer experience can be enhanced by providing personalised suggestions and recommendations about products.

Big data also plays a crucial role in AI and ML, where large datasets are essential for training and improving AI/ML algorithms. The ability to process and analyse data in real time opens up new possibilities for innovation and efficiency in DTs. Essentially, big data can be used to transform raw information into intelligent actions, informed decisions and strategic planning.

At the same time, big data is associated with significant challenges. This data is generally quite unorganised and unstructured. The primary challenge is to store and manage this enormous amount of data volume. Traditional databases are neither designed nor efficient to handle this data. Hence, advanced storage and processing solutions like cloud computing and scalable databases such as NoSQL [31] and Hadoop [32] are essential. Ensuring data quality and accuracy is another significant challenge. Unmanaged and poor data quality can lead to incorrect conclusions and decisions. Moreover, the sensitive nature of the data being processed may lead to privacy and security concerns. Organisations must strictly adhere to regulatory requirements and implement robust security measures to prevent data breaches and misuse.

Big data is a critical component for data processing, AI and smart decision-making. Organisations are continuously innovating to manage and interpret new insights from big data. This will in turn bring more agility and user-friendliness leading to a modern and smarter society.

3.2.2.2 Cloud

Cloud providers provide various computing services such as servers, storage, databases, networking, software and analytics on demand via the internet [33]. These services offer flexible resources and large-scale economies, enabling organisations to access and manage data and applications from a distance rather than on local servers or personal devices. This adaptability allows businesses to scale their operations based on growth without the need for anticipated investment in the physical infrastructure. For example, during peak business times, companies can quickly expand their computing capacity to handle the additional load. Cloud services also promote global collaboration by allowing data and applications to be accessed from anywhere with an internet connection, thereby supporting remote work and boosting productivity.

Cloud computing presents several substantial opportunities for data processing. Some of the most attractive features are dynamic scalability, on-demand resource availability, reduced Capital Expenditures (CapEx) and Operating Expenses (OpEx). Cloud platforms such as Amazon Web Services (AWS), Microsoft Azure and Google Cloud Platform (GCP) enable organisations to process large datasets efficiently by dynamically scaling resources. These features are also vital for big data, where the volume and complexity of data can fluctuate significantly. Cloud services offer advanced data analytics tools and ML frameworks and help businesses gain insights and make data-driven decisions.

The cloud technologies provide vast, scalable storage solutions to manage the large volumes of data generated by DTs. Additionally, it also provides platforms for real-time data processing, advanced analytics and AI-driven insights, enhancing the performance and intelligence of DTs. Furthermore, the integration of DTs with IoT, robotics and drones is possible using cloud platforms to ensure seamless data flow and collaboration across distributed environments which is crucial for DTs' performance and effectiveness [34,35].

All of these opportunities of cloud technologies and platform comes with its challenges [36,37]. The most concerning among them is data security and privacy [38]. Storing data on cloud servers outside the organisational limits raises the concerns related to data ownership, compliance and data breach. This requires organisations to be very sensitive about their data and implement robust security measures to mitigate these risks. Moreover, reliable and high-speed internet access is crucial for optimal cloud performance, which can be a limitation in many areas with limited to poor connectivity [39]. In conclusion, cloud computing is a fundamental element of modern data processing for smart DTs, offering scalable, flexible and cost-effective solutions for managing and analysing data. Despite its inherent challenges, the cloud continues to evolve and provide new tools, capabilities etc. which are driving innovation and efficiency.

3.2.2.3 Artificial intelligence

AI is an attempt to make machines that simulate human intelligence by being programmed to think and behave like humans [40]. This includes cognitive abilities such as learning, reasoning, problem-solving, perception and language comprehension. In many contexts, AI and smartness can be used interchangeably. Though AI has different directions and approaches, ML, deep learning and reinforcement learning are the most popular AI technologies now.

AI enables DTs in various ways. Firstly, AI enables DTs to analyse data, predict outcomes and recommend optimised actions, enhancing operational efficiency and reducing risks. Secondly, self-learning capabilities of AI allows DTs to adapt according to the changing conditions and improve the performance over time. Finally, the simulation capabilities of DTs can be enhanced significantly to evaluate complex scenarios and identify optimal solutions in real-time implementation [41,42].

In a data-driven DTs, AI can handle these massive data volumes in real-time and solve intricate issues that were once out of human grasp to date. A notable advantage offered by AI is in real-time applications, where AI systems augmented by available computing capabilities, generate intelligence through processing data as it is produced and facilitates immediate decisions and reactions. For instance, in healthcare, AI-enabled diagnostic tools evaluate medical images and patient data in real-time, leading to faster and smarter diagnoses. This ability is also vital in financial services, where AI algorithms identify fraudulent transactions as they occur, protecting consumers and financial institutions from potential losses.

Furthermore, AI excels at resolving complex problems involving enormous quantities of data and multiple variables. In scientific research, AI models examine genomics data to pinpoint potential genetic markers for diseases, accelerating the progress of personalised medicine. In engineering, AI designs optimised structures and materials by simulating numerous scenarios and configurations that would be impractical to test manually, adding a layer of intelligent decision-making to the process. AI has helped build autonomous systems like self-driving cars and drones that can operate intelligently in dynamic environments. By leveraging AI's real-time data processing and complex problem-solving capabilities, modern applications are getting smarter and more efficient.

AI's potential is undeniable, but significant hurdles need to be overcome for its responsible and ethical use of AI in any fields including DTs [43]. The major concerns are explainable AI and the exaggeration of any inadvertent biases existing in the data being used for training. Often, AI systems function like *black boxes*, making their decision-making process unclear. This lack of transparency can lead to biased outcomes, especially if the training data itself is biased. Another challenging behaviour with GenAI is *hallucination* where AI generates false facts and information with confidence [44]. Rigorous data checking and mitigation strategies during the training can be helpful to promote fairness and reduce the presence of bias and inaccuracies in the response.

Additionally, data security and privacy are paramount while training the model using data from the Internet and other sources. AI systems must also be designed to withstand cyber-attacks and guarantee secure data handling throughout their life cycle. As AI deals with vast amounts of data, robust safeguards against breaches and unauthorised access are crucial to maintain user trust and adhere to regulations.

Ethical AI is another challenge [45]. The opaqueness of current AI systems threatens the users' freedom and control over their data and understanding of its usage. The massive dataset requirement for effective AI poses the challenge of creating a robust infrastructure for data collection, storage and management. As AI applications grow, efficiently managing this data while maintaining performance and reliability becomes increasingly complex. Addressing these challenges is essential for the sustainable and ethical development of AI.

Data processing: fuelling the intelligence of DTs

Intelligence is the ability to make informed decisions or actions based on data, which relies heavily on effective data processing. As data generation grows exponentially, the importance of data processing becomes increasingly critical to harness and make sense of the vast amounts of information. Data Processing includes managing, computing and making reasonable inferences. Interestingly, over half of the data generated is video [29], which is highly unstructured and compute-intensive. Technologies such as AI, Big Data and Cloud play fundamental roles in data processing to achieve smartness in DTs.

3.2.3 Data presentation

Making the best decision from the given data is only halfway towards smartness but participation and ownership are equally important in fostering commitment, improving outcomes and enhancing satisfaction among the stakeholders. The data presentation tools and technologies transform raw data from DTs into a clear and actionable forms to make informed decisions. The outcomes from DTs can be monitored in a real-time using interactive visualisations tools. We highlight emerging smart technologies and demonstrate how these technologies enhance user interaction by improving participation, feedback and communication by ensuring a smart and efficient experience.

3.2.3.1 Extended reality

Extended reality (XR) are technologies that enable the blending of digital elements, like virtual objects or information with real-world environments, allowing interactive experiences such as gaming, virtual tours and educational simulations. It provides a set of experiences that serve as a bridge between the actual and the simulated world to bring people the real experience [46]. XR describes all real-and-virtual combined environments between human and computer input [47]. It plays an important role in connecting the physical and digital worlds in practically every aspect of development, including design, prototyping, learning, marketing, logistics, maintenance, setups, remote assistance and assembly [48].

XR technology offers various opportunities to revolutionise many industries; within education, the technology provides both immersive and interactive learning. It allows people to interact with the material more visually and experimentally, hence increasing their motivation, interest and comprehension of the subject matter [49]. It has the potential to transform health care by creating immersive experiences for assisting in pain management, therapy, patient education and training to deliver enhanced healthcare [50]. Additionally, it contributes to cross-industry discipline offering opportunities for creativity, digital worlds and knowledge across various sectors [51]. XR is a broad category that includes augmented reality (AR), virtual reality (VR) and mixed reality (MR).

Augmented reality

AR is a technology that allows simultaneous interaction of the actual environment and digital elements, enhancing the user's perception of reality by adding virtual images, objects and information to the existing environment. In short, AR is a technology that projects virtual objects into real physical situations [52]. It allows for the real-time integration of virtual and real-world objects within the range of view allowing users to have a more natural and intuitive sensory experience [53]. The significant advantage of AR is that it eliminates the need to construct everything from the beginning; instead, it can build on what already exists [54].

AR can be present in all aspects of our daily lives, including education and training, the medical field, tourism, manufacturing and more. AR has played a significant influence in evolving the education sector by creating engaging learning and teaching platforms for students and teachers. It has successfully enhanced traditional forms of education and extended learning outside the walls. An application of AR in education is for interactive course material, that enables teachers to bridge the gap between real and virtual [55]. AR can used to improve not only the learning environment but also students' involvement and interest by ensuring proper content understanding. It can help to establish collaborative learning, in which all students participate in the learning process at the same time, resulting in improved teamwork abilities. Additionally, it has helped students retain important facts by bringing teachings to life. In addition, AR can be used to improve training by guiding technicians through challenging tasks, resulting in faster completion and fewer errors. Recent advancements in mobile technology like tablets and smartphones have made AR more accessible for regular maintenance, assembling and installing appliances that have significantly reduced expenses [56].

AR technologies are increasingly recognised as a valuable tool for integrating patients' medical data [54]. The advances in medical imaging have provided vast amounts of data for various activities, including surgery, diagnostics and training tasks [57]. AR enhances symptom diagnosis by providing medical professionals with an accurate picture of the patient's condition through the Real-time Data Offering, enabling observation of a patient's internal organs and disease progression. Virtualisation procedures include combining digital information on a patient's body, enabling physicians to see the patient's interior organs and arrange surgical procedures more precisely.

AR significantly enhances the experience of tourists by helping them move from one place to another, where they can make use of devices like smartphones and tablets that are well-equipped with GPS sensors, fast networks, etc. AR enables travellers to get improved information, navigation assistance and engaging content during their journey [54]. AR has major applications in manufacturing, as it can enhance various processes including assembly, maintenance, training and collaboration between humans and robots [56]. It enhances the assembly processes by reducing completion time, mistakes and workload and cuts maintenance costs by up to 30% allowing machinery suppliers to communicate remotely resulting in real-time data for faster maintenance and inspection.

Virtual reality

VR is a technology that creates a computer-generated environment enabling users to engage with an artificial 3D visual or sensory environment. VR is an artificial, digital environment in which a person can see and interact using a range of additional devices [58]. It is a fully immersive computer-generated world that uses AI to make it feel real and interactive [47]. It facilitates interaction with nonexistent and inaccessible events and objects [59]. The ultimate goal of a virtual environment is to provide the user with a strong sensation of immersion or presence, regardless of how VR is experienced [60]. For example, the application of VR in gaming, where this technology allows players to fully engage themselves in the virtual world by letting them look about, move their bodies and interact with the virtual environment rather than merely controlling a character on a screen.

It has been considered advantageous in a wide range of areas, including education, sciences, archaeology, history, architecture and so on [61]. It allows students to experience difficult-to-describe subject matter, making it more effective than traditional techniques. Here it allows students to repeat experiences without incurring additional fees or difficulties, as well as review challenging circumstances at their own pace [48]. Furthermore, VR has also enabled the exploration of historical locations and microscopic worlds, which has enhanced the learning experience. VR has a wide range of applications in the medical field from giving 3D visualisation that allows medical experts to interact with the human body in a variety of ways [62]. It also assists surgeons in practising procedures and enables ICU medical members to stimulate emergency scenarios. It has played a significant role in pain management, phobia treatment and cancer therapy by providing specific simulations and experiences [62]. It has enhanced medical training, improved surgical skills and fostered better communication among the healthcare professionals. With technological advancements, VR enables the integration of huge datasets from imaging to simulate surgical operations, allowing doctors to rehearse complex surgeries in virtual reality before performing them on real patients [63]. The growing technology of VR has also contributed to tourism industry development.

The use of VR in tourism provides a wide range of benefits, including planning, marketing, entertainment, education, accessibility and historical preservation [64]. It has influenced marketing by offering immersive experiences that improve tourists' choices and expectations. It functions as an entertaining feature at theme parks and other tourist sites.

Mixed reality

MR is a technology that tries to strike a balance between AR and VR by allowing users to physically interact with virtual items in the real world [65]. As we know AR modifies the real environment by adding objects and VR completely involves the user in a virtual world by filtering out the real world. MR allows the entire body to be merged with both real and virtual features across the reality line [66].

MR has always been a viable technology for creating immersive and engaging learning experiences. This can be used as an educational tool that combines physical and computer-generated environments to provide on-site learning experiences and allows students to explore subjects such as science, mathematics and sociology [67]. Using mixed reality for experiential learning, engagement and enjoyment can help to improve students' happiness with learning items and environments. MR has also played an important role in the evolution of the industrial business, helping to maintain and repair machines to assist the operation [68]. With the rise of Industry 4.0, MR has become increasingly popular. The MR integrates with IoT, which supports real-time operational data analytics, aids in the syncing of production lines and assets, and improves remote asset monitoring by allowing field engineers to access real-time data [69].

MR has the potential to change the medical field by replacing the traditional approach with more accuracy. It can be used to view medical imaging that is already in digital format and can be displayed on standard monitors in the operating room to aid surgery [68]. MR can reduce errors, save lives and save healthcare costs by optimising patient care. It promotes experiential learning by creating a rich interactive environment that simulates real-world situations, which benefits medical students, nurses and physicians across a wide range of instructional activities. MR has been used in pharmaceuticals, allowing pharmacist students to see how a specific drug reacts in our bodies, in telesurgery for doctors, where operations were remotely controlled by a robot, and in anatomy education, where it can provide a true sample for effective teaching [70]. MR is utilised for persuasive purposes, including educating tourists about the destination's culture and providing personalised tours. It improves experiential learning, encourages discovery, facilitates reminiscing and allows for re-experience of the journey [71]. This system helps tourists navigate cities or structures by displaying virtual signals that are connected to the real environment [68].

MR integrates AR and VR, creating a seamless blend of physical and virtual environments where users can interact with both simultaneously. The potential of these reality devices in DTs is reviewed in [72] and articulate the possible applications spanning from manufacturing, education, training, as well as safety and productivity in the workplace. A MR interface for a DT-based crane prototype is introduced in [73]. Similarly, the application of reality devices with DTs in the medical field enhances visualisation, interaction and simulation [74]. In [75], the authors explore collaboration between human and robot for automated construction processes using on-site real-time DT of robotic process in a MR construction environment.

Implementing these technologies comes with a variety of challenges. One of the major challenges is the complexity and associated cost along with technical issues such as software/hardware accessibility and support [76–78]. Other significant challenges is cyber-security in the network and privacy where a lot of personal information may be needed to adjust according to the environment to the user's tastes [79]. Many organisations must pay high prices to store this kind of data which reduces the affordability, making users concerned about the theft of their personal information. Additionally, other significant challenges are streaming data over the internet, bandwidth requirements, latency requirements and the complexity of 3D manipulation [80,81]. Furthermore, another challenge is the synchronisation in managing big data with graphic visualisation, dynamic effects and handling issues in applications like sudden environmental changes [82].

3.2.3.2 Holographic communications

Holographic communication is an emerging technology that captures patterns of light to create a 3D image known as a hologram, which can be viewed without the use of special glasses or any other objects [83]. Holograms are unique because their appearances change depending on the viewing angle, creating a perception identical to that of real-world items [84]. It delivers truly sensory immersion for several new applications, like holographic telepresence, healthcare, retail, education, training, entertainment, sports and gaming by displaying multi-view high-resolution 3D holograms of humans or objects/items and creating multi-sensory media (mulsemedia), including audio, haptic, smell and taste [85]. Holography plays an important role in data storage where it has advantages over optical and magnetic data storage by utilising various angles of light to store information in parallel rather than linear ways resulting in higher data transfer speed [86].

The opportunity of holography technology is widely observed in various forms, from 6G wireless networks, holographic entertainment, holographic education, holographic medical healthcare to holographic production [87]. It has contributed to enhancing the quality of learning in education by allowing students to see objects from various perspectives, facilitating teacher exchanges, minimising travel costs and creating a more engaging as well as realistic learning environment [88]. In holographic communication, we make use of a gesture-sensing board which enables users to control a holographic display through hand gestures, without the need for any physical contact [89]. This shows the potential of the technology for interactive learning and future applications of AR. Holography can advance healthcare by speeding imaging procedures, storing digital 3D patient images and enabling monitoring of conditions and substances from diabetes & infections to drug labels and tissue functionality [90]. Similarly, 6G wireless networks enable a comprehensive understanding of the physical world, fostering the integration of virtual reality, increasing the scope for human activity, improving both physical and cognitive abilities, and enabling uninterrupted interaction among a large number of agents, providing a revolution in sensory immersion and a wide variety of advanced applications across domains [91]. This technology can improve entertainment experiences, not only in television, sports broadcasting and gaming but also in 3D content, providing viewers with exclusive views, such as a 3D overview of sports events from any angle and interactive gaming experiences in both non-immersive and immersive virtual worlds.

Holographic communication has immense potential in enhancing the capabilities of DTs in various fields including education [92], construction [93] and more. Therefore, holographic technology allows users to view the DT impressively and interactively, improving the usability and accessibility of DT [94,95].

One major challenge is the bandwidth requirement for transmitting holographic data in real time. Advancements in communication technologies like 5G and 6G, cloud and big data can help address this issue. Another challenge is the need for standardisation in formats and protocols to ensure interoperability between different holographic systems. Collaboration and combined effort between industry stakeholders can help to have a common standard and adoption of the standard. Further, the challenges to overcome for holographic communication are the viewing angle in 360 degrees for effective teaching in the education sector, lack of capability of using outdoor displays, integration in continuously monitoring and adjusting the holographic display based on user interactions and environmental conditions [85].

Data presentation: visualising the power of DTs

Using the latest technologies to make data-driven decisions is only one side of the coin; the other side involves creating a more engaging and interactive user experience through participation and feedback. Data presentation technologies including AR, VR, XR and holographic projection are the third set of technologies that are coupled with smartness. These technologies integrate human factors with Digital Twins, enhancing the relevance of the use case and elevating the overall user experience.

3.3 Security by design, not as overlay

DTs' smartness would be incomplete without security and therefore, security must be included as a part of DT development. All the core technologies and processes discussed in this chapter must be viewed through the lens of security and incorporate necessary design requirements to address the security challenges. Future digital products and services including DTs should be based on the *Security by Design* philosophy to ensure sustainability and enhance user experience. We must adopt a security-by-design approach, rather than the traditional method of adding security as an overlay during or after system design. Security by design is a proactive approach to the development of digital products and services that integrates security measures and considerations throughout the entire development process. Rather than treating security as an afterthought or an add-on, this philosophy embeds security into every phase of the product life-cycle, from initial concept through to deployment and maintenance. This security principle should be applied to all three technology domains of smartness while developing DTs' based products and services.

There is a growing demand for regulating consumer smart products regarding safety [96,97]. Recently, the Product Security and Telecommunications Infrastructure (PSTI) Act came into effect on 29 April 2024 in the UK which requires manufacturers must ensure that all their smart devices meet basic cybersecurity requirements before the sale of the product [96]. The world is watching the effectiveness of this act and many countries will follow this path to protect their economy if it is successful. Therefore, future smart products should anticipate and mitigate security risks and vulnerabilities before they become exploitable.

Achieving product and service security is possible by adhering to key principles. The security should start in the requirement development and design process. The system designer or developer should consider security principles in consideration during the designing of a system or service. They need to identify and understand potential threats and vulnerabilities early in the design phase and also incorporate security requirements as system requirements along with functional requirements. Additionally, the developer should follow best practices while writing code as the growth of software-defined products is rapidly accelerating as businesses increasingly seek flexible, scalable and cost-effective solutions. Therefore, educating developers and stakeholders on security best practices and emerging threats to maintain a security-aware culture. Furthermore, the product or service released in the market should come with the highest possible security setting as a default to support all types of users, ensuring robust protection against potential threats while maintaining ease of use and accessibility for both novice and advanced users. This requirement may be a mandatory demand in the near future to support cyber-security requirements before the sale of products. In addition, there should be a culture of conducting security testing in the organisation to overcome current or emerging threats, ensuring that vulnerabilities are identified and mitigated promptly to maintain the integrity and safety of the product or service throughout its life cycle. Moreover, it is crucial to have a response plan and procedures in place in case a security breach occurs.

The key benefits of using security by design can be viewed from different angles. Firstly, the cost associated and the impact on the economy by cyber-security threats can be reduced significantly by manufacturing products and services using the security by design principle as the cost associated with this approach is cheaper when compared with fixing vulnerabilities after deployment. Secondly, secure products and services can improve trust in the product among the users. Finally, the products and services introduced by using this design principle are resilient to attacks and can easily meet the growing regulatory requirements.

Despite having several benefits and advantages of security by design philosophy as discussed above, it also faces several challenges to implement. Firstly, integrating security into the development process increases complexity in the products and services creation and therefore, requires additional resources and expertise. This initially disturbs the product development life-cycle and is costly compared with traditional products and services. Secondly, security features introduced in the products and services can sometimes impact system performance. Therefore, there is a need for careful balancing of security and performance needs, especially with low latency requirements applications. Finally, keeping up with the latest threats and ensuring the design remains robust against new types of attacks can be challenging in this constantly changing digital landscape.

Incorporating *security by design* requires a philosophical shift in product/service design and development. This approach may also require the development of new security technologies to counter increasingly sophisticated cyber threats and attacks in a rapidly evolving digital landscape. Many of these threats may be unknown at the time of design and development. Some of the emerging security architectures and technologies that address these risks are Zero trust architecture [98], AI and ML [99], blockchain technology [100,101], quantum cryptography [102,103], secure access service edge, homomorphic encryption [104,105], biometric authentication, endpoint detection and response and 5G security enhancements.

Security by design, not as overlay

Adopting a *security by design* philosophy is essential for creating future smartness in DT-based digital products and services which protect data and maintain trust. By integrating security measures from the outset, organisations can ensure sustainability, meet growing demand for product security and provide a superior user experience in an increasingly digital world.

3.4 Sustainability, innovation and lifestyle

In addition to the three technological domains of smartness and security by design, it is crucial that smartness also encompasses other domains essential for the future world. The essential other domains for smartness are represented by three vertices in Figure 3.1 called 3Es (*Environment, Economy* and *Experience*) of Sustainability, Innovation and Lifestyle. DT-based smart systems play a pivotal role in advancing these domains. By improving efficiency and viability, DTs can contribute significantly to global environmental sustainability. Similarly, DT-driven solutions must be economically accessible, enabling wider adoption and benefiting diverse populations. Furthermore, DTs should prioritise enhancing user experience and satisfaction, thus improving the quality of life on a broader scale. In the smartness model depicted in Figure 3.1, the foundational concept of *Sustainability* encapsulates the two domains of environment and economy. Similarly, the model represents the domains of environment and user experience through *Lifestyle*, and the domains of economy and user experience through *Innovation*.

3.4.1 Sustainability

Smartness is sustainable when it supports the global environment and remains economically viable. Therefore, DT's smartness should be linked with the UN Sustainable Development Goals (SDGs). The 2030 Agenda for Sustainable Development by the UN includes 17 SDGs [106]. Two goals (Goal 9 and Goal 11) are directly related to technologies and smartness which include industrialisation, innovation and smart cities but the other goals are indirectly related to technologies and smartness. Goal 9 is defined as 'Build resilient infrastructure, promote inclusive and sustainable industrialisation and foster innovation' [107] and Goal 11 is defined as 'Make cities and human settlements inclusive, safe, resilient and sustainable' [108]. These goals are achievable when smartness takes into account both environmental and economic factors while developing DT-based products and services.

Measuring the impact of smart technology on the global environment and economy is challenging due to the complex interplay of various factors, including the rapid pace of technological advancement, diverse environmental conditions and the multifaceted nature of technological effects. Therefore, there is a need for sustainability modelling to understand, predict and improve the sustainability of

DT-based smart products and services. The model should consider environmental impact, economic viability and social equity to develop strategies that ensure long-term sustainability. The goal of sustainability modelling is to provide insights and solutions that balance these factors to achieve sustainable development. Five-sector sustainability model for assessing the sustainability of production systems is proposed in [109]. The same model is used to measure the correlation between sustainability and smartness indicators in Brazilian cities in [110]. In [111], the authors identify influencing factors for urban sustainability and smartness in their review paper and introduce a theoretical framework to study sustainability and smartness. An evaluation framework for smartness and sustainability in cities is introduced in [112] where a replicable urban regeneration model is introduced, focusing on applying an evaluation framework at both city and project levels, illustrated through its implementation in Valladolid, Spain. These studies are primarily focused on specific, limited areas. Therefore, there is a pressing need for a universal model accepted by the wider community to accurately measure the sustainability of smart technology.

3.4.2 Innovation

Smartness cannot be achieved without innovation. A smart product will deliver an outstanding user experience at an affordable price. No matter how cutting-edge a product might be, if the price tag is not attractive to the masses, it's going to miss out on winning over a wide audience. So, keeping the user experience within reach is key to getting it into as many hands as possible. Therefore, the use of innovative ideas and concepts in DTs development is crucial to making them accessible and valuable to a wider range of stakeholders.

This requires that the DT-based smart products of tomorrow need to be innovative both in their experience and economy. The quest for creating budget-friendly user experiences is driving the wheel of innovation in both technology and business development. Companies are on the hunt for smart ways to cut down on costs and improve their product's appeal, without increasing the price. By reaching the masses, organisations can achieve an economy of scale. As these innovations in technology and strategic planning take off, they end up creating smarter products which are both cost-effective, provide an exhilarating user experience and ensure that organisations do not lose their investment in research and innovation.

3.4.3 Lifestyle

When we discuss the role of economy and innovation as essential contexts of smartness we should not forget the environmental aspect which is intricately connected with our lifestyle in shaping a future that ensures a higher quality of life for all. Sustainability aims to meet the needs of the present without compromising the ability of future generations to meet their own needs, placing a crucial focus on environmental conservation and we need to adopt our lifestyle accordingly. Technology including DTs can play a supportive role in this context by offering tools and innovations that can either protect, save or heal the environment. When leveraged responsibly, technology can significantly reduce humanity's ecological footprint by improving energy efficiency, enabling renewable energy sources and promoting circular economies where waste is minimised and resources are reused.

The impact of technology on people's lifestyles is profound and can lead to more sustainable living practices. Smart homes, for example, utilise IoT devices to optimise energy usage, reducing electricity consumption and lowering carbon footprints. Electric vehicles are another technological advancement transforming transportation, cutting down on greenhouse gas emissions and reducing reliance on fossil fuels. Additionally, advancements in digital communication and remote working tools have reduced the need for daily commuting, thereby decreasing pollution and enhancing work-life balance. These technological shifts not only contribute to environmental sustainability but also enhance human experiences by providing convenience, efficiency and improved well-being.

Ultimately, the integration of sustainable practices, environmental stewardship and innovative technology fosters a lifestyle that aligns with the principles of ecological balance and human advancement. As individuals and communities adopt these lifestyle changes, there is a collective movement towards a healthier planet, an enriched quality of life and a better overall experience for successive generations. By embracing green technologies and sustainable practices in our day-to-day lives, societies can ensure that economic growth and human development go hand in hand with environmental preservation, leading to a more resilient and vibrant future for all. We believe that any technology including DT that supports our journey in this direction is smart. Therefore, By integrating environmental data with user-centred experiences, DTs can facilitate informed decision-making, improved system performance and enhanced usability across industries like urban planning, manufacturing, healthcare, many more areas. These factors are crucial to ensure a higher quality of life for all in future.

3Es for sustainability, innovation and lifestyle

Beyond technical domains, DT smartness also encompasses non-technical contexts. Therefore, technology innovators should focus not only on the technology itself but also on its impact on the *E*nvironment, *E*conomy and user *E*xperience. Sustainability forms the foundational context of smartness, encompassing environmental and economic dimensions. The environmental dimension requires adjustments in lifestyle to preserve our environment, while the economic dimension drives innovation to lower the cost of products and services. Technology can play a crucial role here if chosen and designed wisely. Ultimately, the goal is to achieve an enhanced user experience.

3.5 Towards future smartness

Recent advancements in communication technologies, strides towards AGI and the transformative Industry 5.0 revolution are collectively paving the way for a smarter and more connected future. DTs play a pivotal role in achieving the six bold objectives outlined by the Next-G Alliance (NGA) [113] and align closely with the ITU's vision for IMT-2030 [114]. Additionally, global initiatives such as 3GPP's advancements in 5G technologies [115] further underscore the importance of DTs in delivering innovative use cases and shaping the next wave of technological evolution for the human mankind [116].

Digital twin: pioneering the path to future intelligence
The development in communication technologies, rapid growth towards AGI and Industry 5.0 revolution is driving towards a smarter future. The involvement of DT in ambitious initiatives by Next-G Alliance, ITU's IMT2030 capabilities and usage scenarios and other global efforts are crucial for innovations, sustainable future for humanity. These developments are creating virtual counterparts of physical entities to enable real-time interaction and bringing data-driven insights to optimise various industries' operations.

References

[1] Yao JF, Yang Y, Wang XC, *et al.* Systematic review of digital twin technology and applications. *Visual Computing for Industry, Biomedicine, and Art.* 2023;6(1):10.

[2] Saxony S. What is a Smart System?; 2024. Accessed: 13 December 2024. Available from: https://silicon-saxony.de/en/what-is-a-smart-system/.

[3] Alter S. Making sense of smartness in the context of smart devices and smart systems. *Information Systems Frontiers.* 2020;22(2):381–393.

[4] Albino V, Berardi U, and Dangelico RM. Smart cities: definitions, dimensions, performance, and initiatives. *Journal of Urban Technology.* 2015;22 (1):3–21.

[5] Mukti IY, Iacob ME, Aldea A, *et al.* Defining rural smartness and its impact: a systematic literature review. *Journal of the Knowledge Economy.* 2021;13:1–52.

[6] Halpern O, and Mitchell R. *The smartness mandate.* Cambridge, MA: MIT Press; 2023.

[7] Axelsson K, Melin U, and Granath M. Exploring services in a smart city through socio-technical design principles: revealing five tensions in a smart living context. *Government Information Quarterly.* 2024;41(1):101915.

[8] Radanliev P, De Roure D, Nicolescu R, *et al.* Digital twins: artificial intelligence and the IoT cyber-physical systems in Industry 4.0. *International Journal of Intelligent Robotics and Applications.* 2022;6(1):171–185.

[9] Zayed SM, Attiya GM, El-Sayed A, *et al.* A review study on digital twins with artificial intelligence and internet of things: concepts, opportunities,

challenges, tools and future scope. *Multimedia Tools and Applications*. 2023;82(30):47081–47107.

[10] Correia JB, Abel M, and Becker K. Data management in digital twins: a systematic literature review. *Knowledge and Information Systems*. 2023;65 (8): 3165–3196.

[11] Birk A. What is robotics? An interdisciplinary field is getting even more diverse. *IEEE Robotics & Automation Magazine*. 2011;18(4):94–95.

[12] Intuitive Surgical. Robotic-Assisted Surgery with da Vinci Systems. Intuitive Surgical (Patient Information). Accessed 19 December 2024. Available from: https://www.intuitive.com/en-us/patients/da-vinci-robotic-surgery.

[13] Baidya S, Das S, Uddin M, *et al.* Digital Twin in Safety-Critical Robotics Applications: Opportunities and Challenges. In: *2022 IEEE International Performance. In: Computing, and Communications Conference (IPCCC)*; 2022.

[14] Andrei VC, Li XY, Fees M, *et al.* A Digital Twinning Platform for Integrated Sensing, Communications and Robotics. In: *IEEE 4th International Symposium on Joint Communications & Sensing*; 2024.

[15] Shaaban M, Carfì A, and Mastrogiovanni F. Digital Twins for Human–Robot Collaboration: A Future Perspective. In: *International Conference on Intelligent Autonomous Systems*. Springer; 2023. p. 429–441.

[16] Hentout A, Mustapha A, Maoudj A, *et al.* Key Challenges and Open Issues of Industrial Collaborative Robotics. In: *Proceedings of the 27th IEEE International Symposium on Workshop on Human-Robot Interaction: from Service to Industry (HRI-SI2018) at Robot and Human Interactive Communication*. IEEE; 2018.

[17] Hentout A, Aouache M, Maoudj A, *et al.* Human–robot interaction in industrial collaborative robotics: a literature review of the decade 2008–2017. *Advanced Robotics*. 2019;33(15–16):764–799.

[18] Lee H. Robotics 4.0: challenges and opportunities in the 4th Industrial Revolution. *Journal of Information Systems and Technology Management*. 2022;12(4):39–55.

[19] Hajjaj SSH, Moktar MH, and Weng LY. Review of implementing the Internet of Things (IoT) for robotic drones (IoT Drones). *E3S Web of Conferences*. 2024;477:00016.

[20] Chakraborty M. Drone technology in agriculture. *Agriculture and Food*. 2023;5(2):290–292.

[21] Pugliese LDP, Guerriero F, and Macrina G. Using drones for parcels delivery process. *Procedia Manufacturing*. 2020;42:488–497.

[22] As Q. Applications of medical drones in public health: an overview. *Journal of Human Anatomy*. 2021;5(1):1–9.

[23] Martinez FJ, Kerrache CA, and Lakas A. Guest editorial: drones for smart cities. *IET Smart Cities*. 2022;4(4):229–230.

[24] Majeed R, Abdullah NA, Mushtaq MF, *et al.* Drone security: issues and challenges. *International Journal of Advanced Computer Science and Applications*. 2021;12(5).

[25] Souanef T, Al-Rubaye S, Tsourdos A, *et al*. Digital twin development for the airspace of the future. *Drones*. 2023;7(7):484.
[26] Iqbal D, Buhnova B, and Cioroaica E. Digital twins for trust building in autonomous drones through dynamic safety evaluation. in *Proceedings of the 18th International Conference on Evaluation of Novel Approaches to Software Engineering (ENASE 2023)*, 2023, pp. 1–10. Available from: https://publica.fraunhofer.de/entities/publication/e1a3299f-6043-43d5-bea2-015bef86a358.
[27] To A, Liu M, Hazeeq Bin Muhammad Hairul M, *et al*. Drone-Based AI and 3D Reconstruction for Digital Twin Augmentation. In: *International Conference on Human-Computer Interaction*. Springer; 2021. p. 511–529.
[28] Marr B. How Much Data Do We Create Every Day? The Mind-Blowing Stats Everyone Should Read; 2024. Accessed: 13 December 2024. Available from: https://bernardmarr.com/how-much-data-do-we-create-every-day-the-mind-blowing-stats-everyone-should-read/.
[29] Topics E. How Much Data Is Created Every Day? [2024 Update]; 2024. Accessed: 13 December 2024. Available from: https://explodingtopics.com/blog/data-generated-per-day.
[30] Dash S, Shakyawar SK, Sharma M, *et al*. Big data in healthcare: management, analysis and future prospects. *Journal of Big Data*. 2019;6(1):1–25.
[31] Moniruzzaman ABM, and Hossain SA. NoSQL database: new era of databases for big data analytics—classification, characteristics and comparison. *International Journal of Database Theory and Application*. 2013;6(4):1–14. https://www.earticle.net/Article/A207903.
[32] Ishwarappa I, and Anuradha J. A brief introduction on Big Data 5Vs characteristics and Hadoop technology. *Procedia Computer Science*. 2015; 48:319–324. https://doi.org/10.1016/j.procs.2015.04.188.
[33] Gartner, Inc. What is Cloud Computing? Strategies and Importance for Business;. Accessed: 31 May 2024. https://www.gartner.com/en/topics/cloud.
[34] Paiva Knebel F, Araujo Wickboldt J, and Pignaton de Freitas E. A cloud-fog computing architecture for real-time digital twins. *arXiv e-prints*. 2020; p. arXiv–2012.
[35] Gomes S, Toosi AN, and Ens B. Digital twin of a cloud data centre: an openStack cluster visualisation. In: *New Frontiers in Cloud Computing and Internet of Things*. Berlin: Springer; 2022. p. 209–225.
[36] Zhang Q, Cheng L, and Boutaba R. Cloud computing: state-of-the-art and research challenges. *Journal of Internet Services and Applications*. 2010; 1:7–18.
[37] Kumar S, and Goudar R. Cloud computing-research issues, challenges, architecture, platforms and applications: a survey. *International Journal of Future Computer and Communication*. 2012;1(4):356.
[38] Rong C, Nguyen ST, and Jaatun MG. Beyond lightning: a survey on security challenges in cloud computing. *Computers & Electrical Engineering*. 2013;39(1):47–54.

[39] Wei Y, and Blake MB. Service-oriented computing and cloud computing: challenges and opportunities. *IEEE Internet Computing*. 2010;14(6):72–75.

[40] IBM. Artificial Intelligence; 2024. Accessed: 13 December 2024. Available from: https://www.ibm.com/topics/artificial-intelligence.

[41] Drissi Elbouzidi A, Ait El Cadi A, Pellerin R, *et al.* The role of AI in warehouse digital twins: literature review. *Applied Sciences*. 2023;13(11):6746.

[42] Rathore MM, Shah SA, Shukla D, *et al.* The role of AI, machine learning, and big data in digital twinning: a systematic literature review, challenges, and opportunities. *IEEE Access*. 2021;9:32030–32052.

[43] Marr B. The 15 Biggest Risks of Artificial Intelligence; 2023. Accessed: 13 December 2024. Available from: https://www.forbes.com/sites/bernardmarr/2023/06/02/the-15-biggest-risks-of-artificial-intelligence/?sh=61ac9c892706.

[44] Zhang Y, Li Y, Cui L, *et al.* Siren's song in the AI ocean: a survey on hallucination in large language models. *Computational Linguistics*, 2025;1–46.

[45] Siau K, and Wang W. Artificial intelligence (AI) ethics: ethics of AI and ethical AI. *Journal of Database Management (JDM)*. 2020;31(2):74–87.

[46] Shaikh TA, Dar TR, and Sofi S. A data-centric artificial intelligent and extended reality technology in smart healthcare systems. *Social Network Analysis and Mining*. 2022;12(1):122.

[47] Alnagrat AJA, Zulkifli AN, and Yusoff MF. Evaluation of UUM mobile augmented reality based i-brochure application. *International Journal of Computing, Communication and Instrumentation Engineering*. 2014;2(2):92–97.

[48] Bacca J, Baldiris S, Fabregat R, *et al.* Mobile augmented reality in vocational education and training. *Procedia Computer Science*. 2015;75:49–58.

[49] Khlaif ZN, Mousa A, and Sanmugam M. Immersive extended reality (XR) technology in engineering education: opportunities and challenges. *Technology, Knowledge and Learning*. 2024;29:803–826.

[50] Jones D, Galvez R, Evans D, *et al.* The integration and application of extended reality (XR) technologies within the general practice primary medical care setting: a systematic review. *Virtual Worlds*. 2023;2(4):359–373.

[51] Novakova H, Štarchoň P. Creative industries: challenges and opportunities in XR technologies. *SHS Web of Conferences*. 2021;115:03011.

[52] Leins N, Gonnermann-Müller J, and Teichmann M. Comparing head-mounted and handheld augmented reality for guided assembly. *Journal on Multimodal User Interfaces*. 2024;18(4):313–328. https://doi.org/10.1007/s12193-024-00440-1.

[53] Chen PHC, Gadepalli K, MacDonald R, *et al.* An augmented reality microscope with real-time artificial intelligence integration for cancer diagnosis. *Nature Medicine*. 2019;25(9):1453–1457.

[54] Manuri F, and Sanna A. A survey on applications of augmented reality. *ACSIJ Advances in Computer Science: An International Journal*. 2016;5(1):18–27.

[55] Antonioli M, Blake C, and Sparks K. Augmented reality applications in education. *The Journal of Technology Studies*. 2014;40:96–107.

[56] Plakas G, Ponis S, Agalianos K, *et al*. Augmented reality in manufacturing and logistics: lessons learnt from a real-life industrial application. *Procedia Manufacturing*. 2020;51:1629–1635.

[57] Sielhorst T, Feuerstein M, and Navab N. Advanced medical displays: a literature review of augmented reality. *Journal of Display Technology*. 2008;4(4):451–467.

[58] Vei Siang C, Haron H, Ismail M, *et al*. VR and AR virtual welding for psychomotor skills: a systematic review. *Multimedia Tools and Applications*. 2022;81:12459–12493.

[59] Malik AA, Masood T, and Bilberg A. Virtual reality in manufacturing: immersive and collaborative artificial-reality in design of human-robot workspace. *International Journal of Computer Integrated Manufacturing*. 2019;33(1):22–37.

[60] Alnagrat AJA, Ismail RC, and Idrus SZS. Design safety training using extended reality tracking tools in semiconductor fabrication laboratory furnace. In: Mahyuddin NM, Mat Noor NR, Mat Sakim HA (eds.). *Proceedings of the 11th International Conference on Robotics, Vision, Signal Processing and Power Applications*. Singapore: Springer; 2022; p. 1041–1046.

[61] Christou C. Virtual reality in education. In: Tzanavari A and Tsapatsoulis N (eds.), *Affective, Interactive and Cognitive Methods for E-Learning Design: Creating an Optimal Education Experience*. Hershey, PA: IGI Global Scientific Publishing; 2010. p. 228–243.

[62] Javaid M, and Haleem A. Virtual reality applications toward medical field. *Clinical Epidemiology and Global Health*. 2020;8(2):600–605.

[63] Pensieri C, and Pennacchini M. Virtual reality in medicine. In: Sivan Y (ed.), *Handbook on 3D3C Platforms*. Progress in IS. Cham: Springer; 2016. p. 353–401.

[64] Guttentag DA. Virtual reality: applications and implications for tourism. *Tourism Management*. 2010;31(5):637–651.

[65] Speicher M, Hall BD, and Nebeling M. What Is Mixed Reality? In: *Proceedings of the 2019 CHI Conference on Human Factors in Computing Systems*; 2019. p. 1–15.

[66] Maas MJ, and Hughes JM. Virtual, augmented and mixed reality in K-12 education: a review of the literature. *Technology, Pedagogy and Education*. 2020;29(2):231–249.

[67] Almufarreh A. Exploring the potential of mixed reality in enhancing student learning experience and academic performance: an empirical study. *Systems*. 2023;11(6):292.

[68] Costanza E, Kunz A, and Fjeld M. Mixed reality: a survey. *Lecture Notes in Computer Science*. 2009;5440:47–68.

[69] Ola AF. Impact of IoT integration with mixed reality on manufacturing operations. *OSF Preprints. chs3z*, Center for Open Science. 2023. [Online]. Available: https://ideas.repec.org/p/osf/osfxxx/chs3z.html.

[70] John B, and Wickramasinghe N. A review of mixed reality in health care. In: Wickramasinghe N, and Bodendorf F (eds.), *Delivering Superior Health*

and Wellness Management with IoT and Analytic. Cham: Springer; 2019. p. 375–382.

[71] Čopič Pucihar K, and Kljun M. Augmented reality systems and their future in tourism: before, during and after the journey. In: *Augmented Reality in Tourism, Museums and Heritage: A New Technology to Inform and Entertain*. Berlin: Springer; 2021. p. 49–67.

[72] Kunz A, Rosmann S, Loria E, *et al.* The Potential of Augmented Reality for Digital Twins: A Literature Review. In: *2022 IEEE Conference on Virtual Reality and 3D User Interfaces (VR)*. Piscataway, NJ: IEEE; 2022. p. 389–398.

[73] Tu X, Autiosalo J, Jadid A, *et al.* A mixed reality interface for a digital twin based crane. *Applied Sciences*. 2021;11(20):9480.

[74] Sun T, He X, Song X, *et al.* The digital twin in medicine: a key to the future of healthcare? *Frontiers in Medicine*. 2022;9:907066.

[75] Ravi KSD, Ng MS, Ibáñez JM, *et al.* Real-Time Digital Twin of On-Site Robotic Construction Processes in Mixed Reality. In: *ISARC. Proceedings of the International Symposium on Automation and Robotics in Construction*. vol. 38. IAARC Publications; 2021. p. 451–458.

[76] Obeidallah R, Ahmad AA, and Qutishat D. Challenges of extended reality technology in higher education: a review. *International Journal of Emerging Technologies in Learning*. 2023;18(14):39–50.

[77] Stobiecki P. Augmented reality – challenges and threats. *Ekonomiczne Problemy Usług*. 2018;131:197–205.

[78] Speicher M, Hall BD, Yu A, *et al.* XD-AR. *Proceedings of the ACM on Human-Computer Interaction*. 2018;2(EICS):1–24.

[79] Syal S, and Mathew R. Threats faced by mixed reality and countermeasures. *Procedia Computer Science*. 2020;171:2720–2728.

[80] Rana S, and Jain S. Virtual reality: issues and challenges. *International Journal of Research in Engineering and Applied Sciences (IJREAS)*. 2017;7 (5):105–112.

[81] Cook M, Lischer-Katz Z, Hall N, *et al.* Challenges and strategies for educational virtual reality. *Information Technology and Libraries*. 2019;38(4):25–48.

[82] Rokhsaritalemi S, Sadeghi-Niaraki A, and Choi SM. A review on mixed reality: current trends, challenges and prospects. *Applied Sciences*. 2020;10(2):636.

[83] Sharma N, and Ali K. A review paper on holographic technology three-dimensional visualization. *International Journal of Engineering Research & Technology (IJERT)*. 2016;4. V-IMPACT – 2016.

[84] An J, Won K, and Lee HS. Past, current, and future of holographic video display [Invited]. *Applied Optics*. 2022;61(5):B237–B245.

[85] Akyildiz NIF, and Guo NH. Holographic-type communication: a new challenge for the next decade. *ITU Journal*. 2022;3(2):421–442.

[86] Ghosh A. Significance of holographic technology in modern world. *International Journal of Computer Sciences and Engineering*. 2017;5(2):43–45.

[87] Gong T, Gavriilidis P, Ji R, *et al.* Holographic MIMO communications: theoretical foundations, enabling technologies, and future directions. *IEEE Communications Surveys & Tutorials*. 2023;26:196–257.

[88] Suzanna S. Application of holographic technology in education. *Penelitian Ilmu Komputer Sistem Embedded & Logic*. 2023;11(2):253–266.

[89] Reddy T, Abishai K, and Namassivaya N. 3D holographic display with gesture controller. *International Journal of Research in Engineering and Science (IJRES)*. 2022;10(10):520–523.

[90] Haleem A, Javaid M, and Khan IH. Holography applications toward medical field: an overview. *Indian Journal of Radiology and Imaging*. 2020;30 (03):354–361.

[91] Ishteyaq I, Muzaffar K, Shafi N, and Alathbah MA. Unleashing the power of tomorrow: exploration of next frontier with 6G networks and cutting edge technologies. *IEEE Access*. 2024;12:29445–29463.

[92] Shuguang L, and Lin B. Holographic Classroom Based on Digital Twin and Its Application Prospect. In: *2020 IEEE 3rd International Conference on Electronics and Communication Engineering (ICECE)*. IEEE; 2020. p. 122–126.

[93] Wu J, Zhu J, Zhang J, *et al.* A dynamic holographic modelling method of digital twin scenes for bridge construction. *International Journal of Digital Earth*. 2023;16(1):2404–2425.

[94] Zhang X, Xu M, Tan R, *et al.* Holographic-type communication for digital twin: a learning-based auction approach. *arXiv preprint* arXiv:221101016. 2022.

[95] Zhang X, Xu M, Tan R, *et al.* Learning-based auction for matching demand and supply of holographic digital twin over immersive communications. *IEEE Transactions on Multimedia*. 2023;26:5884–5896.

[96] UK Government. The UK Product Security and Telecommunications Infrastructure Product Security Regime; 2024. Accessed: 13 December 2024. Available from: https://www.gov.uk/government/publications/the-uk-product-security-and-telecommunications-infrastructure-product-security-regime.

[97] The Office of Impact Analysis (OIA). Impact Analysis; 2023. Accessed: 13 December 2024. Available from: https://oia.pmc.gov.au/sites/default/files/posts/2023/12/Impact%20Analysis1.pdf.

[98] Stafford V. Zero trust architecture. *NIST Special Publication*. 2020;800:207.

[99] Prasad R, and Rohokale V. Artificial intelligence and machine learning in cyber security. In:*Cyber Security: The Lifeline of Information and Communication Technology*. Cham: Springer; 2020. p. 231–247.

[100] Guo H, and Yu X. A survey on blockchain technology and its security. *Blockchain: Research and Applications*. 2022;3(2):100067.

[101] Bhutta MNM, Khwaja AA, Nadeem A, *et al.* A survey on blockchain technology: evolution, architecture and security. *IEEE Access*. 2021; 9:61048–61073.

[102] Portmann C, and Renner R. Security in quantum cryptography. *Reviews of Modern Physics*. 2022;94(2):025008.

[103] Pirandola S, Andersen UL, Banchi L, *et al.* Advances in quantum cryptography. *Advances in Optics and Photonics*. 2020;12(4):1012–1236.

[104] Acar A, Aksu H, Uluagac AS, *et al.* A survey on homomorphic encryption schemes: theory and implementation. *ACM Computing Surveys (Csur)*. 2018;51(4):1–35.

[105] Naehrig M, Lauter K, and Vaikuntanathan V. Can Homomorphic Encryption Be Practical? In: *Proceedings of the 3rd ACM Workshop on Cloud Computing Security Workshop*; 2011. p. 113–124.

[106] Union Nations. Sustainable Development Goals; 2024. Accessed: 13 December 2024. Available from: https://sdgs.un.org/goals#.

[107] Union Nations. Goal 9: Industry, Innovation and Infrastructure; 2024. Accessed: 13 December 2024. Available from: https://sdgs.un.org/goals/goal9.

[108] Union Nations. Goal 11: Sustainable Cities and Communities; 2024. Accessed: 13 December 2024. Available from: https://sdgs.un.org/goals/goal11.

[109] Giannetti BF, Sevegnani F, Almeida CM, *et al.* Five sector sustainability model: a proposal for assessing sustainability of production systems. *Ecological Modelling*. 2019;406:98–108.

[110] Pierucci P, Agostinho F, Almeida CM, *et al.* Correlation between sustainability and smartness indicators in Brazilian cities: insights from the 5SenSu model. *Frontiers in Sustainable Cities*. 2024;6:1390735.

[111] Topal HF, Hunt DV, and Rogers CD. Urban sustainability and smartness understanding (USSU) – identifying influencing factors: a systematic review. *Sustainability*. 2020;12(11):4682.

[112] Antolín J, de Torre C, García-Fuentes MÁ, *et al.* Development of an evaluation framework for smartness and sustainability in cities. *Sustainability*. 2020;12(12):5193.

[113] Next G Alliance. National 6G Roadmap; 2024. Accessed: 13 December 2024. Available from: https://nextgalliance.org/working group/national-6g-roadmap.

[114] ITU. IMT-2030: ITU Radiocommunication Sector (ITU-R) Study Groups; 2024. Accessed: 13 December 2024. Available from: https://www.itu.int/en/ITU-R/study-groups/rsg5/rwp5d/imt-2030/Pages/default.aspx.

[115] 5G Americas. 3GPP Technology Trends White Paper; 2024. Accessed: 13 December 2024. Available from: https://www.5gamericas.org/wp-content/uploads/2024/01/3GPP-Technology-Trends-WP.pdf.

[116] Javaid M, Haleem A, and Suman R. Digital twin applications toward Industry 4.0: a review. *Cognitive Robotics*. 2023;3:71–92.

Chapter 4

Digital twins for citizen engagement

Andrew S. Wilson[1] and Adrian Walker[2]

Abstract

This chapter highlights the importance of people-focused place-based research to examine the role and transformative potential of digital twin technologies for local planning authorities. The chapter focuses upon strong partnership working between the City of Bradford Metropolitan District Council and the University of Bradford, UK, through the co-development of 'Virtual Bradford', which has laid the foundations for an open digital twin for Bradford City Centre. Coverage has since been expanded to include outlying areas of Bradford Metropolitan District and localities under other local authority jurisdictions, both in the UK and overseas. The chapter considers the importance of the FAIR principles and open-source methods to foster inclusive data-driven decision-making for a variety of different use cases. These include government-backed initiatives that continue to trial novel approaches for citizen engagement and consultation concerned with heritage conservation, planning and regeneration and public health. Collectively, the chapter emphasises the socio-economic value of 3D geospatial data for shaping equitable, sustainable and culturally enriched urban futures, drawing upon the importance of trust, transparency and capacity building in successful citizen engagement, whilst aligning to the UN Sustainable Development Goals.

Keywords: 3D visualisation; local planning authority; UN Sustainable Development Goals; 3D geospatial modelling; digital co-creation platforms; Geographic Information Systems (GIS)

4.1 Introduction

3D digital tools have existed for some time within the workflows of local authorities, as exemplified by the now widespread use of global navigation satellite systems that have enabled the development of Geographic Information Systems (GIS) for analysing and visualising spatial data. This can stretch to wider societal

[1]Visualising Heritage, Department of Archaeological and Forensic Sciences, University of Bradford, UK
[2]Department of Place, City of Bradford Metropolitan District Council, Britannia House, Hall Ings, UK

shifts in the use of this technology that have been realised through the likes of Google Earth which can trace its origins back to the late 1990s [1].

Whilst GIS is now a mainstay for local authorities and other agencies, the adoption of digital twins by local authorities remains largely aspirational. The UK government outlined this aspiration in the 'Planning for the Future' (https://assets.publishing.service.gov.uk/media/601bce418fa8f53fc149bc7d/MHCLG-Planning-Consultation.pdf) White Paper released in August 2020, signalling a transformational approach that is yet to make it into legislation [2]. Government decisions aside, this represents a momentum that has been gathering for some time, which encourages greater uptake of 3D geospatial and modelling approaches by local authorities. Collectively the relevance of the approach for an array of scenarios in planning helps to connect data with geospatial information, thus helping to make sense of the complexity of the world around us for the benefit of the health and lives of our citizens and the planet.

The emergence of technologies like Google Earth, a technology acquired by Google in 2004 [1], has influenced the expectations of citizens on the Local Authority Planning Service. Whilst we don't live in a two-dimensional world, Local Authority Planning departments have however traditionally relied on 2D drawings, supplemented with 'fixed artist impressions' representing a proposal, used either in formal consultation meetings or the drawings being published on a Local Authority online Planning application website. Given that citizens do not regularly interact with planning proposals, the overlap in skillsets and level of engagement in the interpretation of those 2D drawings are inevitably limited, with very few exceptions. Thus, digital twins have significant potential to assist the planning process, including through the use of new digital co-creation platforms and 3D visualisation technologies to explore proposals within the local context.

In this chapter, we explore the significance of digital twin technologies in the context of the UN Sustainable Development Goals (SDGs), using case study examples to outline the potential approaches used by the team to benefit local communities. In particular, we focus on the development of Virtual Bradford – an open digital twin for the City of Bradford, UK – and a broader set of expectations [3,4] that arise from the citizens and communities that we work with. We also explore in brief the potential across a wide range of applications that collectively aspire to shape future societies and the significance in terms of potential efficiencies and returns for city planning that are starting to be mapped using transformative digital twin technologies [5,6].

4.2 SCORE—the foundations for virtual Bradford

Since the launch of ArcGIS 8.1 in early 2000, which included the 3D Analyst extension [7], City of Bradford Metropolitan District Council has had an aspiration to create and use 3D models within the Local Authority Planning Service. Bradford Council's aspirations to have and use 3D models has been made possible through direct partnership between council officers and researchers in the School of Archaeological and Forensic Sciences at the University of Bradford since 2019. Early in the development of Virtual Bradford in 2020, it became apparent to all involved that the common language and extensive practice and experience in the use of geospatial data that was shared between City of Bradford Metropolitan District Council, as the local authority, and the University of Bradford were also matched in a common set of aspirations for the City of Bradford as a whole.

At the heart of our place-based partnership is a desire to work for the continued improvement of both the physical and social fabric of the city. Our work as a local authority and as the University of Bradford aligns through many related initiatives with other public and private bodies, charitable agencies and community-focused organisations. Collectively, these goals often coalesce around housing, health determinant research, environment and public safety, transportation, conservation and other regeneration matters. However, in the year that Bradford celebrates its role as UK City of Culture, it is also important to emphasise the strategic role that these partnerships have in realising and supporting those activities that enrich, enliven and extend our reach into communities through culturally focused support. These are the elements that bring community cohesion, respect and identity into focus, foregrounding the importance of a people-focused, place-based approach [8].

Although funding to develop an open digital twin for the City of Bradford was originally offered up through a tender process that was won by the University of Bradford, the finances were in reality only pump-priming (using EU funds as part of the Smart Cities & Open Reuse of Data project) that was supported by in-kind contributions from the University. The brief was to develop a LoD3 model [9] for the area of the city centre that was bounded by the Inner Ring Road. Our early joint meetings showed in reality that the Inner Ring Road was too restrictive a boundary that would have ignored both the City Centre Conservation Area boundary and key cultural assets that sit literally across the other side of the A6181 main road from Centenary Square (Figure 4.1). A revised boundary now reflects the importance of these foci that are at the City's cultural heart, including the National Science & Media Museum, The Alhambra Theatre, Bradford Live and principal monuments within the City, including the Bradford Cenotaph War Memorial, the Bradford Pals Memorial and the new Commonwealth Memorial. Transformational infrastructure works in the heart of the city have helped to make the public realm a more cohesive space through enhanced walking and cycling routes into and within the City Centre, that have been realised in large part by funding from the West Yorkshire Combined Authority's Transforming Cities Fund.

The dynamic nature of urban spaces has meant that from the outset we envisioned the need to continue to develop and expand the digital twin incrementally with further phases added through other funding sources. These have also included the ambition to build capacity through placing skillsets where possible within the hands of the local authority. These approaches have needed us to adhere to the FAIR principles – using open-source methods that are copyright-free and free from restrictive intellectual

Figure 4.1 Architectural designs for One City Park, a new principal building within the City Centre, incorporated at design stage into the 3D model of Bradford city centre 3D from Virtual Bradford (credit: University of Bradford, Visualising Heritage and City of Bradford Metropolitan District Council, supplemented by LOD1 background detail derived from Ordnance Survey mapping and data, Blue Sky tree data, and One City Park BIM model courtesy of Sheppard Robson. Published in ESRI ArcGIS Online to highlight development opportunities at UKREiiF 2023

property rights. As mutually invested parties it has been possible to continue to build and host our own model and an open model means that the potential use-cases are limitless and endless, with no intention to restrict use via contracts.

Innovation has been at the core of our collaborative partnership, driving opportunities to use the latest technological advancements, with a focus on sharing and translation of knowledge at grass-roots level. This approach sees partnership as a shared vehicle for positive change, rather than as a transactional arrangement. Our experience has been one that has seen two-way sharing of knowledge to consolidate skills and training, focusing on capacity building to ensure that the local authority has the potential to advance its goals for citizen engagement with continued support from the University.

Replication was one of the fundamental principles of the EU SCORE-funded research, with scope to experiment and scale the work, both in Bradford and elsewhere. In particular, this has offered opportunities via the Arts & Humanities

Research Council (AHRC) Place Programme to capture the entirety of Saltaire World Heritage Site (Figure 4.2) as a second phase of Virtual Bradford (AH/W009102/1), whilst also seeing the importance of education and community-focused activity as part of this work; furthermore, an AHRC scheme responding to the UN Year for the Creative Economy brought the opportunity to advance our capture for the coastal city of Bagamoyo in Tanzania (AH/W006723/1) which is itself a creative cultural hub, with an annual international festival of arts and culture; and a chance to use the AHRC UK-Ireland Collaboration in the Digital Humanities (AH/V002406/1; AH/Y007409/1) to explore the use of digital twins to foster connections via the Heritage Council's Irish Walled Towns Network between Kilmallock in County Limerick and Derry, which as the first UK City of Culture draws further parallels with Bradford's role as City of Culture in 2025. Each of these place-based research opportunities has benefited from the close partnership working with the relevant local authorities, which further extends the network to develop a community with shared experience of the potential of digital twin technologies for citizen engagement and in the innovation steps that sit behind these developments.

4.3 Data-driven decision-making: Bradford's digital strategy

The launch of Bradford's Digital Strategy in 2022 was a watershed moment in the development of Virtual Bradford, since this highlighted the potential of the digital twin as offering key foundations for growth and data-driven decision-making. These elements of underpinning architecture that are embedded within the Council's Digital Strategy [4], include the potential to support the planning of Bradford's new development frameworks and its clean growth objectives, helping to simulate the physicalities of the city centre, and better utilise resources, reducing carbon emissions, optimising supply and transportation networks, and seeking to better understand and predict energy consumption and emissions.

Data from 100 km of streets has already been captured to create the first digital twin of the city, capable of showing accurate levels of detail for the built environment in 3D. Because the data is ultimately freely available to anyone, the potential use cases are limitless. The digital twin makes it possible to design and test city operations virtually before changing the real city environment. This type of policy-supporting instrument helps to make complex urban issues more comprehensible. It also offers scope for co-creation and collaborative decision-making and thus contributes to improving citizen engagement. Drawing upon investment in digital infrastructure for connectivity (IoT and 5G) and AI capabilities, Virtual Bradford provides an environment to develop scalar and interoperable uses for the digital twin, ranging from live-streaming data from in situ sensors spatially located across the district, to use in master planning and with external consultants submitting 3D proposals that can be dropped into the model.

The guiding principles and vision of Open Digital Planning [10] are intended to facilitate wholescale change in the delivery of planning services by local

(a)

(b)

Figure 4.2 *(a) 3D model of Saltaire World Heritage Site derived from airborne drone imagery captured in 2022/2023, aligned to (b) aerial imagery captured by C.H. Wood in 1949 (credit: Joe Moore/ Visualising Heritage; Bradford Museums Photo Archive: image filename F4783)*

authorities. Key to this is the ability to harness new technologies and adapt to the potential of digital approaches that can enhance and speed up decision-making processes, whilst fostering greater understanding and communication through incorporation of 3D datasets.

4.4 Approaches to citizen engagement

4.4.1 Government-backed initiatives

The partnership has been forged through both needs-based and challenge-led use cases. Key examples of this are seen with community-focused work aligned to Virtual Bradford, including several government-backed initiatives that have been key to the development of Virtual Bradford more broadly, with all having elements of citizen engagement at their core.

Heritage assets: strategic investment in infrastructure and researcher time
Infrastructure investment to the University of Bradford from the Strategic Priorities Fund, run by Research England, first enabled us to invest in mobile mapping kit in 2019 that was an initial catalyst for work with Bradford Council and ultimately the development of Virtual Bradford. This was based upon the potential that was seen with the hire of mobile mapping kit used in 2018 as part of research via the British Academy's Cities and Infrastructure scheme that responded to the aftermath of the 2015 Kathmandu earthquake in Nepal and related needs concerned with conflict [11,12].

The potential was further realised with the capture of heritage assets in 2019 within Goitside, Bradford's original 19th-century industrial heartland and a designated conservation area within the city [13]. Access to further funding from the Higher Education Innovation Fund (HEIF), Research England's main funding stream for knowledge exchange, allowed the University to develop the relationship further, offering its own pump-priming that initially supported a range of aspirations from the Council's Landscape, Design & Conservation Team, including support to the Top-of-Town regeneration area; survey of blue–green infrastructure adjacent to Canal Road as part of the EU BEGIN project (https://northsearegion.eu/begin/); 3D capture and reconstruction of stored architectural elements of the former Darley Street market ahead of the new market redevelopment; and digital documentation of the interior of City Hall, Bradford Live and the Richard Dunn Sporting venue to augment the city centre heritage trail and related needs.

Blue–green infrastructure: EU Life Critical Project and Horton Park
This involved University support to baseline tasks relating to Heritage, Physical Terrain/ Water and Community Engagement at historic Horton Park that aligned with the goals of the Council-led EU Life Critical Project (https://www.bradford.gov.uk/planning-and-building-control/landscape-planning/life-critical-projects/). Government funding was secured by the University to enable time contributions for academic staff and researchers via inter-connected work packages, including: (1)

Research England/ Strategic Priorities Fund for the 'Bradford Life Project'; (2) Research England/ HEIF for 'Connected Communities' (Apr–Jul 2021); (3) NERC Hidden Histories for 'Revealing Bradford' (May–Sep 2021); and for (4) a public-facing workshop drawing upon the community-focused work in Horton Park as a response to COP 26.

Of particular relevance to citizen engagement was how interventions have helped to show the importance of Horton Park to many. It is clear that the Park holds a key place in the collective memory of many local people, particularly whilst they were growing up. The history and broader heritage of the park was also found to be of great interest to participants in the various workshop events that were held, with many explaining that the park was also a part of their own personal histories. Many also appreciated the value of the park as a 'green space', with numerous participants highlighting their increased use of the park during the pandemic, recognising its importance in relation to maintaining health and wellbeing.

The project successfully helped to capture comments about what the public would like to see for the park for the future – both informally (during 3D data capture) and during our events and workshops – with many commenting on the improvement of the water features, general upkeep and overall promotion of the park in a positive manner.

3D models and imagery that were produced have been used to guide the decision-making process for the repair and restoration of heritage assets such as the bridge within the park. The pop-up trails that were created for the Horton Heritages event can be expanded and consolidated as part of learning resources to engage with families and local schools and/ or to help with social prescribing, with the potential for further engagement and evaluation of these resources in the future.

Countryside and rights of way

Financial contributions from Bradford Council's Countryside and Rights of Way team, with match-funding from Research England's HEIF contribution to the University enabled the development of new trail content linking the City Centre (Virtual Bradford phase 1) with Saltaire World Heritage Site (Virtual Bradford phase 2) along the Canal Road Greenway. This highly successful project utilised a range of ground-based 360 and aerial capture methods brought into the AGOL environment, using ESRI Experience Builder in order to develop an engaging and immersive approach to new trail content [14], whilst also facilitating knowledge exchange, drawing upon the Council's expertise within the AGOL environment and the developing University's skillsets.

Property technology (PropTech)

More recently, through Council-led Government-backed initiatives it has been possible to build upon the EU SCORE-funded research to promote inclusive growth and to establish and assess key deliverables that help to scale digital solutions which aim to improve citizen engagement within the planning process (PropTech 3 and 4 schemes), with inclusive methods at its core. These focused upon the reuse of data for Saltaire UNESCO World Heritage Site that had been collected as part of AHRC-Place Programme funded research and also new data captured for the Southern Gateway and sites in Leeds.

The Southern Gateway region within Bradford has been identified as a key future location for growth that would extend the City Centre southwards and offer major transformational changes for the city, based upon the development of key infrastructure that includes proposals for a new rail station and mass transit hub. The boundaries of the target regeneration area are currently aligned with physical boundaries (due to topography, major arterial routes into the city, historic rail infrastructure and the inner ring road) and without due consideration these have the potential to reinforce community severance using existing barriers to integration across the city.

The importance of using digital twin technologies for the Southern Gateway and in other trial localities has been to test the use of rapid and scalable digital capture techniques and workflows for local authorities to be able to create and test accessible and engaging 3D immersive visualisation. This has involved building upon groundwork established by the University of Nottingham [15], that help citizens and other stakeholders to better understand proposals as part of master-planning for regeneration.

In conjunction with colleagues at Nottingham Council, Nottingham University, Leeds University and Liverpool University, we have been working collaboratively to fast-track support for other local planning authorities to advance rapid 3D capture using UAV for site identification and assessments and in undertaking street-level capture that scales adoption of digital twin technologies and methods for visualisation and engagement.

4.4.2 Humanities-led place-based research and the UN Sustainable Development Goals

Much of the focus for the research elements that the University of Bradford has led upon is concerned with key narratives that see the use digital twin technologies supporting pathways to health improvement and creative uses towards education, interpretation, outreach and engagement, with a particular emphasis on the relevance of heritage as a vehicle for these approaches [16]. The UN SDGs help to underscore these uses, and were fundamental to a shift in our research and practice that led to the award of a Queens Anniversary Prize in 2021 for our world-leading work and innovation in developing technology and techniques for heritage and archaeology applications and translation of their utility and influence on practice, policy and society (https://royalanniversarytrust.org.uk/winners/building-the-future-by-rebuilding-the-past/). In turn, this also supported the University of Bradford's case for infrastructure investment from the AHRC through the Capabilities for Collections scheme (AH/V01255X/1), which has brought some of the enablers for our digital twin collaborations – not least investment in a Dell Powerscale solution for research data storage, as well as cutting edge vehicle-mounted mobile mapping solutions from Leica (TRK 700 EVO) and Mosaic (X and Viking cameras), and iGloo shared immersion for visualisation.

SDG 3 – Good Health & Wellbeing
Approaches that help to showcase cultural heritage within its contextual setting can offer many valuable contributions, ranging from support to active travel as per our work with the Countryside and Rights of Way team linking up Bradford City Centre and Saltaire World Heritage Site; to access to blue–green infrastructure as with work in Horton Park and at Fountains Abbey); and ultimately with the Healthy Urban Places project.

SDG 4 – Quality Education
The AHRC-funded 'Saltaire: People, Heritage and Place' project helped to showcase the value of digital and creative literacy both in classroom-based activities and during fieldwork. These approaches to active learning have helped to inspire and foster a sense of belonging and identity amongst some of the youngest within our communities [17].

SDG 5 – Gender Equality
Our approaches to workshops using immersive technology to repurpose 3D data of heritage assets as part of the Curious Travellers and BReaTHe – Building Resiliences Through Heritage projects has long focused upon the importance of gender equality to ensure that all voices are heard.

SDG 6 – Clean Water and Sanitation
Digital twin work within some of our historic urban parks that have water courses running through them (Horton Park and Roberts Park) has used geophysical prospection methodologies to understand historic layouts, both to map flood risk and plan infrastructure programmes.

SDG 7 – Affordable and Clean Energy
The establishment of Bradford's Ground Source Heat Network references the importance of below-ground, as well as above-ground assets, with scope to understand the relevance and potential of geophysical prospection methods as an extension of digital twin data.

SDG 8 – Decent Work and Economic Growth
Collectively our digital twin work in Bagamoyo, Tanzania that was funded by an AHRC scheme that was reflective of the UN Year for the Creative Economy; as well as our work with the UNESCO World Heritage Site of Saltaire reinforces the importance of the connections between heritage and tourism [18,19].

SDG 9 – Industry, Innovation and Infrastructure
The British Academy-funded 'Cities and Infrastructure' research that responded to the catastrophic earthquake in 2015 in Kathmandu, Nepal [11] demonstrated the relevance of terrestrial-based mobile mapping technology for rapid and accurate capture that together with airborne capture has been significant in the documentation of the Southern Gateway Regeneration Area and in the contextual capture of heritage assets as part of the enabling works for HS2 in Birmingham [20].

SDG 10 – Reduced Inequalities
Key measures and indices of health, drawing upon health determinants research collaboratives will use digital twin technologies to inform research as part of the assessment of what makes Healthy Urban Places, with recent air quality data emphasising the relevance of spatial modelling for the underpinning research that justified the implementation of Bradford's Clean Air Zone.

SDG 11 – Sustainable Cities and Communities
Digital twins for citizen engagement help to foster civic pride through accessible means of presenting Master plans. A further use of digital twin technologies is seen in the Local Planning Authority's remit to periodically update the management plan for Saltaire World Heritage Site which traditionally has been viewed as a written document, but now can draw from different epochs of survey data derived from airborne or vehicle-mounted capture.

SDG 13 – Climate Action
The threat and pace of climate change places added urgency to the use of digital documentation for infrastructure and heritage assets that are at risk – this ranges from coastal erosion at archaeological sites like Swandro on the island of Rousay [21] to those threatened by flood risk, inclusive of buildings within historic Roberts Park, Saltaire. The recent release of a music video 'Climate and Heritage' with partners from Tanzania emphasises the potential of digital twin technologies as part of messaging that targets and raises awareness amongst wider audiences including youth audiences [22]. The potential of incorporating the use of multispectral imaging alongside digital twin capture technologies is realised through scope for assessing the thermal efficiencies of buildings targeted for retrofitting.

SDG 15 – Life on Land
With increasing awareness of the relevance of nature recovery and biodiversity net gain within the work of local planning authorities and related agencies, the potential offered by some digital twin technologies for which AI protocols and data classification are enablers for viewing access to nature and vegetation coverage.

SDG 16 – Peace, Justice and Strong Institutions
The concept of twinning has long existed as a means to connect communities through common ties. However, the use of digital twins raises the potential for further opportunities. In particular, the value of this is seen in our international work with the Irish Walled Towns Network, inclusive of the capture of the Derry Peace Bridge; and with displaced communities from Syria in Jordan via the Curious Travellers [23] and BReaTHe project [24].

SDG 17 – Partnership for the Goals
This chapter has focused upon the importance of strategic partnerships as being critical in the realisation of key goals for the development of digital twins for citizen engagement. We see this through our regional/national/international networks of collaborators and partners and in ongoing dialogue with varied stakeholders.

4.4.3 Social and health-based contexts

One of the first envisioned use cases for the digital twin was to help to model air quality spatially, using open datasets to help in the justification of the need for a Clean Air Zone in Bradford, based upon the topography of the city which lies within a broad valley catchment commonly referred to as the 'Bradford Bowl'. Recent data evidencing a drop in respiratory appointments with primary health care appointments shows that the Clean Air Zone has already started to make a difference to the lives of many within the City of Bradford [25].

Collectively, the University and the local authority are both part of the £8.62M Medical Research Council-funded Population Health Improvement Network of Clusters for the HUP North project (Healthy Urban Places: a systems approach to understanding how to harness local places as tools to improve population health and reduce inequalities – MR/Y022785/1). Led by the team behind Born-in-Bradford, a major longitudinal cohort study that began in 2007 based out of Bradford Institute for Health Research, this place-based research project seeks to harness the potential of the places in which communities live, work and socialise as tools to improve population health. The project will select four areas within Bradford District and four areas with partners in Liverpool. Fundamental to our contribution is the use of digital twin technologies to help to advance health determinants research collaboration.

4.5 Conclusion

The dynamic nature of place ensures that accessible and rapid capture methods are of particular interest to documenting, consulting on and shaping the future of our cities. Use cases for digital twins and digital twin technologies in support of local authorities and related stakeholders continues to expand. Many of the drivers reflect strategic interests including via key government bodies, including the work of the National Digital Twin Programme led by the Department for Business & Trade; coordination of activity around property technology led by the Ministry of Housing, Communities & Local Government with regeneration interests from Homes England; and research-led activity from UK Research & Innovation, including via the AHRC and in-cross Council initiatives such as the Turing Digital Twin Network.

In 2024, Nottingham Council, Bradford Council and ConsultingWhere, with support from the Ministry of Housing, Communities and Local Government (MHCLG) PropTech Innovation Fund, began a study to assess the socio-economic value of 3D geospatial information for the UK planning sector. The study which was based upon standard cost-benefit analysis and modelled over a 10-year period, interestingly demonstrated that the Return on Investment over a 10- year period, based upon the small sample of use cases within Nottingham related to key internal planning processes was estimated at 2:1. A clear indication that the investment costs are exceeded by the benefits realised [26].

Experience amongst the Bradford-led team has shown that engagement with digital twin outputs is fostered through trust, transparency, openness and inclusivity between communities and stakeholders. We have seen considerable interest in the work that we are undertaking together [27], particularly around the potential for enhanced citizen engagement with the planning process. This is evidenced by continued interest from government and other stakeholders, inclusive of requests for demonstrations and presentations. With further testing we continue to expand our work with young people and wider communities to ensure that we address any gaps around inclusion and access [28,29].

The foundations of the partnership between the Council and the University have been a commitment to knowledge exchange and capacity building. Practices that others point to and aspire to. The partnership allows the Council to sit within the 'wake' of technological advances, benefiting from the University's access to cutting edge 'technologies'. In return, the University has benefited from the Council's expertise with ESRI tools. Without such a supportive partnership the local authority might never have developed the ability to fly drones and to create 3D content and LoD3 models at a landscape scale for incorporation into CityGML format.

Collectively, the partnership between the University and the local authority offers a safe space for the Council, with workshops that have been led by or hosted by the University often resulting in better responses and a more engaged audience, in part because the University offers up a safe, neutral space that supports more balanced engagement as a consequence. The partnership also helps to place the Council and the University in control of needs within the city, without the need for external consultants who may be less invested in the future shape of the city and its citizens.

Acknowledgements

The authors would like to acknowledge infrastructure support from the Arts and Humanities Research Council at the UKRI (AHRC–AH/V01255X/1) and project funding from the EU SCORE project; MHCLG (PropTech schemes); West Yorkshire Combined Authority (Gainshare); AHRC (AH/V002406/1; AH/Y007409/1; AH/W006723/1; AH/W009102/1); and MRC (MR/Y022785/1). The authors would like to thank Visualising Heritage and the following team members at the University of Bradford (UoB) – Richard Dunn, Chris Gaffney, Joe Moore, Ben Jennings, Tom Sparrow, Faye Corbett, Dushyant Naresh, Danielle Taylor, Joe Ogden, Dan Neagu, and Victoria Cotella; and at the City of Bradford Metropolitan District Council (CBMDC) – Joe Ritchings, Syd Simpson, Chris Eaton, and Saira Ali.

References

[1] Kumar, L., and Mutanga, O. 2018. Google Earth engine applications since inception: usage, trends, and potential. *Remote Sensing*, 10(10), 1509. https://doi.org/10.3390/rs10101509.

[2] Boland, P., Durrant, A., McHenry, J., McKay, S., and Wilson, A. 2021. A 'planning revolution' or an 'attack on planning' in England: digitization,

digitalization, and democratization. *International Planning Studies*, 27(2), 155–172. https://doi.org/10.1080/13563475.2021.1979942.

[3] Walker, A. and Wilson, A.S. 2021. *City of Bradford Metropolitan District Council: 'Virtual Bradford' – an open digital twin for the City of Bradford.* https://www.local.gov.uk/case-studies/bradford-district-council-digital-twin (accessed 17 Sep 25).

[4] Wilson, P. 2022. *Digital Strategy for Bradford: Laying the Foundations.* https://www.bradford.gov.uk/media/ftxf0aur/digital-strategy.pdf (accessed 17 Sep 25).

[5] Dunn, M. 2024. Addressing Digital Planning Transformation through 3D, *GeoPlace Conference*, https://static.geoplace.co.uk/downloads/7-Mick-Dunn.pdf (accessed 17 Sep 25).

[6] GEOInsight. 2024, reporting on Wilson, Walker & Sparrow presentation at GeoBusiness 2024 Built Environment Stage - 'Mobile mapping and digital twin technologies in Bradford and beyond', featured in https://www.geobusiness-show.com/mobile-mapping-at-the-forefront-of-university-of-bradfords-innovative-approach-to-heritage-preservation/ and https://www.mosaic51.com/featured/mobile-mapping-at-the-forefront-of-the-university-of-bradfords-innovative-approach-to-heritage-preservation/ (accessed 15 Oct 2025).

[7] Maguire, D.J. 2000. Esri's New ArcGIS Product Family, *ArcNews*. https://www.esri.com/news/arcnews/summer00articles/esrisnew.html (accessed 17 Sep 25).

[8] Madgin, R. and Robson, E. 2023. *Developing a People-Centred, Place-Led Approach: The Value of the Arts and Humanities*, University of Glasgow.

[9] Biljecki, F., Ledouz, H., and Stoter, J. 2016. An improved LOD specification for 3D building models. *Computers, Environment and Urban Systems*, 59, 25–37.

[10] *Open Digital Planning*, 2024. Ten Year Vision. https://opendigitalplanning.org/our-vision (accessed 20 Sep 24).

[11] Coningham, R.A.E., Acharya, K.P., Barclay, C., *et al.* 2019. Reducing disaster risk to life and livelihoods by evaluating the seismic safety of Kathmandu's historic urban infrastructure: enabling an interdisciplinary pilot. *Journal of the British Academy*, 7(s2), 45–82.

[12] Wilson, A.S., Gaffney, V., Gaffney, C., *et al.* 2022. 'Curious travellers: using web-scraped and crowd-sourced imagery in support of heritage under threat', in E. Ch'ng, H. Chapman, V. Gaffney, and A.S. Wilson (eds.) *Visual Heritage: Digital Approaches in Heritage Science*, Springer Series on Cultural Computing, Switzerland. 51–65. https://link.springer.com/book/10.1007/978-3-030-77028-0.

[13] Moore, J., Gaffney, C., Sparrow, T., *et al.* 2022. 'A rapid approach to the digital documentation of Bradford's rich industrial heritage' in Ch'ng, E., Chapman, H., Gaffney, V., Wilson, A.S. (eds.) *Visual Heritage: Digital Approaches in Heritage Science*, Springer Series on Cultural Computing, Switzerland. 375–387. https://doi.org/10.1007/978-3-030-77028-0_18.

[14] White, K. 2024. The Bradford District promotes walking and local heritage. *ThinkGIS issue* 54, p 10. https://www.esriuk.com/content/dam/distributor-restricted/esriuk-com/thinkgis/thinkgis-issue-54.pdf (accessed 17 Sep 25).

[15] Priestnall, G., Gardiner, J., Durrant, J. and Goulding J. 2012. Projection augmented relief models (PARM): tangible displays for geographic information, *Electronic Visualisation and the Arts (EVA 2012)*. https://doi.org/10.14236/ewic/EVA2012.28.

[16] Gaffney, C., Croucher, K., Bates, C.R., *et al.* 2025. Digital Twins at the City and Town Scale: Europe and Beyond. *Internet Archaeology*, 70. https://doi.org/10.11141/ia.70.5.

[17] Croucher, K. Bates, C.R., Booker, O., *et al.* 2025. Place, Identity and Wellbeing: Bradford and Beyond. *Internet Archaeology Issue*: Wellbeing & Heritage.

[18] Cooper, J.P., Ichumbaki, E.B., Blue, L.K., Maligisu, P.C.M., and Mark, S.R. 2022. When the 'asset' is livelihood: making heritage with the maritime practitioners of Bagamoyo, Tanzania. *Heritage*, 5, 1160–1198. https://doi.org/10.3390/heritage5020062.

[19] Schmidt, P.R., and Ichumbaki, E.B. 2020. Is there hope for heritage in former British colonies in Eastern Africa? A view from Tanzania. *Journal of African Cultural Heritage Studies*, 3(1), 26–51. http://doi.org/10.22599/jachs.29.

[20] Sparrow, T., Bain, K., Kimber, M. and Wilson, A.S. 2024. Visualising Heritage: using 3D immersive technologies to innovate, document and communicate rich narratives for HS2, *Internet Archaeology* 65. https://doi.org/10.11141/ia.65.7.

[21] Hilts, C. 2023. The Know of Swandro: Excavating Eroding Archaeology on Rousay. *Current Archaeology*, 396. https://the-past.com/feature/the-knowe-of-swandro-excavating-eroding-archaeology-on-rousay/ (accessed 17 Sep 25).

[22] Chemical 2021. Climate and Heritage (official music video, ft. Abella). https://youtu.be/pHAnLsmx25A?si=yqu5GzQo7pu4Hh4n (accessed 17 Sep 25).

[23] Wilson, A.S., Gaffney, V., Gaffney, C., *et al.* 2019. 'Curious travellers: repurposing imagery to manage and interpret threatened monuments, sites and landscapes' in M. Dawson, E. James, and M. Nevell (eds.) *Heritage Under Pressure, Threats and Solutions: Studies of Agency and Soft Power in the Historic Environment*, Oxbow. 107–122. https://www.jstor.org/stable/j.ctvpmw4hr.13.

[24] Evans, A.A., Croucher, K., Greene, O., and Wilson, A.S. 2020. *Virtual Heritage for Resilience Building*. Published project summary poster. https://doi.org/10.5281/zenodo.3950360.

[25] Mehbrahtu, T.F., Santorelli, G., Yang, T.C., *et al.* 2025. Impact of an urban city-wide Bradford clean air plan on health service use and nitrogen dioxide 24 months after implementation: an interrupted time series analysis. *Environmental Research*, 270, 120988.

[26] ConsultingWhere Ltd 2024. *Assessing the socio-economic value of 3D geospatial information for the UK planning sector*. https://www.arcgis.com/home/item.html?id=fa361ff8d52e446780eccf3932d6c1a0 (accessed 17 Sep 25).

[27] Tenart, J., van der Zee, D. and van Herk, S. 2022. *Open Source for Public Services. Approach, Evidence & Lessons from European Cities*, Barcelona, Bax & Company.

[28] Wilson, A.S. and Croucher, K. 2025. Case study 17: Saltaire, People, Heritage & Place. In James, S., Wood, M. *et al.* (eds.), *A country that works for all children and young people: An evidence-based approach to creating a culture of inclusive opportunity through arts and creativity*, p. 46. https://doi.org/10.48785/100/314 (accessed 15 Oct 2025).

[29] Healthy Urban Places. 2025. Empowering communities and neighbourhoods. In *PHI UK Annual Review 2024–25 'Innovating with People, Places and Communities'*. pp. 6–9. https://phiuk.org/files/directorate/phiuk_annualreview2024-5-web-010725.pdf (accessed 15 Oct 2025).

Chapter 5
Digital twins and smart cities solutions

Asad Khattak[1], Muhammad Ali Raza[2], Hayat Ullah[2], Naila Tabassum[2] and Muhammad Zubair Asghar[2]

Abstract

In this study, we examine the relationship between digital twins (DT) and smart cities by showing how they globally transform urban cities. With the help of DTs, smart cities incorporate real-time optimization and supervision across various aspects such as energy resources, emergency services, transportation, and so many others to improve the quality of life of citizens. DTs, also known as virtual copies of the entire infrastructure, are one of the key factors in smart city ecosystems. DTs integrate live data streaming with modern simulation tools to optimize performance, planning, and prediction. Sustainability, resilience, and effective urban governance planning and management can be achieved by combining DTs and smart city concepts. In this chapter, we also examined the challenges faced by integrating DTs and smart cities. Data privacy and security challenges by discussing the issues that need solutions for cybersecurity threats and regulations, as well as challenges concerned with the integration of a variety of systems and technologies, highlighting interoperability issues, and investing in management and training. This study also examine the adaption of AI-based intelligent Infrastructure and smart cities Asset maintenance but this required advanced expertise and it also raised cyber security concerns. The recent trends like cloud-based solutions and adopting DTs in different sectors are based on the integrated concept of DTs and smart cities. The integrated concept effectively improves efficiency and resilience with innovative technology.

Keywords: Digital twins (DT); Smart cities; Urban transformation; Real-time optimization; Quality of life; Virtual infrastructure; Urban planning and management; Resilient urban ecosystems

5.1 Introduction

Digital twins (DTs) and smart cities are the fundamental concepts for designing advanced and administration urban governance in today's modern era of

[1]College of Technological Innovation, Zayed University, UAE
[2]Gomal Research Institute of Computing, Faculty of Computing, Gomal University, Pakistan

innovative technology and urbanization. The primary objective is to study the relationship between DT and smart cities by examining their complicated mutual capability to globally change the urban environment. Urban cities that make use of advanced and innovative technology the enhance the efficiency and life standard of citizens are known as smart cities [1]. By monitoring and analyzing real-time data from various sensors and the Internet of Things (IoT), smart cities efficiently optimize various areas like effective decision-making and planning.

The integration of smart cities and DT concepts enables administration and city municipal authorities to tackle various areas and generate optimized results to make efficient decisions and effective planning. The urban city-optimized infrastructure and efficient public services increased the overall city resilience [2]. The monitoring of real-time data collected from various sources enables the administration to efficiently tackle trash collection, traffic flow and asset distribution and to skillfully identify the critical hurdles early [3]. Using previous data and modern analytics tools, DT enables to predict future occurrences well precisely like floods, traffic jams, infrastructure breakdowns and disasters [4].

In order to devolve efficient decision-making patterns, the DT encourage more and more citizen to take an interest in local administration via the latest representation tools and by allowing them to access real-time data and express their concerns and experiences [5].

5.2 Smart cities features based on digital twins

With the help of DT, urban cities all over the world are changing into smart cities by effectively enhancing sustainability, optimization response services, and asset management. This section examines the common features of smart cities based on DT that enhance urban city resilience and infrastructure. DT provide a virtual representation of the actual system and infrastructure to find innovative patterns to enhance the characteristics of smart cities [1]. Various features of smart cities are shown in Figure 5.1.

5.2.1 Feedback-driven urban planning

One of the basic features of smart cities is feedback driven urban planning. DT supporting in depth insight into the dynamic and latest environment of the smart cities by constantly analyzing the real-time data collected from various sensors and IoT devices installed in smart cities [6,7]. The urban cities administration and planners used this loop of feedback to effectively design new policies and infrastructure. It also used to take effective and diplomatic measures to tackle the in future challenges [2]. Using feedback-driven (FBD) urban planning, city administrations are able to quickly adapt to changing environments. As one example, Singapore controls DTs that can be used to simulate urban environments. This can be used to predict the effects of new infrastructure on traffic flow and air quality [8].

Figure 5.1 Features of smart cities

The City of Barcelona uses IoT sensors to monitor noise levels and adjust public spaces accordingly to enhance residents' quality of life [9]. As a result of these initiatives, the quality of urban life and sustainability will improve in real time.

5.2.2 Dynamic resource optimization

By designing, modeling and forecasting different resources utilization the DT enable the smart cities to effectively optimize the resource. The constantly data collection and monitoring enable the optimize the resources such as water distribution, traffic flow, and utilization of energy resources with respect supply and demands [3]. This dynamic strategy provides sustainability, minimize the operational cost, and enhance the resources efficiency. For instance, London uses DT to monitor and manage water distribution systems as well as detect early leaks and improve efficiency [10]. DT is used in Amsterdam to predict overcrowding and to adjust traffic signals dynamically [11]. With DT models of Copenhagen, energy demand can be stabilized during risky weather, as well as the supply of energy can be maintained and operational costs can be reduced [12].

5.2.3 Resilience and risk management

The effective risk management of urban is also one of the few key features of the smart cities by measure hazards, designing innovative pattern for encounter and to come over the emergency challenges using DTs [4,13]. The urban area can tackle various challenges by using DT such as disasters, infrastructure damages, emergency and pandemic. The effective risk management approach reduce the its impact on the infrastructure and urban population [5]. DT also support effective planning and monitoring to improve cities resilience [13]. For example, The Tokyo uses DT to assess infrastructure vulnerability for preemptive strengthening in earthquake scenarios [14]. A DT model is used by New York

City to model storm flows and aid flood defense planning following Hurricane Sandy [15]. According to the Wuhan province, DT was used during COVID-19 to predict hospital occupancy and infection hotspots, which improved crisis management [16].

5.2.4 Citizen-centric services

In smart cities, centralized citizen response services are used that are adjustable according to need of each citizen. Using DTs, smart cities make personalized suggestions, real-time responses and warnings, and interactive communication with citizens by integrating data from various sensors, applications, and IoT devices [17]. This enhanced the quality of life as well as citizen participation and satisfaction. DTs and smart city frameworks are improving integration in a number of areas like resilience, resource management, urban design, and citizen services that are outside of urban planning. This study specifies that DTs help smart cities comply more effectively with changing crucial challenges and resource allocation [18,19]. To tackle traffic, emergency and public services, municipal activities, and flood risk, this combination makes it easier [18,20]. In the Dubai model, people can receive real-time notifications about traffic and weather conditions [16]. Citizens of Helsinki are able to suggest improvements to public services using the DT power-driven citizen feedback model [21]. A locality-specific DT route is used during emergencies here in Los Angeles, which enhances safety and reduces confusion.

5.3 Digital twin applications in smart cities

This section examines how DTs effectively work as a reasonable function of smart city operations, as shown in Figure 5.2.

5.3.1 Smart cities management brain

DTs have made it possible for the smart cities management brain to be an integrated platform. Smart cities make it simple to optimize and coordinate activities throughout the city. The centralized system gathers information from many sources and performs in-depth analysis of complicated interlinks. Enhancements in municipal, administration, and government are made possible by the ensuing insights [22].

5.3.1.1 Key features and functions

- **Data fusion and integration**: Using DTs, the smart city management brain integrates all data sources to support a unified perspective of the environment, services, and infrastructure of the city. An example of this would be combining data from heterogeneous sources (such as IoT devices, environmental sensors, public service databases, and citizen feedback systems). Data breakdowns enhance cross-departmental collaboration and ensure

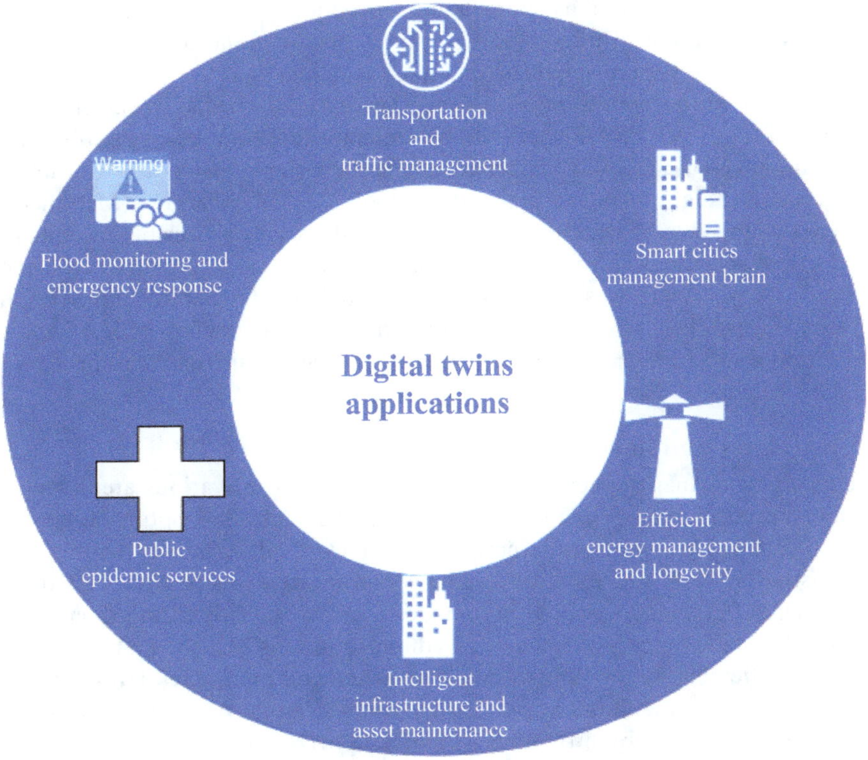

Figure 5.2 Digital twin applications in smart cities

comprehensive situational awareness through the system. In addition, it allows administration to identify correlations between energy usage patterns and transportation needs.

- **Real-time monitoring and analysis**: As the smart city management brain cognitive hub, it offers real-time monitoring and analysis of traffic flow, air quality, energy resource consumption, and public safety by monitoring data received from various sensors and IoT devices installed throughout the city. As a result of real-time insights, emergency responses are faster, resources are allocated more efficiently, and citizen experience is enhanced. As an example, live traffic monitoring can help reduce overcrowding by adjusting traffic lights. Such responsiveness dramatically improves urban livability and operational efficiency.
- **Predictive modeling and simulation**: The smart city management brain is able to predict future patterns, analyze possible obstacles, and tackle policy changes and infrastructure costs by using innovative analytics and simulation strategies. Among these are estimating the effects of extreme weather on infrastructure, and simulating the impact of urban expansion on energy demand. As a result of these predictive capabilities, city planners are able to

make proactive decisions, minimizing disruptions and avoiding costly mistakes. In addition to improving investment planning and urban development strategies, the system simulates multiple scenarios.

- **Decision support and optimization:** The smart city management brain supports data-driven decision-making by recommending the best possible action to improve sustainability, effectiveness, and efficiency using artificial intelligence (AI) algorithms and optimization tools. Machine learning (ML) models are employed to analyze massive datasets and provide actionable insights tailored to specific objectives, such as improving public transportation efficiency or reducing energy waste. To adapt to changing urban dynamics and emerging challenges, the system continuously learns from outcomes and refines its recommendations. In this way, smarter, more adaptive urban environments can be created.

5.3.1.2 Uses and benefits

The smart cities management brain application is used in various areas such as administrative planning, incident response, energy resource optimization, and traffic control. This application increases the lives of citizens by providing local administration data and tools for making optimized decisions and enhancing operational effectiveness, which encourages innovation. This extraordinary ability of DTs in smart city governance and administration is best shown by the smart cities management brain. Smart cities management brain facilitates cities in tackling complexity, minimizing risks, and embracing new possibilities for sustainable urban growth by providing AI and data-driven tools [19]. In Singapore, the Virtual Singapore project uses DTs to simulate and analyze urban planning scenarios, optimize resources, and improve infrastructure efficiency. DTs are also used by Dubai's Smart Dubai initiative to monitor and manage traffic, energy consumption, and public services in real time. With the help of DTs, Barcelona has improved the quality of life of its residents by improving waste management, water distribution, and energy optimization. As shown in these examples, DTs are able to be used in a variety of smart city ecosystems across a wide range of aspects.

5.3.2 Transportation and traffic management

Smart transportation systems may be effectively replaced with DTs. It provides real-time observation, optimization, and study with the use of a dynamic virtual duplicate of the real-time transportation infrastructure system [23]. DTs combine data from several sources, such as sensors, GPS devices, and traffic camera systems, to give complete insights into traffic patterns, barriers, and the efficiency of transportation infrastructure. DT technology may be used by city traffic planners to facilitate better decision-making, increase urban mobility, and provide an efficient transport management system. Making use of virtual twins Transportation and traffic management deal with a wide range of challenges, including reduced traffic and more efficient travel. Some of these are:

DTs connect multiple transportation modes (public transport, bikes, ride sharing) into a single system. This makes travel easier and more efficient for residents by providing access to various modes of transportation.

- **Improve traffic control:** The digital visualization of traffic flow using DT enable the administration to effectively control the traffic. DT have the capability to predict area with traffic jam, control traffic signals and design adoptable traffic control patterns. With IoT, sensors, and GPS data streaming in real time, DT can dynamically adjust signal timing to reduce congestion hotspots, and prioritize emergency vehicle traffic. It is also possible to simulate various traffic management scenarios to test their efficacy before they are implemented, thus reducing disruptions.
- **Predictive maintenance:** DT analyze traffic flow on road, bridges and traffic signals and utilize this data, DT early predict the location where traffic jam may occur to avoid breakdowns. Apart from monitoring infrastructure conditions, DT can also monitor issues like worn roads, bridge cracks, and faulty signal equipment. By using advanced analytics and ML models, authorities are alerted well in advance about potential failures or maintenance needs. As a result, repair costs and downtime are minimized, public safety is enhanced, and public safety is enhanced as well.
- **Integration modeling:** Different transportation modes such as local transport, local train and sharing vehicle can integrated centralized system using DT. This optimizes the travel time and make easier to access different mode of transportation. The DT platform also provides a unified dashboard connecting several transportation providers, allowing seamless coordination and improved routing. Real-time updates are available to passengers about schedules, delays, and alternate routes, while the system itself adapts dynamically to weather conditions and accidents. Integrating modeling also facilitates the development of sustainable transportation networks through the use of eco-friendly modes like electric vehicles.

5.3.2.1 Applications and advantages

Smart cities have numerous compensations when DTs are castoff in traffic and transportation. By designing effective traffic lights and signals controller and traffic regulation smart cities optimize the travel time, traffic jam and outflow traffic. Smart cities enhance response service and minimize accident risk by utilizing DT innovative and latest incident identification and emergency response system. One of the key components of the smart city idea is the attempt to enhance the affordability, safety, and mobility of transport management. Smart cities provide stakeholders with the ability to optimize transportation infrastructure and citizen quality of life via the use of real-time data and predictive analytics. The below Python code shows how to use the DTs concept to visualize a simple traffic flow:

```
import random
import matplotlib.pyplot as plt
# Define road network as a dictionary
road_network = {
    "A": ["B", "C"],
    "B": ["C", "D"],
    "C": ["D", "E"],
    "D": ["E"],
    "E": []
}
# Define car class with location and destination attributes
class Car:
    def __init__(self, location):
        self.location = location
        self.destination = random.choice(road_network[location]) if road_network[location] else location
# Simulate traffic flow for a specific time step
def simulate_traffic(cars):
    for car in cars:
        # Move car towards its destination
        if car.location != car.destination:
            car.location = car.destination
            # Set new destination if the car reaches its current destination
            car.destination = random.choice(road_network[car.location]) if road_network[car.location] else car.location
    return cars
# Initialize cars and simulate for multiple time steps
cars = [Car("A") for _ in range(10)]  # Create 10 cars starting at A
timesteps = 10  # Number of simulation steps
# Simulate and visualize traffic flow over time
all_locations = []  # To track car locations over time
for _ in range(timesteps):
    cars = simulate_traffic(cars)
    locations = [car.location for car in cars]  # Track car locations
    all_locations.append(locations)

# Visualize the traffic flow over time
for timestep in range(timesteps):
    plt.scatter([timestep] * len(all_locations[timestep]), all_locations[timestep], label=f"Timestep {timestep}")
plt.xlabel("Time Steps")
plt.ylabel("Car Locations")
plt.title("Traffic Flow Simulation")
plt.legend()
plt.show()
```

The fundamental idea in modeling and simulating simple traffic patterns using DTs is elaborate in above python code. For smart cities simulations, more complex algorithms, real-time data, and visualization tools integrate can improve the efficiency and precision of the simulation. In this Python code, cars are simulated moving along a road network over a period of time. Road networks are represented as dictionaries, each key (location) pointing to a list of destinations. Cars have a location and a randomly assigned destination that are assigned by a Car class. Simulate_traffic updates a car's location by moving it toward its destination, and if it reaches its destination, it randomly selects a new destination. At each step of the simulation, the cars' locations are recorded, and the simulation continues.

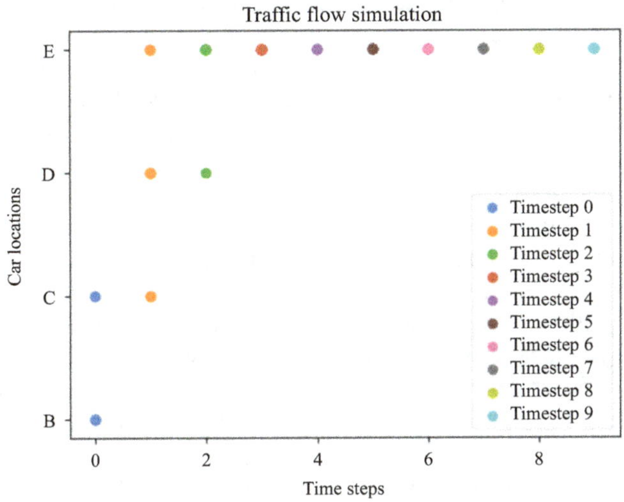

In the plot, the *x*-axis shows the time steps, while the *y*-axis shows the cars' locations over time. On the scatter plot, each point represents the location of a car at a given moment, allowing us to observe how the cars move through the network and how their positions change over time. As a result, a dynamic representation of traffic flow is presented, showing the progression of cars on the simulated roads over time.

5.3.3 Public epidemic services in smart cities

One of the key components of DTs is making public health services more approachable in smart cities. Administrative authorities tracked public health standards, addressed emerging diseases, and implemented targeted treatments using DTs. by combining data from various sources, such as demographics, health monitoring devices, and medical records authorities to get in-depth insights using DTs. Public health may be protected in a proactive manner by taking quick reactions and effective resource allocation made possible by this intuition. By using DTs, smart cities can improve their general determination, planning for epidemics, and ability to adjust to public health emergencies [18]. Integrating DTs in public epidemic systems covers numerous important factors that improved epidemic preparedness and response, such as:

- **Early identification and surveillance:** The real-time data can be analyzed to forecast the pandemic by utilizing DTs. This real-time data can be accessed through laboratory tests and patient admission which provide aid to reveal unusual symptom clusters or patterns that suggest an upcoming epidemic. Analyzing and learning from data streams from laboratories, hospitals, and other healthcare facilities is a key component of DTs. In real time, these data can be analyzed for patterns of symptom clusters that could signal an upcoming epidemic. The use of DTs can also be used to combine environmental sensors, social media, and public health records in order to detect early warning signs and implement proactive measures to combat them.

- **Healthcare planning and resource allocation:** With the use of DTs, the administration of the specified area can allocate the resource efficiently which includes provision of medicines, labor, and other health facilities. On the basis of epidemiological model and demographic changes the demand can also be projected. Using these virtual models, administrators can predict healthcare demands during outbreaks, allowing them to prepare for shortages. As a result of incorporating epidemiological models into DTs, high-risk zones can also be identified, allowing resources to be allocated more effectively. As well as optimizing medical equipment and personal protective gear supply chains, DTs can ensure faster delivery where necessary. Using them, a healthcare system can simulate demographic changes and project long-term resource requirements.
- **Public communication:** DTs contribute by broadcasting information or data about healthcare services and used for the dissemination of information to the selective populace regarding preventive procedures. A DT ensures accurate and timely information reaches affected communities through their ability to provide real-time updates. It includes providing information about vaccination availability, testing centers, and quarantine guidelines. As well as generating localized alerts, they can provide simulation-based visualizations to illustrate the advantages of adhering to public health measures. By engaging specific populations in healthcare initiatives, DTs enhance trust.

5.3.3.1 Advantages and impacts

Smart cities have numerous compensations when DTs are castoff in public epidemic services. By using DTs, the probability of large-scale illness and pressure on public health institution can be moderate by awarding the general public for rapid response to epidemic apprehensions by assimilate predictive analytics and early detection capabilities. The approach for the vaccination, lockdown and testing program can be spot lighted to bar the infections and keep the population out of risk. With the use of DTs, the administration of the specified area can decide on the live stream data to allocate the resource efficiently and effective response to reduce the collateral damage.

Public epidemic services in smart cities are one of the few components of DTs that efficiently enhanced the public health planning. The live streaming data and simulation features enable the government officials to monitor, assess, and respond to epidemic challenges effectively by enhancing public well-being and fostering resilience against emerging health issues. As an example, DTs simulated demand patterns during the COVID-19 pandemic to optimize hospital resources such as ICU beds and ventilators. DTs were used in Singapore to monitor population density to enforce social distance. To optimize outreach and planning efforts, predictive models have been integrated with electronic health records and wearable devices. Personalized healthcare solutions can also be enabled by this technology, which provides chronic disease management and remote patient monitoring [24].

5.3.4 Flood monitoring and emergency response services

One of the few helpful applications of DTs is flood monitoring and emergency response. Additionally, municipal authorities use this technology for monitoring areas that are prone to flooding and taking actions that can minimize this danger. By integrating data from various sources like weather sensors, river gauges, and urban drainage systems, this technology gives a complete description of flood risk components; consequently, it ameliorates readiness and response time. Regions that are prone to flooding can benefit from this technique; therefore, it will promote grit and dynamic decision-making [25].

In order to ameliorate grit against floods and ensure dynamic responses, the utilization of DTs in flood monitoring and emergency response services includes important functionality:

- **Real-time flood monitoring**: DTs give municipal officials early signs of possible dangers and flood situations by ensuring continuous monitoring of river flow rates, water level, and rainfall intensity. With the integration of real-time sensor data, forecasts, and environmental observations, DTs represent flood-prone areas in a dynamic, up-to-date way. Having real-time insights can assist decision-makers in anticipating potential flood risks. A DT can also simulate several flood scenarios based on current conditions, enabling faster identification and timely intervention of critical problem areas. During the early stages of floods, proactive monitoring reduces uncertainty and improves decision-making.
- **Early warning systems**: DTs give warnings and messages to locals and emergency responders in regions that are prone to flooding through their system of early warning systems; this, in turn, helps to evacuate citizens from flood-prone regions and to take other precautionary measures. To utilized this system specialized data analytics and effective predictive AI models are required. In order to use this system effectively, specialized data analytics and predictive AI models are required. The use of DTs combines data from sensors, satellite imagery, and hydrological models to provide more accurate and advanced prediction of flood events. These predictions allow authorities to issue tailored alerts informing of flooding severity and timing, which helps make rapid evacuation plans and allocate resources. Using AI models in DTs, the early warning system can better analyze flood data, weather trends, and changes in urban infrastructure.
- **Risk assessment:** With the help of DT, the highly flood risk region can be identified by utilizing geographical, demographic data and land used pattern. This data can also be used for advance infrastructure investment and measures disasters. The DT provides authorities with a virtual model of flood risk by synthesizing spatial, environmental, and social data. For example, they can

predict flood impacts in densely populated areas or regions with poor infrastructure. In-depth risk assessments help make informed decisions about where to focus flood mitigation efforts and how to prioritize flood barriers and drainage systems. The use of DTs can also help plan for future infrastructure so that it can withstand extreme weather events through simulation of flood scenarios.

- **Adaptive infrastructure management:** DTs model scores of scenarios and optimize operating techniques to maximize grit and minimize flood damage; it allows easy management of urban infrastructure, such as stormwater drainage systems and flood barriers. In order to adapt to changing conditions, DTs are particularly effective. Urban infrastructure can be simulated by simulating storm intensities and water flow patterns. By optimizing stormwater drainage, municipalities can identify vulnerable spots in flood defenses and adjust maintenance schedules accordingly. A DT also facilitates continuous monitoring, ensuring that flood control systems like levees and dams function optimally. The system can control flood flows in real time or temporarily reinforce flood defenses in a disaster.

5.3.4.1 Uses and advantages

There are multiple advantages and uses of DT in flood monitoring and emergency application. The ability of DT to analyze live streaming data and the using forecasting feature the smart cities are able to predict flood risk that are helpful to reduce damages and protect the infrastructure. To minimize the flood impact on infrastructure and to enhance the citizen safety the DT enable the smart cities to early warn the system. The DT have capability to identify flood risk and enable emergency response service using risk assessment tools. The effective decision based on evidence use data analytics and simulation approach. The effective decision optimize the allocation of resources and response pattern. This also improve the effectiveness to tackle and reduce loss during flood.

Smart city resilience and disaster preparation are fundamentally based on the use of DTs in flood monitoring and emergency response services. Urban residents are protected, and sustainable development is promoted by municipal authorities that can monitor, analyze, and react to flood-related threats in a proactive and efficient way thanks to the use of DTs, which combine real-time data with simulation capabilities. Smart city resilience and disaster preparation are basically based on the utilization of DTs in flood monitoring and emergency response services. Urban residents are shielded, and sustainable development is promoted by municipal authorities. Eventually, it can monitor, analyze, and react to flood-related dangers in a dynamic and efficient manner. All in all, the role of DTs, which integrate real-time data with capabilities, cannot be ignored.

5.3.5 Efficient energy management and longevity

Efficient energy management and longevity have a importance in the uses of applications of DTs in smart city. DTs help monitor energy demand forecasting, demand forecasting as well as local authorities implement strategies to improve efficiency and mitigate environmental impact by combining data from Multiple sources such as smart meters, building automation systems and energy renewable sources [26,27]. DTs can provide insights to facilitate proactive energy management techniques and informed decision-making through real-time data collection and analysis [28]. Which is used for promoting sustainable growth of urban areas.

Using DTs for durability and effective energy management includes a number of key capabilities designed to reduced energy and consumption and extend the service life of infrastructure:

- **Predictive maintenance:** Through evaluate the data performance and discovering possible failure location before they occur, the infrastructure of energy maintenance will be predictive with the help of DT, through renewable project of energy and substations. An example is Siemens' implementation of a DT-based predictive maintenance tool for wind turbines. As real-time data is analyzed from turbine sensors, wear-and-tear patterns are detected that indicate potential failures. As a result, downtime can be reduced and efficiency improved by making timely interventions [29].
- **Energy optimization:** By changing consuming patterns, identify inefficiencies and incorporation of renewable energy sources, that is the DT which give an edge in city optimize energy use across industries, including transportations, building and industry. This is achieved through real-time monitoring as well as modeling. As an example, Singapore uses a DT to optimize urban energy consumption. Real-time energy simulations allow the city to adjust power distribution and optimize building efficiency in real time [8].
- **Infrastructure longevity:** DTs play an important role in the infrastructure and assets of energy last longer via maximizing plans of maintenance and operating tactics. DTs also reduce the lower maintenance cost, downtime and the machinery life and system will be increase. Heathrow Airport implements a DT in order to model the entire airport's infrastructure, including HVAC, lighting, and power supplies, predicting their lifespans. As a result of this data, Heathrow has increased asset longevity and reduced maintenance costs [30].

5.3.5.1 Energy uses and advantages

DTs give a helping edge for longevity as well as effective management of energy. Cities can save a more money in the field of energy by using a DT to optimize energy consumption and employ demand response strategies. DT effect on costs of energy and reduces waste, and it will be helpful in both such as customers and utilities. Through integrating energy-efficient technology as well as renewable energy sources DT achieve sustainable development goals by reducing carbon emission furthermore encouraging environmental stewardship. DT prepared systems of energy more reliable and resilient through extending infrastructure life and predictive maintenance. Which means such customers and businessman will experience less disruption and continuous service.

Using of DT for effective energy management and lifecycle is the key to supporting resilience, and effect on economic growth. By using real-time data and simulation capabilities, It enable municipalities to maximize energy efficiency, save money, and extend the life of assets and infrastructure, ultimately promoting more sustainable and livable urban area environment.

5.3.6 Intelligent infrastructure and asset maintenance

DT is essential in the smart cities, especially for smart infrastructure and assets maintenance [31]. By integrating data from multiple sources, such as IoT devices, sensors and maintenance records, local officials can keep tabs on the performance condition as well as use infrastructure patterns. Through this connection, preventative and optimization maintenance are initiatives possible.

For optimize maintenance process and extend asset life, DTs are used in smart infrastructure and asset maintenance. It includes the following key features:

- **Predictive maintenance:** DT can plan maintenance task in advance and predicate possible failure point in infrastructure assets through evaluating previous measurements, performance and sensor data on real- time. With predictive maintenance, you can minimize unplanned downtime and extend asset lifespans by using advanced algorithms and ML techniques. As a result of this proactive approach, maintenance costs are reduced by optimizing schedules and preventing costly emergency repairs.
- **Condition monitoring:** DTs provide insight in the health and state of infrastructure assets through continuous analysis and observation. They point out irregularities and pattern in deterioration that may indicate the need for maintenance or repair. In order to detect abnormal behavior, the system monitors temperature, pressure, vibration, and wear levels. Using the DT, it is possible to identify issues that may lead to equipment failure early and to perform maintenance at the right time, reducing the number of unnecessary interventions and improving operational efficiency.
- **Lifecycle management:** through monitoring using of assets, history maintain and environmental status, it will help in the lifetime of management techniques performance efficient. It will helps the authorities of municipal committee maximize investment of assets, life cycle of assets, and also reduce the lifetime costs. By integrating real-time data and historical performance, better decisions can be made about asset replacement, upgrades, and repair schedules. Using DTs to analyze wear and performance degradation trends, authorities, such as municipal committees, can maximize investment in assets, extend their lifespans, and reduce their overall costs. As a result, smarter budget allocation and resource management can take place, while ensuring optimal performance of assets over their useful life.
- **Risk assessment:** Analyzing of data on the basis of assets performance, environmental status and regulatory compliance, the DTs give a helping edge with mitigation and risk assessment by uncovering potential hazards and vulnerabilities that could compromise safety, regulatory compliance or

dependability. Using predictive analytics, a system can identify high-risk areas for equipment failure or noncompliance, allowing for timely intervention. As a result of simulating several scenarios, DTs can also help implement effective risk management strategies and ensure compliance with industry regulations and safety standards by assessing the potential impact of different risk factors.

5.3.6.1 Maintenance uses and benefits

DTs use for smart cities in intelligent infrastructure and assets maintenance have many advantages. DTs will make Infrastructure assets are more reliable and resilient through predictive maintenance and facilitating condition monitoring. This reduce downtime, minimizes disruption and guarantees continued service to businesses and homes. DTs allow cities to optimize, save costs, resource allocation, and maximize the efficiency of maintenances operation through better maintenance planning and lifecycle management technology. DTs help identify and resolve safety issues, protecting the safety and well-being as well as residents who rely in urban infrastructure of workers. They do this via mitigation activity and streamlining risk assessment.

An important component of smart city application is the development of DT smart infrastructure and asset maintenance to maximize resource utilization, increase reliability and guarantee the longevity of city infrastructure assets. DTs enable municipalities to leverage real-time data and simulation capabilities to proactively manage maintenance tasks, create resilient and reduce hazards and sustainable infrastructure of urban.

5.4 Challenges and opportunities

5.4.1 Concerns about data security and privacy

Data privacy and security have become critical issues in today's digital environment due to increasing the amount of data creating and stored by people and organization. Data breaches and other cyberattacks become more occurring often. In addition to compromising confidential information, these security breaches underline confidence in data handling procedures. Additionally, insiders threats pose serious concerns as insiders may exploit and organizations weaknesses [32]. Changing legislative environments makes data privacy and security more complex. To comply with law such as General Data Protection Regulation, organization must put in place strong safeguard to protect personal data. Failure to comply can result in significant and reputational damage. Additionally, data sharing interoperability issues hinder the maintenance of data security during transfer across multiple platforms [32].

Despite this barrier, there are room for innovation and advancement in privacy and data security. Technological development such as threat detection powered by AI and encryption process offer encouraging alternatives [33]. To overcome these barriers and seize the possibilities collaboration between legislators, cybersecurity expert, and industry participants is critical.

Concern About data privacy and security are only growing due to evolving legal and threats requirements. Still there are opportunities for teamwork and innovation to improve measures of security and reduce risks.

5.4.2 Integration of a variety of systems and technologies

The integration of different systems and technologies create a range of possibilities and strenuousness in multiple areas [34]. Claim that integration process of system is complex such as project, technical, organization, and environmental factors. Heterogeneous nature of the system creates difficulties due to integrated, increased complexity and leading to issues of interoperability furthermore, system nature is heterogeneous being integrated can create difficulties, increased complexity and leading to issues of interoperability. Nonetheless, overcoming these barriers may provide many valuable opportunities to optimize workflow, increase productivity and improve overall efficiency.

The require for smooth technology and system synchronization is one of the principle challenges. Delaney and D'Agostino [35] highlighted that inadequate management and training can make it difficult for organization to adopting new technologies, leading to inefficiency and resistance. Additionally, Aldoseri *et al.* [36] highlighted the importance of rethinking data strategy and integration for ML as well as AI, stating that ineffective integration may affect the efficiency of these technologies. On other way, smooth integration has many advantages. It can affect on communication improvement, data exchanging and decision-making in-between systems and departments. It also provides help in business leverage the benefit multiple technologies, thereby promoting innovation and giving them a competitive edge. Furthermore, interconnected systems give real-time insights and analytics, allowing business to make informed choices and quickly adopt to changing market circumstances [37].

While here difficulties including in integrating disparate technologies and systems, there also multiple opportunities to become more efficient, innovative and competitive for organizations. Organization can effectively use integrated systems to achieve their goals and promote success by through resolving interoperability concerns, issues resources for appropriate training and management and reconsider the strategy of data.

5.4.3 Intelligent infrastructure and asset maintenance

One creative way to address the potential and problems of current assets management is through smart infrastructure and assets maintenance. This application leverages cutting-edge technologies such as IoT, AI, and data analytics to optimize operations and maintenance of critical infrastructure assets [38].

Organization can overcome may of obstacles to traditional asset management approaches due to using intelligent systems. Between multiple infrastructure component these strenuousness included the dependencies and interdependencies, data interoperability and quality issues, alignment of long and short term-goral and modeling uncertainties [38,39].

Decision-based predictive analytics, extended asset life, reduce costs of maintenance and improved operational efficiency have just a few benefit of smart infrastructure and maintenance asset systems [40,41]. Infrastructure owners may now use preventive maintenance methods thanks to these developments, which reduce downtime, boost dependability, and enhance asset performance overall [38].

However, there are a number of obstacles that come with putting intelligent infrastructure and asset maintenance into practice, including the need for a sizable upfront investment in technology and infrastructure, worries about cybersecurity, and the need for qualified staff to handle and analyze the massive volumes of data generated [41,42].

The problems with conventional asset management may be addressed in a promising way by intelligent infrastructure and asset maintenance; nevertheless, in order to fully use new technologies and reap their rewards, these problems must be carefully considered.

5.5 Prospects for the future and emerging trends in digital twins and smart cities

With exciting future possibilities and developing trends, DTs have the potential to completely transform a number of sectors, including urban development. Beyond their uses of conventional in engineering and manufacturing, one notable development is the stretch out of DTs into fields and other industries [43]. As technology advanced, DTs are increasingly being used in multiple industries including health care, agriculture and retail, which shows versatility and how they impact many aspects of society.

The development of cloud-based solution (DTaaS) and DT as a service is another notable development. This model demonstrates a move forward to implementation of DT which are widely available and scalable, enterprises enabling is used to take new technologies without the need for significant infrastructure expenditures [43]. For simulation via using DTs and analytical predictive, enterprises can use DTaaS for improving efficiency of decision-making and operation.

As AI, ML, and advanced data analytics are integrated into this concept, it is expected to evolve considerably, creating even more intelligent, self-optimizing systems. With cloud solutions, DTs can be up-to-date in real time, enabling continuous asset monitoring and management in manufacturing, healthcare, and urban planning sectors. Also, the integration of augmented reality and virtual reality technologies with DTaaS platforms is expected to improve immersive simulations by facilitating better visualization and interaction. As a result of this evolution, cities will become smarter, supply chains will become more efficient, and advanced predictive maintenance systems will become available, ultimately transforming industries into more dynamic and data-driven businesses.

5.5.1 Digital twin technology in urban management and planning

DT technology provides unprecedented prospects for urban management and panning under the smart cities' framework. Planners can build digital models of cities to improve resilience to environmental problems, resource allocation optimizing, and simulate various scenarios [28]. Furthermore, DTs make it easier for monitor and analyze urban systems in real time, helping authorities quick respond to crises and improve overall livability [28].

A DT also improves urban livability and allows authorities to monitor and analyze urban systems in real time. Sensors, IoT devices, and advanced data analytics are integrated into DTs to provide real-time information about a city's infrastructure, energy consumption, traffic, pollution levels, and public services. With this data-driven approach, city officials can detect anomalies, plan emergency responses, and improve public services like waste management and transportation. The use of DTs also contributes to urban sustainability by helping to reduce waste, maximize consumption, and improve resource management.

Integrity DT into city government become increasingly important for sustainable development and citizens welfare as cities continuously expend and change. Taking together, constant acceptance and innovation in multiple fields characterize the future of smart cities and DTs.

By using of cutting-edge technology as well as willingness to embrace new trends, stakeholders can fully realize the oath of DT to solve complex problems and create more livable, resilient, and efficient cities.

5.6 Conclusion

One promising approach to solve modern urban problem is to incorporate DT into smart city framework. Environments of urban are becoming increasingly complex, and cities need to manage them with flexibility, efficiency, and vision. As a result, they might become sustainable and more resilient cities in the digital age. DT has many different and wide-ranging uses in smart cities from traffic and transportation management to the services or public health, energy management and flood monitoring and infrastructure maintenance. It is more critical for smart city planning as well as administration due to resource allocation optimizing, improve resilience to environmental issues, and give real-time monitoring and analysis to quickly respond to crisis.

DT and smart cities have a bright future filled with continuous innovation and adaptability across disciplines. The increasing adaptability of DT, along with potential to revolutionize entire society, is evident as they used conventional domains outside of areas such as healthcare, agriculture and retail.

The emergency of cloud-based solutions and DTs as a service enables better operational decision-making and efficiency among companies, representation a move toward more scalable and accessible implementations. In way to fully harness the potential of DTs and bring about a new era of livable, resilient cities and efficient that are ready tackle complex issues, stakeholders needs to continuous cooperation and innovation.

5.6.1 Technology limitations

- It is difficult to integrate diverse systems and platforms seamlessly because of the limited interoperability.

- The high computational and storage requirements make it difficult for smaller municipalities to implement.
- The increased reliance on connected systems and real-time data increases cybersecurity and privacy risks.
- AI and simulation tools are often unable to adapt to highly dynamic and unpredictable urban environments.
- A lack of infrastructure or sensor networks may result in unavailable or unreliable real-time high-quality data.

With continuous innovation and adaptability across disciplines, DTs and smart cities have a bright future. DTs are being used outside of traditional domains such as healthcare, agriculture, and retail, showcasing their adaptability and potential to revolutionize entire societies.

5.6.2 The future of technology with recent advances

- Enhancing predictive capability for proactive urban planning and crisis response through the integration of AI and ML.
- For real-time decision-making, quantum computing enables faster and more complex simulations.
- In DT systems, blockchain technology can improve data security, privacy, and trustworthiness.
- Using edge computing to reduce latency and improve efficiency in smart cities.
- For more accurate modeling and monitoring, IoT advancements include a broader sensor coverage and more robust data collection.
- Integrated real-time monitoring systems enabled by faster data transmission in 5G and beyond.
- Smart cities must incorporate strategies for reducing carbon footprints and managing renewable energy.

References

[1] A. Caragliu, C. Del Bo, and P. Nijkamp, “Smart cities in Europe,” in M. Deakin and H. Al Waer (eds.), *Creating Smart Cities*. London, UK: Routledge, 2013, pp. 65–82.

[2] M. Mazari, *Transforming Smart Cities and Infrastructure with Digital Twins* (2023). Available: https://www.linkedin.com/pulse/transforming-smart-cities-infrastructure-digital-twins-mehran-mazari-maize [Accessed April 2024].

[3] Ingenuity, *Exploring the Benefits of Digital Twins for Smart City Innovation* (2023). Available: https://www.ingenuityleeds.com/post/exploring-the-benefits-of-digital-twins-for-smart-city-innovation [Accessed December 2024].

[4] M. Finkelde, *The Benefits of a City Digital Twin* (2023). Available: https://vroc.ai/benefits-of-a-city-digital-twin/ [Accessed August 2024].

[5] E. Canorea, *Why Are Digital Twins Essential for Smart Cities?* (2023). Available: https://www.plainconcepts.com/digital-twins-smart-cities/ [Accessed January 2025].

[6] V. Albino, U. Berardi, and R. M. Dangelico, "Smart cities: Definitions, dimensions, performance, and initiatives," *Journal of Urban Technology*, vol. 22, pp. 3–21, 2015.
[7] E. Glaessgen and D. Stargel, "The digital twin paradigm for future NASA and US Air Force vehicles. 53rd structures," in *Structural Dynamics, and Materials Conference: Special Session on the Digital Twin*, 2012, pp. 1–14.
[8] "Smart Nation," 2021. [Online]. Available: https://www.smartnation.gov.sg/. [Accessed November 2024].
[9] "Commission Europa," 2020. [Online]. Available: https://commission.europa.eu/index_en [Accessed July 2024].
[10] "Thames Water," 2022. [Online]. Available: https://www.thameswater.co.uk [Accessed November 2024].
[11] "Amsterdam Smart City," 2021. [Online]. Available: https://amsterdamsmartcity.com/. [Accessed November 2024].
[12] "C40," 2020. [Online]. Available: https://www.c40.org/ [Accessed November 2024].
[13] C. Liu, P. Zhang, and X. Xu, "Literature review of digital twin technologies for civil infrastructure," *Journal of Infrastructure Intelligence and Resilience*, vol. 2, no. 1, p. 100050, 2023.
[14] "Tokyo Metropolitan Government," 2021. [Online]. Available: https://www.english.metro.tokyo.lg.jp/top [Accessed November 2024].
[15] "NYC Resilience Plan," 2020. [Online]. Available: https://www.nyc.gov/ [Accessed November 2024].
[16] "World Health Organization," 2021. [Online]. Available: https://www.who.int/ [Accessed November 2024].
[17] M. Javaid, A. Haleem and R. Suman, "Digital twin applications toward Industry 4.0: A Review," *Cognitive Robotics*, vol. 3, pp. 71–92, 2023.
[18] G. Caprari, G. Castelli, M. Montuori, M. Camardelli, and R. Malvezzi, "Digital twin for urban planning in the green deal era: A state of the art and future perspectives," *Sustainability*, vol. 14, p. 6263, 2022.
[19] M. Batty, K. W. Axhausen, F. Giannotti, *et al.*, "Smart cities of the future," *The European Physical Journal Special Topics*, vol. 214, pp. 481–518, 2012.
[20] E. Macatulad and F. Biljecki, "Continuing from the Sendai Framework midterm: Opportunities for urban digital twins in disaster risk management," *International Journal of Disaster Risk Reduction*, vol. 102, p. 104310, 2024.
[21] "City of Helsinki," 2021. [Online]. Available: https://www.hel.fi/en [Accessed November 2024].
[22] A. Therias and A. Rafiee, "City digital twins for urban resilience," *International Journal of Digital Earth*, vol. 16, pp. 4164–4190, 2023.
[23] F. Josse, K. Laffrechine, and J. Raven, "The Digital Twin, a tool for dynamic planning of an urban resilience," *Copernicus Meetings*, 2023.
[24] A. Vallée, "Digital twin for healthcare systems," *Frontiers in Digital Health*, vol. 5, p. 1251566, 2023.
[25] T. Nam and T. A. Pardo, "Conceptualizing smart city with dimensions of technology, people, and institutions," in *Proceedings of the 12th Annual*

International Digital Government Research Conference: Digital Government Innovation in Challenging Times, 2011, pp. 282–291.

[26] A. A. H. Dani, S. H. Supangkat, F. F. Lubis, I. G. B. B. Nugraha, R. Kinanda, and I. Rizkia, "Development of a smart city platform based on digital twin technology for monitoring and supporting decision-making," *Sustainability*, vol. 15, p. 14002, 2023.

[27] A. Francisco, N. Mohammadi, and J. E. Taylor, "Smart city digital twin–enabled energy management: Toward real-time urban building energy benchmarking," *Journal of Management in Engineering*, vol. 36, p. 04019045, 2020.

[28] H. Wang, X. Chen, F. Jia, and X. Cheng, "Digital twin-supported smart city: Status, challenges and future research directions," *Expert Systems with Applications*, vol. 217, p. 119531, 2023.

[29] "Siemens," [Online]. Available: https://www.siemens.com/global/en/products/services/digital-enterprise-services/analytics-artificial-intelligence-services/predictive-services.html. [Accessed November 2024].

[30] "Airport Technology," [Online]. Available: https://www.airport-technology.com/news/heathrow-nats-aircraft-emissions-optimisation-technology/ [Accessed November 2024].

[31] M. Mahmoodian, F. Shahrivar, S. Setunge, and S. Mazaheri, "Development of digital twin for intelligent maintenance of civil infrastructure," *Sustainability*, vol. 14, p. 8664, 2022.

[32] iPleaders. *Challenges and Opportunities in Technology for Data Security and Privacy* (2023). Available: https://blog.ipleaders.in/challenges-and-opportunities-in-technology-for-data-security-and-privacy/ [Accessed January 2025].

[33] A. Jha, M. Dave, and S. Madan, "Big data security and privacy: A review on issues, challenges and privacy preserving methods," *International Journal of Computer Applications*, vol. 975, p. 8887, 2017.

[34] M. Rajabalinejad, L. van Dongen, and M. Ramtahalsing, "Systems integration theory and fundamentals," *Safety and Reliability*, vol. 39, no. 1, pp. 83–113, 2020.

[35] R. F. Delaney and R. D'Agostino, "The challenges of integrating new technology into an organization," in *Proceedings of the 2015 International Conference on Information Systems (ICIS)*, vol. 8, pp. 159–172, Fort Worth, TX, USA, 2015.

[36] A. Aldoseri, K. N. Al-Khalifa, and A. M. Hamouda, "Re-thinking data strategy and integration for artificial intelligence: Concepts, opportunities, and challenges," *Applied Sciences*, vol. 13, p. 7082, 2023.

[37] J. M. Alvarez-Rodríguez, R. M. Zuñiga, V. M. Pelayo, and J. Llorens, "Challenges and opportunities in the integration of the Systems Engineering process and the AI/ML model lifecycle," in *INCOSE International Symposium*, 2019, pp. 560–575.

[38] W. Serrano, "Smart or intelligent assets or infrastructure: Technology with a purpose," *Buildings*, vol. 13, p. 131, 2023.

[39] S. Daulat, M. M. Rokstad, A. Klein-Paste, J. Langeveld, and F. Tscheikner-Gratl, "Challenges of integrated multi-infrastructure asset management: a review of pavement, sewer, and water distribution networks," *Structure and Infrastructure Engineering*, vol. 20, no. 4, pp. 546–565, 2024.

[40] A. K. Parlikad and M. Jafari, "Challenges in infrastructure asset management," *IFAC-PapersOnLine*, vol. 49, pp. 185–190, 2016.

[41] C. Dominish, *Enhancing Operational Excellence through 'Intelligent' Asset Management* (2021). Available: https://www.linkedin.com/pulse/enhancing-operational-excellence-through-intelligent-asset-dominish [Accessed November 2024].

[42] D. Schraven, A. Hartmann, and G. Dewulf, "Effectiveness of infrastructure asset management: challenges for public agencies," *Built Environment Project and Asset Management*, vol. 1, pp. 61–74, 2011.

[43] N. Sachdeva, *How Will Digital Twins Evolve in the Future? Predictions and Emerging Trends* (2023). Available: https://insights.daffodilsw.com/blog/the-future-of-digital-twins [Accessed April 2024].

Chapter 6

Blockchain for digital twins to empower smart city

Ravi Chandra Koirala[1], *Sujan Sharma*[1], *Santiago Matalonga*[1] *and Keshav Dahal*[1]

Abstract

Rapid global urbanisation is driving the need for a smart city capable of providing more efficient and responsive municipal administration. To realise the full potential of a smart city, it is essential to adopt emerging technologies that are people-centred and foster high-tech innovations. This chapter explores the integration of two transformative technologies: Digital twins (DT) and blockchain, both of which hold the potential to revolutionise smart city development. DT technologies enable real-time virtual simulations, which aid in result prediction, situational control and link to metaverse applications. These simulations create a dynamic, data-driven urban infrastructure that enhances decision-making and operational efficiency. Blockchain technology, on the other hand, contributes to the development of smart cities by improving traceability, transparency and connectivity while establishing a secure, decentralised framework for efficient service management. By ensuring data integrity, blockchain empowers secure and transparent interactions across urban services, helping smart cities offer convenient and secure services to citizens. This chapter investigates how these two technologies can be integrated into a comprehensive smart city model. It begins by explaining the concepts of DT and blockchain, followed by a detailed analysis of their roles in enhancing urban management, resource optimisation and citizen engagement. Through real-world case studies – including applications in transportation, energy management and environmental monitoring – the chapter demonstrates how blockchain-enabled DT systems have been successfully deployed to optimise city operations. Additionally, the chapter delves into the challenges associated with this integration such as scalability, data interoperability and privacy concerns. By addressing these challenges, this research offers insights into building sustainable, resilient and citizen-centric cities of the future. In conclusion, the chapter emphasises the transformative potential of integrating blockchain and DT in smart city development, providing a roadmap towards secure, efficient and sustainable urban ecosystems.

Keywords: Digital twins; blockchain; smart city; municipal administration; urban management

[1]School of Computing, Engineering and Physical Sciences, CEPS, University of the West of Scotland, UK

6.1 Introduction

6.1.1 Smart city and the global urbanisation trend

The rapid pace of global urbanisation has underscored the need for smarter, more resilient cities capable of addressing the dynamic and evolving requirements of urban populations. According to the United Nations, by 2050, approximately 68% of the world's population is expected to live in urban areas, significantly increasing the strain on current urban infrastructures [1]. Urban areas generate nearly 70% of the world's carbon dioxide emissions, where transport and building stand out as the top contributors [2]. Already, many cities face challenges in meeting the demands for housing, transportation, energy consumption and public services [3]. This rapid urbanisation often overwhelms traditional urban management models, which operate in siloed, fragmented systems and struggle to keep pace with the complexity and speed of urbanisation [4]. Conventional urban planning and management approaches, which depend on centralised systems, often fail to efficiently allocate resources or address the growing needs of urban populations. For example, cities often struggle with the high demand for services like public transportation, healthcare and energy distribution, which results in reduced effectiveness and increased operational costs, delays in service delivery, due to the limitations of these models [5]. This has led to the concept of 'Smart' within cities that recognise new frameworks essential to optimising the planning, management and operation of urban spaces.

Smart cities offer a solution to these challenges by integrating advanced technologies into urban planning, enabling cities to evolve into more sustainable, efficient and people-centred environments [6]. Such frameworks are designed to enhance the quality of life for citizens by improving resource management, reducing environmental impacts and ensuring equitable access to public services [7]. As urban systems grow increasingly complex, municipal administrations must adopt real-time resource, service and infrastructure management practices [8]. Yet, traditional centralised infrastructures often struggle to coordinate and manage these diverse systems, leading to inefficiencies in data exchange and integration [9]. Consequently, with growing urban populations and tightening resources, city governments are progressively relying on emerging technologies like blockchain and digital twin (DT) to enhance the management of municipal services [1].

Blockchain technology enables secure, decentralised, tamper-proof storage of data, ensuring transparency and trust in the management of essential services [10]. Its ability to facilitate immutable record-keeping and automated transactions through smart contracts enhances efficiency in smart city operations. DT technology creates dynamic, real-time digital replicas of physical urban systems, enabling predictive modelling, resource optimisation and data-driven decision-making [11]. The integration of blockchain and DT fosters a more intelligent urban management ecosystem by ensuring secure data exchange, improving infrastructure resilience and enhancing service efficiency. Together, these technologies support the development of sustainable, adaptive and citizen-centric smart cities by enabling informed decision-making and optimising critical urban functions.

6.1.2 The role of digital twins in creating people-centred smart city

A key principle in smart city development is the adoption of people-centred approaches that place citizens at the core of urban innovation [12]. Digital methods such as ICT serve as powerful enablers in smart cities by collecting, processing and distributing real-time data for more informed decision-making and efficient resource utilisation [13]. However, as highlighted by the UN 2030 Agenda, a people-first approach to sustainability must guide these technological advancements to strike an appropriate balance between the social, economic and environmental pillars of urban development [14]. By integrating ICT solutions with inclusive governance, social equity measures and environmental safeguards, cities can go beyond mere efficiency gains to address deeper human needs such as safety, quality of life and equitable access to services. In this way, digital methods become catalysts for genuinely people-centred smart cities, where technology supports and augments, rather than merely focusing on technological advancements for efficiency and enhances quality of life, improves access to services and fosters active citizen participation in urban governance [7].

Digital methods are instrumental in achieving these goals, providing collaborative, transparent and user-centric solutions that empower both cities and citizens [5]. One such example in digital technology is DT – a digital version of the city or its components that makes it possible to test the possible suitability of planned service by simulations before deploying it into the real world. Through data-driven emerging technologies and real-time adaptability like DT technology, smart cities can manage resources more effectively, reduce operational inefficiencies and costs and enhance urban resilience, making them better equipped to meet the needs of their citizens [15]. DT provides cities with powerful predictive modelling tools. DT enhances this by providing dynamic, real-time models of physical city infrastructure, enabling planners to simulate and predict the outcomes of different urban projects before implementing them [16]. By integrating citizen feedback into these simulations, cities can align infrastructure development with the actual needs and preferences of their populations. This makes urban planning not only more efficient but also more responsive to the evolving requirements of citizens [15]. Therefore, DT is critical to the future of urban governance, as it not only optimises services but also fosters a participatory and inclusive urban environment. DT enables cities to simulate and optimise various processes, such as traffic flow, energy consumption and infrastructure maintenance, offering a more responsive approach to urban management. As cities continue to expand, the deployment of such cutting-edge technologies will be crucial in overcoming the challenges associated with urbanisation.

6.1.3 The potential of digital twin technologies in smart city development

DT technologies represent a transformative shift in urban management, offering virtual replicas of physical city systems that are continuously updated with real-time data [17]. These digital counterparts enable city administrators to simulate various scenarios and predict outcomes before implementing them in real environments [18]. For example, DT can model and analyse traffic patterns, allowing cities to optimise traffic light timings, reduce congestion and enhance urban mobility [16]. This capability is crucial as congestion in urban areas significantly impacts economic productivity and environmental sustainability [19]. Beyond traffic management, DT can optimise resource allocation by simulating the use of energy, water and waste systems, enabling cities to balance supply with demand efficiently [17]. In the context of disaster preparedness, they offer predictive modelling, allowing authorities to simulate natural disaster scenarios and test emergency response strategies before a crisis occurs [15]. This real-time situational awareness is vital for enhancing urban resilience in the face of increasing climate-related risks [20]. Moreover, DTs are increasingly used in predictive maintenance for critical urban infrastructure [21]. By analysing data from Internet of Things (IoT) sensors, these models can identify early warning signs of potential failures in water distribution, power grids or public transport systems, reducing costly downtimes and improving service delivery [22]. As cities become more complex, the role of DT in maintaining operational efficiency and resilience will grow, making them a cornerstone of smart city development.

6.1.4 The enhancing impact of blockchain in empowering smart city

While DT provides real-time simulations and predictive insights, blockchain technology adds a layer of security, transparency and decentralisation to smart city operations. Blockchain, known for its decentralised and tamper-proof nature, enhances transparency, security and trust in managing urban data and has become essential in creating these platforms [23]. It ensures the integrity of information, which is critical in areas like energy distribution, transportation and public services. Blockchain, with its decentralised and tamper-proof nature, offers a secure and transparent medium for interaction between citizens and city governments [24]. This can ensure trust and accountability in urban management processes, for example, by allowing citizens to securely vote or provide input on municipal decisions via a blockchain-enabled platform. This transparency and decentralisation not only improve trust in governance but also reduce the risks of data manipulation. By utilising distributed ledger technology (DLT), blockchain ensures that all transactions within the city's ecosystem, ranging from resource management to public service delivery, are securely recorded and immutable [25]. This guarantees that critical urban data remains tamper-proof, thereby improving trust between citizens and city administrators.

Blockchain's decentralised architecture eliminates the need for intermediaries in various processes, reducing the risks of corruption and inefficiencies in urban governance [26]. For instance, smart contracts, an application of blockchain, can automate administrative tasks such as utility billing, public procurement and even maintenance contracts, ensuring that transactions occur automatically when predefined conditions are met [27]. This reduces administrative overhead while ensuring the timely and transparent execution of city operations [28]. In addition to improving efficiency, blockchain promotes data traceability, allowing all transactions and interactions within a smart city to be transparent and easily auditable [24]. This can significantly enhance the accountability of urban services. For example, in public services, blockchain can ensure that government contracts are fully executed and payments are made only when all contractual conditions are satisfied, reducing fraud and increasing trust in municipal services [23]. Finally, blockchain also has the potential to enhance citizen engagement by enabling decentralised, peer-to-peer platforms where residents can interact directly with city services. Whether it is registering complaints, accessing personal healthcare records or participating in local elections, blockchain-based systems ensure that these interactions are secure, verifiable and transparent [29]. This fosters greater trust in city governance and encourages citizen participation in urban decision-making processes, ultimately empowering cities to become more inclusive and accountable.

6.1.5 Objectives and scope of this chapter

The primary objective of this chapter is to explore the synergistic potential of blockchain and DT technologies within the context of smart city development. By examining how these technologies can be effectively integrated, the chapter aims to provide insights into enhancing the efficiency, security and sustainability of urban environments. The specific objectives of this chapter include investigating the role of blockchain and DT in Urban Management to improve decision-making and optimise resource allocation. Furthermore, this chapter delves into the technical, financial and governance challenges associated with the integration of blockchain and DT technologies. It will also assess the opportunities these technologies present in addressing complex urban issues such as resource management, infrastructure maintenance and service delivery. In addition, the chapter also includes case studies of successful implementations of these technologies in smart city scenarios with ground analysis in practical applications. These case studies showcase how these technologies have been used to overcome urban challenges and enhance city operations.

Lastly, the chapter proposes a new model for a smart city that leverages blockchain and DT to create secure, resilient and citizen-centric ecosystems. This model prioritises efficiency in service delivery, real-time responsiveness and enhanced citizen participation in urban governance. By focusing on these objectives, this chapter aims to expand the understanding of how cutting-edge technologies can be applied to urban systems, contributing valuable insights for urban planners, policymakers and technologists. The findings are expected to offer practical recommendations for the development of more resilient, secure and people-centred smart cities in the future.

6.2 Digital twins and smart city

6.2.1 Understanding the concept of digital twin

DT technology refers to the virtual model or digital replica of a physical object or system, offering transformative capabilities in urban planning and development [30].

It originated in the manufacturing and aerospace industries, but its potential has now expanded into the broader realm of smart cities, making it a vital component of modern urban design and infrastructure management [18]. In simple terms, a DT is a digital representation of a real-world object, process or system. This virtual model continuously updates through real-time data collected via sensors and IoT devices installed across the physical entity, allowing for a two-way flow of information. In the context of a smart city, DT provide a dynamic and real-time representation of various city infrastructures, including transportation networks, energy grids, water systems and even entire neighbourhoods [8]. This enables the simulation of urban environments, tracks the performance of infrastructure systems and offers predictive insights into potential future conditions or crises. As urban populations continue to grow, DT technology becomes an invaluable tool for municipalities aiming to improve efficiency, sustainability and resilience in managing urban resources.

With urban populations projected to grow significantly, the DT offers an invaluable tool for municipalities aiming to enhance efficiency, sustainability and resilience in managing urban resources [31]. As cities grow more complex, having an accurate and adaptable digital replica can enable decision-makers to test different scenarios, predict future challenges and implement informed solutions before these problems occur in the real world [32]. Furthermore, as artificial intelligence (AI) and machine learning (ML) continue to advance, DTs are becoming more predictive and autonomous, offering cities the ability to address issues such as traffic congestion, environmental pollution and emergency responses with greater precision. This positions cities to become more data-driven, with the DT acting as a cyber-physical system that seamlessly connects and synchronises the physical and digital worlds in real time.

6.2.2 Virtual simulations and result prediction

One of the most significant applications of DT technology in the smart city is its ability to perform virtual simulations and provide accurate result predictions [32]. These simulations offer a virtual environment where city planners and engineers can model and analyse various urban scenarios without the cost, time or risks associated with real-world experimentation. These environments can replicate city infrastructure, from roads to utilities to public services, in real-time, using data generated from IoT sensors and devices deployed throughout the city [33]. In particular, DT excel at predictive modelling, which allows city authorities to simulate the impact of different policies, urban interventions or external shocks, like natural disasters, on city infrastructure [34]. For instance, before implementing a city-wide transportation plan, city managers can simulate the impact of different traffic regulations or new infrastructure on traffic flow, air quality and energy consumption [11]. Similarly, in the field of energy management, virtual simulations powered by DT help cities optimise energy usage by predicting demand patterns and identifying potential system failures before they occur [35].

Moreover, this technology enables cities to proactively address problems. For example, predictive maintenance has emerged as a key advantage of using DT, as cities can identify faults or inefficiencies in infrastructure (such as a failing water pipe or power line) before they escalate into larger issues [21]. By leveraging real-time data and advanced analytics, DT can detect anomalies and foresee such problems, municipalities can reduce downtime, avoid costly repairs and maintain the continuous delivery of essential services [15]. By integrating ML and AI-driven insights, DT enhances the efficiency of resource allocation and maintenance based on impact and urgency, ultimately leading to a smarter, cost-effective approach to urban management. Thus, DT empowers municipalities to shift from reactive to proactive management of urban infrastructure, making cities more resilient and sustainable in the long term.

6.2.3 Situational control and the connected metaverse

DT also enhance situational control, where cities can continuously monitor and manage their systems in real-time, ensuring quick responses to sudden changes or emergencies [36]. Through their real-time data integration, DT provides cities with situational awareness across all sectors – traffic, energy, public safety and more. For instance, in the case of a city experiencing flooding, a DT of the urban drainage system can model how water will flow through the city's infrastructure, allowing authorities to dynamically respond by redirecting traffic or prioritising evacuation routes [37]. This proactive management not only mitigates the impact of emergencies but also saves lives and reduces economic losses. With the integration of DT into the connected metaverse, cities are expanding their ability to manage infrastructure virtually [38].

The metaverse, a highly immersive and interactive virtual space, offers urban planners new tools to visualise, simulate and engage with urban models. Planners and city managers can walk through immersive models of city neighbourhoods or infrastructure projects, manipulating the environment in real-time and predicting the effects of their decisions before implementing them in the real world [39]. This ability to model scenarios in a risk-free setting allows for informed decision-making, minimising unforeseen challenges during the execution phase. The connected metaverse extends the power of DT by adding immersive experiences through augmented reality (AR) and virtual reality (VR) [40]. These technologies allow for advanced collaboration and visualisation in urban planning, where not only city authorities but also citizens and other stakeholders can actively participate in the planning process. For instance, community members can interact with proposed city developments within the metaverse, providing feedback and contributing to co-creation efforts that align with people-centric smart city principles [38]. This inclusive approach fosters a sense of ownership among residents, enhancing social cohesion and ensuring that urban development reflects the needs and desires of the community.

6.2.4 The role of DT in smart city development

The transformative potential of DT technology in smart city lies in its ability to create highly connected, data-driven environments that optimise city services and infrastructure [8]. The use of real-time data in creating digital representations of urban systems leads to greater efficiency in managing resources, improving infrastructure resilience and enabling more sustainable urban development. DT provides a comprehensive digital layer that enhances every aspect of urban life, including transportation, healthcare and environmental monitoring [41]. For instance, in the realm of sustainable urban development, DT can help monitor carbon emissions, optimise energy consumption and promote the adoption of renewable energy sources. By simulating different environmental policies, cities can assess the potential impact of various sustainability measures before implementation, such as the effect of increasing public transportation options on reducing traffic-related emissions, thereby aiding policymakers in making informed decisions [42]. This predictive capability allows cities to align their development goals with sustainability objectives effectively.

Additionally, resilience is a critical aspect of smart city development, especially in the context of climate change and increasing urban risks [31]. DT enable cities to anticipate challenges and develop proactive strategies for responding to natural disasters like floods, earthquakes or wildfires. Through real-time monitoring, cities can dynamically allocate resources and optimise evacuation routes, enhancing their disaster preparedness and response capabilities [43]. Furthermore, by leveraging historical data and predictive analytics, DT can help cities identify high-risk areas and propose long-term infrastructure improvements to minimise potential damage. This capability enhances urban resilience by reducing both the economic and social impacts of disasters while promoting a more adaptive city environment. Additionally, by simulating various emergency scenarios, DT enables authorities to refine contingency plans, enhance coordination among emergency response teams and improve overall crisis management efficiency, ensuring a more effective and timely response to urban risks.

In summary, DT technology is revolutionising smart city development by providing real-time, data-driven insights that enhance urban planning, infrastructure management and disaster preparedness. By integrating AI, IoT and predictive analytics, DT enables cities to transition from reactive problem-solving to proactive decision-making, fostering greater efficiency, sustainability and resilience. Furthermore, the immersive capabilities of the metaverse and AR/VR enhance stakeholder engagement, allowing citizens to actively participate in shaping their urban environments. Beyond technological advancements, DT foster a citizen-centric approach to urban development. By offering a digital platform where citizens can visualise, interact with and provide feedback on public services and infrastructure, DT enhances public participation and transparency in governance. This participatory aspect ensures that a smart city not only prioritises technological advancement but also remains deeply aligned with the needs and desires of its citizens [38]. By fostering engagement, DT not only improves urban planning outcomes but also contributes to a more democratic and inclusive urban governance framework.

6.3 Blockchain technology for smart city

6.3.1 Overview of blockchain technology

Blockchain technology is a decentralised and distributed digital ledger system that records transactions across multiple computers in a way that ensures the security, transparency and immutability of data [44]. Originally developed as the foundational technology behind cryptocurrencies like Bitcoin, blockchain has evolved into a versatile technology with applications spanning various sectors, including finance, healthcare, supply chain management and, crucially, urban governance [45]. At its core, blockchain operates on a network of nodes where each node maintains a copy of the entire blockchain [46]. This decentralised nature not only increases security by eliminating single points of failure but also enhances transparency, as all participants can view and verify the recorded transactions [47]. The use of cryptographic techniques ensures that once data is added to the blockchain, it becomes virtually impossible to alter or delete, thereby fostering trust among users [48].

In the context of a smart city, blockchain technology offers a promising framework for enhancing the management of urban services and improving interactions between city authorities, service providers and citizens [49]. By enabling secure, transparent and efficient data sharing, blockchain can address several critical challenges faced by modern urban environments, including inefficiencies in service delivery, lack of accountability and issues related to data privacy [50]. For example, blockchain can facilitate seamless and tamper-proof record-keeping for land registries, reducing bureaucratic delays and eliminating fraudulent transactions. Additionally, blockchain-based smart contracts can automate various administrative processes, such as tax collection and utility billing, minimising human intervention and errors while ensuring compliance with regulatory standards. Furthermore, by integrating blockchain with the IoT, cities can create real-time, data-driven systems for optimising energy consumption, traffic flow and waste management, ultimately leading to more sustainable and resilient urban infrastructures.

6.3.2 Enhanced traceability and transparency in smart city

One of the most compelling benefits of blockchain technology is its capacity for enhanced traceability and transparency, both crucial for effective urban governance [50]. In a smart city, where multiple stakeholders are involved in service delivery, ensuring accountability is vital. Blockchain's immutable nature provides a reliable mechanism for tracking the provenance and history of data, assets and transactions [51]. For instance, in the context of waste management, cities can utilise blockchain to monitor the entire waste disposal process, from collection to processing and recycling [52]. Each step can be recorded on the blockchain, allowing citizens and authorities to verify whether waste is being managed correctly. This level of transparency can deter corruption and mismanagement while empowering citizens to hold authorities accountable for their actions [52].

Moreover, blockchain can also enhance transparency in public procurement processes. By recording contracts and procurement transactions on a blockchain, cities can ensure that all bids are accessible for review and that contract fulfilment is traceable. This transparency helps to eliminate fraud and ensures that public resources are allocated efficiently, ultimately leading to better service delivery for residents [53]. Additionally, blockchain-based procurement systems can reduce bureaucratic inefficiencies by automating processes such as contract approvals and payments, ensuring compliance with regulations while minimising delays. The use of smart contracts further strengthens integrity, as funds can be automatically disbursed only when contractual obligations are met, reducing the risk of financial mismanagement. By fostering an open and verifiable system, blockchain can enhance public trust in government operations and encourage greater citizen participation in urban development initiatives.

6.3.3 Improved connectivity and efficient service management

Blockchain technology facilitates improved connectivity among various systems and stakeholders in a smart city ecosystem [54]. The integration of blockchain with IoT devices enhances the ability of city managers to gather and analyse data from different sources, allowing for more efficient service management [55]. For example, in the realm of transportation, blockchain can enable seamless data sharing between different transportation systems, such as public transit, ride-sharing and pedestrian networks, enhancing overall mobility solutions [56]. This connectivity can facilitate real-time updates regarding traffic conditions, public transportation schedules and availability of ride-sharing services, improving the overall commuting experience for citizens.

Additionally, blockchain can streamline urban service management by enabling decentralised applications (dApps) that facilitate direct transactions between service providers and residents [57]. For instance, smart contracts, self-executing contracts with the terms of the agreement directly written into code, can automate service delivery in areas like utility management, enabling instantaneous billing and payment processing based on actual consumption data recorded on the blockchain [27]. This automation reduces human intervention, lowering the potential for errors, disputes and delays associated with traditional billing systems. Furthermore, blockchain-powered solutions can enhance transparency and trust between stakeholders by providing tamper-proof records of service transactions, ensuring accountability in service provision. In emergency response management, for example, blockchain can be leveraged to coordinate real-time data sharing between emergency services, hospitals and local authorities, ensuring a faster and more efficient response to crises. By enabling automated, transparent transactions and fostering seamless communication among various urban entities, blockchain can reduce administrative burdens and minimise delays in service delivery, ultimately leading to a more efficient urban ecosystem.

6.3.4 Establishing a foundation for secure and efficient smart city operations

In addition to enhancing transparency and connectivity, blockchain technology provides a robust foundation for secure and efficient smart city operations [50]. The security features inherent to the blockchain, such as encryption, decentralised storage and consensus mechanisms, make it exceptionally well-suited to handle the vast amounts of sensitive data generated in urban environments [58]. Security is particularly crucial when dealing with citizen data, which is often collected through various IoT devices and services in a smart city [50]. With rising concerns about data breaches and unauthorised access to personal information, implementing a secure data management system is paramount. Blockchain's decentralised approach minimises the risk of data loss or manipulation, as compromising a single node in the network does not jeopardise the integrity of the entire system [24].

Moreover, blockchain can empower citizens by providing them with greater control over their data. With self-sovereign identity models based on blockchain, individuals can securely manage their identities and share only the necessary information with service providers, thereby enhancing privacy and reducing the likelihood of data misuse [59]. This user-centric approach not only fosters trust between citizens and authorities but also encourages greater participation in smart city initiatives. As cities strive to build sustainable and resilient urban environments, the ability to implement efficient and secure operational frameworks becomes increasingly vital [60]. By leveraging blockchain technology, urban administrators can create data-driven policies and solutions that are not only transparent and accountable but also secure and citizen-centric [61].

In summary, blockchain technology presents a transformative opportunity for smart city to enhance their operational capabilities and foster more effective governance. By providing enhanced traceability, improving connectivity among systems and establishing secure data management practices, blockchain can significantly improve the efficiency and transparency of urban services. As cities continue to embrace digital innovation, the integration of blockchain will be essential in creating resilient, sustainable and citizen-focused urban ecosystems.

Beyond operational improvements, blockchain has the potential to drive economic efficiency by minimising bureaucratic hurdles, streamlining transactions and reducing fraud in public service management. Its decentralised structure enhances trust between citizens and authorities by ensuring that data remains secure, verifiable and tamper-proof. However, for widespread adoption, cities must address challenges such as regulatory compliance, system integration and public acceptance. By strategically implementing blockchain solutions, urban administrations can foster a future where digital services are more transparent, efficient and inclusive, ultimately improving the overall quality of life in the smart city.

6.4 Integrating blockchain and DT in smart city development

6.4.1 Blockchain-enabled trust in digital twin smart city applications

The integration of blockchain and DT technologies represents a significant leap forward in the evolution of smart city frameworks [62]. This synergy between the two technologies can lead to the development of a new model for a smart city that is more resilient, efficient and responsive to the needs of citizens and government. In this new model, blockchain enhances the capabilities of DT by providing a secure and immutable record of data exchanges between various stakeholders in a smart city ecosystem [63]. This means that every interaction, whether it is the monitoring of energy consumption in a smart building or the management of traffic flow, can be recorded transparently on the blockchain. Such a system not only increases the reliability of the data but also helps to ensure accountability and trust among different parties involved [50].

The convergence of these technologies allows for the creation of a collaborative data environment [63]. Cities can harness data from a multitude of sources – including IoT sensors, infrastructures such as transportation systems, communication systems, energy grid, health system, business and finance, digital platforms and citizen feedback – while ensuring that this data is both secure and accessible. This leads to improved urban planning and resource allocation, as decision-makers can simulate various scenarios using DT to assess potential outcomes before implementing changes in the real world. For example, urban planners can utilise this integrated model to optimise public transport routes by simulating various traffic scenarios and understanding the potential impacts of changes on overall city traffic flow [64]. The inclusion of blockchain technology ensures that all data used in these simulations is tamper-proof and can be audited, fostering a higher level of trust among stakeholders.

6.4.2 The potential benefits of combining blockchain and DT

The combination of blockchain and DT offers several benefits that can transform urban environments into more efficient and responsive systems.

(i) **Enhanced data integrity:** Data integrity is a critical requirement for a smart city. DT rely on accurate, real-time data for monitoring and simulations. Blockchain ensures this data remains immutable and trustworthy by preventing tampering. For instance, in public safety and infrastructure management, reliable data is essential to avoid inaccurate decision-making that could have severe consequences. Blockchain's cryptographic protocols safeguard the integrity of the data used by DT [65].

(ii) **Improved decision-making**: Integrating blockchain with DT allows for more advanced data analytics, enabling city administrators to simulate and predict the impact of their decisions. ML algorithms applied to this data can help visualise the interaction of various urban factors, leading to more informed, data-driven policies. For example, urban planners can model the effects of new policies on traffic, energy consumption or pollution, ensuring decisions align with sustainable urban development goals [66].

(iii) **Increased citizen engagement**: Blockchain fosters transparency and trust in city governance by providing citizens with access to real-time data on urban operations. This transparency enhances citizen engagement, as individuals can contribute feedback on urban projects via digital platforms. By integrating this citizen feedback into DT simulations, cities can adopt a more participatory governance model that reflects public needs and concerns, enhancing the overall effectiveness of urban planning [67].

(iv) **Resource optimisation**: Both technologies can contribute to optimising resources. In energy management, for example, a DT can simulate energy consumption across different sectors, while Blockchain verifies the accuracy of energy usage data. This allows cities to implement demand-response strategies that reduce energy waste and costs while minimising environmental impact. Blockchain also ensures that energy transactions between suppliers and consumers are secure and efficient [68].

(v) **Resilience to disruptions**: The integration of blockchain and DT can improve urban resilience by offering real-time insights and control mechanisms during crises. For instance, in the event of a natural disaster, DT can simulate damage and plan recovery efforts, while blockchain ensures that resource allocation data is secure, preventing fraud or mismanagement. This combination allows cities to respond more effectively to disasters and other emergencies [69].

6.4.3 Challenges and considerations in implementation

While the integration of blockchain and DT in smart city development holds great promise, several challenges must be addressed to ensure successful implementation.

(i) **Interoperability issues**: Smart cities involve a wide array of technologies and systems that must interact seamlessly. One major challenge lies in ensuring interoperability between different blockchain platforms and DT applications. A lack of standardised protocols may result in fragmented systems that cannot communicate effectively, limiting the potential benefits of integration. Establishing common standards and protocols is essential for achieving seamless data sharing and system integration [70].

(ii) **Data privacy and security**: While blockchain provides enhanced data security through its decentralised nature, privacy concerns remain, particularly regarding the protection of sensitive citizen data. As smart cities generate and collect vast amounts of personal data, ensuring compliance with privacy regulations like the General Data Protection Regulation is crucial. Developing privacy-preserving blockchain solutions, such as zero-knowledge proofs and secure multiparty computation, can help strike a balance between transparency and privacy [71].

(iii) **Scalability**: Blockchain's scalability remains a significant challenge, particularly when applied to large urban environments. While blockchain can handle smaller-scale implementations, scaling up to manage the vast amount of data generated by IoT devices and DT can lead to performance issues, such as slower transaction speeds and higher costs. Research and development into more scalable blockchain solutions, such as sharding and Layer 2 protocols, are critical to overcoming these limitations [72].

(iv) **Regulatory and legal frameworks**: The use of blockchain in public administration introduces complex regulatory and legal issues. Governments must establish clear regulatory frameworks that encourage innovation while protecting public interests. This may involve developing new legislation or adapting existing laws to accommodate the unique features of blockchain technology, such as decentralised governance and smart contracts [24].

(v) **Public acceptance**: Public trust and acceptance are critical to the success of smart city initiatives. Citizens must be made aware of the benefits of blockchain and DT technologies, and efforts must be made to build trust in the systems managing their data. Engaging the public through education campaigns and demonstrating the tangible benefits of these technologies can increase acceptance and promote widespread adoption [24,73].

In conclusion, the integration of blockchain and DT technologies presents a transformative opportunity for smart city development. By creating a robust model that enhances data integrity, improves decision-making and fosters citizen engagement, cities can build more resilient and efficient urban environments. Furthermore, the synergies between these technologies can act as a catalyst for achieving global sustainability goals by optimising resource usage and reducing environmental impact. By adopting a proactive approach to these innovations, cities can position themselves as pioneers in smart urban development, setting benchmarks for others to follow. However, addressing the challenges related to interoperability, data privacy, scalability, regulatory frameworks and public acceptance is essential for realising the full potential of this integrated approach. As urbanisation continues to accelerate, the need for innovative, technology-driven solutions and collaboration among stakeholders will become increasingly pressing, making the integration of blockchain and DT not just advantageous but essential and more inclusive.

6.5 Characteristics and technologies of a blockchain-enabled digital twin city

Integrating blockchain technology with DT systems offers a transformative approach to urban management and service delivery. As cities worldwide face increasing pressures from urbanisation, integrating these advanced technologies can create more efficient, transparent and responsive urban environments. This section explores the key characteristics of a blockchain-enabled DT city, the technological infrastructure required for its implementation and various real-world application scenarios.

6.5.1 The key characteristics of a blockchain-enabled smart city

A blockchain-enabled DT city possesses several defining characteristics that distinguish it from traditional urban models. These characteristics ensure that the city can effectively manage resources, engage citizens and maintain transparency and security in its operations.

(i) **Data integrity and security**: One of the most critical characteristics of this model is the robust security framework provided by blockchain. Since blockchain is inherently decentralised and tamper-proof, it enhances data integrity by ensuring that any data fed into the DT system is verified and immutable. This characteristic is particularly important for applications involving sensitive information, such as health data in healthcare systems or personal data in citizen engagement platforms [74].

(ii) **Interoperability**: A blockchain-enabled DT city emphasises the importance of interoperability among various data sources, systems and stakeholders. By adopting standardised protocols and APIs, cities can create a cohesive ecosystem where data from IoT devices, urban infrastructure and citizen feedback can be seamlessly integrated into the DT framework. This interoperability is crucial for optimising urban operations and enhancing decision-making [75].

(iii) **Real-time analytics and insights**: The integration of DT with blockchain enables real-time data processing and analytics. With access to live data streams from various urban systems, decision-makers can leverage the predictive capabilities of DT to simulate different scenarios and assess potential outcomes before implementing changes. This feature allows cities to respond swiftly to emerging challenges, ensuring that they can adapt to dynamic urban conditions [15].

(iv) **Transparency and accountability**: Transparency is a hallmark of a blockchain-enabled model. By providing open access to data recorded on the blockchain, cities can foster trust among citizens and stakeholders. This transparency not only enhances accountability but also encourages citizen engagement in urban governance. Citizens can access information related to public services, infrastructure projects and city planning, enabling them to hold authorities accountable for their actions [76].

(v) **Sustainability and resource optimisation**: Sustainability is a core objective of modern urban development. A blockchain-enabled DT city supports sustainable practices by facilitating efficient resource management. For example, cities can use DT to monitor energy consumption, optimise traffic flows and reduce waste generation. The transparency and traceability provided by blockchain allow cities to track resource usage, identify inefficiencies and implement corrective measures [77].

(vi) **Citizen-centric approach:** The integration of blockchain and DT promotes a people-centred approach to urban management. By prioritising citizen engagement and participation, cities can tailor their services to meet the needs of the community. Blockchain enables secure, transparent channels for citizen feedback, while DT allow for the simulation of various scenarios based on this feedback, ensuring that urban development aligns with the priorities of residents [8].

6.5.2 Technological infrastructure for a DT city

The successful implementation of a blockchain-enabled DT city relies on a robust technological infrastructure that encompasses various components. Key elements of this infrastructure include:

(i) **Internet of Things devices**: IoT devices play a crucial role in collecting real-time data from the urban environment. These devices can include sensors for monitoring air quality, traffic conditions, energy consumption and public safety. The data collected by IoT devices serves as the foundation for creating and updating DT, ensuring that they reflect the current state of urban systems [78].

(ii) **5G networks**: The vast amount of data generated by IoT devices and DT requires high-speed, low-latency communication networks. 5G technology is essential for supporting the real-time data exchange that DT cities require. The high bandwidth of 5G networks allows for seamless communication between IoT devices, DT and blockchain nodes, ensuring that all city operations are synchronised in real-time [79].

(iii) **Cloud computing and edge computing**: Cloud computing provides the necessary and on-demand capacity of computational services and resources for processing and storing vast amounts of data generated by IoT devices through external cloud servers over the internet, ensuring flexibility, scalability and cost-efficiency. It enables real-time analytics and simulations conducted by DT. Edge computing complements cloud solutions by processing data closer to its source, reducing latency and enhancing the responsiveness of urban systems [29]. Edge computing enables time-sensitive applications, including autonomous vehicles, real-time surveillance and industrial automation, to operate with minimal delays by processing essential data directly at the network's edge. It also facilitates offline operations and localised decision-making in situations where connection to cloud servers is unreliable or temporarily unavailable. Together, these technologies build a hybrid architecture where edge devices process time-sensitive data locally and leverage the cloud for storage and deeper analysis, enabling an efficient, seamless and adaptive solution.

(iv) **Blockchain infrastructure**: At the heart of a blockchain-enabled DT city is the blockchain infrastructure itself. This consists of a decentralised network of nodes that verify and record transactions, ensuring data integrity and security. The choice of blockchain consensus mechanism – such as Proof of Work, Proof of Stake (PoS) or Delegated Proof of Stake – will depend on the specific needs of the city in terms of scalability, energy efficiency and security [80]. Additionally, smart contract platforms, such as Ethereum or Hyperledger, provide the necessary framework for automating processes and transactions within the city.

(v) **Artificial intelligence and machine learning**: AI and ML technologies are essential for analysing the vast amounts of data generated by DT, enabling cities to identify patterns, predict future trends and optimise operations in real-time. For instance, AI can analyse traffic patterns to forecast congestion, while ML algorithms can enhance energy consumption efficiency based on historical data [81]. Additionally, advanced analytics and ML techniques are crucial for extracting actionable insights from both historical and real-time data, facilitating improved resource allocation and urban resilience [82]. Furthermore, blockchain technology ensures that the data utilised by AI and ML algorithms remains accurate and verifiable, enhancing the overall decision-making process.

(vi) **User interfaces and visualisation tools**: To facilitate effective communication between decision-makers and the DT system, intuitive user interfaces and visualisation tools are essential. These tools allow stakeholders to interact with the DT, explore different scenarios and visualise the impacts of various decisions on urban systems. Effective visualisation aids in better understanding complex data and enhances collaborative decision-making [83].

(vii) **Cybersecurity measures**: As cities become increasingly reliant on digital technologies, the importance of cybersecurity cannot be overstated. Protecting sensitive data and ensuring the integrity of urban systems is critical. Implementing robust cybersecurity measures, such as encryption, access controls and continuous monitoring, will help safeguard against potential threats and vulnerabilities [84].

6.5.3 Real-world application scenarios

Numerous cities worldwide are already leveraging the integration of blockchain and DT technologies to enhance urban management. This section highlights key application areas, including transportation and traffic management, energy consumption and resource optimization, healthcare, governance, and environmental monitoring, demonstrating how these technologies improve efficiency, transparency, and decision-making in smart cities.

6.5.3.1 Transportation and traffic management

In a smart city, effective transportation management is critical for reducing congestion, enhancing mobility and minimising environmental impacts. The integration of DT with blockchain can significantly improve traffic management systems. For example, the city of Singapore has implemented a comprehensive smart traffic management system that utilises DT technology to create real-time simulations of traffic flow [85,86]. By integrating blockchain, the system enables secure and transparent sharing of data among various stakeholders, including traffic agencies, public transport operators and citizens. This collaboration allows for the development of responsive traffic control strategies that adjust signal timings based on real-time traffic conditions, reducing congestion and improving overall mobility [87].

Moreover, the use of smart contracts on the blockchain can automate processes such as toll payments or ride-sharing services, ensuring secure transactions and efficient resource allocation. The data collected from vehicles and IoT sensors can be analysed through the DT to predict traffic patterns, enabling proactive measures to mitigate congestion and enhance public transport reliability. Blockchain's immutable ledger ensures transparency and trust in data handling, while dynamic pricing mechanisms and seamless coordination with autonomous vehicles optimise traffic flow and enhance urban mobility. Together, DT and blockchain technologies create adaptive, data-driven solutions for smarter and more efficient transportation systems.

6.5.3.2 Energy consumption and resource optimisation

Energy consumption is a critical challenge for urban areas, and cities are increasingly turning to technology to optimise resource usage. A notable example is Amsterdam, which has adopted a blockchain-enabled DT model for energy management. In this initiative, Amsterdam utilises DT to monitor energy consumption across various buildings and public infrastructure. The city employs IoT devices to gather real-time data on energy usage and integrates this data into a DT of the urban environment. By employing blockchain technology, the city ensures that energy consumption data is securely recorded and can be verified by all stakeholders [88].

This integrated approach allows for dynamic pricing models based on real-time energy consumption, enabling residents to make informed decisions about their energy usage. Additionally, the city can identify inefficiencies and implement targeted interventions to reduce energy waste. The transparency provided by blockchain fosters trust among residents and stakeholders, encouraging collaboration in achieving sustainability goals. This effort highlights how technology can be used to bridge the gap between energy management and environmental responsibility, creating a scalable model for other cities to emulate.

6.5.3.3 Healthcare and emergency services

In cities like Dubai, blockchain and DT are being used to improve healthcare services by securely storing patient data and enabling real-time simulations of healthcare infrastructure. DT can simulate the spread of diseases or model emergency response scenarios, while blockchain ensures that sensitive healthcare data remains secure and compliant with data protection regulations [81].

The integration of these technologies facilitates an efficient and secure exchange of data, minimising administrative inefficiencies and improving patient care. In emergency services, DTs can model disaster response scenarios, enabling authorities to evaluate and optimise strategies before real-world deployment. By leveraging blockchain to ensure the reliability and accessibility of healthcare data, cities can build trust among citizens and healthcare providers while promoting smarter, data-informed healthcare innovations.

6.5.3.4 Governance and citizen engagement

Blockchain and DT can also enhance governance and citizen engagement. For instance, Estonia has implemented blockchain-based systems for e-governance, allowing citizens to vote, pay taxes and access public services securely online [89]. DT can further enhance this by simulating the effects of government policies before they are implemented, ensuring data-driven decision-making and improving public trust [8].

Integrating blockchain with DT strengthens governance by establishing a transparent and data-focused foundation for decision-making. Blockchain safeguards the integrity and accuracy of the data used in DT simulations, which, in turn, provide realistic visualisations of potential policy outcomes. This synergy enables governments to embrace more inclusive governance models, encouraging citizen participation and feedback informed by simulated scenarios.

6.5.3.5 Environmental monitoring and sustainability

DT cities can help monitor environmental factors like air quality, water usage and waste management. In cities like Amsterdam, DT are used to model the environmental impact of urban projects, while blockchain ensures that data related to sustainability efforts is transparent and verifiable [18]. This enables cities to meet their sustainability goals and engage citizens in environmental initiatives.

The combination of DT and blockchain offers a transformative approach to promoting sustainability in urban settings. DT enable real-time simulations of environmental factors, helping cities predict and assess the impact of urban projects, while blockchain ensures the data used in these simulations is secure, transparent and verifiable. By integrating these technologies, cities can make well-informed, accountable decisions and actively engage citizens by providing reliable and accessible information about sustainability efforts.

In summary, the characteristics and technological infrastructure of a blockchain-enabled DT city to present a compelling framework for enhancing urban management and sustainability. By ensuring data integrity, interoperability, real-time analytics and transparency, this integrated model addresses the challenges faced by modern urban environments. The practical applications in transportation and energy management demonstrate the transformative potential of combining these technologies, paving the way for more efficient, resilient and citizen-centric cities. Furthermore, this integration framework also demands collaboration among stakeholders. By promoting citizen engagement and sustainability, this will improve the quality of life among citizens and help cities meet global sustainable development goals. Hence, as cities continue to evolve, the integration of blockchain and DT technologies will be essential for creating smarter and sustainable urban ecosystems.

6.6 Case studies and examples

As the integration of blockchain and DT technologies advances, several cities have successfully implemented these technologies in different sectors, particularly urban planning, such as event management, construction and building, disaster management and citizen involvement towards governance, transport and traffic management, energy consumption and healthcare. These case studies not only highlight the benefits of combining these innovations but also offer valuable lessons on scalability and potential for future urban planning.

6.6.1 *Successful implementation of blockchain and DT in smart city*

6.6.1.1 Case 1: digital twin implementation in Dublin Docklands, Ireland [90]

The Dublin Docklands area in Ireland serves as a leading example of how DT technology can revolutionise urban planning and governance. Through the development of a publicly accessible DT, this initiative aims to improve city planning and engage citizens in the decision-making process. By leveraging advanced technologies such as IoT devices, building information models (BIM) and urban data systems, Dublin is transforming its approach to urban development. This case study explores the concept and design of the DT project, applications and use cases, experimental setup, results and impacts, limitations and challenges, highlighting its role in enhancing transparency, fostering citizen involvement and utilising real-time simulations to inform urban governance and policy-making.

Concept and design of the digital twin

The DT of the Dublin Docklands incorporates multiple layers of information, organised into a six-layer model. These include terrain, buildings, infrastructure, mobility, the digital layer (smart city data) and the virtual layer (DT simulations). Each layer builds upon the previous one to provide a comprehensive understanding of the urban environment.

The terrain layer maps the physical attributes such as elevation, soil quality and water bodies. The building layer includes detailed 3D BIM of structures in the Docklands, while the infrastructure layer covers transport systems, utilities and public amenities. The mobility layer adds dynamic simulations of pedestrian and vehicle movements. Finally, the digital and virtual layers collect and process data from IoT devices to run simulations, such as urban mobility, flooding and building impact on skylines.

Applications and use cases

The DT model of the Dublin Docklands offers a diverse range of applications in urban planning, disaster management, mobility optimisation and citizen engagement. Its integration of real-time data, interactive simulations and community feedback creates a comprehensive framework for smarter, more sustainable cities.

One key application is skyline planning and development, where the DT allows urban planners to simulate the visual and functional impacts of new buildings on the cityscape. By incorporating building information modelling data, proposed structures can be integrated into the model to assess their effect on sunlight access and aesthetics. Public officials and citizens can virtually explore these changes from various perspectives, providing feedback through online forms. This approach not only enhances transparency but also incorporates community input into urban design. For instance, concerns about a building being ‘too tall’ or mismatched with Dublin’s architectural style can guide redesign efforts.

Green space planning is another significant use case, emphasising the role of parks and recreational areas in improving urban quality of life. The model utilises environmental data, such as air quality, noise levels and pedestrian flow, to identify optimal locations for new green spaces. Citizens are actively involved in the design process, suggesting features like gym equipment or additional seating through interactive simulations. This participatory approach ensures that green spaces meet community needs while sensors in smart cities monitor the success of added amenities, providing valuable data for future enhancements. The model also addresses disaster preparedness, particularly through its flooding simulations. By modelling water level rises in the River Liffey, the DT identifies areas at risk of inundation, guiding the placement of flood defences like sandbags and informing evacuation strategies. Historical and real-time data integration ensures accuracy, while dynamic updates help predict flooding timelines. This capability not only aids immediate responses but also informs long-term infrastructure improvements, such as drainage systems or river diversions.

In the realm of mobility optimisation, the DT evaluates pedestrian behaviour and urban infrastructure. Simulations track metrics like waiting times and distances travelled, accounting for demographic variations such as elderly populations. These insights guide the design of accessible streetscapes and public spaces. For example, planners can test how footpath gradients or street furniture affect pedestrian flow, ensuring that urban environments accommodate diverse needs. Additionally, the model can simulate the impact of large events, such as concerts at Dublin's Three Arena, to optimise traffic and crowd management. The DT also fosters citizen engagement through user tagging and feedback mechanisms. Residents can interact with the virtual city to report issues like broken streetlights or litter, with precise geolocation data forwarded to relevant authorities. This system streamlines maintenance workflows and creates a repository of recurring issues, enabling better resource allocation and policy decisions. Beyond problem reporting, citizens actively participate in shaping urban policies by voting on proposed developments and offering suggestions. This participatory model ensures that urban planning aligns with community values and expectations.

Integration with IoT and real-time data further enhances the model's capabilities. IoT sensors continuously update the twin with data on traffic, noise and crowd dynamics, enabling simulations to reflect current conditions. This adaptability makes the DT a living model that evolves alongside the city. For instance, real-time traffic data can guide congestion management during major events, while data from private citizens and businesses enriches the simulation's accuracy and scope. The DT proves invaluable for future event simulations. By modelling scenarios such as increasing a stadium's capacity or managing fire evacuations, planners can anticipate challenges and test solutions. For example, simulating an influx of attendees to the Three Arena provides insights into parking, public transport and emergency response needs, ensuring smoother experiences for both residents and visitors.

Overall, the Dublin Docklands DT demonstrates the transformative potential of data-driven urban planning. Its applications extend across planning, disaster management and community engagement, making it a replicable model for cities worldwide aiming to improve infrastructure, inclusivity and resilience.

Experimental setup

The DT's development relied on open-source tools like Unity3D and SUMO for mobility simulations. Publicly available datasets, including BIM files and data from Dublin's Dublinked portal, were utilised to ensure the model's accuracy and alignment with real-world conditions. Pedestrian mobility models were integrated, with agent-based simulations distinguishing between adult and elderly pedestrians based on movement characteristics from prior studies.

Various simulations were conducted to explore the DT's capabilities. A skyline simulation tested the integration of proposed buildings into the cityscape, evaluating their visual and functional impacts. Citizens were invited to provide feedback on these changes via an online interface. A green space simulation focused on developing parks and other recreational areas, allowing users to propose and vote on features such as seating, gym equipment or children's play areas. Simulations were further extended to include user tagging, enabling citizens to interact with the model to report real-world issues like streetlight malfunctions or potholes. Flooding simulations modelled rising water levels in the River Liffey, identifying at-risk areas and potential evacuation routes. Finally, crowd mobility simulations analysed pedestrian movement patterns, evaluating the effects of urban design elements on different demographic groups.

The DT was made publicly accessible via an online platform, encouraging citizen participation. This setup created a feedback loop where insights from simulations and public input informed urban planning decisions.

Results and impacts

The results of the project demonstrated the DT's significant potential to enhance urban planning, citizen engagement and disaster preparedness. Skyline simulations revealed the model's ability to visually and quantitatively evaluate the impact of proposed buildings. Feedback collected from 30 citizens on a new building proposal showed that 78% approved of the design, while the remainder expressed concerns about height and architectural compatibility. This data provided actionable insights for urban planners, showcasing how public sentiment could influence design revisions. The green space simulations highlighted the importance of community involvement in urban design. Citizen feedback resulted in the inclusion of additional features such as a children's play area, which was not part of the original proposal. The ability to track park usage and engagement through smart city sensors further demonstrated how the DT could monitor the success of implemented changes, ensuring that urban spaces meet evolving community needs.

The flooding simulations had a direct impact on disaster management strategies. The model accurately predicted areas most vulnerable to rising water levels, guiding the placement of defences like sandbags and informing evacuation plans. These simulations also underscored the value of integrating real-time data to refine predictions and optimise responses during emergencies. The mobility and crowd simulations provided valuable insights into how urban infrastructure affects pedestrian behaviour. For instance, elderly pedestrians were found to have longer waiting times due to reduced mobility, suggesting the need for design adjustments such as wider footpaths or smoother gradients. These results can inform the design of more inclusive urban environments. Similarly, crowd simulations during hypothetical events, such as concerts at Dublin's Three Arena, demonstrated how the DT could optimise pedestrian and vehicle traffic flow, reducing congestion and improving safety.

The implementation of user tagging proved effective in identifying and resolving urban issues. Citizens reported problems with precise geolocations, enabling faster response times and better resource allocation by city authorities. Over time, this feature can create a valuable database of recurring issues, guiding long-term infrastructure improvements. In terms of broader impacts, the project fostered transparency and inclusivity in urban planning by enabling public access to the DT. It empowered citizens to participate actively in shaping their city, ensuring that developments aligned with community values and needs. Additionally, the model's adaptability and scalability make it a replicable solution for other cities aiming to implement data-driven, participatory approaches to urban management.

Limitations and challenges

Despite the promising outcomes, the Dublin Docklands DT project faced several limitations and challenges. One major limitation was the incomplete representation of certain areas, such as older buildings and open spaces, which were only depicted as generic grey boxes. Additionally, the model lacked some urban mobility systems, like the city's light rail system, and key details like bus stops and road markings were missing, limiting the scope of certain simulations. The reliance on publicly available and sometimes aggregated data from the Dublinked platform posed challenges in creating highly accurate simulations, as finer-grain data was often needed. Furthermore, the integration of real-time data from IoT devices was still in its early stages, and the model would benefit from more granular, up-to-date information. Lastly, while citizen feedback was valuable, ensuring broad participation and addressing diverse community needs remained a challenge in a large-scale urban setting.

In conclusion, the Dublin Docklands DT project represents a significant step towards transforming urban planning and management through the integration of advanced technologies and citizen engagement. By simulating real-world urban scenarios – ranging from skyline developments to flooding events – the project demonstrated the powerful potential of DTs to enhance decision-making, improve city infrastructure and foster inclusivity. The ability to collect real-time feedback from citizens through interactive simulations and user tagging empowers communities to actively participate in shaping their environment, ensuring that urban development aligns with their needs and preferences. Despite challenges related to data completeness and real-time integration, the project showcases the immense value of DTs in creating more responsive, sustainable and transparent cities. Moving forward, the lessons learned from this initiative will guide future improvements, enabling the DT model to evolve into an even more comprehensive tool for urban innovation and management.

6.6.1.2 Case 2: blockchain technology implementation in healthcare system in Saudi Arabia

Saudi Arabia is spearheading transformative efforts in its healthcare sector by integrating blockchain technology to overcome systemic challenges and fulfil the goals of Vision 2030 [91]. This study highlights the deployment of a multi-layer blockchain framework, eHealth system to manage electronic health records (EHR) effectively which is currently deployed in Al Qassim province. The case study explores the design, applications, experimental approach, outcomes and limitations of the system, drawing inspiration from global practices such as the European Health 2020 framework.

Design and architecture of the blockchain framework

The architecture of the blockchain framework for Saudi Arabia's healthcare system is multi-layered, addressing the need for secure, efficient and interoperable EHRs. integrates several entities, including patients, healthcare providers and research institutions. It is designed to store, manage and share EHRs securely. The system is built on three primary layers: constrained nodes (IoT, sensors, gateways, patients), authorities (hospitals, research institutes and labs) and an EHR storage layer (cloud providers and data banks). The blockchain's decentralised structure ensures data integrity, reduces dependence on third parties and enhances transparency.

Practical applications and benefits

The blockchain framework has introduced transformative changes across multiple domains in the healthcare system:

(i) **Empowering patients**
Patients have control over their health records, allowing selective sharing with healthcare providers for specific durations and purposes.

(ii) **Seamless data exchange and enhanced security**
The system bridges communication gaps between private and public healthcare facilities, eliminating redundant testing and improving efficiency. Blockchain's decentralised and encrypted architecture minimises the risks of unauthorised access and data breaches.

(iii) **Fostering medical research**
Anonymised data from the blockchain serves as a valuable resource for advanced studies in epidemiology, genetics and disease prevention.

(iv) **Optimising resources**
Enhanced data sharing allows for better allocation of medical resources, reducing strain on emergency services and primary care centres. Blockchain technology also reduces operational costs associated with data management and security, benefiting healthcare institutions and patients.

Experimental implementation

The system was initially tested in the Qassim region, leveraging existing IT infrastructures to integrate blockchain capabilities. Key components of the pilot included:

- **Data capture**: Patient information was collected through IoT devices and patient interactions at healthcare facilities. The MIRACL library was used for secure communication in blockchain.

- **Verification**: Digital signatures and cryptographic protocols ensured secure validation of records. Elliptical curve approach was used for cryptography.
- **Storage**: Data was stored on a decentralised blockchain platform, maintaining accuracy and privacy. Health records, medication, images and reports were stored as blockchain data with an index having metadata.
- **User engagement**: Patients utilised secure portals to manage their health records and share information with authorised healthcare providers. Patient identity is kept anonymous using patient virtual blocks.

The system begins with the collection of health data through IoT devices, sensors and healthcare providers. This data is encrypted and stored in blockchain blocks, ensuring security and immutability. Each patient is assigned a unique identifier, linking all their medical data chronologically within the blockchain. Patients have complete control over their data and can set granular permissions to decide who can access, update or view specific records. These permissions are managed using cryptographic keys, adding a layer of privacy and security.

When a patient visits a healthcare provider, new medical information, such as tests, diagnoses and prescriptions, is added to their blockchain record. This data is securely stored in the cloud and synchronised across the network, enabling seamless sharing between authorised healthcare entities like hospitals and research institutions. The system also allows patients to use pseudonyms, protecting their identities when sharing data for research or other purposes. Blockchain's decentralised nature ensures that data integrity is maintained, unauthorised access is prevented and redundancies such as repeated medical tests are eliminated. Notifications are sent to patients whenever updates are made to their records, ensuring transparency and fostering trust in the system. This approach not only enhances the efficiency of healthcare services but also empowers patients by giving them control over their health information.

Results and outcomes

The proposed multi-level blockchain architecture demonstrated its potential to address key issues like interoperability, security and privacy in healthcare data management. The implementation provided seamless access and control over EHRs for patients, empowering them with secure data-sharing capabilities. It also aimed at integrating healthcare providers, patients and research entities under a unified digital infrastructure. The use of blockchain ensured data immutability and security, making it a reliable solution for health data exchange. This system was noted to reduce administrative costs and improve the efficiency of healthcare service delivery.

Challenges and limitations

The healthcare system in Saudi Arabia faces significant challenges in implementing a robust eHealth infrastructure. A major issue is the lack of technical expertise and resistance to adopting advanced health information systems. Data interoperability remains limited, preventing seamless sharing of health records between entities. Security and privacy concerns, alongside cultural barriers, further hinder progress. Financial constraints, especially for smaller facilities, complicate the adoption and maintenance of eHealth systems. Patients in government hospitals have minimal access to their records, and data-sharing mechanisms between institutions are often absent, leading to redundant medical tests and delays. Overcrowding in emergency departments strains resources, necessitating the redirection of cases to primary care centres. These limitations highlight the urgent need for secure, interoperable solutions that enhance patient access, improve data sharing and overcome systemic, technical and cultural barriers for a more efficient healthcare system.

Saudi Arabia's adoption of blockchain technology in healthcare marks a significant step towards addressing longstanding inefficiencies and empowering both patients and providers. By aligning with Vision 2030, the system enhances data security, streamlines operations and improves patient satisfaction. The pilot program in Qassim serves as a foundation for broader implementation, showcasing how advanced technologies can revolutionise public health. Despite the challenges, the framework offers a replicable model for other nations seeking to modernise their healthcare systems. Continued investment in technology, infrastructure and workforce training will be crucial to sustaining progress and achieving the ambitious goals of Vision 2030. This initiative exemplifies the potential of innovation to create a more inclusive, transparent and efficient healthcare landscape.

6.6.1.3 Case 3: transport and traffic management in Singapore

Singapore is a global leader in the adoption of smart city technologies [92]. One of the most notable initiatives is its **Virtual Singapore** project, which uses DTs to simulate urban dynamics in real-time, particularly focusing on transport and traffic management. DTs of the city's infrastructure, roads and transport networks are integrated into a single platform to monitor and predict traffic patterns based on real-time data from IoT sensors embedded throughout the city. This enables authorities to manage traffic flow more effectively and reduce congestion, ultimately improving citizens' quality of life [18]. Blockchain technology enhances this system by providing secure, decentralised data management, which ensures that the massive data collected from sensors, traffic lights and vehicles remains tamper-proof. With the introduction of blockchain, transport data is encrypted and distributed across a decentralised network, ensuring transparency and trust. For example, blockchain can record vehicle maintenance, driving behaviour and traffic violations on a transparent ledger that can be accessed by regulatory bodies without compromising data privacy. This system also facilitates the automation of toll payments and parking fees using smart contracts [25]. Moreover, Singapore has also integrated blockchain to improve vehicle-sharing platforms. This guarantees more secure peer-to-peer transactions, reducing the dependency on intermediaries and thus lowering costs for consumers [93]. Blockchain enables transparent vehicle histories, including maintenance records and usage statistics, which helps users make informed decisions when renting or sharing vehicles.

6.6.1.4 Case 4: energy consumption and resource optimisation in Helsinki

Helsinki, Finland, has made significant strides in leveraging blockchain and DTs to improve energy consumption and resource optimisation. Helsinki's energy infrastructure is one of the most advanced in the world, with a strong focus on sustainability and efficiency. The city uses DT technology to create virtual models of energy grids, public buildings and residential areas, which are connected to real-time data streams from IoT sensors [94]. These DTs provide real-time insights into energy consumption patterns across different sectors of the city. They allow city planners and energy providers to predict energy demands, optimise resource allocation and reduce wastage. For example, DTs can simulate the energy consumption of a new residential area, helping planners decide the most efficient way to distribute resources [95].

Blockchain further enhances this system by offering a secure, decentralised platform for energy transactions. Helsinki has implemented a blockchain-enabled smart grid, allowing consumers to participate in decentralised energy trading. Households and businesses equipped with renewable energy sources, such as solar panels, can use blockchain to sell excess energy to the grid securely and transparently. The transactions are recorded in real-time and automated through smart contracts, ensuring that consumers are fairly compensated for the energy they supply without the need for intermediaries [95]. By integrating blockchain, Helsinki has created a more transparent and efficient energy market, which is essential for the city's sustainability goals. The technology has also enabled dynamic pricing models, where energy costs fluctuate based on real-time demand and supply, incentivising more responsible energy use.

6.6.2 Lessons learned from real-world deployments

Several important lessons have emerged from the successful deployment of blockchain and DTs in these smart city applications:

- **Data integrity and security**: Both Singapore and Helsinki's experiences highlight the critical role that blockchain plays in securing data in DT environments. In these systems, massive amounts of data are continuously generated by IoT devices and used for real-time simulations. Ensuring the integrity and authenticity of this data is crucial for the reliable operation of smart city services. Blockchain's immutable ledger system provides a solution, ensuring that data cannot be tampered with once it is recorded [29].
- **Scalability challenges**: While blockchain is instrumental in providing secure and decentralised data management, its scalability remains a challenge, particularly in environments with high data volumes, such as smart cities. Both Singapore and Helsinki have had to address issues related to transaction speeds and the computing power required to maintain blockchain networks. For instance, traditional blockchains, like Bitcoin, are often too slow to handle the real-time demands of smart city applications. Solutions such as PoS and Layer 2 scaling technologies are being explored to mitigate these challenges [96].

- **Interoperability**: One of the key lessons learned from above case studies is the importance of **interoperability** between blockchain and DT technologies. In smart city, various systems – transportation, energy, waste management, healthcare – must interact seamlessly. Blockchain's ability to provide a common, trusted platform for data exchange is critical in achieving this interoperability. Cities need to establish standardised frameworks for integrating different systems, ensuring that data from diverse sources can be securely shared and analysed.

6.6.3 Potential for scaling and expanding the model

The successful implementation of blockchain and DTs in smart city applications offers immense potential for scaling and expanding these models into other areas of urban management. Several key considerations for scaling these technologies include:

- **Transport and traffic management**: Beyond Singapore's success, other major metropolitan areas, such as London and New York, are exploring the integration of blockchain with DTs to address urban transportation challenges. Blockchain can facilitate cross-border data sharing, allowing cities to coordinate on transportation initiatives, such as smart logistics and autonomous vehicle deployment. As more cities adopt electric vehicles (EVs), blockchain can help standardise EV charging stations and enable decentralised, peer-to-peer energy trading.
- **Healthcare and emergency services**: The potential for scaling blockchain and DTs in healthcare is significant, particularly in cities that aim to improve emergency response times and healthcare infrastructure. DTs can simulate emergency scenarios, while blockchain ensures the secure sharing of sensitive medical data across institutions. For instance, cities like Dubai are implementing blockchain to create decentralised health records, enabling doctors to access patient information securely in real-time during emergencies [94].
- **Environmental monitoring and sustainability**: Cities like Amsterdam are exploring how blockchain and DTs can be used for environmental monitoring and sustainability [97]. DTs can model air quality, water management and waste disposal systems, while blockchain ensures the transparency of sustainability efforts. This model can be scaled to other cities aiming to meet climate goals, allowing them to benchmark their environmental performance and collaborate on global sustainability initiatives [18].
- **Governance and citizen engagement**: Blockchain-enabled governance models, such as those in Estonia, can be expanded to more cities [89]. By combining blockchain with DTs, cities can simulate policy outcomes and engage citizens in decision-making processes. For example, DTs can model the impact of new zoning laws, while blockchain ensures transparent voting and secure public consultations. This approach can be scaled to large, complex urban areas, allowing for more participatory governance [8].

The future of blockchain and DTs in smart cities is promising. As these technologies continue to evolve, cities will be able to scale their smart city initiatives, resulting in more efficient, transparent and sustainable urban environments.

6.7 Proposing a new model

Building upon the insights from the case studies and lessons learned, we propose a new model for a smart city that integrates blockchain and DT technologies into a modular, scalable and citizen-focused framework. This model, as seen in Figure 6.1, not only addresses current technological and operational limitations but also positions smart cities as dynamic, adaptive ecosystems capable of meeting the demands of the future. It is designed to balance technological innovation with inclusivity, sustainability and governance.

6.7.1 Layers of the proposed model

1. **Physical layer**: **urban infrastructure and IoT devices**
   This foundational layer encompasses the city's physical assets, including transportation systems, energy grids, healthcare facilities and environmental monitoring stations. These assets are equipped with IoT devices such as sensors and actuators that collect real-time data.
2. **Digital twin layer**: **virtual representation**
   DTs serve as virtual counterparts to the physical assets, continuously receiving and processing data from the IoT devices. They provide real-time monitoring, simulation and analysis capabilities, enabling city planners and managers to make informed decisions.

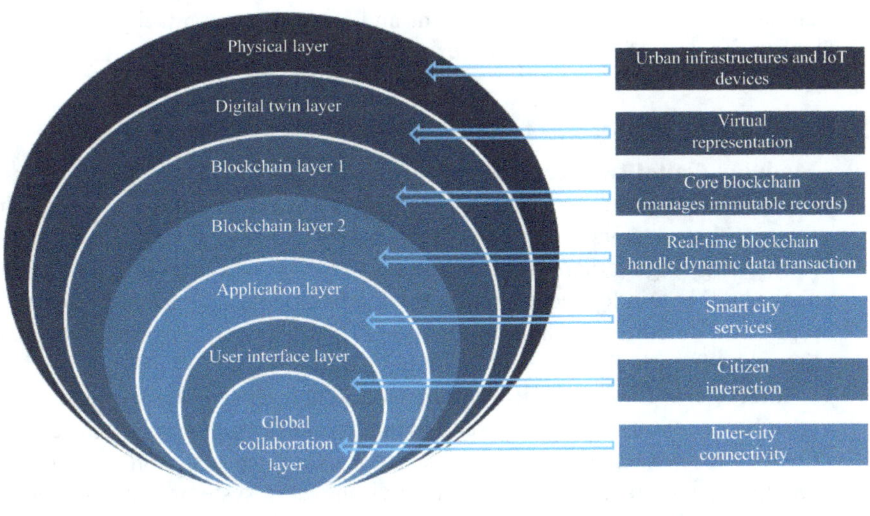

Figure 6.1 Proposed conceptual model of smart city

3. **Blockchain layers: secure data management**
   This layer enables data integrity, security and transparency across the system, and the smart contracts automate processes like toll payments, energy trading and access permissions. This layer is divided into two sub-layers: core blockchain (Layer 1) and real-time blockchain (Layer 2). Core blockchain or Layer 1 manages immutable records such as policy frameworks, regulatory compliance documents and historical data. Whereas the Real-Time blockchain or Layer 2 handles dynamic data transactions, including IoT sensor updates and resource exchanges, ensuring scalability and speed.
4. **Application layer: smart city services**
   This layer extends across multiple domains, including transportation, where it facilitates real-time traffic management, autonomous vehicle coordination and predictive maintenance. In the energy sector, it enables smart grids, peer-to-peer energy trading and optimised consumption. Healthcare benefits from this layer through patient monitoring, emergency response optimisation and secure medical records management. Governance applications include transparent voting systems, citizen engagement platforms and policy simulations. Additionally, in environmental monitoring, it supports resource optimisation, pollution tracking and sustainability assessments.
5. **User interface layer: citizen interaction**
   The user interface layer provides platforms for citizens to interact with smart city services, access personalised data and participate in governance. It emphasises data ownership, privacy controls and decentralised identity (DID) management.
6. **Global collaboration layer: inter-city connectivity**
   This layer facilitates interoperability between different cities' systems through blockchain bridges, allowing for data sharing, collaborative policy development and coordinated responses to regional challenges. Overall, this model emphasises a layered approach, ensuring that each component integrates seamlessly to create a secure, efficient and responsive smart city ecosystem. The key features of the model are explained below.

6.7.2 Key features of the model

(i) **Modular digital twin ecosystem**
   The proposed model introduces a modular architecture for DTs, where different urban sectors – such as transportation, energy, healthcare, waste management, governance and public safety – are represented as interconnected but independent modules. Each module operates as a digital replica of its corresponding urban system, continuously updated with real-time data from IoT sensors and external databases.

   Interoperability and integration: Blockchain ensures secure and interoperable communication between these modules, creating a unified yet flexible ecosystem. For instance, data from the transportation module can seamlessly integrate with energy and environmental systems to support green mobility initiatives, such as EV infrastructure optimisation.

Customisable deployment: Cities can prioritise specific modules based on their most pressing challenges. For instance, a city facing severe traffic congestion might focus initially on the transportation module, whereas one with high energy costs might start with the energy module. Additional modules can be integrated as resources and needs evolve, allowing for incremental scaling.

(ii) **Layered blockchain infrastructure**

To address the scalability challenges of traditional blockchain systems in data-intensive environments, the model employs a layered blockchain architecture:

Layer 1: core blockchain

This foundational layer is responsible for high-value, low-frequency transactions. It provides an immutable ledger for critical data, such as property records, regulatory compliance and legal frameworks.

Layer 2: scalable solutions

Layer 2 solutions, such as state channels, sidechains and rollups, handle high-frequency, real-time transactions like sensor data updates, energy trading and mobility service usage. These solutions reduce the computational load and improve transaction speeds, making the system responsive and efficient.

Cross-chain connectivity

To ensure interoperability with legacy systems and foster collaboration between cities, the model incorporates cross-chain bridges. These enable the exchange of data and services between different blockchain networks, supporting international partnerships, such as cross-border EV charging and collaborative urban sustainability projects.

(iii) **AI-enhanced decision-making**

AI is deeply integrated with the DT ecosystem, providing enhanced analytics, predictive capabilities and real-time decision-making support. For example:

Predictive analytics: AI-powered DTs can forecast traffic congestion, energy demands or public health emergencies, enabling proactive resource allocation.

Transparent AI models: Blockchain is used to record AI training datasets, decision-making processes and outcomes, ensuring transparency, accountability and fairness in AI-driven decisions. This is particularly critical for urban governance, where trust in technology is paramount.

(iv) **Citizen-centric services**

At the heart of the model is a commitment to empowering citizens by placing them in control of their data and fostering direct engagement with smart city systems.

Decentralized identity management: Blockchain-based DID solutions allow citizens to own and manage their personal data. They can selectively grant access to specific information, such as health records, educational qualifications or mobility usage, without compromising privacy.

Participatory governance: Blockchain-backed systems enable secure voting and transparent public consultations, ensuring that citizens have a voice in urban planning decisions. For example, residents can participate in virtual referendums modelled through DTs to explore the impact of proposed zoning laws, infrastructure projects or environmental policies.

Enhanced urban services: Blockchain ensures efficient delivery of public services, such as issuing permits, managing subsidies and providing access to education and healthcare records.

(v) **Decentralised energy and resource networks**

Expanding on Helsinki's blockchain-enabled smart grid, this model envisions decentralised networks for essential resources like electricity, water and internet connectivity.

Peer-to-peer trading: Blockchain smart contracts facilitate automated, secure and transparent transactions between producers and consumers of resources. For instance, households with solar panels can sell excess energy directly to the grid or other consumers without intermediaries, reducing costs and enhancing resource efficiency.

Digital twin optimisation: DTs simulate and optimise these decentralised networks, predicting peak demand periods and suggesting measures to minimise resource wastage.

(vi) **Dynamic policy simulation**

The model allows policymakers to use DTs as experimental platforms for testing the potential outcomes of new regulations or urban interventions. Blockchain ensures the integrity of these simulations by maintaining a tamper-proof record of the parameters and results.

Scenario testing: Cities can simulate various scenarios, such as the introduction of new public transportation routes or carbon taxation policies, to predict their socio-economic and environmental impacts before implementation.

Stakeholder collaboration: By making simulation data accessible through blockchain, cities can engage stakeholders, including businesses, NGOS and citizens, fostering a collaborative approach to urban development.

6.7.3 Benefits of the model

1. **Scalability**

   The modular and layered approach allows cities to expand their smart city initiatives at their own pace, accommodating the growing complexity and data volumes associated with urban environments.

2. **Transparency and trust**

   Blockchain's decentralised and tamper-proof nature ensures data integrity, fostering trust among citizens, businesses and government entities.

3. **Sustainability**

   By promoting resource optimisation and decentralised systems, the model aligns with global sustainability goals, reducing environmental footprints while enhancing urban resilience.

4. **Inclusivity**
   The model prioritises equitable access to services and fosters citizen engagement, ensuring that all demographics benefit from smart city innovations.
5. **Global collaboration**
   The interoperable nature of the model encourages cities to share data, experiences and solutions, paving the way for global networks of smart cities that collaborate on challenges such as climate change, disaster management and public health crises.

6.7.4 Implementation pathway

The implementation of this model requires a phased and collaborative approach to ensure its effectiveness and sustainability. Cities should begin by deploying the model in specific sectors or neighbourhoods through pilot programs, allowing for iterative testing and refinement before scaling up. Public-private partnerships play a crucial role in this process, as collaboration with private tech firms, academia and international organisations is essential for developing, standardising and funding these systems. Additionally, regulatory frameworks must be established by governments to address key concerns such as data privacy, cybersecurity and cross-border collaborations, ensuring the secure and ethical use of blockchain and DT technologies. Equally important is citizen education and engagement, where public awareness campaigns and participatory workshops can help communities understand and embrace these technologies, fostering trust and inclusivity in smart city initiatives. By integrating blockchain and DTs into a holistic, adaptable framework, this new model redefines how cities manage resources, engage citizens and plan for the future, creating smarter, more resilient urban environments.

6.8 Summary and future directions

6.8.1 Recap

This chapter explored the integration of blockchain and DT technologies to empower the development of smart cities, focusing on how these tools offer transformative solutions in urban management and citizen engagement. Some key findings include:

- **Digital twins**: Through high-fidelity virtual simulations, DTs provide real-time insights into city systems, enabling predictive analytics, situational control and data-driven decision-making. By creating virtual replicas of physical infrastructure, cities can optimise resource use, traffic flows and emergency responses [18].
- **Blockchain**: Blockchain enhances security, traceability and transparency across smart city infrastructures. It provides a decentralised ledger for secure data sharing and ensures that sensitive data, such as energy usage, healthcare records or traffic data, remains tamper-proof [50]. Additionally, smart contracts enable automated and trustworthy service management, reducing the need for intermediaries.

- **Integration of blockchain and digital twins**: The integration of these two technologies forms a robust foundation for secure, efficient and resilient urban ecosystems. Blockchain addresses the privacy and data integrity challenges posed by DTs, while DTs enhance the predictive and real-time monitoring capabilities needed for advanced urban management [25].
- **Real-world applications**: Case studies in Singapore and Helsinki demonstrate the power of these technologies in solving critical urban challenges like traffic management and energy consumption. These cities have used blockchain and DTs to decentralise energy markets, optimise transportation networks and secure data flows across municipal systems.

These findings underline the tremendous potential of blockchain-enabled DT cities, showcasing how this integrated approach can lead to efficient municipal operations, improved citizen engagement and sustainable resource management.

6.8.2 The implications for future smart city development

The synergy between blockchain and DTs offers significant implications for future smart city developments, potentially reshaping the way cities are designed, managed and experienced by citizens. Here are some of the major implications:

- **Enhanced decision-making**: The combination of real-time data from DTs and the immutable records from blockchain will allow urban planners and administrators to make more informed, data-driven decisions. Whether in urban mobility or energy management, this will enable cities to dynamically respond to changing conditions and predict future needs.
- **Decentralised governance and civic engagement**: Blockchain's ability to decentralise services will lead to a more inclusive and transparent governance system. Citizens can directly participate in decision-making processes via blockchain-based voting systems and civic engagement platforms, while also maintaining greater control over personal data [50].
- **Security and data sovereignty**: As cities increasingly rely on IoT and big data, ensuring the security of vast datasets is essential. Blockchain provides a secure platform for data exchanges, guaranteeing that data is not altered or accessed without consent. This can be especially relevant in sectors like healthcare and public safety, where data integrity is critical.
- **Scalability and global replication**: The success of blockchain and DT implementations in Singapore and Helsinki points towards their scalability and potential for global adoption. These models can be replicated and customised based on different urban needs, whether in developed metropolises or emerging cities. The use of blockchain ensures that city services can be extended without compromising on efficiency or security, while DTs provide the flexibility needed to model complex urban environments.
- **Sustainability and climate goals**: As cities prioritise sustainability, the integration of blockchain and DTs will play a key role in achieving net-zero goals. By improving energy distribution and resource optimisation through decentralised systems, cities can reduce their environmental impact while maintaining

high service standards. This technology will also be instrumental in monitoring environmental conditions and supporting global climate commitments [94].

6.8.3 Closing remarks and the way forward

The integration of blockchain and DTs in smart cities represents a fundamental shift in urban planning and service delivery. These technologies have the potential to redefine how cities operate by ensuring transparency, security and efficiency. The journey towards a smart city is still in its early stages, and challenges such as interoperability, scalability, and regulatory compliance need to be addressed to achieve widespread adoption.

Looking forward, smart city models will likely evolve to become more decentralised, with blockchain empowering local communities to manage their resources and services. Blockchain-based systems could allow citizens to own and share data responsibly, participate in governance decisions directly and contribute to the sustainable development of their environments. At the same time, DTs will continue to serve as a critical tool for simulating urban scenarios, providing insights into how different policies and innovations might impact city ecosystems.

Future research should focus on:

1. Improving the scalability of blockchain systems to handle large volumes of real-time city data.
2. Establishing standards for DT and blockchain implementations to ensure interoperability across different cities and regions.
3. Addressing privacy concerns and ensuring citizen trust in smart city data systems, especially when sensitive data is involved.

References

[1] UN DESA. Around 2.5 billion more people will be living in cities by 2050, projects new UN report [Internet]. 2018 [cited 2024 Oct 1]. Available from: https://www.un.org/uk/desa/.

[2] IPCC. Climate Change 2022: Impacts, Adaptation and Vulnerability [Internet]. 2022 [cited 2024 Oct 1]. Available from: https://www.ipcc.ch/report/ar6/wg2/.

[3] Paes VDC, Pessoa CHM, Pagliusi RP, *et al.* Analyzing the challenges for future smart and sustainable cities. *Sustainability*. 2023;15(10):7996.

[4] UN DESA. 2018 Revision of World Urbanization Prospects [Internet]. 2018 [cited 2024 Oct 1]. Available from: https://www.un.org/en/desa/2018-revision-world-urbanization-prospects.

[5] Albino V, Berardi U, and Dangelico RM. Smart cities: Definitions, dimensions, performance, and initiatives. *J Urban Technol*. 2015;22(1):3–21.

[6] Mohanty M. Sustainable Urban Planning and Making Sustainable Cities. In: Leal Filho W, Azul AM, Brandli L, Özuyar PG, and Wall T, editors. *Sustainable Cities and Communities* [Internet]. Cham: Springer International

Publishing; 2020 [cited 2025 Feb 12]. p. 1–12. (Encyclopedia of the UN Sustainable Development Goals). Available from: http://link.springer.com/10.1007/978-3-319-71061-7_62-1.

[7] Caragliu A, Del Bo C, and Nijkamp P. Smart cities in Europe. *J Urban Technol*. 2011;18(2):65–82.

[8] Mazzetto S. A review of urban digital twins integration, challenges, and future directions in smart city development. *Sustainability*. 2024;16(19):8337.

[9] Duan Y, Edwards JS, and Dwivedi YK. Artificial intelligence for decision making in the era of big data – evolution, challenges and research agenda. *Int J Inf Manag*. 2019;48:63–71.

[10] Singh AP, and Kulkarni V. Bitcoin – upsides, downsides and bone of contention – a deep dive. *Theor Econ Lett*. 2019;09(05):1383–92.

[11] Tao F, Zhang H, Liu A, and Nee AYC. Digital twin in industry: state-of-the-art. *IEEE Trans Ind Inform*. 2019;15(4):2405–15.

[12] Jakonen O. People-Centric and Inclusive Approach to Planning of Smart Cities. *CSID J Infrastruct Dev* [Internet]. 2023 June 29 [cited 2025 Feb 12];6(1). Available from: https://scholarhub.ui.ac.id/jid/vol6/iss1/9/.

[13] Zheng C, Yuan J, Zhu L, Zhang Y, and Shao Q. From digital to sustainable: A scientometric review of smart city literature between 1990 and 2019. *J Clean Prod*. 2020;258:120689.

[14] UN DESA. Transforming our World: The 2030 Agenda for Sustainable Development [Internet]. 2015[cited 2024 Oct 1]. Available from: https://sdgs.un.org/publications/transforming-our-world-2030-agenda-sustainable-development-17981.

[15] Batty M, Axhausen KW, Giannotti F, *et al*. Smart cities of the future. *Eur Phys J Spec Top*. 2012;214(1):481–518.

[16] Grieves M, and Vickers J. Digital Twin: Mitigating Unpredictable, Undesirable Emergent Behavior in Complex Systems. In: Kahlen FJ, Flumerfelt S, and Alves A, editors. *Transdisciplinary Perspectives on Complex Systems* [Internet]. Cham: Springer International Publishing; 2017 [cited 2025 Feb 12]. p. 85–113. Available from: http://link.springer.com/10.1007/978-3-319-38756-7_4.

[17] Lehtola VV, Koeva M, Elberink SO, *et al*. Digital twin of a city: Review of technology serving city needs. *Int J Appl Earth Obs Geoinform*. 2022;114:102915.

[18] Fuller A, Fan Z, Day C, and Barlow C. Digital twin: Enabling technologies, challenges and open research. *IEEE Access*. 2020;8:108952–71.

[19] Yigitcanlar T, Kamruzzaman Md, Foth M, Sabatini-Marques J, Da Costa E, and Ioppolo G. Can cities become smart without being sustainable? A systematic review of the literature. *Sustain Cities Soc*. 2019;45:348–65.

[20] Ramirez Lopez LJ, and Grijalba Castro AI. Sustainability and resilience in smart city planning: A review. *Sustainability*. 2020;13(1):181.

[21] Mahmoodian M, Shahrivar F, Setunge S, and Mazaheri S. Development of digital twin for intelligent maintenance of civil infrastructure. *Sustainability*. 2022;14(14):8664.

[22] Qi Q, and Tao F. Digital twin and big data towards smart manufacturing and Industry 4.0: 360 degree comparison. *IEEE Access*. 2018;6:3585–93.

[23] Zhang Y, and Wen J. An IoT Electric Business Model Based on the Protocol of Bitcoin. In: *2015 18th International Conference on Intelligence in Next Generation Networks* [Internet]. Paris, France: IEEE; 2015 [cited 2025 Feb 12]. p. 184–91. Available from: http://ieeexplore.ieee.org/document/7073830/.

[24] Bhushan B, Khamparia A, Sagayam KM, Sharma SK, Ahad MA, and Debnath NC. Blockchain for smart cities: A review of architectures, integration trends and future research directions. *Sustain Cities Soc*. 2020;61:102360.

[25] Zhao JL, Fan S, and Yan J. Overview of business innovations and research opportunities in blockchain and introduction to the special issue. *Financ Innov*. 2016;2(1):28.

[26] Swan M. *Blockchain: Blueprint for a New Economy*. 1st ed. Beijing, Cambridge, Farnham, Köln, Sebastopol, Tokyo: O'Reilly; 2015. 1 p.

[27] Miglani A, Kumar N, Chamola V, and Zeadally S. Blockchain for Internet of Energy management: Review, solutions, and challenges. *Comput Commun*. 2020;151:395–418.

[28] Kundu D. Blockchain and trust in a smart city. *Environ Urban ASIA*. 2019;10(1):31–43.

[29] Khan SN, Loukil F, Ghedira-Guegan C, Benkhelifa E, and Bani-Hani A. Blockchain smart contracts: Applications, challenges, and future trends. *Peer-Peer Netw Appl*. 2021;14(5):2901–25.

[30] Shahat E, Hyun CT, and Yeom C. City digital twin potentials: A review and research agenda. *Sustainability*. 2021;13(6):3386.

[31] Negri E, Fumagalli L, and Macchi M. A review of the roles of digital twin in CPS-based production systems. *Procedia Manuf*. 2017;11:939–48.

[32] Rasheed A, San O, and Kvamsdal T. Digital twin: Values, challenges and enablers from a modeling perspective. *IEEE Access*. 2020;8:21980–2012.

[33] Marai OE, Taleb T, and Song J. Roads infrastructure digital twin: A step toward smarter cities realization. *IEEE Netw*. 2021;35(2):136–43.

[34] Ye X, Du J, Han Y, *et al*. Developing human-centered urban digital twins for community infrastructure resilience: A research agenda. *J Plan Lit*. 2023;38(2):187–99.

[35] Agostinelli S, Cumo F, Guidi G, and Tomazzoli C. Cyber-physical systems improving building energy management: Digital twin and artificial intelligence. *Energies*. 2021;14(8):2338.

[36] Cheng R, Hou L, and Xu S. A review of digital twin applications in civil and infrastructure emergency management. *Buildings*. 2023;13(5):1143.

[37] Ariyachandra MRMF, and Wedawatta G. Digital twin smart cities for disaster risk management: A review of evolving concepts. *Sustainability*. 2023;15(15):11910.

[38] Xu H, Berres A, Shao Y, Wang C (Ross), New JR, and Omitaomu OA. Toward a Smart Metaverse City. In: Durbha SS, Sanyal J, Yang L, *et al* (eds.), *Advances in Scalable and Intelligent Geospatial Analytics* [Internet]. 1st ed. Boca Raton: CRC Press; 2023 [cited 2025 Feb 12]. p. 245–57. Available from: https://www.taylorfrancis.com/books/9781003270928/chapters/10.1201/9781003270928-18.

[39] Ham Y, and Kim J. Participatory sensing and digital twin city: Updating virtual city models for enhanced risk-informed decision-making. *J Manag Eng*. 2020;36(3):04020005.

[40] Geroimenko V, editor. *Augmented and Virtual Reality in the Metaverse* [Internet]. Cham: Springer Nature Switzerland; 2024 [cited 2025 Feb 12]. (Springer Series on Cultural Computing). Available from: https://link.springer.com/10.1007/978-3-031-57746-8.

[41] Mylonas G, Kalogeras A, Kalogeras G, Anagnostopoulos C, Alexakos C, and Munoz L. Digital twins from smart manufacturing to smart cities: A survey. *IEEE Access*. 2021;9:143222–49.

[42] Tyagi AK, Tiwari S, and Naithani K. Blockchain, AI, and IoT for Smart Road Traffic Management System. In: Tyagi AK, editor. *Digital Twin and Blockchain for Smart Cities* [Internet]. 1st ed. Wiley; 2024 [cited 2025 Feb 12]. p. 197–214. Available from: https://onlinelibrary.wiley.com/doi/10.1002/9781394303564.ch10.

[43] Fan C, Zhang C, Yahja A, and Mostafavi A. Disaster city digital twin: A vision for integrating artificial and human intelligence for disaster management. *Int J Inf Manag*. 2021;56:102049.

[44] Habib G, Sharma S, Ibrahim S, Ahmad I, Qureshi S, and Ishfaq M. Blockchain technology: Benefits, challenges, applications, and integration of blockchain technology with cloud computing. *Future Internet*. 2022;14(11):341.

[45] Shen C, and Pena-Mora F. Blockchain for cities – a systematic literature review. *IEEE Access*. 2018;6:76787–819.

[46] Komalavalli C, Saxena D, and Laroiya C. Overview of Blockchain Technology Concepts. In: Saravanan Krishnan, Balas VE, Golden Julie E, Harold Robinson Y, Balaji S, and Raghvendra Kumar (eds.), *Handbook of Research on Blockchain Technology* [Internet]. Elsevier; 2020 [cited 2025 Feb 12]. p. 349–71. Available from: https://linkinghub.elsevier.com/retrieve/pii/B9780128198162000149.

[47] Gao W, Hatcher WG, and Yu W. A Survey of Blockchain: Techniques, Applications, and Challenges. In: *2018 27th International Conference on Computer Communication and Networks (ICCCN)* [Internet]. Hangzhou: IEEE; 2018 [cited 2025 Feb 12]. p. 1–11. Available from: https://ieeexplore.ieee.org/document/8487348/.

[48] Leng J, Zhou M, Zhao JL, Huang Y, and Bian Y. Blockchain security: A survey of techniques and research directions. *IEEE Trans Serv Comput*. 2022;15(4):2490–510.

[49] Sun J, Yan J, and Zhang KZK. Blockchain-based sharing services: What blockchain technology can contribute to smart cities. *Financ Innov*. 2016; 2(1):26.

[50] Xie J, Tang H, Huang T, *et al.* A survey of blockchain technology applied to smart cities: Research issues and challenges. *IEEE Commun Surv Tutor.* 2019;21(3):2794–830.

[51] Yue K, Zhang Y, Chen Y, *et al.* A survey of decentralizing applications via blockchain: The 5G and beyond perspective. *IEEE Commun Surv Tutor.* 2021;23(4):2191–217.

[52] Ahmad RW, Salah K, Jayaraman R, Yaqoob I, and Omar M. *Blockchain for waste management in smart cities: A survey* [Internet]. 2021 [cited 2025 Feb 12]. Available from: https://www.techrxiv.org/articles/preprint/Blockchain_for_Waste_Management_in_Smart_Cities_A_Survey/14345534.

[53] Ning X, Ramirez R, and Khuntia J. Blockchain-enabled government efficiency and impartiality: Using blockchain for targeted poverty alleviation in a city in China. *Inf Technol Dev.* 2021;27(3):599–616.

[54] Singh S, Sharma PK, Yoon B, Shojafar M, Cho GH, and Ra IH. Convergence of blockchain and artificial intelligence in IoT network for the sustainable smart city. *Sustain Cities Soc.* 2020;63:102364.

[55] Atzori L, Iera A, and Morabito G. Understanding the Internet of Things: Definition, potentials, and societal role of a fast evolving paradigm. *Ad Hoc Netw.* 2017;56:122–40.

[56] Paiva S, Ahad M, Tripathi G, Feroz N, and Casalino G. Enabling technologies for urban smart mobility: Recent trends, opportunities and challenges. *Sensors.* 2021;21(6):2143.

[57] Riggs W, Vyas V, and Sethi M. Blockchain and distributed autonomous community ecosystems: Opportunities to democratize finance and delivery of transport, housing, urban greening and community infrastructure[Internet]. Mineta Transportation Institute; 2022 July [cited 2024 Oct 10] p. 76. Report No.: 22 -34. Available from: https://scholarworks.sjsu.edu/mti_publications/413/.

[58] Zheng Z, Xie S, Dai H, Chen X, and Wang H. An Overview of Blockchain Technology: Architecture, Consensus, and Future Trends. In: *2017 IEEE International Congress on Big Data (BigData Congress)* [Internet]. Honolulu, HI, USA: IEEE; 2017 [cited 2025 Feb 12]. p. 557–64. Available from: http://ieeexplore.ieee.org/document/8029379/.

[59] Stockburger L, Kokosioulis G, Mukkamala A, Mukkamala RR, and Avital M. Blockchain-enabled decentralized identity management: The case of self-sovereign identity in public transportation. *Blockchain Res Appl.* 2021;2 (2):100014.

[60] Desouza KC, and Flanery TH. Designing, planning, and managing resilient cities: A conceptual framework. *Cities.* 2013;35:89–99.

[61] Tsampoulatidis I, Bechtsis D, and Kompatsiaris I. Moving from e-Gov to we-Gov and beyond: A Blockchain Framework for the Digital Transformation of Cities. In: Komninos N, Kakderi C, editors. *Smart Cities in the Post-Algorithmic Era* [Internet]. Edward Elgar Publishing; 2019 [cited 2025 Feb 12]. Available from: https://china.elgaronline.com/view/edcoll/9781789907049/9781789907049.00016.xml.

[62] Sadri H, Yitmen I, Tagliabue LC, *et al*. Integration of blockchain and digital twins in the smart built environment adopting disruptive technologies – a systematic review. *Sustainability*. 2023;15(4):3713.

[63] Tao F, Zhang Y, Cheng Y, *et al*. Digital twin and blockchain enhanced smart manufacturing service collaboration and management. *J Manuf Syst*. 2022; 62:903–14.

[64] Matei A, and Cocoşatu M. Artificial internet of things, sensor-based digital twin urban computing vision algorithms, and blockchain cloud networks in sustainable smart city Administration. *Sustainability*. 2024;16(16):6749.

[65] Pervez Z, Khan Z, Ghafoor A, and Soomro K. SIGNED: Smart cIty diGital twiN vErifiable Data Framework. *IEEE Access*. 2023;11:29430–46.

[66] Ahmed I, Zhang Y, Jeon G, Lin W, Khosravi MR, and Qi L. A blockchain- and artificial intelligence-enabled smart IoT framework for sustainable city. *Int J Intell Syst*. 2022;37(9):6493–507.

[67] Deng T, Zhang K, and Shen ZJ (Max). A systematic review of a digital twin city: A new pattern of urban governance toward smart cities. *J Manag Sci Eng*. 2021;6(2):125–34.

[68] Khatoon A, Verma P, Southernwood J, Massey B, and Corcoran P. Blockchain in energy efficiency: Potential applications and benefits. *Energies*. 2019;12(17):3317.

[69] Tyagi AK, Kumari S, and Surve T. Integration of Digital Twin and Blockchain for Smart Cities. In: Tyagi AK, editor. *Digital Twin and Blockchain for Smart Cities* [Internet]. 1st ed. Wiley; 2024 [cited 2025 Feb 13]. p. 81–100. Available from: https://onlinelibrary.wiley.com/doi/10.1002/9781394303564.ch5.

[70] Alasbali N, Azzuhri SRB, Salleh RB, *et al.* Rules of smart IoT networks within smart cities towards blockchain standardization. *Mob Inf Syst.* 2022;2022:1–11.

[71] Ishai Y, Kushilevitz E, Ostrovsky R, and Sahai A. Zero-knowledge proofs from secure multiparty computation. *SIAM J Comput*. 2009;39(3):1121–52.

[72] Croman K, Decker C, Eyal I, *et al.* On Scaling Decentralized Blockchains: (A Position Paper). In: Clark J, Meiklejohn S, Ryan PYA, Wallach D, Brenner M, and Rohloff K, editors. *Financial Cryptography and Data Security* [Internet]. Berlin, Heidelberg: Springer Berlin Heidelberg; 2016 [cited 2025 Feb 13]. p. 106–25. (Lecture Notes in Computer Science;vol. 9604). Available from: http://link.springer.com/10.1007/978-3-662-53357-4_8.

[73] Michalik D, Kohl P, and Kummert A. Smart cities and innovations: Addressing user acceptance with virtual reality and digital twin city. *IET Smart Cities*. 2022;4(4):292–307.

[74] Kanawade S, Patil S, Gavhane S, Jagtap NS, and Bhanushali A. Blockchain-Based Secure Digital Twin Framework for Smart Healthy City. In: Tyagi AK, editor. *Digital Twin and Blockchain for Smart Cities* [Internet]. 1st ed. Wiley; 2024 [cited 2025 Feb 13]. p. 135–58. Available from: https://onlinelibrary.wiley.com/doi/10.1002/9781394303564.ch8.

[75] Silva BN, Khan M, Jung C, *et al*. Urban planning and smart city decision management empowered by real-time data processing using big data analytics. *Sensors*. 2018;18(9):2994.

[76] Viale Pereira G, Cunha MA, Lampoltshammer TJ, Parycek P, and Testa MG. Increasing collaboration and participation in smart city governance: A cross-case analysis of smart city initiatives. *Inf Technol Dev*. 2017;23(3):526–53.

[77] Majeed U, Khan LU, Yaqoob I, Kazmi SMA, Salah K, and Hong CS. Blockchain for IoT-based smart cities: Recent advances, requirements, and future challenges. *J Netw Comput Appl*. 2021;181:103007.

[78] Ketu S, and Mishra PK. A contemporary survey on IoT based smart cities: Architecture, applications, and open issues. *Wirel Pers Commun*. 2022;125(3):2319–67.

[79] Nguyen HX, Trestian R, To D, and Tatipamula M. Digital twin for 5G and beyond. *IEEE Commun Mag*. 2021;59(2):10–5.

[80] Yadav AK, Singh K, Amin AH, Almutairi L, Alsenani TR, and Ahmadian A. A comparative study on consensus mechanism with security threats and future scopes: Blockchain. *Comput Commun*. 2023;201:102–15.

[81] Alam KM, and El Saddik A. C2PS: A digital twin architecture reference model for the cloud-based cyber-physical systems. *IEEE Access*. 2017;5:2050–62.

[82] Varshney H, Khan RA, Khan U, and Verma R. Approaches of artificial intelligence and machine learning in smart cities: Critical review. *IOP Conf Ser Mater Sci Eng*. 2021;1022(1):012019.

[83] Capra CF. The smart city and its citizens: Governance and citizen participation in Amsterdam smart city. *Int J E-Plan Res*. 2016;5(1):20–38.

[84] Vempati S. Securing smart cities: A cybersecurity perspective on integrating IoT, AI, and machine learning for digital twin creation. *J Electr Syst*. 2024;20(5s):2817–27.

[85] Kumar S, Verma AK, and Mirza A. Artificial Intelligence-Driven Governance Systems: Smart Cities and Smart Governance. In: *Digital Transformation, Artificial Intelligence and Society* [Internet]. Singapore: Springer Nature Singapore; 2024 [cited 2025 Feb 13]. p. 73–90. (Frontiers of Artificial Intelligence, Ethics and Multidisciplinary Applications). Available from: https://link.springer.com/10.1007/978-981-97-5656-8_5.

[86] Wajid MS, Terashima-Marin H, Najafirad P, Pablos SEC, and Wajid MA. DTwin-TEC: An AI-based TEC district digital twin and emulating security events by leveraging knowledge graph. *J Open Innov Technol Mark Complex*. 2024;10(2):100297.

[87] Chavhan RD, and Sambare DGB. AI-driven traffic management systems in smart cities: A review. *Educ Adm Theory Pract*. 2024 May;30(5):105–16.

[88] Tahmasebinia F, Lin L, Wu S, Kang Y, and Sepasgozar S. Exploring the benefits and limitations of digital twin technology in building energy. *Appl Sci*. 2023;13(15):8814.

[89] Semenzin S, Rozas D, and Hassan S. Blockchain-based application at a governmental level: disruption or illusion? The case of Estonia. *Policy Soc*. 2022;41(3):386–401.

[90] White G, Zink A, Codecá L, and Clarke S. A digital twin smart city for citizen feedback. *Cities*. 2021;110:103064.

[91] Albahli S, Khan RU, and Qamar AM. A blockchain-based architecture for smart healthcare system: A case study of Saudi Arabia. *Adv Sci Technol Eng Syst J.* 2020;5(1):40–7.

[92] Aloupogianni E, Doctor F, Karyotis C, Maniak T, Tang R, and Iqbal R. An AI-Based Digital Twin Framework for Intelligent Traffic Management in Singapore. In: *2024 International Conference on Electrical, Computer and Energy Technologies (ICECET)*. 2024. p. 1–6.

[93] Ben Tolila C, Hovav Y, Danilchenko K, and Daltrophe H. Blockchain-enabled car sharing: Enhancing reliability and vehicle history management. *Eng Rep.* 2025;7(1):e13125.

[94] Mohamed M, and Alosman K. *An IoT-Enabled Framework for Smart City Infrastructure Management* [Internet]. Preprints; 2024 [cited 2025 Feb 12]. Available from: https://www.techrxiv.org/users/747731/articles/719445-an-iot-enabled-framework-for-smart-city-infrastructure-management?commit=14bcc363d241e1edc42c2eb667e6e7dce013f783.

[95] Sayed AN, Bensaali F, Himeur Y, Dimitrakopoulos G, and Varlamis I. Enhancing building sustainability: A digital twin approach to energy efficiency and occupancy monitoring. *Energy Build.* 2025;328:115151.

[96] Hafid A, Hafid AS, and Samih M. Scaling blockchains: A comprehensive survey. *IEEE Access*. 2020;8:125244–125262.

[97] Singh B, and Nayyar A. Exploring Diverse Use Cases of Digital Twins Projecting Digital Transformation: Unlocking Potential, Addressing Challenges and Viable Solutions. In:Sailesh I, Anand N, Anand P, and Naved M (eds.), *Digital Twins for Smart Cities and Villages* [Internet]. Elsevier; 2025 [cited 2025 Feb 20]. p. 631–55. Available from: https://linkinghub.elsevier.com/retrieve/pii/B9780443288845000270.

Chapter 7

Emerging technologies for securing digital twins

Raman Singh[1] *and Bhisham Sharma*[2]

Abstract

A digital twin is a virtual representation of a structure in the real world that emulates both its behaviour and performance in a real-time scenario, based on its characteristics, allowing analysis, monitoring and optimisation. The applications of digital twins have extended to include manufacturing and health care, supply chain and many others, there have now arisen concerns about the security of these digital twins. In this chapter, we discuss vulnerabilities in the architecture of digital twins and the requirement for serious security frameworks concerning sensitive data protection and system integrity. We analyse possible attack vectors such as data breaches, unauthorised access and manipulation of virtual representation and propose a multi-layered security approach. The chapter also explores applications of emerging technologies like blockchain technology, artificial intelligence and quantum computing for securing the digital twin. We discuss research carried out in this domain to industry standards that can also develop secure environments for digital twins. This will allow organisations to amplify cyber resilience and ultimately fully benefit from the technology.

Keywords: Digital twin; cyber security; artificial intelligence; blockchain technology; internet of things; supply chain security; smart city

7.1 Introduction

The digital twin (DT) has been one of the most important innovations during the age of Industry 4.0, and it has the potential to change how industries design, operate and maintain systems and processes. A DT can be considered as a software model of a physical object, which may be any product, system or process, offering interaction with its physical counterpart. This is an innovative technology which enables further integration of data from sensors, simulation and machine learning

[1]School of Computing, Engineering and Physical Sciences, University of the West of Scotland, United Kingdom
[2]Centre for Research Impact and Outcome, Chitkara University Institute of Engineering and Technology, Chitkara University, India

algorithms [1]. That said, this technology can also enable organisations to create valuable insights for making informed decisions through comprehensive analysis.

This concept of a DT initially came from NASA back in the early 2000s to enhance reliability concerning systems on spacecraft. However, these applications have extended beyond the space program and have mushroomed in manufacturing, health, city planning and supply chain management in the modern digital era. For instance, in manufacturing, DTs make it possible to simulate production processes. Therefore, this helps manufacturing companies to locate inefficiencies in the process of production and hence optimise their operations [2]. If there is a digital equivalent of the assembly line, a company can analyse it in advance, without actually making any changes in the corresponding physical environment, hence. Not affecting its productivity or resource usage. Such a proactive strategy not only ensures better efficiency of operations but also saves money and time usually spent when resolving issues through trial and error.

It is also possible to develop patient DTs in healthcare by building from a growing amount of data from wearable devices, medical equipment and electronic health records. Researchers have proposed DT-based Internet of Medical Things (IoMT) simulators, which consist of touch screens, cameras, markers, headsets, surgical instruments and computing devices which assist doctors in training or performing surgeries. This surgical operation platform improved the overall accuracy of surgeries [3]. Researchers also discussed the use of virtual reality, extended reality and mixed reality in various medical devices to enhance their capabilities in healthcare sectors. For example, applications in spinal surgery, 3D printed devices for patient-specific applications, implantable cardiac defibrillators, stroke rehabilitation, remote patient monitoring, robotic surgery, connected inhalers, smart connected contact lenses, hand hygiene monitoring, etc. [4]. Virtual models may allow customised medicine based on virtual testing of the different treatment options using individual features of patients. Healthcare providers will be able to use DTs to predict responses to medicines, monitor chronic conditions, tailor their interventions and improve outcomes of patients, together with a reduction of hospital readmission.

Even urban planners and city managers are embracing this race to create smart cities with DT technology. This could be modelling an urban environment that includes infrastructure, transportation systems and energy usage, through which city officials will be able to parse data for improving resource allocation, enhancing sustainability and creating resilient, adaptive urban landscapes by simulating traffic patterns or other emergency response strategies. To support this understanding, researchers proposed urban digital twin known as DeepLabV3, which is a deep learning integrated model for pixel-level semantic segmentation to support sustainable urban planning [5].

Figure 7.1 shows a typical system architecture of a DT system. We can define a DT system using a three-layer architecture, hardware layer, software layer and middleware. The hardware layer includes physical components of a DT system, for example, Internet of Things (IoT) sensors, network devices like routers, switches, edge servers and actuators. The hardware level also includes devices like computing infrastructure and industrial machines. The software layer is a crucial component of a DT system, which translates captured raw data into business insights using analytics engines. Artificial Intelligence and Machine Learning play

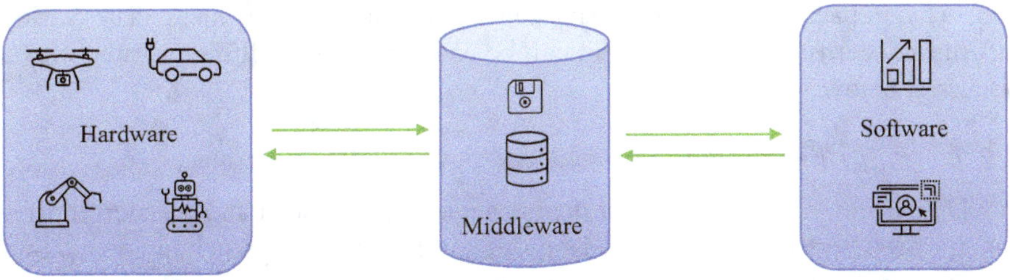

Figure 7.1 System architecture of digital twin technology

an important role in this layer to generate business-critical information. This layer also includes a dashboard and simulation tool. The middleware connects the hardware and the software layers and is used to store data repositories in a centralised manner. This layer also has an important role in various functionalities like connectivity, data processing, data visualisation and data integration.

Admittedly, there are also challenges with DT technology. With the comprehensive application of DT technology, major concerns also arise in the areas of data security and privacy [6]. Since DTs operate a great deal with real-time data interlinked across multiple devices, it invites a wide window of opportunity for cyberattacks and data breaches. Ensuring the integrity and confidentiality of such sensitive information and key compliance with regulatory standards becomes necessary. Moreover, complete transformation with DT technology requires a cultural shift within organisations. More precisely, stakeholders must be open to data-driven decision-making and invest in relevant infrastructures, tools and training. Interdisciplinary collaboration is a crucial fact that, by and large, development and management require cooperation among a range of competencies, from engineers to data scientists and business leaders, all working together to align technology with organisational objectives. One grave concern for a DT system is cyber threats. Such systems are prone to cyberattacks, which can have a serious impact on DT system adoption. These cyber threats are discussed in section 2 of the chapter. Addressing the cybersecurity issues of a DT system will help in expanding this technology's adoption with greater confidence.

The rest of the chapter is organised as follows. We begin by introducing the DT system and discussing the associated cybersecurity challenge. Section 7.2 discusses the security threats in a DT system. Section 7.3 explores the use of Blockchain technology in a DT system, whereas Section 7.44 inspects the role of artificial intelligence in securing the DT systems. Section 7.5 examines how quantum encryption can be used in securing a DT system. Finally, the study is concluded in Section 7.6.

7.2 Security threats in digital twin

The wide variety of applications of the DT system offers numerous benefits, however, the security threats associated with DTs present significant challenges also. The impact of security threats can affect their effectiveness. The various security concerns of the DT system can be categorised into different categories as discussed below.

7.2.1 Data breaches

In a DT system, a large amount of data is acquired, produced and transferred. If an unauthorised person accesses this data, this can lead to data breach incidents. Such data breaches can cause a data leak situation and can compromise the integrity of the system. Figure 7.2 shows a basic data management arrangement in a DT system. Data is acquired at the physical twin side and transferred to the DT for processing. DT processes this data and transmits information back to the physical twin. DT can also be networked with external sources like a secondary data repository, a secondary analytics centre or a command & control centre, mostly situated in distant geographic locations. This architecture of a DT system makes it vulnerable to data breach attacks.

Researchers in one study [6] discussed data breaches and privacy issues of a DT system for the automotive industry. This study focused on presenting ways to make a DT system General Data Protection Regulation (GDPR) compliant. Data security and making a DT system GDPR compliant are crucial to increasing the acceptance of the technology in the industrial ecosystem. A DT system is prone to attacks on data sources, for example, compromising devices by installing rootkits or pushing malicious updates. It is also possible to attack the knowledge base of a DT system by tampering with process knowledge, domain knowledge or historical data. Such a type of attack can contribute to wrong or biased decision-making and can incur huge financial losses [7]. In a DT system, data leakage can occur from the training data of a large language model (LLM). The sensitive data leakage because of an LLM attack can significantly harm a DT system [8]. There is also a significant risk of data breaches during the data lifecycle in a DT system. Data breaches can occur at any layer of a DT system, and researchers emphasise securing the system's full life cycle. Researchers arranged a DT system in four different layers: data dissemination & acquisition layer, data management & synchronisation layer, data modelling & additional services layer and data visualisation & accessibility layer. Layer 1 is used to acquire the data from the physical space. Layer 2 normalises and enriches the acquired data and also prepares the heterogeneous data for further processing. Layer 3 runs a digital model in order to specify states, behaviour

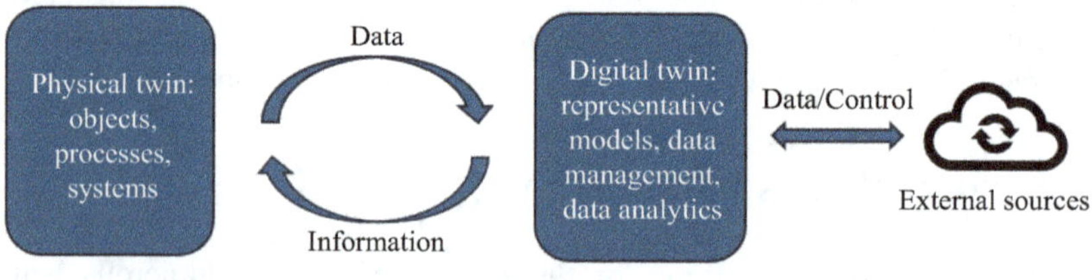

Figure 7.2 Data management in a digital twin system

and geometric shapes. Layer 4, which is the data visualisation layer, consists of supply chain management software, enterprise resource planning and manufacturing execution systems to visualise simulation results from digital models. These four layers make a DT's life cycle [9]. Researchers in one study [10] discussed the various security threats that existed in a DT system, including threats related to data theft. The same study also suggests countermeasures to mitigate the security threats.

7.2.2 Cyberattacks

DT systems are vulnerable to cyberattacks like ransomware, distributed denial of services (DDoS) and data breaches, with the possibility of compromising the integrity of the virtual model. Ransomware is an attack in which a hacker gains access to DT systems and encrypts critical data. This can lead to a system hostage situation, and hackers demand ransom to decrypt the data, hence known as a ransomware attack. In 2021, manufacturing plants like Colonial Pipeline were targeted by ransomware attacks [10,11], and with the growth of DT technology usage, the ransomware threat to such systems also grows. In a DDoS attack, multiple systems (known as zombies) are used to flood a target system, such as servers, with a large volume of traffic. This can overwhelm the server, making it unavailable to legitimate users. It has also been analysed that a DDoS attack can cause more destruction to a DT system and organisation than a malware attack. Organisations with a DT system tend to suffer more damage because of a DDoS attack, but can strengthen their security using a strong firewall [12].

A DT system heavily relies on third-party components and associated software to run those components. Because of this, the DT system can become a victim of cyberattacks like reverse engineering, buffer overflows and manipulations in computing sections. The possibility of such attacks increases manifold if the source codes are made public. On various occasions, DT systems faced attacks like PLC-Blaster worm, Dragonfly, Stuxnet, BlackEnergy, LockerGoga, REvil, etc. PLC Blaster Worm is a threat that targets Programmable Logic Controllers (PLCs) of various cyber-physical systems, such as Supervisory Control and Data Acquisition (SCADA). This worm has the capability to manipulate commands and settings as well as destroy or modify data. Dragonfly attack is a series of cyberattacks from a well-established espionage group that has the capability to infiltrate and disrupt critical infrastructure, for example, the energy sector, manufacturing and utilities. This attack has targeted PowerGrid operators, oil & gas companies and utilities with various attack methods like phishing emails, exploiting software vulnerabilities and remote access tools. The Stuxnet attack is another example of PLC Worm which can threaten critical infrastructure, particularly the nuclear and energy sectors. This worm was first discovered in 2010 and targeted a nuclear program. It can spread through USB drives and network connections. BlackEnergy is a suite of malware which was used to carry out a series of cyberattacks on Ukrainian infrastructure, particularly electricity grids. It is a multi-functional malware suite which can be used for cyber espionage, data theft and service disruption. LockerGoga is a ransomware attack that primarily targets businesses and industrial organisations and has the potential to become highly destructive. This worm can infect a system and encrypt its files, along with displaying a ransom note. This worm primarily targets manufacturing units, energy sectors and utilities. REvil is another ransomware attack which is highly destructive and targets large organisations, corporations and critical infrastructure. This ransomware also supports the ransomware-as-a-service model and other hackers can work on profit share models. This ransomware delivers its payload through various infection vectors such as phishing emails, malicious attachments, remote desktop protocols and virtual private networks. It is also found that REvil is notorious for demanding double extortion: one for decryption and a second for exfiltration of sensitive data [9].

Researchers in one study noted that two common attacks on a DT system are malware attacks and DDoS attacks. A malware attack is a cyberattack carried out using malicious software (malware). A malware attack can be used to steal data, damage a system, compromise a system or disrupt the normal functioning of a server. This attack is typically designed to perform harmful actions, for example, taking control of a system or stealing data, as well as damaging the critical infrastructure. [12] A DT system is also vulnerable to a Man-in-the-middle (MitM) attack, and researchers have demonstrated its impact in the application of remote surgery. In an MitM attack, an attacker intercepts, alters or monitors the communication between two parties without their consent or knowledge. The main goal of this attack is to steal sensitive information, alter data or inject a malicious payload. The various operations performed during this attack include interception, data sniffing, data modification, impersonation, payload injection and relaying. The application involved a real-time remote control over mobile networks and used DTs for surgery. The impact of a MitM attack can be catastrophic in such an application [13]. Rogue devices can also be a greater security concern in a DT system. These rogue or cloned devices can be inserted or replaced physically by an imposter or insider. A rogue device threat refers to a security risk in a DT system that is posed by an unauthorised or compromised device. A hacker can replace an original device with a compromised device. These rogue/cloned devices can lead to various attacks like data leakage, model manipulation, information exfiltration, etc. The data leakage in a DT can be caused by a rogue device because of unauthorised access and data manipulation. If a device is added without proper authentication, the device can gain access to the sensitive data. Model manipulation is also a serious threat from a rogue device attack. This attack can potentially inject manipulated data into a system, which can lead to biased decisions. Information exfiltration is unauthorised data transfer or data theft, which can be caused by a rogue device attack in a DT system [14].

7.2.3 Other security threats

Model manipulation attack for a DT is used to describe a deliberate modification or distortion of the underlying model or data with the intent to confuse, degrade or sabotage the performance of the physical asset or the entire system it represents

[15]. Various examples can be modifying temperature readings, tweaking parameters of analytics algorithms, skewing result outputs etc. Multiple researchers in studies like [15], [16] and [17] have discussed threats to a DT system in terms of model manipulation. In [15], researchers discussed a novel fake traffic injection attack which can compromise a distributed network digital twin (NDT) system. In a fake traffic injection attack, attackers deliberately generate or inject bogus network traffic data into a network or system to achieve different objectives, like disrupting services. Researchers in [16] discussed false injection of sensor data and node capture attacks for a DT system. In a false injection attack, an attacker needs physical access or remote access to the sensor in order to inject false data. For example, in a patient monitoring system, an attacker can capture a sensor remotely or physically and generate false vital information such as blood pressure, temperature, sugar level, etc., which can impact the patient's diagnosis. Node capture is another attack which can be first carried out to inject false data. In the node capture attack, an attacker takes full charge of the key nodes of a DT system. One more threat in a DT system is the intentional adversarial attack, which is discussed by researchers in [17]. This attack refers to a deliberate attempt to manipulate or corrupt the operations of a DT system. This attack can impact the integrity of a DT system and can be carried out by exploiting vulnerabilities.

An insider threat in a DT system is the risk posed by those with authorised access (employees, contractors and partners) who intentionally or unintentionally use their credentials to harm the system. Because DTs are intricately tied to the physical assets they represent, an insider attack can cause real-world damage to the physical infrastructure or less kinetic damage, such as misinformation or disruption. Insider attackers can carry out various attacks like tampering with data by authorised staff, intentional manipulation of data, intellectual property theft, etc. The impact of a cyberattack on a DT system can be far-reaching and significant because, in many cases, a DT system is an integral part of real-time monitoring and part of decision-making processes. Various attacks can increase the downtime of a DT system, making it overwhelming, unavailable or unresponsive. This significant operational downtime can impact industries like manufacturing or services. Cyberattacks can also cause loss of real-time data, leading the system to an inconsistent state or bias in decision-making. A ransomware attack can cause significant financial and reputation loss for an organisation. Industries like manufacturing, energy and healthcare can face safety-related issues because of cyberattacks on their DT systems. A data theft attack can lead to intellectual property loss or cause business closures [9].

7.3 Application of blockchain for securing the digital twins

DTs are at the core of Industry 4.0 and call for appropriate, secure data-sharing models among the interacting parties. Decentralised applications adopt the solution by using distributed ledgers and decentralised databases for storage and processing.

In one research, an owner-centric, decentralised sharing model is proposed. A formal access control model covers integrity and confidentiality. To implement the complex data sharing of a DT system, a fine-grained blockchain-based access control model is proposed. An access control mechanism or model is a framework used to manage the permissions of data access on a computer network or system. It is a model which is used to authorise users' access to specific data and regulate their access. The proposed access control model is coupled with encrypted off-chain data storage. The prototype EtherTwin demonstrates decentralised data sharing in order to handle DT components. The evaluation of an industrial use case and expert interviews shows the validity of the approach [18]. Resource constraints in industrial IoT (IIoT) result in brute-force attacks, forming botnets for DDoS attacks. A brute force attack refers to an attack which can systematically attempt all possible combinations of passwords and encryption keys. For example, if a password is a four-digit number, a brute force attack will try all possible 10,000 combinations (0000 to 9999). A botnet is an essential part of a DDoS attack, which is a compromised device often referred to as a zombie or bot. Because these IIoT devices are small, lack computation power/resources and have less opportunity to have sophisticated cyber countermeasures, attackers can easily attack them to take over control to use them as zombies.

Delayed detection hinders it from stopping malware spread, hence raising the risk of large-scale cyberattacks. In this respect, the research proposes an early bot-detection framework based on Blockchain for Smart Factories. In the proposed system, early bot/zombie detection is encouraged by adding a packet auditor and DT registration steps. A packet auditor is used to detect corrupt data transmission, smart contract authentication and to ensure malicious node exclusion in data transmission. Packet auditors use a random value and a hash to authenticate devices before data transmission. The second step of registration is used to first register the DT before it is used. It registers a DT system and smart contract using digital certificates. In line with this, a DT performs device data monitoring at the edge layer, analyses packet headers with deep learning methods and identifies suspicious connections. Data syncing between the DT and Packet Auditor will prevent corrupt data transmissions. Smart Contracts ensure secure data exchange to avoid the expansion of botnets. In blockchain technology, a smart contract is a self-executing contract in which terms and conditions are mentioned as computer codes, and it gets executed automatically when a certain pre-defined condition is met. This contract runs on a decentralised and distributed ledger blockchain and can be verified by anyone; hence, it does not require any central entity's intervention to enforce. It ensures data integrity for training the bot detection model by ensuring data privacy by inspecting packet headers only [19]. Thus, the integration of DT with IIoT may be said to be developing data analytics by the creation of virtual representations. However, large data generation in IIoT introduces security threats in view of unreliable communication and a lack of trust between users. A framework is proposed for blockchain and Deep Learning [20]. The proposed framework would consist of a new model of DT for simulating the processes in IIoT, blockchain-based data transmission for data integrity and Deep Learning for intrusion detection system (IDS).

LSTMSAE is the proposed DL technique for attack detection with the algorithm MHSA-BiGRU. This framework develops a significant enhancement in the security of communication and data privacy in IIoT. The improvement includes storing the encrypted data on an interplanetary file system (IPFS) based on off-chain storage, which can minimise the communication and computation overhead, enhancing real-time data access speed. A deep learning-based intrusion detection is also integrated, which uses validated data obtained from the blockchain. These improvements ensure data privacy and offer secure data communication [20].

While the features of DT have increased its adoption in several sectors, at the same time they have opened possibilities for security breaches. A blockchain-based two-factor authentication protocol was analysed and proved inefficient [21]. The present schemes proved inefficient because they cannot provide desirable security and fail to protect against offline password-guessing attacks. The reported literature review suggests that many two-factor-based authentication mechanisms cannot support forward secrecy and user anonymity properties. Many of these methods cannot withstand user and server impersonation attacks. For that purpose, a three-factor privacy-preserving authentication scheme was designed for DT environments. The proposed solution has been proven efficient through Burrows–Abadi–Needham (BAN) [22] logic and the Real-or-Random (ROR) [23] model. The BAN model is a formal framework which can be used for analysing the security properties of a security mechanism to validate its applicability and usability. This model was developed in 1989 by Michael Burrows, Martín Abadi and Roger Needham and can be used to prove the correctness of the security of a communication protocol. The benefits of using this model are that it supports clear formalism, simplified reasoning and security verification. Another model, ROR, can also be used to analyse the security of a cryptographic framework. This model works on a game-based approach and can support real-world or random-world scenarios. The ROR model is best suited for security frameworks based on concepts like public-key encryption or digital signatures. The proposed framework provides better security features with a low computation cost and comparable communication cost when compared to the existing schemes [21]. Researchers in one paper propose an Ethereum blockchain-based solution for DTs, presenting performance and cost analyses [24]. A smart contract is designed in the proposed scheme, which ensures secure information management and access control. The implementation will be done on Ethereum and IPFS, storing the stakeholders' details on the storage server. A real-world use-case application about a smartphone production line proves the system's efficiency and safety with low consumption of resources and transaction costs [24]. Applications of unmanned aerial vehicles are increasing in air-ground integrated networks. DT technology integrates cyber-physical networks with virtual models and offers real-time simulation for decision-making. Cyber-physical networks also need security and reliability services. A secure federated aerial learning for an air-ground integrated network is used along with blockchain technology. A layered structure is proposed for integrated networks of DTs, defining construction, communication, aggregation, analysis and operation layers. A real-world case study will be demonstrated to prove this approach's efficacy [25].

Simulations involve a lot of sensitive information, so sharing real-time data must be done securely. A potential leakage to an adversary might lead to serious privacy issues. It is been argued to secure efficient and verifiable data sharing using cloud computing and blockchain [26]. Communication schemes guarantee privacy and security over wireless channels. Security analysis is performed using informal and formal methodologies: BAN logic and automated validation of internet security protocols and applications (AVISPA) [27], among others. BAN logic and AVISPA are software validation tools which are used for formal security analysis of security mechanisms. AVISPA tool can help automatically validate the security of a protocol or a system by checking against various attacks such as MiTM and DDoS. Various features of this tool include automated verification, comprehensive attack modelling, scalability and formal verification support. Thus, the proposed protocol fits DT environments, which have been elaborated and compared to related protocols [26]. Proposal for the blockchain-based creation of decentralised transactions ensures secure traceability, accessibility and immutability utilising smart contracts. Researchers utilise the IPFS for decentralised storage. Details on system design, implementation, security analysis, cost analysis and availability of smart contract code [28]. The research concentrates on enhancing the security of the Internet of Vehicles (IoV) with the help of blockchain technology. In the IoV concept, vehicles are connected to the Internet, each other and also to roadside infrastructures like smart traffic management systems, traffic lights, etc. Design an IoV DTs model comprising big data, DTs, a Wasserstein distance-based generative adversarial network (WaGAN) and a Group Authentication and Privacy-preserving scheme. To secure communication in IoV, a secure communication architecture is proposed using blockchain data with WaGAN for risk forecasting. A Group Authentication and Privacy-preserving scheme is proposed to handle network congestion. A huge number of in-vehicle devices can connect to IoV simultaneously to a base station, and hence can result in network channel congestion. Therefore, a group authentication and privacy-preserving scheme can help reduce network congestion. In conclusion, Blockchain used in IoV will further improve the accuracy and efficiency of intelligent transportation driven by DTs [29].

Researchers have also proposed an integrated blockchain-based framework with Cloud storage for secure big digital twin data (BDTD) sharing [30]. In this architecture, all the data will be encrypted and stored in the Cloud, and the hash and transaction records will be kept in the blockchain. A hash is a fixed-length string of characters which is generated by a mathematical function known as a hash function. This hash code is irreversible, which helps in maintaining the integrity and immutability of a blockchain. A transaction record is a record of all the transactions of a particular batch, which stores important information such as the addresses of the sender & receiver, the amount of the transaction, the timestamp, the transaction hash and the transaction fee. Each transaction is verified by miners before being added to the blockchain, and transaction records provide a transparent history of all transfers in a blockchain network. In addition, new block generation rules enhance the speed of processing. Finally, an algorithm for choosing the optimal sampling rate aims at the maximum selection of social benefits. Simulation and evaluation of a prototype system prove to improve the feasibility and security of BDTD sharing [30]. Researchers proposed a scheme named BPDATA (abbreviation for Blockchain-based Privacy-preserving Authentication scheme for Digital Twin for Aviation) that enables the sharing of data over the cloud in a secure manner, and the integrity of the data is guaranteed with blockchain. The resistance to attacks comes through BAN logic and security analysis. The proposed BPDATA mechanism has a lower computation cost and a lower communication cost, hence providing an effective counter to the attacks on stolen devices, anonymity and un-traceability. BPDATA seems efficient in aerospace industry applications, as proved by Raspberry Pi testing [31]. Researchers have also proposed an improved blockchain-based trust mechanism, proof of authority (PoA), to provide better security with improved data privacy for IIoT applications [32]. Besides, DPRG was proposed for the creation of a genesis block creation and PoA-based master nodes can improve data security with reduced energy consumption in simulation. One researcher made use of blockchain and Web3 for data sharing on a tamper-proof platform while protecting intellectual property rights using non-fungible tokens (NFTs) and decentralised autonomous organisations (DAOs). AN NFT is a unique way of certification and authenticity of ownership of a particular item or content with digital identifiers. NFTs are recorded on a blockchain, which makes them tamper-proof and verifiable. NFTS can be used to prove the ownership of items such as games, arts, collectables, real estate, music, videos and domain names. A DAO is an example of an organisation that uses blockchain technology to manage itself without a central authority. A DAO, in simple terms, is a governance system developed to decentralise the decision-making, management and entity ownership different from traditional organisations. A DAO is a decentralised, automated, transparent and inclusive organisation. Other areas the study seeks to develop further are idea ownership and decentralised governance, besides testing other solutions such as federated learning and fundraising tools. In addition, this work uses methodologies like the random oracle model and BAN logic to check the DT projects regarding security issues, opening the door to further enhancements [33]. In this research, the cross-domain authentication protocol in IIoT relies on blockchain-maintaining domain accumulators for less overhead. The proposed protocol efficiently validates the identity of devices, with much better results than other protocols, showing a gain in computation cost efficiency and communication cost efficiency, respectively [34].

7.4 Application of artificial intelligence for securing the digital twins

Industry 4.0 is all about managing the data and automation of tasks with the help of AI. A DT is an obvious representative of a cyber-physical system. It works on key technologies like edge, fog and 5G by integrating physical processes with computing and networks. In each technology domain, AI is playing a very important role, especially in the prediction of robotic arm movement, experimentally validated with real data [35]. In this paper, the introduction of an enhanced DT framework empowered by AI has been proposed to enhance the 6G IoV network security and efficiency. This includes advanced feature engineering using stacked sparse autoencoders (SSAE) and Feature Selection. An SSAE is a neural network type used in unsupervised learning. It is a combination of many autoencoders arranged in a stacked manner with sparsity constraints applied to each layer of a neural network. The SSAE method is widely used in many techniques such as feature selection, dimensionality reduction and deep learning network training. Autoencoder consists of an encoder and decoder and is a type of artificial neural network which is used to efficiently perform the dimensionality reduction of a dataset. Feature selection is a pre-processing step in a machine learning technique in which relevant features are selected out of all available features. The main aim is to reduce the number of features by removing the irrelevant and redundant features while keeping the most important ones that contribute to the decision-making. Online learning has been performed for the exact attack detection. This can detect attacks with a success rate of 98%. It decreases system latency by 12%, energy consumption by 15%, RAM usage by 20% and enhances packet delivery rates by 6.1%. This would increase the robustness and responsiveness of 6G IoV systems [36]. The automatic network guardian for electrical systems (ANGEL) DT for cyber-physical system security introduces state-of-the-art critical and non-critical infrastructure security through the implementation of DT technology [37], which is usually found in aviation, manufacturing and automotive. This architecture uses the DT model to enhance microgrids' security by applying real-time physics-based simulations that provide constant monitoring and control. ANGEL DT can model both the cyber and physical layers of the microgrid in an integrated environment with real-time data visualisation. The integration hence allowed the evaluation of the status and behaviour of the physical plant under a variety of conditions. It may be helpful for system diagnosis and healing to reduce failures and cyberattacks [38]. One research study investigates the security challenges of distributed network DT systems that affect the reliability of network applications such as wireless traffic forecasting [15], It focuses on weak attackers where limited knowledge about the victim network is required, and even without access to the network data, they can interact with the server-level model. Accordingly, a kind of fake traffic injection attack against the distributed NDT system is proposed, and a defence mechanism called global–local inconsistency detection is brought about. Various experiments with real-world data show that the effectiveness of both the attack and defence strategy calls for a need to incorporate security mechanisms while designing DTs in 5G networks [15]. The aim of the paper is the security of critical infrastructures against physical and digital kinds of threats, especially the vulnerabilities made by PLCs and SCADA systems. SCADA is an industrial control system which is used to monitor, control and optimise industrial processes and infrastructure. This system is widely used in various industries, for example manufacturing sector, the energy sector, water treatment, telecommunication, mining, the oil & gas sector and environmental monitoring. SCADA is capable of performing various functions such as monitoring, control, data logging, alarm handling and reporting. It discloses digital doubles for the possible ways of enhancing such kinds of security due to the application of AI algorithms in the detection and remediation processes of safety attacks like DoS, injection and data tampering. It efficiently classifies data in critical infrastructure based on DTs. For the efficient and effective detection of network traffic in order to identify intrusions, an AI model has been deployed on intrusion detection systems [39].

7.5 Application of quantum encryption for securing the digital twins

The integrated quantum-enhanced blockchain and DT architecture will ensure the health data concerning the integrity and confidentiality of medical records. The proposed architecture will use the concepts of quantum computing, quantum key distribution (QKD) protocols and lattice-based cryptography to offer protection against quantum attacks. In the DT Framework, encryption and access control are used for protecting patient data, which includes but is not limited to the healthcare encryption algorithm. These steps are outlined by the quantum-enhanced blockchain and digital twin integration process for the integration between quantum-enhanced blockchain and DT for secure management against cyberattacks, scalable in the field of medical records [37]. The application of DTs is of paramount importance in the healthcare sector as a means of digital transformation. They consider digitising both individual patient data and treatment schedules. Due to the nature of the data, diagnosis can be improved by helping physicians in their prescribed line of treatment. Data bears much significance in a DT, arising from both physical and virtual sources. In the medical context, securing records is a big challenge. The encryption of medical records prevents retrieval. Therefore, this requires a cloud-based solution using post-quantum searchable encryption through physical unclonable functions (PUFs). A PUF is a cryptographic function that can generate a unique identifier for a device. This is a hardware-based security feature and is used during the manufacturing process of a device. PUF considers microscopic variations in the semiconductor fabrication process and creates a unique identifier for each device. This unique identifier is used to identify the device to distinguish between a real and a cloned device. In this way, indeed, DTs, integrated with cloud encryption, blockchain verification and cloud retrieval, may well play a significant role in transforming health care into an impenetrably safe and ultra-efficient system [40]. Polarisation-encoded QKD has secure keys, but commercial devices have insufficient precision to allow the final key exchange rate (KER). QKD is a secure communication method of cryptographic key distribution/ exchange using quantum physics. QKD is different from the traditional key distribution method and is considered to be more secure. Eavesdropping and environmental events provide a larger quantum bit error rate (qBER) and reduced KER. a DT for polarisation-encoded QKD (named DARIUS) is proposed to serve as the DT of QKD systems for addressing component imperfections, distinguishing eavesdropping from qBER and compensating dynamically for environmental events [41]. A qBER is a parameter which is used to measure the performance of a frequency-coded QKD system. It is a metric to measure the proportion of quantum bits (qbits) received incorrectly during the transmission and is calculated as a ratio of wrongly received bits to the total number of detected bits. KER is another metric used to measure the speed at which a secure cryptographic key is generated and exchanged with shared parties using quantum principles. It measures the speed of a successfully established key per unit of time and is usually expressed in bits per second. Cloud computing of IIoT provides computation and storage services. In addition, because of separate trust domains, the confidentiality of DT data should be well protected. The access is managed based on public key encryption, while traditional methods face searching and sharing encrypted DT data in application scenarios, a proxy re-encryption scheme with plaintext checkable encryption for data access control (PRE-IBSC-PCE) is proposed to solve all issues of supply chains in terms of privacy, integrity and efficiency for the applications of DT in IIoT [42].

7.6 Conclusions and future research directions

The DT is a software model which closely resembles its physical counterpart-object, system or process, and mimics the real-world characteristics of the latter in real time to monitor and optimise performance. They leverage sensor and IoT data. DTs are of considerable importance in questions of security, given their potential control over critical infrastructures, energy grids and transportation systems serious compromise would be extremely dangerous. In this chapter, we discussed security issues in a DT system, architecture, data management and various security threats associated with DT technology. This chapter also discussed the use of blockchain technology in securing the DT technology. Various researchers have used blockchain technology to enhance its security in terms of data security, data integrity and authentication. Artificial Intelligence has also proven its application in securing the DT systems, which is also discussed in this chapter. Finally, the application of quantum computing in the digital system has also been explored.

Future research directions

DT is an evolving technology and is gaining momentum in various applications, as discussed in this article. The article discussed various technologies used for securing a DT system, however, as the usability of a DT system expands, security aspects should also be explored accordingly. Based on this study, various future research directions are listed here as a guide to prospective future research, as given below:

- **Shifting to quantum cryptography**: Quantum computers are slowly becoming a reality and have started taking shape now. It is feared that classical encryption techniques will become obsolete within one decade. NIST has recommended a few quantum encryption algorithms which need to be tested for DT systems, also for their applicability. More quantum encryption algorithms specific to DT systems are required.
- **Integration of quantum computing and blockchain technology**: Blockchain technology has been used in securing a DT system, however, blockchain technology in itself uses hashing and encryption, which need to be replaced by

quantum computing-based encryption. There is a need for the development and testing of Quantum encryption-based blockchain technology for DT systems.

- **Edge security**: DT system uses on-premises servers, cloud infrastructure and is often distributed across edge devices. Securing these layers is essential for holistic DT security. There is a requirement for the development of lightweight security protocols for the security of edge devices, considering their integration with other layers such as cloud computers, on-premises servers, etc. Also, edge computing security is a challenging task because of its decentralisation nature.
- **Edge AI/tiny machine learning**: Machine Learning and Deep Learning are among the most popular technologies used in DT systems for intrusion detection. Because of the resource-constrained nature of edge devices of a DT system, traditional machine learning/ deep learning algorithms face challenges like overheads, slow learning and delayed response. There is a requirement for the development of lightweight machine learning algorithms known as Edge AI and Tiny Machine Learning (TinyML).
- **Zero trust architecture**: More research is required in developing zero-trust architecture-based security frameworks for DT systems. In a zero-trust security architecture, each access request is authenticated and verified rather than authenticated once to allow full access. Integration of multiple devices makes it difficult to develop a zero-trust security architecture for a DT system.
- **Cross-domain security**: The DT system often consists of various components such as multiple platforms, devices and technologies with lots of interoperability. Many times, these multiple components are controlled by different entities and run on different technologies. They can also have different security frameworks. All these characteristics make a DT system a challenging task to provide holistic security. More research is required to propose a security framework that can support cross-domain security for DT systems.
- **Regulatory compliance**: Applications of a DT system include healthcare, manufacturing, defence and aviation. These sectors are government-regulated and should comply with government/industry regulations, including the GDPR). There is a need for standardisation in security policies and a need for more research on how to make such DT systems compliant with government regulations/ policies. The development of automated audit tools is also a need of the hour.

References

[1] VanDerHorn, E., and Mahadevan, S., Digital twin: Generalization, characterization and implementation. *Decision Support Systems*. 2021; 145:113524.

[2] Sharma, A., Kosasih, E., Zhang, J., Brintrup, A., and Calinescu, A., Digital twins: State of the art theory and practice, challenges, and open research questions. *Journal of Industrial Information Integration*. 2022;30:100383.

[3] Tai, Y., Zhang, L., Li, Q., *et al.*, Digital-twin-enabled IoMT system for surgical simulation using rAC-GAN. *IEEE Internet of Things Journal*. 2022; 9(21):20918–20931.

[4] Rowan, N.J., Digital technologies to unlock safe and sustainable opportunities for medical device and healthcare sectors with a focus on the combined use of digital twin and extended reality applications: A review. *Science of the Total Environment*. 2024;926:171672.

[5] Luo, J., Liu, P., Xu, W., Zhao, T., and Biljecki, F., A perception-powered urban digital twin to support human-centered urban planning and sustainable city development. *Cities*. 2025;156:105473.

[6] Damjanovic-Behrendt V., A digital twin-based privacy enhancement mechanism for the automotive industry. In *2018 International Conference on Intelligent Systems (IS)*, 2018 (pp. 272–279). IEEE.

[7] Suhail S., Iqbal M., Hussain R., and Jurdak R., ENIGMA: An explainable digital twin security solution for cyber-physical systems. *Computers in Industry*. 2023;151:103961.

[8] Carlini N., Tramer F., Wallace E., *et al.*, Extracting training data from large language models. In *30th USENIX Security Symposium (USENIX Security 21),* 2021 (pp. 2633–2650).

[9] Alcaraz C., and Lopez J., Digital twin: A comprehensive survey of security threats. *IEEE Communications Surveys & Tutorials*. 2022;24(3): 1475–1503.

[10] Karaarslan E., and Babiker M., Digital twin security threats and countermeasures: An introduction. In *2021 International Conference on Information Security and Cryptology (ISCTURKEY)*, 2021 (pp. 7–11). IEEE.

[11] Easterly, J. and Fanning, T. (2023). The attack on colonial pipeline: What we've learned & what we've done over the past two years. [online] Cybersecurity and Infrastructure Security Agency. Available at: https://www.cisa.gov/news-events/news/attack-colonial-pipeline-what-weve-learned-what-weve-done-over-past-two-years. Last accessed on: 04 Jan 2024.

[12] Mustofa, R., Rafiquzzaman, M., and Hossain, N.U.I., Analyzing the impact of cyber-attacks on the performance of digital twin-based industrial organizations. *Journal of Industrial Information Integration*. 2024;41:100633.

[13] Laaki H., Miche Y., and Tammi K., Prototyping a digital twin for real time remote control over mobile networks: Application of remote surgery. *IEEE Access*. 2019;7:20325–20336.

[14] Biham E., Bitan S., Carmel A., Dankner A., Malin U., and Wool A., *Rogue7: Rogue Engineering-Station Attacks on s7 Simatic PLCs*. Black Hat USA. 2019. Available at: https://ee.tau.ac.il/sites/engineering.tau.ac.il/files/media_server/Engineering/Elect/us-19-Bitan-Rogue7-Rogue-Engineering-Station-Attacks-On-S7-Simatic-PLCs-wp.pdf.

[15] Zhang, Z., Fang, M., Chen, M., Li, G., Lin, X., and Liu, Y., Securing distributed network digital twin systems against model poisoning attacks. *IEEE Internet of Things Journal*. 2024;11(21):34312–34324.

[16] Shaikh E., Mohammad N., Al-Ali A., and Muhammad S., A probabilistic model checking (PMC) approach to solve security issues in digital twin (DT). In *2023 International Conference on Intelligent Data Communication Technologies and Internet of Things (IDCIoT)*, 2023 (pp. 192–197). IEEE.

[17] Zhou Y., Ge Y., and Jia L., Double robust federated digital twin modeling in smart grid. *IEEE Internet of Things Journal*. 2024;11(24):39913–39931.

[18] Putz B., Dietz M., Empl P., and Pernul G., Ethertwin: Blockchain-based secure digital twin information management. *Information Processing & Management*. 2021;58(1):102425.

[19] Salim M.M., Comivi A.K., Nurbek T., Park H., and Park J.H., A blockchain-enabled secure digital twin framework for early botnet detection in IIoT environment. *Sensors*. 2022;22(16):6133.

[20] Kumar P., Kumar R., Kumar A., Franklin A.A., Garg S., and Singh S., Blockchain and deep learning for secure communication in digital twin empowered industrial IoT network. *IEEE Transactions on Network Science and Engineering*. 2022;10(5):2802–2813.

[21] Thakur G., Kumar P., Jangirala S., Das A.K., and Park Y., An effective privacy-preserving blockchain-assisted security protocol for cloud-based digital twin environment. *IEEE Access*. 2023;11:26877–26892.

[22] Monniaux, D., Analysis of cryptographic protocols using logics of belief: An overview. *Journal of Telecommunications and Information Technology*. 2002;(4):57–67.

[23] Srinivas, J., Das, A.K., Kumar, N., and Rodrigues, J.J., TCALAS: Temporal credential-based anonymous lightweight authentication scheme for Internet of drones environment. *IEEE Transactions on Vehicular Technology*. 2019; 68(7):6903–6916.

[24] Onwubiko A., Singh R., Awan S., Pervez Z., and Ramzan N., Enabling trust and security in digital twin management: A blockchain-based approach with ethereum and ipfs. *Sensors*. 2023;23(14):6641.

[25] Dai M., Wang T., Li Y., Wu Y., Qian L., and Su Z., Digital twin envisioned secure air-ground integrated networks: A blockchain-based approach. *IEEE Internet of Things Magazine*. 2022;5(1):96–103.

[26] Son S., Kwon D., Lee J., Yu S., Jho N.S., and Park Y., On the design of a privacy-preserving communication scheme for cloud-based digital twin environments using blockchain. *IEEE Access*. 2022;10:75365–75375.

[27] Armando, A., Basin, D., Boichut, Y., *et al.*, The AVISPA tool for the automated validation of internet security protocols and applications. In *Computer Aided Verification: Proceedings of the 17th International Conference, CAV 2005*, Edinburgh, Scotland, UK, July 2005. (pp. 281–285). Springer Berlin Heidelberg.

[28] Hasan H.R., Salah K., Jayaraman R., *et al.*, A blockchain-based approach for the creation of digital twins. *IEEE Access*. 2020;8:34113–341326.

[29] Liu J., Zhang L., Li C., Bai J., Lv H., and Lv Z., Blockchain-based secure communication of intelligent transportation digital twins system. *IEEE*

Transactions on Intelligent Transportation Systems. 2022;23(11):22630–22640.

[30] Shen W., Hu T., Zhang C., and Ma S., Secure sharing of big digital twin data for smart manufacturing based on blockchain. *Journal of Manufacturing Systems*. 2021;61:338–350.

[31] Aggarwal P., Narwal B., Purohit S., and Mohapatra A.K., BPADTA: Blockchain-based privacy-preserving authentication scheme for digital twin empowered aerospace industry. *Computers and Electrical Engineering*. 2023;111:108889.

[32] Sasikumar A., Vairavasundaram S., Kotecha K., *et al.*, Blockchain-based trust mechanism for digital twin empowered Industrial Internet of Things. *Future Generation Computer Systems*. 2023;141:16–27.

[33] Bamakan S.M., and Far S.B., Distributed and trustworthy Digital Twin platform based on blockchain and Web3 technologies. *Cyber Security and Applications*. 2024;3:100064.

[34] Mahmood K., Shamshad S., Saleem M.A., *et al.*, Blockchain and PUF-based secure key establishment protocol for cross-domain digital twins in industrial Internet of Things architecture. *Journal of Advanced Research*. 2024;62: 155–163.

[35] Groshev M., Guimarães C., Martín-Pérez J., and de la Oliva A., Toward intelligent cyber-physical systems: Digital twin meets artificial intelligence. *IEEE Communications Magazine*. 2021;59(8):14–20.

[36] Yigit Y., Maglaras L., Buchanan W.J., Canberk B., Shin H., and Duong T. Q., AI-enhanced digital twin framework for cyber-resilient 6G internet-of-vehicles networks. *IEEE Internet of Things Journal*. 2024;11(22):36168–36181.

[37] Danilczyk W., Sun Y., and He H., Angel: An Intelligent Digital Twin Framework for Microgrid Security. In *2019 North American Power Symposium (NAPS)* 2019 (pp. 1–6). IEEE.

[38] Patel T., Jadav N.K., Rathod T., Tanwar S., Garg D., and Shahinzadeh H., AI-Based Secure Intrusion Detection Framework for Digital Twin-Enabled Critical Infrastructure. In *2023 14th International Conference on Information and Knowledge Technology (IKT)* 2023 Dec (pp. 24–29). IEEE.

[39] Bose R., Sutradhar S., and Roy S., Quantum-Enhanced Blockchain and Digital Twin Integration for Enhanced Healthcare Data Security. Preprint available at Research Square, https://doi.org/10.21203/rs.3.rs-4707183/v1.

[40] Yi H. Improving cloud storage and privacy security for digital twin based medical records. *Journal of Cloud Computing*. 2023;12(1):151.

[41] Ahmadian M., Ruiz M., Comellas J., and Velasco L., DARIUS: A digital twin to improve the performance of quantum key distribution. *Journal of Lightwave Technology*. 2024;42(5):1356–1367.

[42] Hadabi A., Qu Z., Elhabob R., *et al.*, Proxy re-encryption with plaintext checkable encryption for integrating digital twins into IIoT. *Computers and Electrical Engineering*. 2024;116:109164.

Chapter 8

Digital twin technology in Industry 4.0: revolutionising quality control in intelligent manufacturing

Tahir Mahmood[1]

Abstract

This chapter addresses the essential role of digital twin (DT) technology in improving intelligent manufacturing systems (IMS) as part of Industry 4.0. As businesses evolve towards highly adaptive, efficient and autonomous production environments, DT offers real-time communication between physical assets and their digital equivalents, fostering a dynamic interchange of data that promotes decision-making and operational efficiency. IMS uses disruptive technologies such as the Internet of Things, artificial intelligence and cloud computing to promote innovations that meet shifting demands and retain system flexibility. The chapter introduces a systematic five-layer framework for DT implementation, including important components such as digital models, shadows and twins, which permit complex data integration together. By integrating DT into quality control, manufacturing operations can proactively resolve quality concerns, monitor system health and optimise production cycles. The DT-based predictive methodology replaces traditional reactive quality assurance approaches, allowing for real-time problem diagnosis, predictive maintenance and increased uniformity in product standards. Moreover, the chapter illustrates how DT-driven quality control may increase supply chain integrity, reduce downtime and extend asset lifespan, thereby supporting sustainability goals and regulatory compliance. As manufacturing ecosystems grow increasingly, networked DT technology stands as a revolutionary force, integrating production techniques with the ideals of Industry 4.0. Through a deep assessment of DT applications and practical guidance, this chapter gives insights into implementing DT to boost modern production systems' resilience, intelligence and adaptability.

Keywords: Control chart; digital twin; Industry 4.0; intelligent manufacturing; quality control; statistical process control

[1]School of Computing, Engineering and Physical Sciences, University of the West of Scotland, United Kingdom

8.1 Introduction

Intelligent manufacturing systems (IMS) embodies a revolutionary production methodology driven by the amalgamation of disruptive technologies and is consistent with the principles of Industry 4.0 [1]. These systems seek to establish highly adaptable, efficient and autonomous production environments that adjust dynamically to fluctuations in demand, resource availability and operational conditions. The concept of IMS is depicted in Figure 8.1. This shows that the growth of IMS is directly tied to the rapid advancements and adoption of disruptive technologies during the past twenty years. As we transition into Industry 4.0, the convergence of technologies such as the Internet of Things (IoT), cloud computing, artificial intelligence (AI), blockchain and advanced robots is revolutionising how industrial processes are designed, operated and optimised [2].

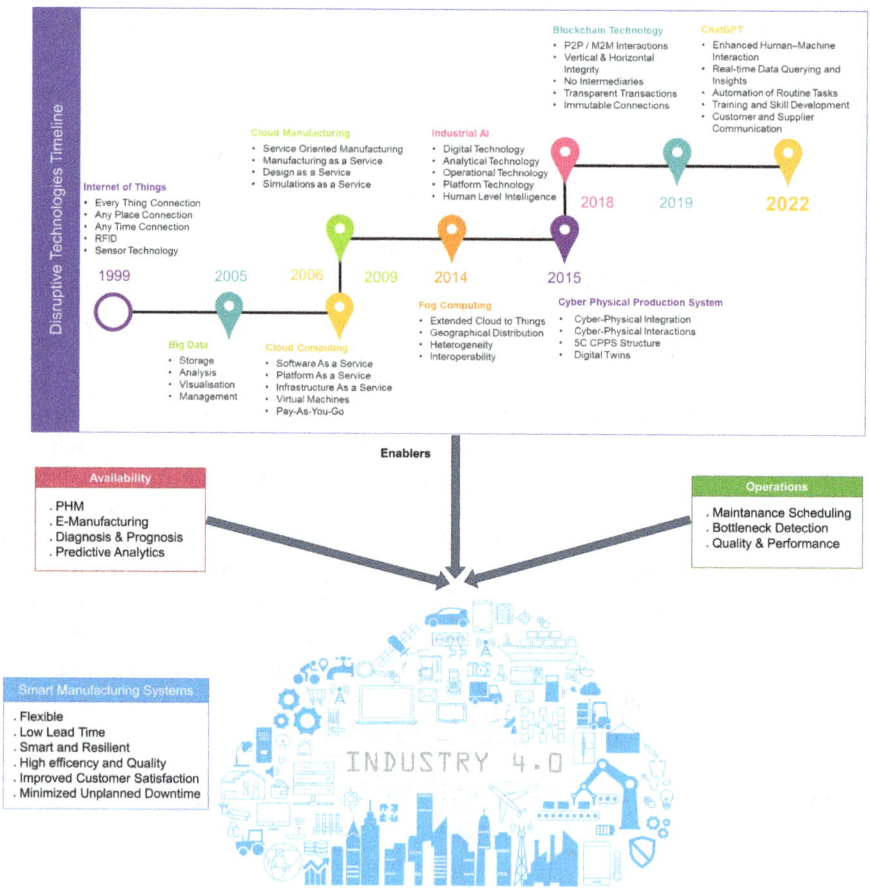

Figure 8.1 The concept of intelligent manufacturing systems

The chronology of these advancements commences with the advent of IoT in 1999 [3], which revolutionised manufacturing by facilitating real-time data interchange among interconnected devices. This connectivity facilitated more efficient operations, enabling devices to communicate effortlessly across geographical areas and time zones. The advent of big data in 2005 significantly bolstered these capabilities by providing improved storage, analytical and management tools, allowing manufacturers to leverage extensive data for strategic decision-making. [4]. In 2006, cloud computing transformed the manufacturing environment by introducing scalable services like Infrastructure as a Service and Platform as a Service, which allowed organisations to innovate and expand without significant initial investments [5]. In 2009, the emergence of fog computing enhanced cloud functionalities by bringing them nearer to the data source, facilitating expedited processing for geographically distributed manufacturing activities.

By 2014, the rise of industrial AI allowed manufacturers the capabilities to automate complicated decision-making activities, while the introduction of cyber-physical systems (CPS) in 2015 created seamless interactions between physical production systems and digital networks. These technologies enabled systems to adjust in real-time to changes in demand, resources and external influences, resulting in better efficiency. Blockchain technology made its mark in 2018, enabling increased security, transparency and traceability in manufacturing, notably in sectors like supply chain management and peer-to-peer transactions [6]. More recently, advanced AI models such as ChatGPT, released in 2022, have further improved human-machine interactions, simplifying jobs such as data searching, automating regular operations and boosting communication between customers and suppliers. This continuing chronology of disruptive technologies emphasises the revolutionary potential of IMS. With the continual integration of cutting-edge digital technologies, manufacturing is set to become increasingly intelligent, interconnected and autonomous in the framework of Industry 4.0.

This chapter is intended to provide an in-depth analysis of the notion of the digital twin (DT), concentrating on its vital role in the digital transformation of modern industries. It looks into the fundamental components of DT technology, starting with its description and going into the five major factors that govern its implementation. Readers will get insights into the basic information necessary for producing DTs, the many implementation levels involved and how this technology matches the ideas of Industry 4.0. Additionally, the chapter addresses the vital function of DTs in quality control procedures, emphasising their usefulness in establishing efficient, adaptive and IMS. Through this detailed assessment, the chapter underlines the transformative potential of DTs in transforming product creation and operational efficiency in the era of smart manufacturing.

8.2 Digital transformation products

In the context of digital transformation, terminology like digital models, digital shadows and DTs are commonly misunderstood, but they represent distinct products with varying levels of data integration [7]. Digital transformation applies to

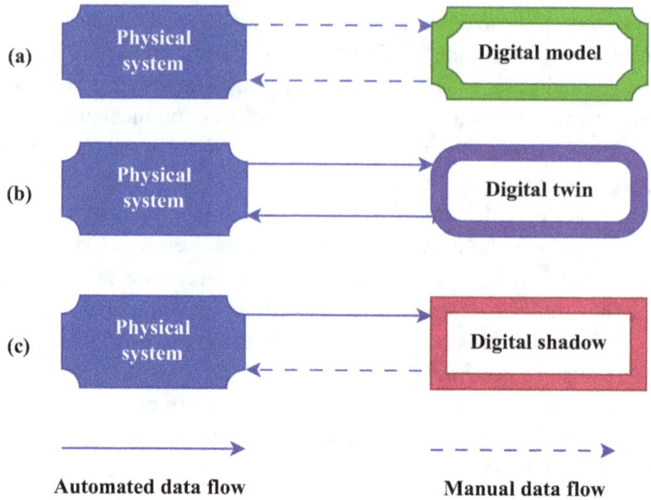

Figure 8.2 The digital transformation products: (a) digital model; (b) digital twin; and (c) digital shadow

machines, processes or systems; depending on the need, it creates one of these three outcomes (cf. Figure 8.2).

A digital model is the simplest form, acting as a static digital representation of a real object, such as computer-aided design models, but lacks automatic data synchronisation with the physical system (cf. Figure 8.2(a)). A digital shadow provides one-way data flow from the physical object (PO) to the digital equivalent, updating the digital representation in reaction to physical changes (cf. Figure 8.2(c)). The most advanced type is the DT, which incorporates bi-directional data flow, allowing real-time interaction between the physical system and its digital representation, impacting both sides (cf. Figure 8.2(b)). These distinctions help decide how deeply data is integrated and exploited in digital transformation. For example, a manufacturing unit might utilise a digital model for initial design, a digital shadow to monitor real-time performance and a DT for increased control and adaptability. Understanding these variances is crucial to matching digital transformation with specific operational needs.

8.3 Digital twin and its five dimensions

In a 2016 Product Lifecycle Management lecture at the University of Michigan, Michael Grieves first proposed the idea of the digital twin. [8]. A DT is an integrated multi-physics, multi-scale, probabilistic simulation of an as-built vehicle or system that uses physical models, sensor updates and historical data to represent the life of the corresponding flying twin [9]. NASA quickly adopted this concept for its next-generation aircraft and offered a generally recognised definition. The DT has since been modified by industry to suit their requirements, leading to various interpretations.

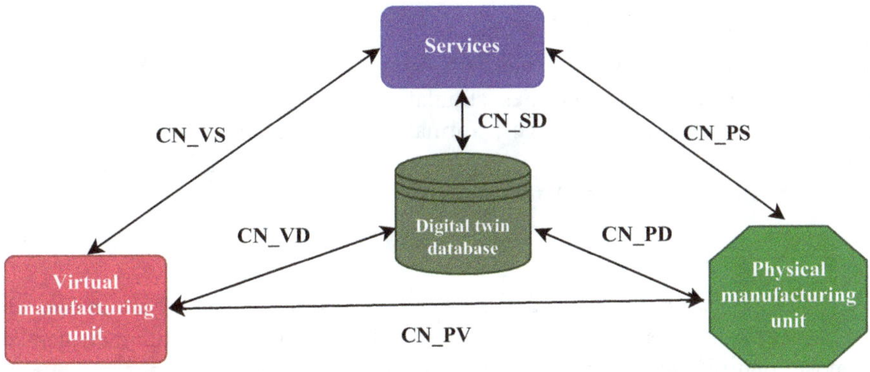

Figure 8.3 The five dimensions of digital twin

Tao *et al.* [10] presented a framework based on DTs to connect virtual and real items in manufacturing, one of the first industries to use them, improving sustainability, intelligence and efficiency. Virtual testing and Product Lifecycle Quality are likewise based on the idea of the DT [11]. The real product, the DT in a virtual setting and the link that permits data and information sharing between them are the three main parts of the DT model. To ensure that the DT precisely replicates the behaviour and performance of its real-world counterpart, virtual testing in the digital twin environment (DTE) necessitates that the DTE closely resemble the actual environment.

Five essential elements comprise the five-dimension DT model: POs, virtual models (VMs), digital twin database (DTD), services (S) and connections (CN). The mathematical representation of this model, $DT = (PO, VMU, DTD, S, CN)$, simulates behaviours by capturing interactions between the virtual and physical worlds [12]. These five dimensions are presented in Figure 8.3 and detailed discussed as follows.

8.3.1 Physical objects

POs serve as the DT foundation. These entities can be systems, processes, technologies, goods or even organisations that operate in unpredictable situations while adhering to physical rules. They are divided into three levels: system, unit and system of systems levels, according to their structure and purpose. In Figure 8.3, the PO is considered as the physical manufacturing unit.

8.3.2 Virtual models

VMs mimic the geometry, characteristics, behaviours and laws of real-world objects. The physics models capture phenomena like corrosion and deformation, the behaviour models explain state transitions and performance degradation, the rule models allow for reasoning, judgment and decision-making based on past data and expert input, and the 3D geometric models depict the entity's shape and structure. In Figure 8.3, the VM is presented as the virtual manufacturing unit.

8.3.3 Digital twin database

At the heart of the DT is the database (cf. Figure 8.3). It includes both static and dynamic data from physical entities, simulation data from VMs and data pertaining to services, among other sources, formats and temporal scales. Furthermore, knowledge data comes from specialists or pre-existing data, while fusion data is the outcome of merging these different sources.

8.3.4 Service

The DT framework relies heavily on services (cf. Figure 8.3), which are in line with the Everything-as-a-Service (XaaS) philosophy [13]. Prognostic health management, diagnosis, optimisation, monitoring and simulation are just a few of the functions that the DT provides. Third-party services, such as data, knowledge and algorithm services, are also required to assist in the creation and functioning of the DT. Platform services also make software development, model creation and service delivery easier.

8.3.5 Connections

The dynamic interplay of data, services, VMs and POs is made possible by CN, which are represented by arrows (↔) in Figure 8.3. POs and VMs (CN_PV), POs and database (CN_PD), POs and services (CN_PS), virtual models and database (CN_VD), VMs and services (CN_VS) and services and data (CN_SD) are the six most important relationships. Within the DT ecosystem, these linkages guarantee the constant flow of information, facilitating efficient simulation, operation and analysis.

8.4 Information required for digital twin development

It is essential to collect basic data before putting a DT into practice. Psarommatis and May [14] provided complete guidelines regarding the basic information required to form a DT. Determine the industry for which the DT will be created first, as this may affect the design and legal issues. Although the DT may be relevant across numerous sectors, like automotive, composite materials and aerospace, certain businesses, such as pharmaceuticals, medical devices and aircraft, have special requirements that must be followed. Next, specify the application's overall objective to establish the DT's purpose. If the DT is a component of a larger system, it is crucial to determine the system's overarching goal, which may be to streamline production control, improve product quality, improve process efficiency or refine product design.

It is also necessary to specify precisely which process or asset the DT will model. A milling machine, the cutting procedure that goes along with it, scheduling tools, inspection procedures, flaw detection and defect prediction are a few examples. How the DT will be used in the future as well. This entails figuring out how often the DT will be used, whether it will run continuously, only be utilised as necessary, or work in a hybrid mode, and whether it will be static or dynamic, adjusting to changes in the starting conditions.

Another crucial phase is determining which technologies will be used in the development of the DT. These could be knowledge-based systems, AI, machine learning (ML) techniques or experimental design. Additionally, the DT's input parameters must be specifically defined, as must the kind of data that each parameter will process, such as real-time data, historical time series data or a single value. Indicate the name of the parameter, the units that apply, the kind of data and the interval rate at which fresh values will be sent for every input parameter.

Finally, it is crucial to specify the DT's output parameters, which must have the same requirements as the input parameters. These include the parameter name, units (if appropriate), data type and interval rate for newly created values. By obtaining this data, a thorough grasp of the DT's capabilities and requirements is ensured, opening the door for successful deployment.

8.5 The digital twin implementation layers

In order to successfully apply DT technology, a five-layer structured model is suggested by Jeong *et al.* [15], which will direct the creation, use and upkeep of DTs. By facilitating a deliberate approach to deployment, these layers were presented in Figure 8.4, which will make sure that every component of the DT is carefully considered and performance optimised.

8.5.1 Layer 1: digital virtualisation

As the base layer, digital virtualisation concentrates on the digital depiction of real-world elements like people, things and settings. This procedure entails gathering and moving data into a digital format, after which it is examined and displayed. Since it establishes the foundation for all other levels, the importance of this layer cannot be overstated. Through precise emulation of the traits and actions of tangible objects, companies may produce a strong digital equivalent that replicates the intricacies of the actual world. This entails using sophisticated sensors, data-gathering techniques and visualisation software to produce a multi-dimensional picture of the intended environment.

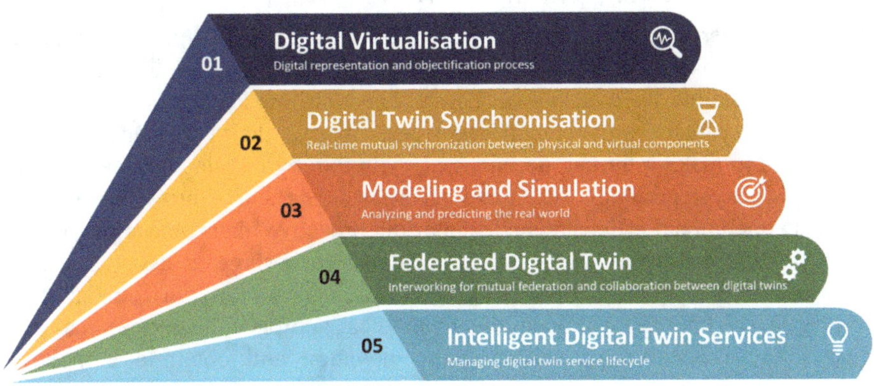

Figure 8.4 The digital twin implementation layers

8.5.2 Layer 2: digital twin synchronisation

The goal of the second layer is to connect digital and physical components in real-time. This layer ensures the synchronisation of static and dynamic elements in both worlds using sophisticated data transfer and information verification mechanisms. Synchronisation is essential for preserving the DT's relevance and accuracy since it enables real-time monitoring and modifications based on real-time data. This layer may use technologies such as cloud computing for data management, high-speed data transmission protocols and data validation algorithms to guarantee the data's integrity between the physical and digital worlds.

8.5.3 Layer 3: modelling and simulation

In order to tackle real-world problems, modelling and simulation make digital models and simulate both tangible and intangible objects. This layer optimises system performance by utilising a variety of modelling approaches, scenario development and verification procedures. Without having to worry about upsetting the physical environment, organisations can assess the effects of changes by modelling various circumstances and factors. In sectors where accuracy and productivity are critical, like manufacturing, aerospace and healthcare, this skill is especially beneficial. Through data-driven insights, stakeholders may improve decision-making, forecast results and streamline procedures thanks to the modelling and simulation layer.

8.5.4 Layer 4: federated digital twin

The notion is expanded by federated DTs, which allows numerous DTs to collaborate. It unifies disparate digital models into a single system, allowing for the sharing of information between parties and guaranteeing efficient administration and governance of these linked organisations. This federated strategy empowers firms to tackle intricate problems spanning multiple industries by encouraging interconnection and facilitating thorough analysis across several domains. For example, several DTs representing public services, utilities and transportation can collaborate in smart city projects to maximise resource allocation and enhance overall urban administration.

8.5.5 Layer 5: intelligent digital twin services

Intelligent DT services include managing DT services generally and using intelligent technology to make them run smoothly. This layer makes learning and self-healing capabilities possible by focusing on defect detection, predictive maintenance and service resource management. Organisations can improve their DTs' functioning and enable them to make informed decisions on their own by utilising ML and AI techniques. This layer prolongs the life of physical assets and reduces downtime by enhancing operational efficiency and supporting proactive maintenance programs.

With different technological components at each stage to assist successful deployment and operation, these five layers provide a thorough foundation for adopting DT technology. By using this methodical approach, businesses may fully utilise DTs to boost productivity, spur innovation and obtain a competitive advantage in a digital environment that is becoming more and more complicated. Incorporating DT technology into corporate processes simplifies operations and promotes a continuous improvement culture, which helps firms react quickly to changing market needs and obstacles.

8.6 Role of digital twin in Industry 4.0 principles

Fundamentally, Industry 4.0 seeks to build smart factories that improve productivity, adaptability and response to shifting consumer needs. Technical support, decentralised decision-making, connectivity, information transparency, intelligence, knowledge and interoperability are some of the fundamental tenets of this shift [16], which are briefly discussed in the following subsections. These ideas are strongly tied to the idea of DTs and are essential to changing conventional production methods.

8.6.1 Technical assistance

The term technical assistance describes the application of intelligent systems to assist human operators in their work. This idea is shown in the context of DTs by VMs that offer insights and suggestions based on real-time data, enabling operators to improve efficiency and make well-informed decisions.

8.6.2 Decentralised decision-making

Decentralised decision-making allows local devices and systems to decide on their own using predetermined criteria and data analysis. This idea is made possible by DTs, which enable real-time scenario analysis and simulation. This enables localised solutions to operational problems without depending on centralised control.

8.6.3 Interconnection/connectivity

A key component of Industry 4.0 is interconnection/connectivity, which emphasises the smooth integration of machines, devices and systems. By building a digital model of tangible assets that interacts with their real-world counterparts constantly, DTs take advantage of this idea. Better monitoring and control are made possible by the free flow of data across systems, which this connectivity ensures.

8.6.4 Information transparency

Information transparency promotes a culture of shared knowledge by guaranteeing that all interested parties have access to pertinent data and insights. By showing real-time data from physical assets, DTs improve information transparency and offer a clear, thorough picture of operational performance.

8.6.5 Intelligence and awareness

Systems that possess intelligence and awareness are able to analyse data and draw conclusions that can be put into practice. This idea is embodied by DTs, which use sophisticated analytics and algorithms to process enormous volumes of data and turn it into knowledge that can inform decisions.

8.6.6 Knowledge

As businesses want to use data for ongoing innovation and improvement, knowledge is crucial to Industry 4.0. Through their ability to record the performance and behaviour of physical systems, DTs help enterprises create new information and improve operations in the future.

8.6.7 Interoperability

The ability of various technologies and systems to function together without any problems is known as interoperability. By offering a common digital representation of physical assets, DTs facilitate interoperability by enabling efficient communication and collaboration between different systems, irrespective of the underlying technologies.

8.7 Connection of quality control, Industry 4.0 and digital twin

Quality control is essential to Industry 4.0, utilising new technologies such as IoT, AI and real-time data analytics to improve accuracy and efficiency in monitoring and improving manufacturing processes. These advances provide predictive maintenance, problem identification and ongoing enhancement, connecting quality management with intelligent manufacturing concepts. In this modern era, manufacturing is revolutionised by incorporating quality control into Industry 4.0 and DT frameworks, improving output, efficiency and product quality. In contrast to conventional reactive quality checks, this method allows for continual improvement and proactive, data-driven, real-time monitoring. Manufacturing companies may swiftly identify anomalies using DTs, which serve as intricate digital copies of real assets and procedures, guaranteeing operational integrity and customer satisfaction. A culture of continual improvement is fostered by this networked environment, which also makes it easier to coordinate the supply chain. By using predictive analytics, manufacturers may turn quality control into a competitive advantage by anticipating and resolving quality issues before they arise. For more details on recent advancements in quality control, one may see studies [17–20].

8.7.1 A real-time monitoring framework

The diagram presented in Figure 8.5 depicts a DT framework employed for the real-time monitoring and enhancement of production quality. The system unifies virtual and physical manufacturing units, interconnected via a DT database. This configuration allows for ongoing data gathering, analysis and feedback to enable real-time management of the manufacturing process. The virtual production unit produces many kinds of data, including simulated data for forecasting production results, quality prediction and traceability data and real-time perception data. It also gathers diverse process design data, encompassing processing parameters (parameter type, values and variations), equipment status (machine accuracy,

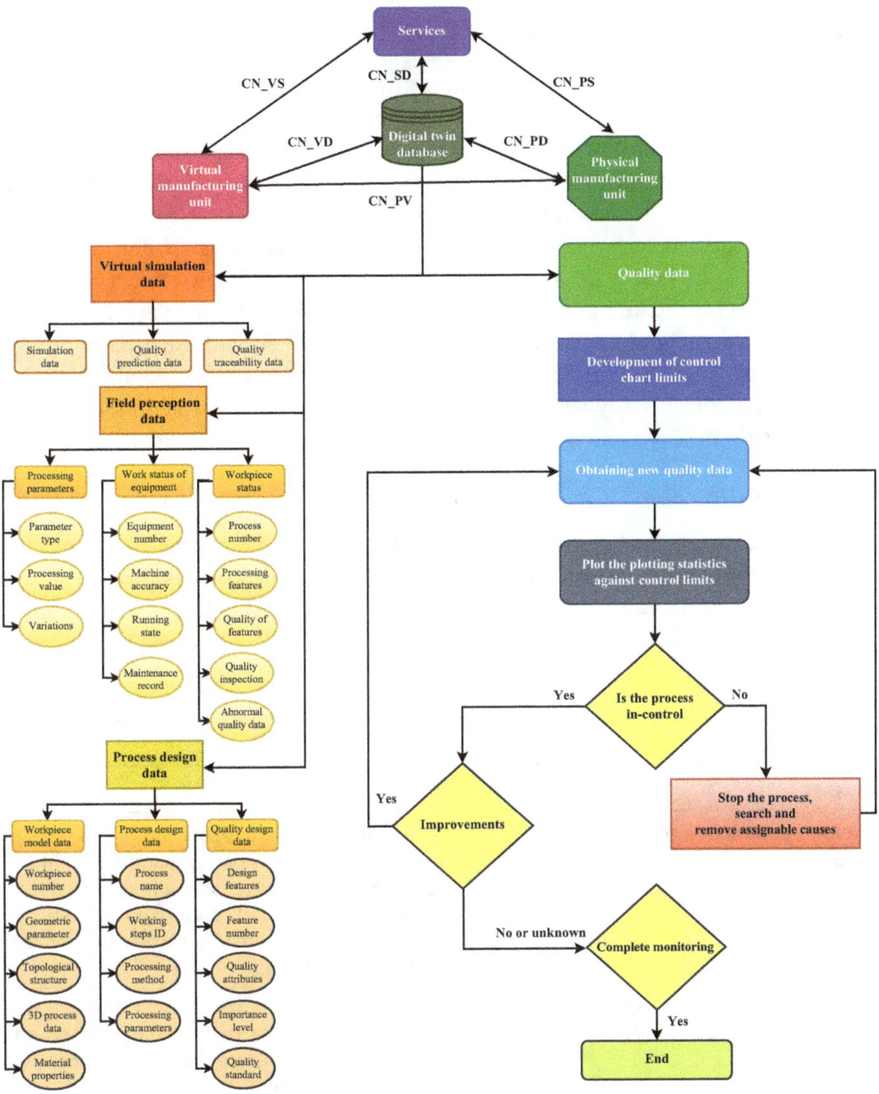

Figure 8.5 The digital twin with quality control setup

operational state and maintenance), and workpiece status (process number, processing characteristics and quality assessments). Moreover, comprehensive workpiece model data and process design data are incorporated, delineating parameters such as geometric configuration, material characteristics, processing stages and quality features. The physical manufacturing unit immediately gathers quality data from the manufacturing environment. This information, in conjunction with data from the virtual unit, is preserved in the DT database, a central repository facilitating interaction between the virtual and physical components of the process. The services component subsequently engages with this database, providing insights, forecasts and suggestions for process enhancements.

Control charts is a well-known online monitoring tool, which is commonly used to detect any abrupt changes in the quality characteristics of the process [21–26]. The framework's quality control flow begins with the physical manufacturing unit delivering quality data to build control chart boundaries. New quality data is then regularly plotted against these restrictions to establish whether the process is in control. If the process is stable, it advances towards improvements; if not, the system stops the process and seeks for assignable causes to fix. After improvements are made, the process is re-evaluated to see if complete monitoring is achievable. The process terminates if all conditions are met; otherwise, it cycles back for further monitoring or improvements. Overall, this DT system provides real-time quality control and continuous improvement by dynamically predicting, recognising and addressing quality concerns inside the production process.

8.7.2 Quality measures in a digital twin

Quality assessments between physical and virtual manufacturing units in a DT framework concentrate on matching VMs with real-world production outputs to guarantee consistency, predictability and high product standards. The potential quality metrics are listed in Table 8.1.

Table 8.1 Performance measures used for the quality monitoring of digital twin

Measure	Sub-measures	Example
Matching parameters in real time	Process parameters	Verify that the virtual simulation matches the real process by comparing parameters like temperature, pressure, speed and feed rate.
	Tool wear and condition	To update the virtual model and preserve performance consistency, track and forecast tool wear in the actual unit.
Dimensional tolerances and accuracy	Dimensional consistency	Verify that the physical product's dimensions, including thickness, surface flatness and hole sizes, correspond to the parameters specified in the virtual model.
	Tolerance matching	To make sure items fulfil design requirements, confirm that physical dimensions remain within permitted tolerances as indicated by the virtual model.
Identification and forecasting of defects	Real-time defect identification	Find surface imperfections and misalignments in the physical unit, then modify the virtual model to anticipate and avoid similar problems.
	Predictive flaw modelling	By using real-time physical data and predictive analytics, you can find possible flaw patterns in the virtual model and make proactive corrections.

(Continues)

Table 8.1 (*Continued*)

Measure	Sub-measures	Example
Efficiency and cycle time	Process timing consistency	To evaluate alignment and improve process flow, compare the cycle times of virtual and physical processes.
	Throughput matching	Verify that cycle rates and production throughput match the projections of the virtual model, indicating possible areas for efficiency gains.
Energy use and resource consumption	Comparison of energy usage	Monitor the physical unit's energy usage and contrast it with online forecasts to ensure sustainability and cost effectiveness.
	Resource consumption	To guarantee conformity with the virtual model and facilitate effective resource planning, track the physical unit's raw material and tool utilisation.
Vibration and stability analysis	Vibration monitoring	Track actual vibration levels to forecast any failures or disruptions and adjust the virtual model appropriately.
	Structural stability	To avoid unanticipated failures, make sure that the physical unit's structural responses, such as stress and strain, correspond with virtual models.
Predictive maintenance and downtime analysis	Maintenance predictions	To maximise predictive maintenance and save downtime, monitor the condition of physical machines and compare them with virtual maintenance schedules.
	Failure rate and downtime tracking	To improve dependability, measure and contrast component failure rates and downtime incidents between virtual and real units.
Environmental impact and compliance	Monitoring of emissions and waste	Keep tabs on emissions and waste in the actual process to make sure they correspond with the predictions of the virtual model, allowing for adherence to environmental laws.
	Checks for safety and compliance	To make sure safety regulations are being followed, compare virtual expectations with actual production safety measures (such as noise and emissions).
Supply chain quality synchronisation	Supply chain consistency	Verify that suppliers and sub-components in the actual production process adhere to the same quality standards upheld in the virtual model.
	Material and component traceability	Monitor material and component traceability in virtual and physical systems to improve supply chain quality control.

8.7.3 Existing quality control studies using digital twin

For exploring the literature, the PRISMA technique was used to investigate the integration of quality control into DT systems, with the 'Web of Science' [27] serving as the main search engine. On 16 September 2024, 166 articles were found using the search query 'Digital Twin' AND ('Quality Control' or 'Control Chart' or 'Statistical Process Control') (All Fields). Following a screening process based on the relevancy criteria 'Digital Twin' AND 'Quality Control Application', these first results were reduced to 56 articles. Most of these publications were either introductory or literature reviews; however, this inquiry focused on studies showing how DTs can be integrated into offline or real-time monitoring applications. As a result, only 16 articles satisfied these particular requirements, which are listed in Table 8.2. The majority of the 16 chosen articles discussed engineering applications. These papers examined offline monitoring, mostly ML methods, while seven used control charts to show real-time monitoring. Remarkably, only one study used a multivariate control chart in the real-time monitoring subset; the others used univariate control charts instead.

8.8 Summary and concluding remarks

In today's quickly evolving industrial world, the integration of DT technology into IMS exhibits a transformative leap towards fulfilling the goals of Industry 4.0. By linking the physical and digital realms, DTs offer a linked ecosystem that permits real-time communication and feedback between VMs and physical production units. This bi-directional flow of information promotes predictive and proactive maintenance, quality control and operational efficiency, thus setting a new benchmark for adaptation and resilience in industrial processes.

DTs provide a comprehensive and detailed understanding of production processes, from mimicking physical behaviour to forecasting and diagnosing quality concerns before they arise. Monitoring metrics like tool wear, dimensional accuracy and process timing consistency allow manufacturers to improve workflows, eliminate faults and decrease downtime. Furthermore, the predictive insights created by DT technology enable manufacturing systems to adjust to fluctuations in demand, resource limits and environmental variables in real-time, fostering a flexible and responsive environment to external changes. The organised five-layer framework provided in this chapter underlines the significance of a methodical approach to DT implementation, addressing important components from digital virtualisation to intelligent service layers. This architecture facilitates the seamless integration of varied technology parts and ensures that each stage of DT deployment contributes to overall system efficiency and performance. By combining advanced analytics, AI and cloud-based data synchronisation, DTs provide a stable foundation for sustainable and self-optimising production systems.

Quality control, a historically reactive process, is transformed by DT-enabled proactive quality management, enabling for real-time identification and resolution of anomalies. The inclusion of predictive analytics further ensures that any flaws

Table 8.2 List of literature which consisting of integration of quality control into digital twin systems

Year	Article title	Source title	Physical system	Model(s)	Quality tool	Variables	Monitoring
2020 [28]	A Digital Twin-Driven Approach for On-line Controlling Quality of Marine Diesel Engine Critical Parts	International Journal of Precision Engineering and Manufacturing	Critical parts of Diesel Engine	Neural Network	–	Tool Life, cutter diameter, number of teeth, cutting width, cutting depth, feed per tooth, cutting speed	Offline
2020 [29]	Digital DNA in quality control cycles of high-precision products	CIRP Annals-Manufacturing Technology	Injection System	Elastic Net and OLS Regression (linear and squared)	Specification Limits	Injected fuel, injection volume	Offline
2020 [30]	Quality Prediction and Control of Assembly and Welding Process for Ship Group Product Based on Digital Twin	Scanning	Welding Process of Ship	BP neural network	–	Welding deformation	Offline
2021 [31]	A digital twin-driven approach towards traceability and dynamic control for processing quality	Advanced Engineering Informatics	Connecting Rod of Diesel Engine	Bayesian Network, BP neural network and SVM	–	cutting speed, cutting depth, feed rate, spindle speed, cutting width, milling cutter diameter, number of teeth and centre distance deviation	Offline

(Continues)

Table 8.2 (Continued)

Year	Article title	Source title	Physical system	Model(s)	Quality tool	Variables	Monitoring
2021 [32]	A new intelligent and data-driven product quality control system of industrial valve manufacturing process in CPS	Computer Communications	Ball Valve	BP neural network	–	stem torque, valve flow, pressure leakage, valve leakage and Fault (no fault, torque fault, spring fault, valve seat processing fault and valve body trachoma)	Offline
2022 [33]	A digital twin-driven method for online quality control in process industry	International Journal of Advanced Manufacturing Technology	Optical Fibre Drawing Process	RNN, Bi-RNN, LSTM, Bi-LSTM, GRU, Bi-GRU, Bi-GRU with AM	–	time, temperature, power, feeding speed, drawing speed and rotation speed.	Offline
2022 [34]	Fully automated coal quality control using digital twin material tracking and statistical model predictive control for yield optimisation during production of semi soft coking- and station coal	Journal of the Southern African Institute of Mining and Metallurgy	Coal Yield	–	Shewhart Chart	Yield based on PSC and SSCC methods	Real-time

(Continues)

2022 [35]	Manufacturing Operator Ergonomics: A Conceptual Digital Twin Approach to Detect Biomechanical Fatigue	IEEE Access	Biomechanical Fatigue	–	EWMA Chart	Dynamic Time Warping (DTW) Algorithm based Distances	Real-time
2023 [36]	Offline digital twin for simulation and assessment of product surface quality	International Journal of Advanced Manufacturing Technology	Stainless Steel Machining	Adaptive Neurofuzzy Inference System (ANFIS)	–	Surface Roughness	Offline
2023 [37]	Digital Twin-Enabled Monitoring of Mining Haul Trucks with Expert System Integration: A Case Study in an Experimental Open-Pit Mine	2023 5th Global Power, Energy and Communication Conference, GPECOM	Mining Haul Trucks	–	Shewhart Chart	Logged Data	Real-time
2023 [38]	An Intelligent Control Model Based on Digital Twin Technology and Optimised Least-Squares Support Vector Regression for Predicting Electromagnetic Brake Assembly Quality	IEEE Access	Electromagnetic Brake Assembly	GRA-IPSO-LSSVR (grey relational analysis (GRA), least-squares support vector regression (LSSVR), improved particle swarm optimisation (IPSO)) Method	–	Friction plate square hole diameter, Inside diameter of upper cover, Resistance value, Clearance between the armature and the stator , Flatness of armature , Brake thickness, Clearance from the loam cake to	Offline

(Continues)

Table 8.2 (Continued)

Year	Article title	Source title	Physical system	Model(s)	Quality tool	Variables	Monitoring
						the friction plate, The flatness of the loam cake, Clearance between the loam cake and armature, Concentricity of the friction plate, Spring installation height, Torque of the lock screw, Static friction braking torque	
2023 [39]	Updating digital twins: Methodology for data accuracy quality control using machine learning techniques	Computers in Industry	Fresnel solar field	Principal components analysis (PCA), Adaptive Neurofuzzy Inference System (ANFIS), DNN, LSTM	–	direct solar radiation, ambient temperature, water flow rate, inlet temperature and outlet temperature	Offline
2023 [40]	Simulation-based digital twins monitoring: an approach focused on models' accreditation	International Journal of Advanced Manufacturing Technology	Production flow	K-near neighbours (K-NN) classifier	p control chart	Production flow time data	Real-time
2023 [41]	Physic-based vs data-based digital twins for bush bearing wear diagnostic	Wear	Bush Bearing Wear Diagnostic	Boussinesq's and Archard's equations	Shewhart Chart	Wear Rate	Real-time

(Continues)

2024 [42]	Digital Twin simulation models: a validation method based on machine learning and control charts	International Journal of Production Research	Production flow	K-near neighbours (K-NN) classifier	p control chart	Production flow time data	Real-time
2024 [43]	Real-Time Monitoring of Human and Process Performance Parameters in Collaborative Assembly Systems using Multivariate Control Charts	Journal of Intelligent & Robotic Systems	Human Stress Response Assessment	–	Hotelling T2 and Generalised Variance charts	Assembly time, Quality control time, Total defects and Stress	Real-time

are discovered and remedied at early stages, which greatly improves product quality, lowers waste and promotes compliance with high regulatory standards. As a result, manufacturing businesses can maintain high consistency and reliability standards, ultimately boosting customer satisfaction and competitive advantage. Looking to the future, the promise of DT extends beyond individual manufacturing units to bigger, federated systems where many DTs interact across the supply chain and across sectors. This collaborative strategy lays the path for smarter, more sustainable industry ecosystems that expedite manufacturing and contribute to broader economic and environmental goals. As DT technology evolves, its applications in areas like supply chain quality synchronisation, resource efficiency and environmental impact monitoring will likely fuel continuous innovation and expansion in smart manufacturing.

References

[1] Lee J, Ni J, Singh J, Jiang B, Azamfar M, and Feng J. Intelligent maintenance systems and predictive manufacturing. *Journal of Manufacturing Science and Engineering*. 142(11), 110805 (2020). doi:10.1115/1.4047856.

[2] Zhong RY, Xu X, Klotz E, and Newman ST. Intelligent manufacturing in the context of industry 4.0: A review. *Engineering*. 3(5), 616–30 (2017). doi:10.1016/J.ENG.2017.05.015.

[3] Madakam S, Ramaswamy R, and Tripathi S. Internet of Things (IoT): A literature review. *Journal of Computer and Communications*. 3(5), 164–73 (2015). doi:10.4236/jcc.2015.35021.

[4] Chen M, Mao S, and Liu Y. Big data: A survey. *Mobile Networks and Applications*. 19, 171–209 (2014). doi:10.1007/s11036-013-0489-0.

[5] Qian L, Luo Z, Du Y, and Guo L. Cloud computing: An overview. *Cloud Computing: Proceedings of the First International Conference, CloudCom 2009*, Beijing, China, Springer; December 2009. p. 626–31.

[6] Yu T, Lin Z, and Tang Q. Blockchain: The introduction and its application in financial accounting. *Journal of Corporate Accounting & Finance*. 29(4), 37–47 (2018). doi:10.1002/jcaf.22365.

[7] Yousif I, Burns L, El Kalach F, and Harik R. Leveraging computer vision towards high-efficiency autonomous industrial facilities. *Journal of Intelligent Manufacturing*. 36(16), 2983–3008 (2024). doi:10.1007/s10845-024-02396-1.

[8] Grieves M, and Vickers J. *Origins of the Digital Twin Concept*. Melbourne, FL: Florida Institute of Technology/NASA. (2016). doi:10.13140/RG.2.2.26367.61609.

[9] Kosse S, Vogt O, Wolf M, König M, and Gerhard D. Digital twin framework for enabling serial construction. *Frontiers in Built Environment*. 8, 864722 (2022). doi:10.3389/fbuil.2022.864722.

[10] Tao F, Cheng J, Qi Q, Zhang M, Zhang H, and Sui F. Digital twin-driven product design, manufacturing and service with big data. *The International*

Journal of Advanced Manufacturing Technology. 94, 3563–76 (2018). doi:10.1007/s00170-017-0233-1.

[11] Grieves MJM. Digital twin certified: Employing virtual testing of digital twins in manufacturing to ensure quality products. *Machines*. 11(8), 808 (2023). doi:10.3390/machines11080808.

[12] Qi Q, Tao F, Hu T, *et al*. Enabling technologies and tools for digital twin. *Journal of Manufacturing Systems*. 58, 3–21 (2021). doi:10.1016/j.jmsy.2019.10.001.

[13] Sigler L, Ubach PA, Mora J, and Oñate E. A review of technologies and challenges for integrated modeling analysis. *Archives of Computational Methods in Engineering* 32(2), 1733–1762 (2025). doi:10.1007/s11831-024-10187-3.

[14] Psarommatis F, and May G. A literature review and design methodology for digital twins in the era of zero defect manufacturing. *International Journal of Production Research*. 61(16), 5723–43 (2023). doi:10.1080/00207543.2022.2101960.

[15] Jeong D-Y, Baek M-S, Lim T-B, *et al*. Digital twin: Technology evolution stages and implementation layers with technology elements. *IEEE Access*. 10, 52609–20 (2022). doi:10.1109/ACCESS.2022.3174220.

[16] Cañas H, Mula J, Díaz-Madroñero M, and Campuzano-Bolarín F. Implementing industry 4.0 principles. *Computers & Industrial Engineering*. 158, 107379 (2021). doi:10.1016/j.cie.2021.107379.

[17] Zwetsloot IM, Mahmood T, and Woodall WH. Multivariate time-between-events monitoring: An overview and some overlooked underlying complexities. *Quality Engineering*. 33(1), 13–25 (2020). doi:10.1080/08982112.2020.1788717.

[18] Mahmood T, and Xie M. Models and monitoring of zero-inflated processes: The past and current trends. *Quality and Reliability Engineering International*. 35(8), 2540–57 (2019). doi:10.1002/qre.2547.

[19] Ahmed F, Mahmood T, Riaz M, and Abbas N. Comprehensive review of high-dimensional monitoring methods: Trends, insights, and interconnections. *Quality Technology & Quantitative Management*. 22(14), 727–751 (2025). doi:10.1080/16843703.2024.2395745.

[20] Ali S, Pievatolo A, and Göb R. An overview of control charts for high-quality processes. *Quality and Reliability Engineering International*. 32(7), 2171–89 (2016). doi:10.1002/qre.1957.

[21] Zwetsloot IM, Mahmood T, Taiwo FM, and Wang Z. A real-time monitoring approach for bivariate event data. *Applied Stochastic Models in Business and Industry*. 39(6), 789–817 (2023).

[22] Mahmood T, and Erem A. A bivariate exponentially weighted moving average control chart based on exceedance statistics. *Computers and Industrial Engineering* 175, 108910 (2023).

[23] Hussain S, Mahmood T, Riaz M, and Nazir HZ. A new approach to design median control charts for location monitoring. *Communications in Statistics-Simulation and Computation*. 51(7), 3553–77 (2023). doi:10.1080/03610918.2020.1716245.

[24] Erem A, and Mahmood T. A bivariate CUSUM control chart based on exceedance statistics. *Quality and Reliability Engineering International*. 39 (4), 1172–91 (2023). doi:10.1002/qre.3285.

[25] Mahmood T, Iqbal A, Abbasi SA, and Amin M. Efficient GLM-based control charts for Poisson processes. *Quality and Reliability Engineering International*. 38(1), 389–404 (2022).

[26] Mahmood T. On the enhanced surveillance methods for high-quality processes. *2022 IEEE International Conference on Industrial Engineering and Engineering Management (IEEM)*: IEEE; 2022. p. 0369–73.

[27] Birkle C, Pendlebury DA, Schnell J, and Adams J. Web of Science as a data source for research on scientific and scholarly activity. *Quantitative Science Studies*. 1(1), 363–76 (2020).

[28] Cheng D-J, Zhang J, Hu Z-T, Xu S-H, and Fang X-F. A digital twin-driven approach for on-line controlling quality of marine diesel engine critical parts. *International Journal of Precision Engineering and Manufacturing*. 21, 1821–41 (2020). doi:10.1007/s12541-020-00403-y.

[29] Wagner R, Haefner B, Biehler M, and Lanza G. Digital DNA in quality control cycles of high-precision products. *CIRP Annals*. 69(1), 373–6 (2020). doi:10.1016/j.cirp.2020.03.020.

[30] Li L, Liu D, Liu J, Zhou H-g, and Zhou J. Quality prediction and control of assembly and welding process for ship group product based on digital twin. *Scanning*. 2020(1), 3758730 (2020). doi:10.1155/2020/3758730.

[31] Liu J, Cao X, Zhou H, *et al*. A digital twin-driven approach towards traceability and dynamic control for processing quality. *Advanced Engineering Informatics*. 50, 101395 (2021). doi:10.1016/j.aei.2021.101395.

[32] Pang J, Zhang N, Xiao Q, Qi F, and Xue X. A new intelligent and data-driven product quality control system of industrial valve manufacturing process in CPS. *Computer Communications*. 175, 25–34 (2021). doi:10.1016/j.comcom.2021.04.022.

[33] Zhu X, and Ji Y. A digital twin–driven method for online quality control in process industry. *The International Journal of Advanced Manufacturing Technology*. 119, 3045–64 (2022). doi:10.1007/s00170-021-08369-5.

[34] Coetzee B, and Sonnendecker PW. Fully automated coal quality control using digital twin material tracking and statistical model predictive control for yield optimization during production of semi soft coking-and power station coal. *Journal of the Southern African Institute of Mining and Metallurgy*. 122(8), 429–36 (2022). doi:10.17159/2411-9717/2002/2022

[35] Sharotry A, Jimenez JA, Mediavilla FAM, Wierschem D, Koldenhoven RM, and Valles D. Manufacturing operator ergonomics: A conceptual digital twin approach to detect biomechanical fatigue. *IEEE Access*. 10, 12774–91 (2022). doi:10.1109/ACCESS.2022.3145984.

[36] Seid Ahmed Y, and ElMaraghy H. Offline digital twin for simulation and assessment of product surface quality. *The International Journal of Advanced Manufacturing Technology*. 127(5), 2595–615 (2023). doi:10.1007/s00170-023-11662-0.

[37] Elbazi N, Tigami A, Laayati O, El Maghraoui A, Chebak A, and Mabrouki M. Digital twin-enabled monitoring of mining haul trucks with expert system integration: A case study in an experimental open-pit mine. *2023 5th Global Power, Energy and Communication Conference (GPECOM)*: IEEE; 2023. p. 168–74.

[38] Shi Y, Pang J, Chen Y, Dai J, and Li Y. An intelligent control model based on digital twin technology and optimized least-squares support vector regression for predicting electromagnetic brake assembly quality. *IEEE Access*. 11, 137303–16 (2023). doi:10.1109/ACCESS.2023.3331734.

[39] Rodríguez F, Chicaiza WD, Sánchez A, and Escaño JM. Updating digital twins: Methodology for data accuracy quality control using machine learning techniques. *Computers in Industry*. 151, 103958 (2023). doi:10.1016/j.compind.2023.103958.

[40] dos Santos CH, Campos AT, Montevechi JAB, de Carvalho Miranda R, do Amaral JVS, and de Queiroz JA. Simulation-based digital twins monitoring: An approach focused on models' accreditation. *The International Journal of Advanced Manufacturing Technology*. 124(7), 2423–35 (2023). doi:10.1007/s00170-022-10674-6.

[41] Regis A, Arroyave-Tobón S, Linares J-M, and Mermoz E. Physic-based vs data-based digital twins for bush bearing wear diagnostic. *Wear*. 526, 204888 (2023). doi:10.1016/j.wear.2023.204888.

[42] dos Santos CH, Campos AT, Montevechi JAB, de Carvalho Miranda R, and Costa AFB. Digital Twin simulation models: A validation method based on machine learning and control charts. *International Journal of Production Research*. 62(7), 2398–414 (2024). doi:10.1080/00207543.2023.2217299.

[43] Verna E, Puttero S, Genta G, and Galetto M. Real-time monitoring of human and process performance parameters in collaborative assembly systems using multivariate control charts. *Journal of Intelligent & Robotic Systems*. 110(3), 126 (2024). doi:10.1007/s10846-024-02162-8.

Chapter 9

The role of digital twins in realising circular economy in the era of Industry 4.0 and Industry 5.0

Julius Sechang Mboli[1]

Abstract

Technological advancements contribute to increased waste and greenhouse gas emissions through e-waste, energy-intensive manufacturing and infrastructure, and increased consumption. However, technology also offers solutions for mitigating these impacts through improved efficiency, waste management optimisation and environmental monitoring. This chapter explores the transformative role of digital twins (DTs) in realising the circular economy (CE) within the paradigms of Industry 4.0 (I4.0) and Industry 5.0 (I5.0). It begins by examining the advancements brought by I4.0, characterised by automation, IoT, AI and cyber-physical systems, aimed at enhancing efficiency and productivity. Transitioning to I5.0, the narrative shifts towards a human-centric and sustainable industrial approach, emphasising collaboration between humans and machines. DTs, as virtual replicas of physical systems or processes, emerge as pivotal enablers of CE by facilitating real-time monitoring, predictive maintenance and optimisation. The integration of DTs with CE principles supports resource efficiency, waste reduction and lifecycle extension. Key technologies such as AI, IoT, 5G and edge computing enhance the potential of DTs, enabling applications like supply chain transparency, energy efficiency and product lifecycle management. The chapter delves into the synergy between DTs and I5.0, highlighting how DTs empower mass customisation, personalised production and ethical sustainability. Real-world case studies, spanning aerospace, automotive and urban planning, demonstrate the practical impact of DTs in driving CE objectives. Despite challenges like data security, high implementation costs and standardisation gaps, the chapter identifies promising opportunities in predictive maintenance, energy optimisation and healthcare innovations. Concluding, the chapter asserts that DTs represent a cornerstone of sustainable industrial practices, bridging physical and digital realms to foster a resilient, human-centred and eco-friendly future. Their

[1]Centre of Excellence for Data Science, Artificial Intelligence and Modelling (DAIM), University of Hull, UK

integration with evolving technologies ensures their relevance in shaping industries and achieving CE goals.

Keywords: Digital twins; circular economy; Industry 4.0; Industry 5.0; sustainability; waste reduction

9.1 Introduction

Technological advancements often bring challenges like increased carbon footprints, waste generation and heightened energy and material consumption. The positive is that these advanced and cutting-edge technologies could be employed to pursue enhanced sustainability initiatives through circular economy (CE) principles. For instance, innovations such as SpaceX's 2024 achievements in reusing the Falcon 9 first stage, payload fairings, starship and raptor engines [1] demonstrate how technology can also promote sustainability. Similarly, while the development and use of AI raise concerns about energy consumption and intense resource utilisation, companies like NVIDIA are tackling these issues through initiatives focused on energy efficiency, renewable energy, data centre optimisation and AI for climate action [2]. Additionally, leading tech firms such as Google, Apple, IBM, Dell, Microsoft and Amazon are making significant strides in addressing AI's sustainability concerns through various impactful measures [3,4]. Hence, this chapter explores the role of some of these cutting-edge technologies, focusing on digital twins (DTs) in realising CE in the era of Industry 4.0 (I4.0) and Industry 5.0 (I5.0).

9.1.1 Overview of Industry 4.0 and Industry 5.0

I4.0 also known as the beginning of the fourth industrial revolution, is typically categorised by the integration of advanced technologies such as the Internet of Things (IoT), artificial intelligence (AI), big data analytics, cyber-physical systems, additive manufacturing, autonomous robots, augmented reality (AR), simulations and Industrial Internet of Things [5–7]. I4.0 centres on creation of intelligent factories where machines, systems and humans are interconnected to enable autonomous decision-making and optimised production processes. The main objective is to drive efficiency, productivity and flexibility, enabling real-time data-driven decision-making and operations [8].

As the industrial landscape continues to rapidly evolve, I5.0 surfaces 10 years after the launch of I4.0, as a transformative phase that extends the principles of I4.0. Whereas I4.0 emphasises automation and efficiency, I5.0 focuses on human-centricity and sustainability [9]. The primary goal of I5.0 is to foster collaboration between humans and machines, leveraging the strengths of both to drive innovation, creativity and personalised manufacturing. I5.0 also prioritises sustainable practices and ethical considerations, ensuring that technological advancements benefit both society and the environment [10]. Hence, by bringing in I5.0, the various concerns of I4.0 which considers only automation and efficiency can be addressed. How this can be achieved with the help of DTs and CE will be explored in this chapter.

9.1.2 Introduction to circular economy

The CE represents a paradigm shift from the traditional linear economic model, which is based on a 'take-make-dispose' approach to a model that is circular in nature [11]. CE aims to reduce the amount of waste generation and resource consumption through the creation of closed-loop systems that prioritise reuse, repair, remanufacture, recycling, cascade and regeneration [12,13]. According to a report by Ellen MacArthur Foundation, the key principles of the CE include designing out waste, keeping products and materials in use for as long as possible while driving maximum value and regenerating natural systems [14]. From the same report, one core principle of CE is material circularity which is based on a butterfly model where a technical circle should mimic the organic cycle closely, thereby minimising wastes.

Digital transformation plays a crucial role in realising CE by enabling data-driven decision-making and enhancing transparency across supply chains [12,15]. By leveraging advanced technologies, businesses are able to optimise resource utilisation, extend product lifecycles and reduce environmental impact and make data driven business decisions. The integration of CE principles with I4.0 and I5.0 initiatives highlights the importance of sustainable practices in shaping the future of industries [16].

9.1.3 Introduction to digital twins

In simple terms, DTs are essentially virtual representations of physical assets, processes or systems that enable real-time monitoring, simulation and analysis [17]. Dating back to 1960 when NASA wanted to monitor and simulate spacecraft systems remotely, DTs have evolved to become a critical component of modern industrial applications [18].

DTs integrate data from sensors and other sources to create a dynamic, real-time digital replica of their physical counterparts illustrated in Figure 9.1. This integration allows for continuous monitoring, predictive maintenance and optimisation of assets and processes [17,18]. In the context of I4.0 and I5.0, DTs can play a crucial role in increasing efficiency, enabling customisation and fostering innovation while aligning with the principles of the CE [19] as introduced previously.

By bridging the physical and digital worlds, DTs provide a comprehensive view of systems and processes, enabling organisations to make data-driven decisions, reduce downtime and improve product quality dynamically and globally [18]. The growing significance of DTs in modern industries emphasises their potential to transform the way businesses operate, innovate and compete in an increasingly digital and sustainability-driven world. The aim is to meet the needs of the present without compromising the needs of future generations. This can be achieved via sustainability-driven innovation, which involves creating new products, services or processes that reduce the use of natural resources and the release of harmful substances into the environment [20].

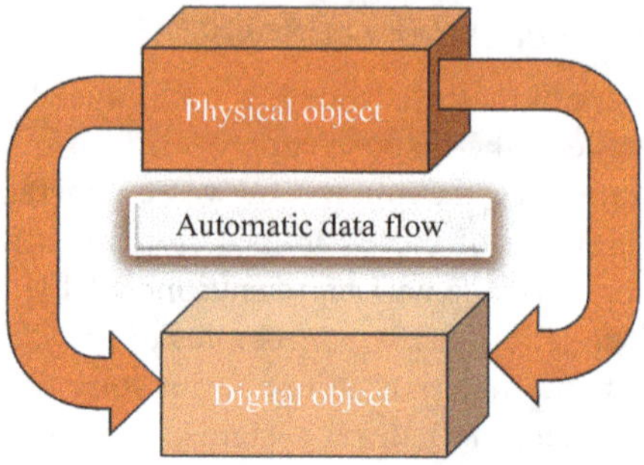

Figure 9.1 Digital twin illustration

9.2 Digital twins in Industry 4.0

9.2.1 Key components and technologies

DTs are powered by a combination of cutting-edge technologies that enable real-time data integration, analysis, visualisations and other capabilities. The aim of this section is to briefly highlight some of the key components for enhancing these capabilities as follows:

- **IoT and sensors**: IoT devices and sensors can enable the collection of data from physical assets, offering near real-time or real-time insights into their condition and performance [21,22]. Sensors and actuators embedded in physical assets gather real-time data, which is crucial for creating accurate DTs. This data from the unified repository (UR) linking a physical asset or process to its digital replica as described in [18] is crucial for monitoring resource usage and identifying opportunities for waste reduction among other benefits.
- **Artificial intelligence and machine learning**: AI and ML algorithms can analyse data from DTs/UR, enabling predictive maintenance, anomaly detection and process optimisation [23]. With DT, this can even happen in real-time where errors can be spotted and corrected before the manufacturing process is completed thereby preventing any future failure and wastes. ML models can identify patterns and trends that facilitate sustainable practices such as reuse, repair, remanufacture, recycle and cascade of products, components and materials [12].
- **Cyber-physical systems**: These systems integrate physical processes with digital technologies, allowing for seamless interaction between machines and DTs [17,24,25]. Cyber-physical systems enable the implementation of closed-loop systems and circular supply chains that lead to the enhancement of circular practices which has the potential of minimising wastes related to supply chain management.
- **Data platforms**: DT platforms manage and process data, providing a centralised hub for analytics and visualisations. These data platforms are akin to what Grieves referred to in the white paper as UR that links the a physical asset or process to its virtual counterpart [18]. These platforms enable businesses to track and optimise resource flows, aligning with CE principles.

- **Big data analytics**: This technology processes and analyses large volumes of unstructured data generated by IoT devices. Volume, velocity, variety, veracity and value are key Vs of big data and are pivotal in driving real-time or near real-time insights from the data [26]. It helps in extracting valuable insights and making data-driven decisions for the DT that can be applied in several domains.
- **Cloud computing**: Cloud platforms provide the necessary storage and computational power to handle the vast amounts of data generated by DTs. They also enable remote access and collaboration needed for global access for DTs [25,27].
- **Edge computing**: Edge computing processes data closer to the source (in the case of DT, the physical asset or the physical process) to reduce latency and bandwidth usage. This is especially important for real-time applications of DTs as some networks may not quite real-time analytics [25,28]. Researchers are already exploring deep learning models for hybrid 5G services in mobile edge computing with the aim of optimising user association and reducing resources and energy usage [29]. Though the adoption of cloud and edge computing for DTs are still in its infancy in the oil and gas industries, it still has the potential to be used in several different areas [30]. Acquisition, storage and sharing of big data are critical for collaborations and implementation of DTs.
- **5G/6G networks**: These advanced communication networks offer high-speed, low-latency data transmission, which is crucial for the real-time operation of DTs [31]. This is crucial for DTs as any simulator deployed on a low speed and high latency can lead to inaccurate outcomes thereby resulting in wrong decisions [32].
- **3D modelling and simulation**: 3D modelling creates detailed virtual representations of physical objects, while simulation tools allow for testing and analysis of different scenarios within the DT. For instance, it can be used for structural vulnerability assessment of heritage structures. This is a crucial part of risk mitigation strategy for preserving the treasured assets for the nations and thereby minimising that wastes from such assets [33].
- **Augmented reality (AR) and virtual reality (VR)**: AR and VR technologies enhance the visualisation and interaction with DTs, providing immersive experiences for users. As already described, the benefits of DT covers different fields of manufacturing, such as production and design, remote diagnostics and services [18]. It relies on the constantly accrued data and real-time presentation of the collected data so as to instantaneously update and adapt with its physical counterpart. But presenting massive amount of data and information collected in a DT in an intuitive manner is still a major challenge [34].
- **Blockchain**: DT may be employed for the configuration, monitoring, diagnostics and prognostics of a physical asset, equipment or process. It is estimated that this new technology will become more popular in the conceivable future that will take critical roles in I4.0 and beyond. Today's methods, systems and technologies employed for DTs' creation are however, generally centralised thereby lacking trusted data provenance, audit and traceability. Additionally, transactions data, logs and history are not tamper-proof/secure. Blockchain technology ensures the security and integrity of data by providing a decentralised and tamper-proof ledger [35]. This is crucial for maintaining

trust in the data used by DTs in a world that is increasingly becoming vulnerable to cyber threats.

- **Digital thread**: One major aspect that can promote the transition to CE is to address the risks associated with product residual value uncertainty [12]. With DT, the digital thread connects data across the entire lifecycle of a product, from design and manufacturing to operation and maintenance thereby providing the opportunity for transparent circular supply chains. It ensures that the DT remains up-to-date and accurate [36].
- **System integration**: Four crucial domains interactions challenges for DTs, I4.0 and beyond are (i) man-to-man, (ii) man-to-machine, (iii) machine-to-man interaction and (iv) machine-to-machine interaction. System integration involves integrating various technologies and systems to ensure seamless communication and interoperability to achieve these interactions [37]. Effective system integration is crucial for the successful implementation of DTs and enhanced opportunity for carbon footprints and waste minimisation.

The synergy between these technologies forms the backbone of DTs, facilitating the creation of dynamic, responsive and intelligent systems that is capable of enabling sustainable practices via the CE initiatives.

9.2.2 Applications and use cases

From resource optimisation and waste reduction, to supply chain transparency and optimisation, DTs have found several applications across industries, revolutionising processes and driving sustainability already. Some of the key use cases are now discussed below:

Resource optimisation and waste reduction

DTs enable real-time monitoring of resource consumption, identifying opportunities for waste reduction and resource efficiency. By simulating different scenarios, businesses can optimise resource flows and minimise environmental impact [37,38]. For instance, in agriculture, farmers are considering adopting smart farming techniques to improve the efficiency of farming process that will lead to optimising resources usage and waste reduction. This will also help in addressing agricultural challenges that depends on natural conditions, such as weather, seasons, diseases, soil conditions and climate change. Other use cases in agriculture includes weather modelling [39], soil management [40] and livestock monitoring and optimisation [39,41]. Most of these uses and more are still in their infancy stages, but certainly potential impacts and contributions for sustainable practices are there and will become clear and better as DTs continue to gain popularity and become more standardised.

Product lifecycle management and closed-loop systems

CE principles includes designing out waste and relying on non-toxic materials for products manufacturing [11]. From product design to process design, DTs provide insights into product lifecycle stages, enabling businesses to extend product lifecycles and implement closed-loop systems. This approach supports reuse, repair, recycling, remanufacturing and refurbishment initiatives [12]. It also provides a virtual replica of a manufacturing asset that can collects data, offering the opportunity of creating, building, testing and validating products and incorporating feedback that will help in eliminating waste [18,38].

Energy efficiency and environmental monitoring
DTs monitor energy consumption and environmental parameters in real-time, identifying opportunities for energy savings and efficiency improvements. This capability supports sustainability goals and reduces carbon footprints. Research has shown that DT has the potential of effectively reducing collective energy demand by at least 20.4%, and can also lower average energy cost per household by up to 17.7% [42]. This is certainly encouraging at a time that energy cost is rising with high inflation and households are struggling.

Supply chain transparency and optimisation
The bottom lines of all supply chain players are affected by constantly increasing logistics costs. Retailers and manufacturers are always seeking for financial sustainability by lowering supply chain costs. Studies have shown that a good supply chain performance has the potential of reducing costs and increasing revenue, productivity, profits and sustainability [12]. By providing real-time insights into supply chain operations, DTs enhance visibility and enable efficient resource management. This transparency facilitates sustainable sourcing and logistics practices [43].

These are just few applications that demonstrate the transformative potential of DTs in I4.0, driving sustainability and competitiveness in the modern industrial landscape.

9.2.3 Benefits and challenges

While the integration of DTs in I4.0 with CE principles offers numerous benefits, there are still several challenges. Some of these benefits are:

Enhanced sustainability
Global market report [44] suggest that real-time monitoring and optimisation as key aspects of DT support resource efficiency and waste reduction, aligning with CE principles [23,44,45].

Improved decision-making
Data-driven insights enable informed decision-making, enhancing strategic planning and resource allocation [46]. With DT and I4.0, decisions can be made based on real-time data through the product lifecycle to avoid uncertainties and risks that could lead to financial and resources lost.

Increased efficiency
Real-time monitoring and optimisation reduce downtime, enhance productivity and lower operational costs. DT also provides the innovative solutions to visualise, track and enhance numerous operational and business processes, that can improve productivity and efficiency [47].

While these benefits and more can be so enticing to businesses, there however, several challenges that cannot be ignored at this stage. To fully benefit from the potentials of DTs, appropriate steps including investment in research and development to address these challenges. This is because DT's technology just like its key enabling technologies has many shared challenges some of which include data security and privacy. DT technology relies heavily on data and digital link between the physical asset and its digital replica. In the industry environment, it is obvious that everyone is concerned with the privacy and security of the system. With constant collection of data that is accumulated and stored digitally or on the cloud, cyber threats remained a challenge. This is because of the enormous amount of data the system uses and the risk this poses to sensitive classified and/or system data. Protecting sensitive data from cyber threats is crucial, requiring robust security measures and protocols [48]. Another challenge is Interoperability. Ensuring seamless integration with existing systems and technologies poses a significant challenge, requiring standardised protocols and frameworks. There are several challenges that are related to legacy systems, updating old IT infrastructures and connectivity challenges. Other challenges are related to scalability as implementing DT may start in small scale but grow rapidly due to accumulation of data and simulations [38,48]. Scaling DT solutions across large enterprises will even require significant investment in infrastructure and resources and this may be challenged by managers since the benefits of DTs are still as popular, they would like.

Despite these challenges, the benefits of DTs in I4.0 are undeniable that it is able to drive innovation and sustainability in the modern industrial landscape.

9.3 DTs in Industry 5.0 and the circular economy

9.3.1 Human-centric and sustainable approach

The term I5.0 is still under substantial considerations by both the academia and the industry as it is still in its infancy. However, back in 2021, the European Commission put forth its definition largely, because of the anticipated influence that the concept will have in the future for both the world and the European industry itself [49]. The concept aims to address some aspects of I4.0 that are considered controversial or at least not defined properly due to missing out on some essential values such as sustainability and social fairness. The European Commission then considered this as an opportunity to align the main concepts of I5.0 with societal goals and to seek for higher benefits that goes beyond just economic growth and jobs satisfaction. This should also address what was missing in I4.0 and that is why I5.0 is not conceived as a complete industrial revolution, rather an amalgamation of the two paradigms for a win-win society [50] As a result, the focus of I5.0 is on one hand, sustainable manufacturing and the other hand, industrial operator well-being therefore complementing each other as emerging concepts [51]. Essentially, the main goal of the I5.0 framework is to enhance the efficiency of smart factories through technological advancements while simultaneously minimising environmental and social impacts to the greatest extent possible. Hence, it introduces a human-centric paradigm shift, emphasising collaboration between humans and machines [49]. Based on the key components of DTs previously discussed, it can play a crucial role in I5.0 transition by some of the ways highlighted in the following paragraphs.

Augmenting human capabilities: DTs empower workers by providing real-time insights and decision-support tools, enhancing their capabilities and productivity [52]. This empowerment supports sustainable practices and CE initiatives. For instance, BMW has created DT factories where about 15,000 of its employees can access data via BMW Factory Viewer and use it for collaborations, virtual inspections and precise measurements simultaneously [53]. The digital platform supports sustainability, efficiency and digital transformation goals [52].

Facilitating collaboration: By integrating human expertise with digital insights, DTs foster collaboration, innovation and creativity. This collaboration supports the development of sustainable solutions and products [54]. DTs can revolutionise human-robot collaboration by enabling real-time simulation, monitoring and control, but there are potential advantages and challenges associated with collaborative environments.

Enhancing user experience: With the level of technological integrations, DTs can enable the creation of personalised products and services that are capable of enhancing customer satisfaction and loyalty that can support sustainability [38,48]. This personalisation aligns with CE principles by promoting sustainable consumption and production patterns. When products and services are smart and customised and personalised to best suit the need of individual users, they tend to stay in use for longer period, thereby offering the best value possible [12].

The human-centric approach of I5.0 emphasises the importance of human skills, creativity and innovation, leveraging DTs to create a harmonious synergy between humans and machines for sustainable outcomes. These are the features of I5.0 that the European Commission believes the foundations of I5.0 should complement those missing links between the society and I4.0.

9.3.2 Customisation, personalisation and circularity

DTs enable the development of personalised products and services, aligning with the goals of I5.0 and the CE. Key applications include mass customisation, product personalisation and circular design and manufacturing which are discussed in the following paragraphs.

DTs are instrumental in enabling mass customisation while supporting sustainability and CE goals [48]. By creating accurate virtual models of products and production processes, DTs allow manufacturers to adapt production lines in real time to meet varying customer demands without overproducing or wasting materials [38,54]. This flexibility reduces excess inventory and minimises the use of raw materials, aligning with sustainability goals by ensuring that products are manufactured only when needed and to precise specifications. Additionally, DTs enable better forecasting of material requirements and production timelines, reducing energy consumption and waste associated with trial-and-error manufacturing processes [55]. In the broader context of the CE, mass customisation powered by DTs helps manufacturers create products designed for longevity, reuse, repair, remanufacture and eventual cascading to a third party, contributing to a more sustainable production ecosystem [12,19].

Product personalisation, when enhanced by DTs, also promotes sustainability by reducing waste and unnecessary resource consumption. DTs allow manufacturers to create individualised products based on real-time data, ensuring that each product meets the exact specifications of the consumer without overproduction or excessive use of materials [5]. This precision helps eliminate wasteful practices and reduces the environmental footprint of manufacturing processes. Furthermore, DTs can enable the integration of CE key principles into personalised production, allowing companies to design products with disassembly, recycling, reuse, repair or remanufacture in mind. By leveraging real-time insights from DTs, manufacturers are able to ensure that personalised products not only meet consumer preferences but also align with sustainable production goals by optimising the use of resources and minimising material waste throughout the product lifecycle.

Another potential application is in circular design and manufacturing. DTs also drive the adoption of circular design and manufacturing principles, which aim to minimise waste and extend product lifecycles through sustainable practices. By simulating the entire lifecycle of a product, DTs provide insights into how materials can be reused, repurposed or recycled at the end of a product's life, facilitating more sustainable production methods [37,52]. They allow manufacturers to optimise resource use, reduce material waste and ensure energy efficiency throughout the manufacturing process. Furthermore, the data captured and analysed by DTs enables companies to design products with circularity in mind from the outset, ensuring that components can be disassembled and materials recovered for future use. This minimises environmental impact and contributes to the broader goal of sustainable manufacturing, where products are designed for longevity, reuse, repair, recyclability, cascading before energy recovery, all while maintaining efficiency and reducing costs.

These applications and more demonstrate the potential of DTs to drive customisation and personalisation, aligning with the human-centric and CE goals of I5.0.

9.3.3 Ethical and environmental considerations

Based on the definition of I5.0 from the European Commission, it emphasises sustainability and ethical considerations, leveraging DTs to create environmentally responsible and socially equitable systems [49]. The Commission clearly states that

> 'The new concept of I5.0 could not come at a better time. Many European industries are reinventing themselves, adapting to the new COVID reality, increasingly embracing digital and green technologies to remain the solution provider for all Europeans. Now is the time to make workplaces more inclusive, build more resilient supply chains and adopt more sustainable ways of production'. [49]

Some of the key areas demanding critical attentions include sustainable manufacturing, energy efficiency and ethical considerations [38]. DTs enable the optimisation of resource usage, reducing waste and minimising environmental impact. This optimisation supports sustainable production practices and CE initiatives as discussed in previous sections [47]. Energy efficiency can also be achieved by continuous monitoring of energy consumption in real-time to identify opportunities for energy savings and efficiency improvements. This capability supports sustainability goals and reduces carbon footprints [42]. Just like other digital technologies, DTs also raise ethical considerations, such as data privacy, transparency and accountability, requiring careful consideration and governance [38,48]. Addressing these considerations ensures that DT solutions align with ethical and sustainability goals as the core values of I5.0.

The integration of sustainability and ethical considerations into DT solutions aligns with the goals of I5.0, promoting responsible and equitable industrial practices.

9.4 Case studies and industry examples

DTs appear ready to fulfil their vast potential across various industries, such as automotive, aerospace, construction, agriculture, mining, utilities, retail, healthcare, military, natural resources and public safety sectors [38]. One example from the aerospace is Boeing. Boeing created an AR-powered aircraft inspection application using a DT of one of its planes. This DT enabled Boeing to generate over 100,000 synthetic images to better train the machine learning algorithms of the AR application which can easily be adopted for circular and sustainable practices [56]. Another case study is from architecture. The award-winning SHoP Architects and JDS Development Group, a firm specialising in real estate development, construction and acquisitions, are leveraging real-time data through Unity to accelerate decision-making among all project stakeholders, providing opportunity for incorporating CE principles. This is how a DT of The Brooklyn Tower, a 93-story, 1,073-foot skyscraper in New York City, helps save time, reduce costs and lower the project's carbon footprint [56], a crucial aspects of CE. Yet another case study that can be considered powerful is from the automotive industry. Volvo Cars adopted DT technology to enhance communication and collaboration between design and engineering teams, minimise dependence on physical prototype vehicles and create more immersive and impactful buying experiences [57]. All these case studies not demonstrate the capability of DTs but present opportunities for enabling CE principles such as designing out waste, designing for reuse, using renewable energy and enhancing energy efficiency.

Focusing on CE and sustainable practices, the buildings and infrastructure industry is where digital is poised to make a substantial impact. DTs are used to optimise energy consumption in buildings and ensure the resilience of critical infrastructure. The digital replicas mirror physical assets and systems, offering a transformative approach to understanding, managing and optimising various aspects of construction, building and infrastructure management [58]. These are just few and publicly available case studies and examples the potential impact of DTs, I4.0 and I5.0 and the CE. The main target remains a win-win ecosystem for both the society and the industry.

9.5 Future directions and trends

Technological innovation often brings challenges like increased energy consumption, resource depletion and waste generation. Yet, groundbreaking advancements show how technology can align with sustainability objectives [1]. SpaceX exemplifies this by revolutionising aerospace with reusable components such as the Falcon 9 first stage, payload fairings, starship system and raptor engines. These innovations drastically reduce the need for new materials, lower costs and minimise environmental impacts [59]. By integrating reusability into its operations, SpaceX has set a benchmark for how cutting-edge technologies can drive environmental responsibility while advancing industrial capabilities, hence, could an area to explore the application DTs further.

DTs, AI and other technological components face similar concerns about energy use and resource efficiency. However, companies such as NVIDIA are addressing these issues through targeted initiatives. For instance, NVIDIA's energy-efficient GPUs, reliance on renewable electricity and efforts to optimise datacentre operations illustrate a commitment to reducing AI's environmental footprint [2]. Beyond internal measures, NVIDIA also leverages AI to tackle global challenges like climate adaptation and resource management, showcasing how AI can be a powerful tool for sustainability as AI is key component of DTs.

Tech leaders like Google, Microsoft, IBM, Amazon and Apple are similarly transforming AI into a force for environmental good [3,4]. Google has significantly reduced energy use in datacentres through AI-driven cooling systems [60]. Microsoft's AI for Earth initiative supports environmental monitoring and conservation [60], while IBM employs AI for weather prediction and resource optimisation. Amazon uses AI to enhance logistics and renewable energy integration, and Apple's supply chain AI fosters energy efficiency, with hundreds of its suppliers committing to renewable energy [4].

These examples illustrate how industries are using technology to address environmental concerns. By embedding sustainability into the core of innovation, companies demonstrate that progress and environmental stewardship are not mutually exclusive but complementary drivers of a sustainable future.

9.5.1 Evolution of digital twin technology

The evolution of DT is rapidly advancing, offering new opportunities for innovation across various sectors. As DTs become more sophisticated, their integration with emerging technologies and expansion across industries is shaping the future of digital operations. Below are some of the most significant trends in the adoption and evolution of DT technology.

Integration with AI and machine learning

DTs are increasingly being enhanced by AI and ML technologies, which significantly improve their predictive capabilities [37]. This integration enables more accurate simulations, advanced analytics and real-time optimisation of processes. With AI and ML, DTs can predict system failures, optimise workflows and enable better decision-making, making them indispensable in industries that require high precision and efficiency [23,55]. The following sections highlights how the evolution of DTs with other technologies can facilitate the realisation of CE in I4.0 and I5.0.

Expansion across industries
Originally pioneered in sectors like manufacturing and aerospace, DT technology is now expanding rapidly into diverse industries, including healthcare, smart cities and energy management [38]. In healthcare, for example, DTs are being used to simulate patient-specific treatments, offering more personalised and effective healthcare solutions [37,61]. The flexibility of DT applications in new domains is unlocking significant potential for innovation, operational efficiency and enhanced service delivery. The key is innovation and creativity for DTs to penetrate new sectors.

Real-time data and IoT integration
The integration of the IoT with DTs is becoming increasingly common, providing DTs with real-time data from physical assets and environments [21]. This allows for dynamic, accurate simulations and enhanced monitoring capabilities [62]. By using IoT sensors to continuously feed data into DT systems, businesses can gain a comprehensive, real-time view of their operations, enabling rapid responses to changes and improving overall system performance.

Enhanced predictive maintenance
One of the most impactful applications of DT technology is in predictive maintenance. By leveraging real-time data and advanced analytics, DTs can accurately predict equipment failures and identify maintenance needs before issues arise [63]. This predictive capability reduces unplanned downtime, extends equipment lifespan, reduces waste and cuts maintenance costs, ultimately enhancing operational reliability and environmental sustainability across industries like manufacturing, energy and logistics [44,45,47].

Sustainability and energy efficiency
DTs are becoming essential tools in sustainability efforts, helping organisations reduce their carbon footprints and optimise energy usage. By simulating energy consumption patterns and identifying inefficiencies, DTs enable companies to fine-tune their operations for greater sustainability [42,45]. These capabilities are increasingly valuable as industries strive to meet environmental goals and comply with stricter regulations on emissions and resource usage.

Improved supply chain management
The incorporation of DTs into supply chain management is revolutionising logistics, offering enhanced visibility and control over supply chain processes. DTs provide real-time tracking, predict supply chain disruptions and optimise the movement of goods [48,63]. This allows companies to increase efficiency, reduce costs and improve the resilience of their supply chains by responding swiftly to disruptions.

Cybersecurity enhancements
As DT technology becomes more integral to critical infrastructure and operational systems, ensuring the security of DTs and their data is becoming increasingly important.

Future trends in DT technology will likely focus on bolstering cybersecurity measures to protect sensitive data and operational integrity. This includes implementing advanced encryption protocols, real-time threat detection systems and secure data sharing frameworks to safeguard DTs from cyber threats [64]. Now, may also be the right time to start considering quantum computing cybersecurity enhancements for future DTs.

User-friendly interfaces and accessibility
A key trend in the evolution of DT technology is the development of more intuitive, user-friendly interfaces [65]. This progress is making DTs more accessible to a broader range of users, including those without specialised technical knowledge. By simplifying the user experience and reducing the technical barrier to entry, DT technology can be adopted more widely across various sectors, driving further innovation and efficiency [55].

These trends underscore the growing importance of DT technology as it continues to evolve. From enhancing operational efficiency and sustainability to improving decision-making and security, DTs are poised to become integral to the future of various industries, transforming how businesses manage their assets, operations and resources. As DT adoption expands, the technology will continue to play a critical role in driving innovation, improving business performance and supporting sustainable practices across the global economy.

9.5.2 Digital twin integration with Industry 5.0 technologies

The convergence of DTs with I5.0 is set to revolutionise numerous sectors, driving advancements in human–machine collaboration, sustainability and operational efficiency as defined by the European Commission [49]. I5.0 emphasises a human-centric approach that integrates advanced technologies, offering significant opportunities for the evolution of key industries which can be achieved through integration with CE principles. Below are some of the most promising future applications and technological developments arising from this integration.

Human-centric manufacturing
I5.0 focuses on the seamless collaboration between humans and machines. DTs will play a pivotal role in manufacturing by creating virtual replicas of production processes, enabling real-time monitoring and dynamic adjustments [66] leading to integration of sustainable practices. This leads to more personalised, efficient production lines where human workers and robots collaborate effortlessly, optimising both productivity and worker satisfaction. The ability to simulate production environments will allow manufacturers to make rapid, data-driven decisions to fine-tune operations and eliminate resource waste beforehand.

Advanced supply chain management
The integration of DTs with blockchain technology promises to revolutionise supply chain management by enhancing transparency, security and efficiency. Blockchain provides immutable transaction records, while DTs enable real-time tracking and simulation of supply chain processes [66]. This combination will

allow organisations to monitor and optimise every stage of their supply chains, improving reliability and responsiveness while reducing costs, minimising resources waste and enhancing operational integrity. The integration. Of blockchain could tackle the issue of trust, security and privacy which is a common issue for digital technologies and crucial for transition to CE.

Smart agriculture
In the context of Agriculture 5.0, DTs offer the potential to optimise livestock production systems through the integration of IoT devices and cyber-physical systems. Farmers can monitor animal health, track environmental conditions and manage resources more efficiently, ultimately boosting productivity. The ability to simulate agricultural environments and processes allows for precision agriculture, improving decision-making related to crop growth, resource allocation and sustainable farming practices that include waste reduction [67].

Enhanced predictive maintenance
DTs, powered by AI and big data analytics, will revolutionise predictive maintenance by providing more accurate forecasts of equipment failures and maintenance needs [68]. This capability will significantly reduce unplanned downtime, lower maintenance costs and enhance the overall efficiency of industrial operations. By continuously collecting and analysing real-time data, DTs can optimise the lifecycle management of machinery and infrastructure, extending their useful life and reducing operational disruptions. It also ensures that equipment are maintained before failures so reuse, repair, remanufacture, recycle and even cascade are made possible which all reduces waste generation and materials use [12].

Sustainable energy management
DTs can play a crucial role in optimising energy usage across industries, helping organisations meet sustainability targets. By simulating and optimising energy consumption, DTs will enable companies to reduce their carbon footprints and improve energy efficiency [68]. Integrating DTs with advanced communication protocols such as 6G will provide real-time data and actionable insights, empowering organisations to make data-driven decisions that support both operational excellence and environmental sustainability [67].

Healthcare innovations
In healthcare, DTs offer significant potential for personalised medicine by creating patient-specific models that simulate treatments and predict health outcomes. It can also be employed for predicting and maintaining medical equipment status and failures thereby minimising medical wastes which can be very hazardous [69]. This technology allows for individualised treatment plans based on real-time data, improving patient outcomes and reducing the reliance on physical prototypes in drug development and medical device testing, leading to efficiency and waste reductions [66]. The use of DTs in healthcare can streamline diagnostics, treatment planning and even the design of patient-specific surgical procedures, advancing the field of precision medicine and potentially minimising medical equipment waste.

Urban planning and smart cities
DTs will also be integral to the future of urban planning and the development of smart cities. Virtual city models can simulate various urban dynamics such as traffic flow, energy consumption and waste management [70] with CE principles at its core. These simulations allow city planners to make informed decisions that improve infrastructure, enhance sustainability and reduce environmental impact. DTs can also help in optimising public services, ensuring more efficient and resilient city systems in the face of population growth and climate change.

Cybersecurity enhancements
As DTs become increasingly integrated into critical infrastructure and industrial systems, cybersecurity becomes paramount. Ensuring the protection of DT data and operations from cyber threats will be a key priority. Future advancements in cybersecurity for DTs will focus on developing robust protocols and security architectures to safeguard sensitive information and ensure the integrity of these digital systems in real time, protecting against emerging cyber risks [70].

These emerging trends demonstrate the transformative potential of integrating DT technology with I5.0 to promote CE initiatives. By driving innovation, efficiency and sustainability across various sectors, DTs will be pivotal in shaping the future of industries ranging from manufacturing and agriculture to healthcare and urban planning and beyond. As these technologies evolve, their applications will continue to expand, unlocking new possibilities for research, collaboration between humans and machines and contributing to a more sustainable and efficient future through the principles of CE.

9.5.3 Challenges and opportunities

The future of DT technology with its key enabling technologies, I4.0, I5.0 and CE presents both challenges and vast opportunities as also already discussed in previous sections. As industries continue to explore its potential, overcoming these hurdles while capitalising on emerging possibilities will be key to accelerating the adoption and effectiveness of DTs across various sectors. The following paragraphs will now look at some of these key challenges that must addressed.

9.5.3.1 Challenges

Data security and privacy
DTs depend on large volumes of data, much of which can be sensitive or proprietary. Ensuring the security and privacy of this data is critical to prevent breaches and unauthorised access [38]. Robust cybersecurity measures must be developed to protect data integrity, safeguarding the trust of users and stakeholders in line all major laws such as the GDPR and data protection laws. A proactive approach to data protection will be crucial to DT adoption, particularly as more industries integrate these systems into their operations.

High implementation costs
The high initial costs of setting up and integrating DTs pose a significant challenge, especially for small and medium-sized enterprises [37,48]. However, as DT

technology matures and becomes more widespread, these costs are expected to decrease as it is the case with new technologies. McKinsey reported that, '75 percent of large enterprises are actively investing in DTs to scale AI solutions. Each technology has immense potential, and together they could unlock trillions in total economic value' [55]. In addition, highlighting the long-term cost savings, efficiency improvements, operational and human-centric benefits that DTs and the enabling technologies offer can help justify the upfront investment, making them a more attractive option for businesses of all sizes [23,54].

Standardisation issues
The lack of standardised protocols and procedures across industries hinders the seamless integration of DTs [33,38]. Just DTs and I5.0, the CE model is still a new paradigm shift with no standard taxonomy, there adding to the complexities and challenges [71]. This challenge limits interoperability between different systems and reduces the overall efficiency of DT applications. Establishing industry-wide standards and best practices is vital to addressing this issue, facilitating smoother adoption and integration while enhancing the effectiveness of DTs in diverse environments.

Complexity and scalability
Creating and managing DTs for complex systems presents challenges, particularly when scaling up for larger operations [19,47]. This is where advancements in AI and machine learning can play a crucial role. These technologies can simplify the creation, management and scaling of DTs, allowing for easier handling of complex systems and ensuring that DTs remain effective, even as operations expand.

9.5.3.2 Opportunities

Enhanced predictive maintenance
One of the most promising opportunities presented by DTs is their ability to enhance predictive maintenance [49]. By accurately forecasting equipment failures and maintenance needs, DTs can help organisations reduce downtime and minimise maintenance costs. This not only improves operational efficiency but also extends the lifespan of equipment which is core model of the CE. However, continuous data collection and analysis are essential to ensure the accuracy and reliability of these predictions.

Sustainability and energy efficiency
DTs offer significant potential for optimising energy usage and reducing carbon footprints, making them valuable tools in achieving sustainability goals [38,43]. By simulating and optimising energy consumption, DTs contribute to more efficient resource use and environmentally friendly practices. Integrating DTs with existing energy management systems can be complex, but the potential benefits make this opportunity worth pursuing, particularly in industries seeking to reduce their environmental impact which of course cut across every industry.

Improved resource decision-making
DTs can enhance decision-making by providing real-time data and simulations across various industries. This capability allows organisations to test scenarios, predict outcomes and make informed resource circularity decisions quickly and

avoid risking human lives in some context. However, ensuring the accuracy and timeliness of the data and simulations is crucial for reliable decision-making [47,62]. Ongoing updates and data verification processes will be needed to maintain the relevance and accuracy of the insights generated by DTs.

Personalised healthcare for waste reduction

In the healthcare sector, DTs offer the opportunity to simulate patient-specific treatments, advancing personalised medicine and improving health outcomes. By creating virtual models of patients, DTs can help predict the efficacy of treatments, allowing healthcare providers to tailor interventions more effectively [38]. Furthermore, DTs can play a crucial role in optimising the circularity of medical resources. By tracking the lifecycle of medical devices and equipment, DTs can facilitate predictive maintenance through early identification of potential failures and allow for timely repairs or refurbishment, extending the lifespan of medical equipment and reducing the need for premature replacements. Optimal utilisation is also possible by using DTs to analyse usage patterns and identify underutilised equipment, enabling better resource allocation and minimising waste. Efficient reprocessing can also be achieved by monitoring device usage and sterilisation cycles since DTs can ensure optimal reprocessing workflows, maximising the reuse of single-use devices and minimising waste generation. DTs can facilitate the creation of closed-loop systems for medical devices, enabling efficient repair, recycling, recovery, refurbishment and reuse of valuable materials. Integrating diverse data sources and ensuring the accuracy, security and privacy of patient data remain complex challenges that must be addressed to fully unlock these opportunities.

By addressing these challenges and harnessing the associated opportunities, DT technology is poised to transform industries and provide significant value across sectors. As organisations continue to innovate and refine DT applications, their potential to enhance efficiency, sustainability and decision-making will only grow.

9.6 Conclusion

This chapter has explored the transformative potential of DTs in driving the CE within the frameworks of I4.0 and I5.0. DTs, as virtual replicas of physical assets and processes, provide real-time monitoring, simulation and optimisation, making them powerful enablers of efficiency, customisation and sustainability. DTs are pivotal in bridging the gap between the physical and digital worlds, enhancing decision-making, operational and efficiency, and efficient resource management. Integration of technologies like IoT, AI, 5G and a host of others as discussed in this chapter, with DTs supports real-time data analysis, enabling advance predictive maintenance, resource optimisation and waste reduction through various routes. I5.0's human-centric and sustainable approach expands the potential of DTs, fostering collaboration between humans and machines, supporting personalised production and promoting CE principles such as reuse, repair, remanufacture, recycle and cascade.

With the rapidly evolving nature of digital technologies which DTs depend on, the challenges and future directions of DTs remain intriguing. While the integration of DTs with I4.0 and I5.0 presents numerous opportunities, challenges such as data security, interoperability and high implementation costs must be addressed. To unlock the full potential of DTs, standardisation and scalable solutions are essential. As the technology evolves, the convergence of AI, machine learning and blockchain will further enhance DT capabilities, driving innovation in industries ranging from manufacturing to healthcare, urban planning and beyond.

In conclusion, DTs represent a critical innovation for industries aiming to achieve sustainability, efficiency and resilience. As businesses and governments continue to embrace DT technology, its role in fostering a CE and realising I5.0's vision of a human-centred, sustainable future will only become more prominent.

References

[1] BBC. 'Elon Musk's Starship booster captured in world first.' https://www.bbc.co.uk/news/articles/c8xe7exjy1go (accessed 12/11/2024).

[2] Nvidia. 'NVIDIA Sustainability Report Fiscal Year 2024.' https://images.nvidia.com/aem-dam/Solutions/documents/FY2024-NVIDIA-Corporate-Sustainability-Report.pdf (accessed 03/12/2024).

[3] C. Mega. 'AI Sustainability: How Microsoft, Google Cloud, IBM & Dell Are Working on Reducing AI's Climate Harms.' https://www.techrepublic.com/article/tech-giants-ai-sustainability/ (accessed 10/12/2024).

[4] Research and Markets. 'Sustainable Data Center Industry Outlook & Forecast 2024–2029: Cloud Data Center Tech Giants such as Google, Microsoft, Oracle, IBM, Tencent, Meta, and AWS Are Leading the Charge – ResearchAndMarkets.com.' https://www.businesswire.com/news/home/20241220909755/en/Sustainable-Data-Center-Industry-Outlook-Forecast-2024-2029-Cloud-Data-Center-Tech-Giants-such-as-Google-Microsoft-Oracle-IBM-Tencent-Meta-and-AWS-are-Leading-the-Charge—ResearchAndMarkets.com (accessed 20/12/2024).

[5] R. Agrawal, V. Wankhede, A. Kumar, *et al.*, 'Progress and trends in integrating Industry 4.0 within circular economy: A comprehensive literature review and future research propositions', *Business Strategy and the Environment*, 2022, https://doi.org/10.1002/bse.2910.

[6] L. Wang, M. Törngren, and M. Onori, 'Current status and advancement of cyber-physical systems in manufacturing', *Journal of Manufacturing Systems*, vol. 37, pp. 517–527, 2015.

[7] M. Rüßmann, M. Lorenz, P. Gerbert, *et al.*, 'Industry 4.0: The future of productivity and growth in manufacturing industries', *Boston Consulting Group*, vol. 9, no. 1, pp. 54–89, 2015.

[8] L. S. Dalenogare, G. B. Benitez, N. F. Ayala, and A. G. Frank, 'The expected contribution of Industry 4.0 technologies for industrial performance', *International Journal of Production Economics*, vol. 204, pp. 383–394, 2018, https://doi.org/10.1016/j.ijpe.2018.08.019.

[9] J. Leng, W. Sha, B. Wang, *et al.*, 'Industry 5.0: Prospect and retrospect', *Journal of Manufacturing Systems*, vol. 65, pp. 279–295, 2022.

[10] X. Xu, Y. Lu, B. Vogel-Heuser, and L. Wang, 'Industry 4.0 and Industry 5.0—Inception, conception and perception', *Journal of Manufacturing Systems*, vol. 61, pp. 530–535, 2021, https://doi.org/10.1016/j.jmsy.2021.10.006.

[11] EMF. '*Towards circular economy.*' https://www.ellenmacarthurfoundation.org/assets/downloads/publications/Ellen-MacArthur-Foundation-Towards-the-Circular-Economy-vol.1.pdf (accessed 07/02/2018).

[12] J. S. Mboli, D. Thakker, and J. L. Mishra, 'An Internet of Things-enabled decision support system for circular economy business model', *Software: Practice and Experience*, vol. 52, pp. 772–787, 2020.

[13] EMF. 'Towards the Circular Economy Vol. 3: Accelerating the scale-up across global supply chains.' https://www.ellenmacarthurfoundation.org/assets/downloads/publications/Towards-the-circular-economy-volume-3.pdf (accessed 05/04/2018).

[14] EMF. 'Towards the Circular Economy Vol. 2: opportunities for the consumer goods sector.' https://www.ellenmacarthurfoundation.org/assets/downloads/publications/TCE_Report-2013.pdf (accessed 05/03/2018).

[15] S. Bag, L. Wood, A. Telukdarie, *et al.*, 'Application of Industry 4.0 tools to empower circular economy and achieving sustainability in supply chain operations', *Production Planning & Control*, 2021, https://doi.org/10.1080/09537287.2021.1980902.

[16] C. M. V. B. Almeida, F. Agostinho, D. Huisingh, and B. F. Giannetti, 'Cleaner production towards a sustainable transition', *Journal of Cleaner Production*, vol. 142, pp. 1–7, 2017, https://doi.org/10.1016/j.jclepro.2016.10.094.

[17] M. Mashaly, 'Connecting the twins: A review on digital twin technology & its networking requirements', *Procedia Computer Science*, vol. 184, pp. 299–305, 2021.

[18] M. Grieves, 'Digital twin: manufacturing excellence through virtual factory replication', *Digital Twin White Paper*, vol. 1, no. 2014, pp. 1–7, 2014.

[19] A. Preut, J. Kopka, and U. Clausen, 'Digital twins for the circular economy', *Sustainability*, 2021. [Online]. Available: https://www.mdpi.com/2071-1050/13/18/10467.

[20] Scottish Enterprise. 'Sustainability-driven innovation: how it can help your business.' https://www.scottish-enterprise.com/learning-zone/business-guides/sustainability-driven-innovation (accessed 12/06/2024).

[21] R. Minerva, G. M. Lee, and N. Crespi, 'Digital twin in the IoT context: A survey on technical features, scenarios, and architectural models', *Proceedings of the IEEE*, vol. 108, no. 10, pp. 1785–1824, 2020, https://doi.org/10.1109/JPROC.2020.2998530.

[22] J. E. Ibarra-Esquer, F. F. González-Navarro, B. L. Flores-Rios, L. Burtseva, and M. A. Astorga-Vargas, 'Tracking the evolution of the internet of things concept across different application domains', *Sensors*, vol. 17, no. 6, p. 1379, 2017.

[23] Z. Huang, Y. Shen, J. Li, M. Fey, and C. Brecher, 'A survey on AI-driven digital twins in industry 4.0: Smart manufacturing and advanced robotics', *Sensors*, vol. 21, no. 19, p. 6340, 2021.

[24] A. Ahmed, M. Nazzal, and B. Darras, Cyber-physical systems as an enabler of circular economy to achieve sustainable development goals: A comprehensive review (*International Journal of Precision Engineering and Manufacturing*). Springer, vol. 9, pp. 955–975, 2021.

[25] Q. Qi, D. Zhao, T. W. Liao, and F. Tao, 'Modeling of cyber-physical systems and digital twin based on edge computing, fog computing and cloud computing towards smart manufacturing', in *International Manufacturing Science and Engineering Conference*, 2018, vol. 51357: American Society of Mechanical Engineers, p. V001T05A018.

[26] J. Anuradha, 'A brief introduction on Big Data 5Vs characteristics and Hadoop technology', *Procedia Computer Science*, vol. 48, pp. 319–324, 2015.

[27] J. Cheng, W. Chen, F. Tao, and C. L. Lin, 'Industrial IoT in 5G environment towards smart manufacturing', (in English), *Journal of Industrial Information Integration*, vol. 10, pp. 10–19, 2018, https://doi.org/10.1016/j.jii.2018.04.001.

[28] C. L. Stergiou and K. E. Psannis, 'Digital twin intelligent system for industrial IoT-based big data management and analysis in cloud', *Virtual Reality & Intelligent Hardware*, vol. 4, no. 4, pp. 279–291, 2022.

[29] R. Dong, C. She, W. Hardjawana, Y. Li, and B. Vucetic, 'Deep learning for hybrid 5G services in mobile edge computing systems: Learn from a digital twin', *IEEE Transactions on Wireless Communication*, vol. 18, no. 10, pp. 4692–4707, 2019.

[30] F. P. Knebel, R. Trevisan, G. S. do Nascimento, M. Abel, and J. A. Wickboldt, 'A study on cloud and edge computing for the implementation of digital twins in the oil & gas industries', *Computers & Industrial Engineering*, vol. 182, p. 109363, 2023.

[31] H. X. Nguyen, R. Trestian, D. To, and M. Tatipamula, 'Digital twin for 5G and beyond', *IEEE Communications Magazine*, vol. 59, no. 2, pp. 10–15, 2021.

[32] H. Ahmadi, A. Nag, Z. Khar, K. Sayrafian, and S. Rahardja, 'Networked twins and twins of networks: An overview on the relationship between digital twins and 6G', *IEEE Communications Standards Magazine*, vol. 5, no. 4, pp. 154–160, 2021.

[33] A. Shabani, M. Skamantzari, S. Tapinaki, A. Georgopoulos, V. Plevris, and M. Kioumarsi, '3D simulation models for developing digital twins of heritage structures: Challenges and strategies', *Procedia Structural Integrity*, vol. 37, pp. 314–320, 2022.

[34] Z. Zhu, C. Liu, and X. Xu, 'Visualisation of the digital twin data in manufacturing by using augmented reality', *Procedia Cirp*, vol. 81, pp. 898–903, 2019.

[35] H. R. Hasan, K. Salah, R. Jayaraman, *et al.*, 'A blockchain-based approach for the creation of digital twins', *IEEE Access*, vol. 8, pp. 34113–34126, 2020.

[36] T. Y. Pang, J. D. Pelaez Restrepo, C.-T. Cheng, A. Yasin, H. Lim, and M. Miletic, 'Developing a digital twin and digital thread framework for an 'Industry 4.0' shipyard', *Applied Sciences*, vol. 11, no. 3, p. 1097, 2021.

[37] J. Kaivo-oja, O. Kuusi, M. S. Knudsen, and T. Lauraeus, 'Digital twins approach and future knowledge management challenges: where we shall need system integration, synergy analyses and synergy measurements?', in *Knowledge Management in Organizations: Proceedings of the 14th International Conference, KMO 2019, Zamora, Spain*, 2019: Springer, pp. 271–281.

[38] M. Attaran and B. G. Celik, 'Digital twin: Benefits, use cases, challenges, and opportunities', *Decision Analytics Journal*, vol. 6, p. 100165, 2023, https://doi.org/10.1016/j.dajour.2023.100165.

[39] S.-K. Jo, D.-H. Park, H. Park, Y. Kwak, and S.-H. Kim, 'Energy planning of pigsty using digital twin', in *2019 International Conference on Information and Communication Technology Convergence (ICTC)*, 2019: IEEE, pp. 723–725.

[40] R. G. Alves, G. Souza, R. F. Maia, *et al.*, 'A digital twin for smart farming', in *2019 IEEE Global Humanitarian Technology Conference (GHTC)*, 2019: IEEE, pp. 1–4.

[41] V. Erdélyi and L. Jánosi, 'Digital twin and shadow in smart pork fetteners', *International Journal of Engineering and Management Sciences*, vol. 4, no. 1, pp. 515–520, 2019.

[42] Y. Fathy, M. Jaber, and Z. Nadeem, 'Digital twin-driven decision making and planning for energy consumption', *Journal of Sensor and Actuator Networks*, vol. 10, no. 2, p. 37, 2021.

[43] Y. Blomkvist and L. Ullemar Loenbom, 'Improving supply chain visibility within logistics by implementing a digital twin: A case study at Scania Logistics,' Master of Science Thesis, School of Industrial Engineering and Management, KTH Royal Institute of Technology, 2020.

[44] G. M. Insight, 'Digital twin market size, share & trends analysis report by end use (manufacturing, agriculture), by solution (component, process, system), by region (North America, APAC), and segment forecasts, 2022–2030, 2021', Online: https://www.grandviewresearch.com/industry-analysis/digital-twin-market, (accessed 10/02/2024) 2021.

[45] R. Beltramo, E. Vesce, and S. Duglio, 'Utilisation of digitalisation in sustainable manufacturing and the circular economy', In M. Wojnarowska, M. Ćwiklicki, and C. Ingrao (eds.), *Sustainable Products in the Circular Economy: Impact on Business and Society*. Routledge; 2022, https://doi.org/10.4324/9781003179788-9.

[46] S. Ma, Y. Zhang, Y. Liu, H. Yang, J. Lv, and S. Ren, 'Data-driven sustainable intelligent manufacturing based on demand response for energy-intensive industries,' *Journal of Cleaner Production*, vol. 274, p. 123155, 2020.

[47] L. Barth, L. Schweiger, R. Benedech, and M. Ehrat, 'From data to value in smart waste management: Optimizing solid waste collection with a digital twin-based decision support system', *Decision Analytics Journal*, vol. 9, p. 100347, 2023, https://doi.org/10.1016/j.dajour.2023.100347.

[48] A. Fuller, Z. Fan, C. Day, and C. Barlow, 'Digital twin: Enabling technologies, challenges and open research', *IEEE Access*, vol. 8, pp. 108952–108971, 2020.

[49] European Commission. '*Industry 5.0: Towards more sustainable, resilient and human-centric industry.*' https://research-and-innovation.ec.europa.eu/news/all-research-and-innovation-news/industry-50-towards-more-sustainable-resilient-and-human-centric-industry-2021-01-07_en (accessed 20/05/2024).

[50] D. Paschek, A. Mocan, and A. Draghici, 'Industry 5. 0 – the expected impact of next industrial revolution,' in *Management Knowledge Learning International Conference*, 2019, pp. 125–132.

[51] S. Nahavandi, 'Industry 5.0—A Human-Centric Solution', *Sustainability*, vol. 11, no. 16, p. 4371, 2019. [Online]. Available: https://www.mdpi.com/2071-1050/11/16/4371.

[52] S. Overby. 'Digital Twins at Work: 8 Examples.' https://www.sap.com/uk/insights/viewpoints/digital-twins-at-work.html (accessed 25/07/2024).

[53] BMW. 'This is how DIGITAL the BMW iFACTORY is.' https://www.bmwgroup.com/en/news/general/2022/bmw-ifactory-digital.html (accessed 23/01/2024).

[54] M. Shaaban, A. Carfì, and F. Mastrogiovanni, 'Digital twins for human-robot collaboration: A future perspective', in *Intelligent Autonomous Systems*, 18, Cham, 2024: Springer Nature Switzerland, pp. 429–441.

[55] McKinsey. 'Digital twins and generative AI: A powerful pairing.' https://www.mckinsey.com/capabilities/mckinsey-digital/our-insights/tech-forward/digital-twins-and-generative-ai-a-powerful-pairing (accessed 03/08/2024).

[56] Unity. 'Digital twin applications and use cases.' https://unity.com/topics/digital-twin-applications-and-use-cases (accessed 12/08/2024).

[57] Unity. 'Unity's real-time technology helps drive Volvo Cars into the future.' https://unity.com/case-study/volvo (accessed 01/08/2024).

[58] Twinview. 'Digital twins in action: unveiling the best use cases for buildings and infrastructure.' https://www.twinview.com/insights/digital-twins-in-action-unveiling-the-best-use-cases-for-buildings-and-infrastructure (accessed 05/06/2024).

[59] C. Zack. 'Boosting rocket reliability at the material level.' https://news.mit.edu/2023/boosting-rocket-reliability-material-level-1128 (accessed).

[60] A. Varghese, 'AI-driven solutions for energy optimization and environmental conservation in digital business environments', *Asia Pacific Journal of Energy and Environment*, vol. 9, no. 1, pp. 49–60, 2022.

[61] G. A. Moreno López, H. Recaman Chaux, and P. A. Molina Parra, 'Digital twins, metaverse, and learning. Review and proposal of conceptual framework', in *Immersive Learning Research Network*, 515–532, 2024: Cham, Springer Nature Switzerland.

[62] A. Gharaei and D. Kiritsis, *Digital Twin as a decision-making tool to opt for the most promising Product Design Strategies in a Circular Economy* (2nd Smart Services Summit). flore.unifi.it, 2019.

[63] M. Attaran, S. Attaran, and B. G. Celik, 'The impact of digital twins on the evolution of intelligent manufacturing and Industry 4.0', *Advances in*

Computational Intelligence, vol. 3, no. 3, p. 11, 2023, https://doi.org/10.1007/s43674-023-00058-y.

[64] R. Zhang, F. Wang, J. Cai, Y. Wang, H. Guo, and J. Zheng, 'Digital twin and its applications: A survey', *The International Journal of Advanced Manufacturing Technology*, vol. 123, no. 11, pp. 4123–4136, 2022, https://doi.org/10.1007/s00170-022-10445-3.

[65] M.-E. Iliuţă, M.-A. Moisescu, E. Pop, A.-D. Ionita, S.-I. Caramihai, and T.-C. Mitulescu, 'Digital twin—a review of the evolution from concept to technology and its analytical perspectives on applications in various fields', *Applied Sciences*, vol. 14, no. 13, p. 5454, 2024. [Online]. Available: https://www.mdpi.com/2076-3417/14/13/5454.

[66] Z. Zhen and Y. Yao, 'The confluence of digital twin and blockchain technologies in Industry 5.0: Transforming supply chain management for innovation and sustainability', *Journal of the Knowledge Economy*, vol. 16, pp. 5295–5321, 2024, https://doi.org/10.1007/s13132-024-02151-0.

[67] P. Fraga-Lamas, S. Lopes, and T. Fernández-Caramés, 'Green IoT and edge AI as key technological enablers for a sustainable digital transition towards a smart circular economy: An industry 5.0 use case', *Sensors*, vol. 21, p. 5745, 2021. [Online]. Available: https://www.mdpi.com/1244922.

[68] O. A. A. Modad, J. Ryska, A. Chehade, and G. Ayoub, 'Revolutionizing sheet metal stamping through industry 5.0 digital twins: A comprehensive review', *Journal of Intelligent Manufacturing*, vol. 36, pp. 3717–3739, 2024, https://doi.org/10.1007/s10845-024-02453-9.

[69] H.-y. Shi and P.-y. Wang, 'Thermal plasma medical waste treatment: Data-ML driven system performance and product prediction', *Waste and Biomass Valorization*, vol. 16, pp. 299–317, 2024, doi:10.1007/s12649-024-02593-2.

[70] J. Barata and I. Kayser, 'How will the digital twin shape the future of industry 5.0?', *Technovation*, vol. 134, p. 103025, 2024, https://doi.org/10.1016/j.technovation.2024.103025.

[71] V. Julianelli, R. Caiado, L. Scavarda, *et al.* 'Interplay between reverse logistics and circular economy: Critical success factors-based taxonomy and framework,' *Resources, Conservation and Recycling*. Elsevier, vol. 158, p. 104784, 2020.

Chapter 10

Digital twins services architectural design: practical implementation

Gayan Dihantha Kuruppu Kuruppu Appuhamilage[1], *Maqbool Hussain*[1], *Wajahat Ali Khan*[1], *Ben Anderson*[2] *and Asad Masood Khattak*[3]

Abstract

The rapid growth of digitisation of business workflows using Industry 4.0 (4IR) has transformed the way businesses interact with products, processes and people. As an emerging technology, the digital twin can establish two-way communication to simulate attributes and behaviours between physical and virtual entities. The ability to synchronise the state in real-time, model using ontologies, combined with other 4IR technologies such as the Internet of Things, cloud computing, big data and artificial intelligence, has enabled these digital models for self-generation, self-optimisation and self-configuration based on the physical state. Much research followed this data-driven approach of simulating physical entities with 4IR technologies to solve fundamental problems such as intelligent automation, revolutionise industries, value addition, reduce power consumption and climate change using historical and real-time multi-model data. Based on the existing literature, the study has identified the key aspects of a digital twin service such as components, data, models, technologies, architectures and challenges to overcome to ensure the digital twin service achieves the organisational requirements. Researchers used open-source, commercial or custom digital twin platforms to overcome the challenges associated with the digital twin process. These platforms are categorised according to the code availability for core services, acceptable use and licencing by the vendors. Despite having many advantages, as an emerging technology majority of these technologies are not mature or not widely used by the industry and pose many limitations. It is required to follow decision-making mechanisms to select the right digital twin platforms. Furthermore, this chapter is categorised into two parts as the digital twin service and digital twin platforms, and multiple subsections will briefly discuss to lay the foundation of the practical digital twinning process to build either commercial or academic proof of concepts.

[1]School of Computing, College of Science and Engineering, University of Derby, UK
[2]Addqual Ltd., Derby, UK
[3]College of Technological Innovation, Zayed University, Dubai, UAE

Keywords: Digital twinning process; digital twin architectures; digital twin platforms; vendor selection process; modelling and simulation; digital twin challenges.

10.1 Overview

10.1.1 What are digital twin services?

The most cost-effective way to represent a complex dynamic system is through simulating the virtual models. Many experts across various disciplines use simulation of complex systems to optimise physical entities such as products and processes [1]. According to ISO 23247-1:2021, standards provide the terms and definitions for digital twins (DT) in the manufacturing sector. According to the ISO definition, DT are a layered architecture observing physical manufacturing elements by constantly updating operational and environmental data [2,3]. In simple terms, a DT is a digital replica of a physical system [3]. Wu *et al.* presented a DT as a virtual model or representation of a physical entity synchronised with real-time data at a specific frequency and fidelity [4]. But Björnsson *et al.* argue that a DT is distinct from simulation due to its analytical and predictive capabilities [5]. Parle *et al.* defined a DT as a digital representation that includes the features, functionalities and behaviour of the physical asset [3].

There is an increasing number of academic research studies associated with DTs to simulate the physical entities. Jeremiah *et al.* have grouped the existing research into products (consumer goods), systems (factories, buildings and cities), processes (complex processes such as manufacturing and logics to optimise the process and avoid bottlenecks), Internet of Things (IoT, integration of sensors and physical objects), humans (replica of biological systems using health records for personalised medicine) and services (operating and maintaining service environments) DTs [6]. Attaran *et al.* have identified a broad use of cross-disciplinary implementation of DT applications, such as manufacturing (design [7] and optimisation of products and processes [8], supply chain management [9], preventive maintenance [10], cross-functional collaboration), agriculture (farm management [11], resource optimisation, weather modelling, soil management, supply chain management [12], livestock monitoring), healthcare and life sciences (drug development, advanced diagnosis and preventive treatment [13], clinical research, personalised medicine [5,14]), facility and operations design, education and training, diagnosis and therapy [15]), automotive & aviation industry [16], construction and real estate (urban environment [1], automate project control, resource planning and logistics [17], construction safety, quality control and assessment and building performance assessment utilities [18–20]) and mining [21] sectors. Rizqi *et al.* proposed an asset administration shell, which is a smart warehouse based in Taiwan to manage assets, including automated guided vehicles, forklifts and storage [22]. Yu *et al.* [23] proposed a smart charging framework to enable smart features for electric vehicle charging infrastructure. Li *et al.* [24] introduced a novel approach to integrate large-scale hydro steel structures in hydraulic engineering to make it easier for safe, reliable and durable operation and maintenance processes. The research works done by Ismail *et al.* and Koirala *et al.* have mentioned that DT technology will play an important role in managing assets, systems and actors in the urban multi-energy systems in the future [19,20].

The DT technology is unique due to its capability to model individual physical elements and simulate these virtual objects in real time. This unique characteristic has helped to lay the foundation for precision medicine, where DTs can simulate therapies and monitor their results and progression of the disease for each patient [14]. In healthcare, DTs can be used to simulate patients or their anatomy, or hospital environment using dynamic data sources such as electronic health records (EHR), patients' disease registries, omics data as well as physical markers, demographic and lifestyle data [14]. Many existing research is more likely to be digital shadows that simulate the physical entity by using existing datasets or mapping the physical entity using a data stream. But recent advancements in cloud computing to gather and store IoT data and analyse big data using machine learning or artificial intelligence (AI) have the potential for advancements in DTs [14]. For example, Brahmi *et al.* introduced a context-aware framework to monitor air quality and human activity in indoor environments using the sensors, IoT, edge computing and cloud computing [25]. Jin *et al.* have discussed analysis, optimisation, defect detection and sustainability in machine learning's role in DTs [26].

10.1.2 What is digital twin architecture?

A DT architecture is a process of virtually replicating the physical assets or processes by using multiple layers or key components to support operational requirements. According to a white paper published by Grieves a DT consists of a physical object, a virtual object and a digital thread [27]. According to Liu *et al.* [28], the process of DT includes modelling the physical object, real-time connection between the physical and virtual objects, testing and validation, continuous adjustments and feedback to the model. Jeremiah *et al.* [6] argues that a DT is a virtual representation of a physical object, simulating and analysing using mathematical modelling, application programming and specification-based technologies. They have suggested that a DT must cover the operational requirements such as security (confidentiality, integrity, availability and other fault tolerant mechanism aspects), interoperability (compossibility, heterogeneity and scalability aspects), dependability (maintainability and safety aspects), predictability (compositionality and accuracy aspects), reliability (robustness aspect) and sustainability (adaptability, resilient, efficiency, reconfigurability aspects) attributes.

10.1.2.1 Key components

The key characteristic in a DT service is continuous data connectivity between the physical entity with its virtual replica. This unique feature differentiates from simulation, where it does not contain any two-way communication. But with the emergence of edge and distributed computing, researchers can showcase real-time communication between these two entities. Hakiri *et al.* [1] have suggested the following components in DT services.

Network

The *network* is composed of physical hardware, protocols and software tools to manage the connectivity with the edge devices in the physical world with their virtual counterparts. The concepts such as latency, stability, coverage, availability, security and cost play a major role when establishing the connectivity between the two entities.

Physical entity

The *physical entity* is an asset, an object, an entity, a process or a product to represent in a DT service. The physical entity may have multiple entities interacting with each other or relationships crucial to describe the real-world phenomena as required by the operational requirements.

Physical environment

The *physical environment* is the environment where the physical entity exists such as a factory setting for the Cobot or a hospital environment for a patient. When deciding the architecture, it is important to identify the relationships associated with the physical entities. Also, weather elements (such as temperature, illuminance, pressure and noise), pathways, processes, culture, ethics, safety, laws and regulations have to be considered to depict a more accurate picture of the physical environment.

Physical process

The *physical* process is a broader term that represents processes with the physical entity associated in the physical environment. These processes may change or impact the state of the physical entity or environment. For example, the adjustable movements of a Cobot or the progress of the treatment process associated with a patient can be identified as physical processes.

Virtual entity

The *virtual* entity is a model that describes the physical entity, where the state of each instance is synchronised with their physical entity. For example, a Cobot virtual entity can have multiple static entities such as joints to connect arms with its base, and a tool to interface that is necessary to describe a Cobot physical entity or a patient virtual entity can have dynamic entities for the treatment process, disease and anatomy to describe the patient physical entity.

Virtual environment

The *virtual environment* consists of a visual representation of the physical environment. The technologies such as VR/AR, 3D CAD models and dashboards can be used to visualise and analyse virtual entities and the environment for the end-users.

Virtual process

The *virtual process* is a computational process such as analytics, algorithms and functions associated with the virtual entity that can change or impact the state of the virtual entity and virtual environment.

Synchronisation

The *synchronisation* involves two-way communication between the virtual entity and the physical entity. The states associated with the physical processes should be reflected in their virtual entity and vice versa. The IoT is a key technology associated with enabling the synchronisation between two entities.

Synchronisation rate

The *synchronisation* rate is the frequency at which data from the physical entity is reflected on its virtual entity. The most common way to reflect this is hertz, which number of cycles in a second. The synchronisation rate is vital for a more accurate description of the state of the virtual entity. The increasing number of cycles might cause expensive infrastructure for low-latency communication and computer processing requirements.

State

The *state* describes the attributes associated with an entity. For example, attribute describing a joint position of a Cobot may indicate the physical state of the mechanical arm.

Fidelity

The *fidelity* describes the accuracy of the state of the virtual entity at each point in time. Based on the operational requirements, developers can increase the synchronisation rates to the point of more update cycles per second to function near real-time analytics.

Data

The *data* is an important component in a DT architecture. Here, *data* describes all types of data, such as metadata, telemetry, which is used to describe the state of a DT service. The operational requirements, such as accuracy, security, privacy, laws and regulations, are applicable when deciding the data that is going to be collected by the DT service. For example, monitoring a Cobot does not involve laws or regulations to describe the state, but it is important to get accurate information about the Cobot to make an accurate decision regarding employee well-being. For health DTs collecting patient-related clinical and para-clinical data with biomarkers specific to a treatment process for passive patient monitoring, biological and behavioural parameters can cause a lot of ethical and privacy issues [14].

Armeni *et al.* have described that the data sources for health care-related DTs can be sources from a wide range of sources such as EHR, digital health devices (smart watches, wearables for blood pressure and oxygen levels), surveys, datasets, non-health and non-clinical sources (air quality), healthcare processes [14].

10.1.2.2 Data requirements

The data stored in the DT services is in digital formats, represented as JSON to store DT metadata [1]. The DT platforms use two types of data: *telemetry* type and *property* type. The telemetry data type is a data event that does not have any storage. However, property data type saves the data associated with the attribute in the virtual entity. Hakiri *et al.* categorised the data used to denote the DT properties [1].

Time series data

The *time series data* are timestamped historical data used to represent and analyse a virtual entity [29]. This type of data is primarily stored in NoSQL databases, due to the number of records is based on the synchronisation rate of the physical entity [1].

For example, sensor data such as temperature, illuminance and pressure are collected based on the timestamp at the time they are generated by the physical entity. In a DT service, property associated with time series data is initialised as a telemetry data type due to data is collected as telemetry update events with timestamps. If the update event has a high synchronisation rate, then an individual event is not significant to demonstrate the state of the virtual entity. Because the state of the physical entity will translate into the next synchronisation.

Master data

The *master data* is stored in enterprise data stores for resource planning or asset management [1]. Unlike time series data, the DT services associate master data in property data type. The update event is significant to demonstrate the state of the virtual entity.

Transactional data

Unlike master data, operational data consists of business transactions, which are significant to demonstrate the state of the virtual entity [1]. The update event is significant to demonstrate the state of the virtual entity.

10.1.2.3 Digital twin model types

When developing a DT architecture, the nature of the physical entity must be reflected in the virtual entity. In digital twinning, we use different types of models to describe a virtual environment. Hakiri *et al.* proposed different types of DT models [1].

Physics-based models

Ritto and Rochinha introduced physics-based models to DTs in their research on applying machine learning to detect damage in buildings [30]. Most common uses are predicting damage, uncertainty, maintenance for simulation and co-simulation. The physics-based models are used to synchronise virtual entities with real-time operational parameters for calculations using discrete physics for the prediction of physical structures such as buildings and vehicles.

Analytics-based models

Kharchenko *et al.* used machine learning, and mathematical and statistical models to predict the state of the physical entity [31]. Most common uses are prediction, recommendation, simulation and analytics.

Visual models

The visualising technologies, such as augmented reality, virtual reality, metaverse and 3D modelling, can be used to integrate data elements into digital twin architecture [32]. The visual models are used to describe the physical entities as visual elements such as colours, shapes, animations and movements in a visualising environment.

Discrete event simulation models

The discrete event simulation (DES) models abstract the behaviours of physical entities into event-driven operations [33]. These models are used in production and manufacturing domains to create high fidelity simulations for higher accuracy, analysis and prediction.

10.1.2.4 Technology aspects

Attaran and Celik [34] have identified that DT services use four technologies. These technologies have been used to collect and store real-time data generated by physical entities, to provide insights and to create a virtual entity.

Internet of Things

The IoT manages the connectivity between the physical entity and the virtual entity. This technology creates a two-way communication channel to send telemetry data to the virtual entity and execute commands in the physical entity by using networking protocols and software development kits (SDKs) associated with the frameworks. It is useful in systemisation aspect of a DT architecture. The popular examples for the IoT are Azure IoT (proprietary), AWS IoT (proprietary) and Eclipse IoT (open source).

Cloud computing

Cloud computing is a distributed computing framework that provides services such as the IoT, DTs, data storage, computing, machine learning and AI based on dynamic pricing. The main advantages of using cloud computing for building DTs are scalability, availability, support, security and disaster recovery. The popular examples for cloud computing are Azure, AWS and Oracle.

Artificial intelligence

AI is used to achieve human-like intelligence using statistical analysis for decision-making in a DT service. The logical reasoning and data analysis based on the current state and the temporal data of DTs are a few aims to achieve in a DT service.

Extended reality

The immersive technologies, such as virtual reality, augmented reality and mixed reality, are used in DT services to provide a more detailed representation of the virtual entities for non-technical personnel involved in the decision-making process.

10.1.3 What are the different architectures?

10.1.3.1 Levels

In 2014, Grieves *et al.* defined DT services as having three major elements: a physical object in a real space, a virtual object in a virtual space and a digital thread. Here, the physical object can be an object, a process, a person or a phenomenon. The virtual object is a model defined the physical object. The digital thread allows data flows from real space to virtual space, and information flows from virtual space to real space [27]. According to ISO/IEC 30173:2023, a standard DT service has a data collection and control entity for the device, core entity and user entity [3,35]. Since each entity is scattered across the network physically and conceptually, the standard architecture evolves around breaking the whole system into manageable pieces of applications. Jeremiah *et al.* [6] mentioned that DTs follow a layered architecture. The technologies associated with each layer are mentioned in Table 10.1.

Table 10.1 The technologies associated with each digital twin layer [6]

Layer	Technology
Acquisition	MQTT, IoT sensors, wearable devices, TCP-IP, OPC UA, Space Air Ground Integrated (SAGIN) Network, ModBus, Arduino
Synchronisation	Cloud services (Azure/AWS), databases (relational and non-relational databases), data warehouses, data lakes, cloud storage
Modelling	Agent-based simulation, discrete system dynamics, event simulation, IronCAD, FlexSim, Enterprise SolidWorks, AutoCAD, FreeCAD
Visualisation	Virtual reality, augmented reality, desktop web portals (ASP NET Core, Java Spring, Python Flask, React and Angular), mobile apps (Android/iOS), dashboarding and reporting tools (such as Microsoft Power Apps)

10.1.3.2 Architectures

Jeremiah *et al.* have expanded the existing DT ecosystem from a traditional point of view which has three components such as physical object, virtual object and data link, to a broad definition: digital representation, data collection devices, software platforms, user interfaces, communication, data storage and processing, statistics and AI algorithms, and security access control components [6]. These key features are then implemented as either an edge or a distributed architecture.

Edge architecture

The edge architecture defines an independently deployable component from multiple networks and repositories, unifying through enabling horizontal and vertical scalability, and deployment independence [1]. Unlike the cloud architecture, these deployments are unified as a single service. This provides security, mitigates attacks, a modular architecture for deployment, and network efficiency to overcome the complexities associated with distributed systems due to communication failures. Brahmi *et al.* proposed a context-aware framework to monitor indoor climate and human activity using an edge architecture-based framework [25]. There are very few notable examples to provide a fully implementable edge architecture. For example, Ditto by the Eclipse Foundation is a main open-source alternative for DTs. By combining Ditto with other Eclipse Foundation's Eclipse IoT projects such as Hono, Mosquitto and Streamsheets, researchers have come up with solutions such as medical treatments [36], wireless networks [37] and logistics [38]. These edge-based architectures can be easily deployed in their edge nodes to get the benefits of maximum performance from a DT service [39].

The main advantage of edge architecture is the ability to perform real-time analysis due to no noise from the network. Since all the components are deployed at the edge, the framework can extract features and respond faster with accuracy due to low network-related noise or redundant data [40]. There are many limitations such as lack of security, unable to access from external computers, lack of features, reduce performance, hardware limits associated with implementing machine learning or AI algorithms, increased in maintenance and operation costs, scalability issues and external environmental factors such as power failures, fires and data theft. Picone *et al.* [39] introduced the edge-based DTs' architecture represented by using the *Core Engine* concept with the following manages communication and protocol, resource, data, behaviour, composition, metric and logs.

Communication and protocol manager
The *communication and protocol manager* (CPM) layer consists of managing communication and protocols associated with networking, such as implementing standards, protocols and patterns such as RESTful, CoAP, Pub/Sub broker-based communications using MQ Telemetry Transport messaging protocol to publish and subscribe data over a network. The CPM layer allows for communication of available properties, behaviours and relationships of the connected devices using protocols, data formats and interfaces associated with resources, measurements and actions.

Resource manager
The *resource manager* layer manages resources by handling selection, digitisation, enrolment and maintenance of the physical asset by using resources such as sensors and actuators of the physical asset through the networking functionalities provided by the CPM layer.

Data manager
The *data manager* layer supports processing data, storage. This layer manages packets and messages in the *communication and protocol manager* layer and RM layer from physical and digital layers, and internal data structures such as properties, relationships and actions.

Behaviour manager
The *behaviour manager* layer provides the execution of functions associated with the state of the DTs by analysing the available information and descriptions. Each function is associated with a behaviour or achieves the targeted goals by manipulating the virtual and physical entities.

Composition manager
The *composition manager* layer provides interfaces to navigate and explore the composition and relationships of the DTs.

Metric & logs manager
The *metric and logs manager* layer has shared and structures set of functionalities to collect, track, export metrics and logs associated with the DT service to observe the resource allocation, consumption and overview of each layer for monitoring, diagnostic and anomaly detection.

Distributed architecture
The DT platforms by big tech companies such as Microsoft's Azure, Amazon's AWS and Google's Google Cloud Platform (GCP) have emerged as the software intermediary between the physical entities and their growing number of applications. The main feature of these cloud platforms is that they are distributed by nature and accessible from application programming interfaces using REST

architecture and SDKs in multiple programming languages to link their growing number of services to custom-built DT solutions [41]. The product developers can harness these feature-rich, production-grade services to provide customers a scalable DT service without acquiring hardware and adopting micro services and serverless computing to address challenges associated with edge architecture. Jin *et al.* discuss the potential of applying big data using cloud computing to analyse real-time telemetry and historical temporal data associated with the physical assets to analyse materials, optimise design, optimise process parameters, detect defects, and monitor sustainability in the additive manufacturing domain [26]. For healthcare, distributed computing is essential to reduce expenses regarding maintaining an extensive portfolio of hardware, scalability aspects, querying multiple sources of data and powerful computing power that is needed to manage the DT infrastructure [14].

The primary technology associated with distributed architecture is cloud computing services. The big tech companies have introduced their cloud computing platforms such as Microsoft's Azure, Amazons' AWS, Google's GCP and Nvidia's Omniverse. The main advantage of the distributed architecture is the ability to use microservices and serverless computing, which can address various challenges regarding edge architecture, which are security, scalability, accessibility and ability to integrate with many services. The main limitations are load imbalances and network faults [41]. By nature, distributed architecture relies on data flow, and many cloud services are accessed through various networks. The main problem is the network latency and transmission speeds. This reduces the ability to perform the DT framework in real time. Even though these proprietary services are available 24/7, failures and outages could shut down some services. Also, the technology cannot be replicated across other platforms.

The architecture is composed of cloud services such as IoT, DTs, database and static storage, compute, and AI and machine learning tools. The IoT provides the capability to establish and maintain the functionality and changes over time by the physical entity [14]. The DT service helps to describe the virtual entities, relationships using modelling languages and mapping the physical characteristics with virtual attributes. The databases and static storage store temporal data generated by the physical entity and the data that defines the internal structures. The compute services are a containerised microservice platform to execute source code depending on the demand. This reduces the need for virtual machines to execute a program by using triggers and bindings such as Hyper Text Transfer Protocol (HTTP), queue, blob, service bus, timer, event or custom triggers. One of the main limitations of edge computing is that it is expensive to set up the hardware that is required to run machine language and AI frameworks. But distributed computing resolves this issue with its integrated machine learning and AI tools. The tools provide functionalities such as large language models and image recognition to analyse historical data and provide intelligence recommendations based on the real-time state of the DT. Also, the application programming interfaces could be used to virtually represent the physical environment using Unity 3D, AR/VR and metaverse tools [1]. Finally, the analytics services provide useful metrics such as availability, ingress and egress connections and traffic about each service to optimise and secure the network.

10.1.4 What are the challenges?

Currently, challenges regarding DT technology are ethical and policy issues, technical limitations and society [14]. Meijer *et al.* presented data acquisition and integration, data privacy and security, data quality and accuracy, data bias and fairness, ethical considerations, DT modelling, computing infrastructure and business models as challenges [34,42]. Jeremiah *et al.* [6] identified the main causes for security vulnerabilities are real-time connectivity, isolation assumption and heterogeneity. They discussed threats facing DTs such as physical, privacy, criminal, political and financial threats. These vulnerabilities can be caused by power failures, equipment sabotage, unprotected components, jamming and noise, insecure protocols and access points, exposed devices, insecure operating systems and software, network attacks such as DOS, firewalls, rogue human and software attacks, malwares, backdoor exploitations, exposed symmetric keys and unencrypted credentials. Many researchers have provided solutions to overcome challenges such as confidentiality, integrity, availability, safety and intellectual property theft in DTs by enabling blockchain-based DTs and gamification. First, blockchain-based DT frameworks are based on blockchain technology to oversee the coordination in the communication between parties by smart contracts for secure lifecycle data communication between the physical and virtual DT. This method will establish tamper tamper-proof methodology using audit trails for all DTs-based operations in the framework to enhance the security and trustworthiness. Second, gamification helps to identify security vulnerabilities and provides means for security analysts to develop strategies to prevent attacks. Also, it provides a learning environment for the staff members to train [6].

Currently, many challenges we discussed earlier remain unsolved due to many reasons. The high development costs of implementing a robust DT framework have hindered the growth in the industry. The costs related to hardware, software frameworks and trained staff members to develop and maintain these critical systems are enormous due to the lack of supply in the technology. Also, real-time interaction, which is to establish two-way communication between the physical and virtual entities, is impossible due to power failures and natural disasters affecting the communication network's latency and the capacity in a particular geographic area. Next, complexity and technical limitations for modelling physical entities that require dynamic changes and biological entities such as humans are impossible due to the lack of ontologies developed to model the changes and behaviours. The lack of standardisation of policies regarding the knowledge and decisions made by DT entities to follow specific procedures against different scenarios is also a critical challenge. The physical environment dynamically changes based on the scenarios, and the DT frameworks must be designed to work alongside human specialists in the respective field. The human–computer interaction and design of the DT are also critical when human-in-the-loop scenarios. When designing and developing a DT framework, developers must prioritise making the DT framework easier to understand by the non-technical personnel who interact with the system. The insider threats associated with employees, contractors or third-party vendors could steal data or misuse the framework. To overcome this issue, the DT framework should be designed in a way inaccessible to rogue entities using access controls [6].

10.1.4.1 Security and vulnerability

The *security and vulnerability* are access to confidential data by unauthorised bodies. Accessing classified data such as patient healthcare information could cause leakage and vulnerability that would result in catastrophic consequences [14]. To overcome this challenge, organisations encrypt the sensitive data, authorisation roles, limit data accessibility and responsibilities are granted only for authorised users [14,43]. The technical implementations, such as role-based access control, can be used to restrict access based on the user role [1]. For example, Microsoft's Entra and Amazon Cognito provide user directories, authentication servers, authorisation services, private access points, virtual private networks, a firewall for ingress and egress and in-house servers for developers to secure different aspects of the DT service.

10.1.4.2 Privacy

The *privacy* aspect of the DT service expects data integrity and protection from rogue users in the network [1]. This does not limit technical factors, but human factors like screening for criminal history, affiliation with external organisations and employment history should also be considered before engaging anyone to access the sensitive data.

10.1.4.3 Ethics

The *ethics* aspect aimed at providing data integration and prediction while achieving data transparency and avoiding data bias [1]. Also, responsibility, decency and morality are essential to enhance the DT innovation.

10.1.4.4 Scalability and complexity

The *scalability and complexity* involve applying efficient and cost-effective tools and software to model the different DT services. Higher scalability, big data analysis and a computing framework are required to achieve more accurate and better performance in a large-scale DT service [1].

10.1.4.5 Real-time communication

The *real-time communication* is expected to communicate real-time information for real-time synchronisation between the physical entity and virtual entity. But networks offer different quality of service based on various reasons, which could affect higher latency and lower bandwidth, which is essential to provide real-time processing of the information of the DTs [1].

10.1.4.6 Interoperability

The *interoperability* expects providing common data standards and industry standards for interoperability to widespread adoption across various domains. This includes open and standardised interfaces, pre-built models and common methods, as well as models and mechanisms to reduce the fragmentation and heterogeneity of the DT services [1].

10.1.4.7 Modelling complexities

The *modelling complexities* discuss that the models should be flexible and expandable to compose and extend based on dynamic requirements to support the large-scale adoption of DT services [1].

10.1.4.8 Data coherence

The *data coherence* ensures the high fidelity of data. But data coherence and model revision are key challenging issues in preserving the data coherence in a DT service [1].

10.1.4.9 Data quality

It should fit the purpose for which they have been collected or designed to ensure that DT applications continue to work correctly, and update and upgrade to meet the needs they are used for [1]. The *data quality* requires that the data collected by a DT service must meet the operational requirements. The DT service expects continuous operation, updates and upgrades accordingly based on changing requirements.

10.2 Digital twin platforms

A DT is a process of replicating a physical entity with features, functions and behaviours in a virtual entity. This requires software tools to manage the connectivity between the physical entity and the virtual entity, store data and internal structures associated with models, event mechanisms and security protocols. So, creating a DT platform from scratch is expensive and infeasible for many use cases. To overcome these challenges, many companies have provided open-source and proprietary solutions to create, manage and maintain DT solutions. Also, these platforms have their own services and capabilities to integrate with other platforms for further improvements to the DT service for insights and analytics behaviour [3]. This section will discuss the advantages and limitations caused by using DT platforms and selection criteria when selecting a suitable DT platform. Finally this chapter will discuss different types of DT platforms such as open-source, commercial and custom and popular products associated with each classification.

10.2.1 What are the limitations?

The most common limitations associated with DT platforms are platform dependence, required specialised skillset, costs and benefits, lack compelling factors to lure companies to invest in training and development, network issues, availability due to technical failures and depends on big tech companies for critical infrastructure can be recognised as a few limitations [3].

10.2.1.1 Platform dependence

The code infrastructure used in building DT services using these platforms limits its capabilities to the same platform. The code and architecture used to develop these applications cannot be incorporated with other platforms.

10.2.1.2 Special skillset

The process of building and maintaining these DT systems requires specially trained workers who specialised in the specific areas of cloud technologies. The lack of tutorials, coding samples and multi-model training facilities is common in this domain to employ these technologies.

10.2.1.3 Costs and benefits

The costs associated with migrating to the cloud require considerable investments to employ the technology to make it widely available and retire old systems. Cloud computing involves rapid modernisation of the tech stack used to build these services. So many legacy applications cannot be deployed in this modern architecture without a rebuild or significant updates to their codebase. At the end, employing all these changes to an already stable operational mechanism has a high risk of losing customers due to the unavailability of the requested service.

10.2.1.4 Lack of willingness for integration

By considering limitations associated with DT services, many companies are hesitant to use DT technology for their processes since it is an emerging technology. Converting the existing organisational process by retraining the workforce, educating the vendors and building trust in partners is expensive and high-risk due to the novel nature of the technology.

10.2.1.5 Network issues

Achieving near real-time calibration between the physical entity and virtual entity requires seamless connectivity with low-latency and high-bandwidth networks. For many companies situated in rural areas and geographically isolated areas, having a fibre network is expensive and most of the time is unavailable. The radio wave-based communication creates a lot of interference due to weather conditions and has a high latency rate, which is not suitable for real-time DT services.

10.2.1.6 Relying on external organisations for critical infrastructure

The DT services in nature are a critical infrastructure in an organisation. So, organisations always consider applying standalone applications, where they can have control of the infrastructure. Relying on an external organisation to manage the infrastructure can be critical when the service is unavailable.

10.2.2 What are the advantages?

Parle *et al.* [3] mentioned many advantages of using DTs in net-zero manufacturing. First, the ability to integrate various sources of data in real time. This allows a holistic view of the processes, which enables better decision-making and more efficient operations by identifying inefficiencies, predicting failures and suggesting optimal operational parameters which help to reduce the energy consumption. Second, the ability to simulate the physical environment. This simulation capability is crucial for exploring the impact on energy consumption before implementing it in the physical environment. Third, the capability to support automation and autonomous control of the manufacturing process. This reduces the requirement of human factor while minimising the errors, while having consistent performance in the manufacturing process. Fourth, its ability to scalability and flexibility to model physical entities in real time. This has helped to integrate a diverse set of physical entities, ranging from sensors, machines, to humans in a DT service for a comprehensive management, monitoring and control of the resources. Finally, DT services can be used to integrate with visualising tools such as 3D models, virtual reality, augmented reality, metaverse and web-based dashboards to make it easier to identify trends and anomalies.

Ismail *et al.* [19] mentioned that DTs research in the energy sector is aimed at optimising operations, diagnosing faults, monitoring, controlling and simulation energy assets in renewable and non-renewable sectors. Jeremiah *et al.* [6] identified that DTs have the potential to solve security testing and validation, improve patch management, manage risks, active monitoring and incident response in cyber defence, virtual commissioning of products and services, and autonomy and predictive analysis. According to the literature review, the advantages of using appropriate DT platforms are as follows.

- real-time integration of multiple data sources,
- simulation of the physical environment,
- support for automation and autonomous control,
- scalability and flexibility,
- integration of visualising tools,
- ability to diagnose faults and monitor, and
- virtual commissioning of required resources without changing the framework.

Next, the section will discuss on criteria associated with the selection of a DT platform.

10.2.3 How to select a digital twin platform?

Parle *et al.* suggested that the selection of a digital platform must consider if the selected platform must be aligned with the strategic and technology objectives, trustworthiness and usefulness, features and MCDM [3]. They have mentioned different ways we can select a DT platform. Although the author compares the approaches based on general manufacturing and net-zero manufacturing, these approaches could be used in many other domains.

10.2.3.1 Multi-criteria decision-making

The *multi-criteria decision-making* approach (MCDM) aimed at evaluating and determining the DT platform for a case study by considering and comparing based on criteria such as cost, scalability, integration, support, traffic flow, environmental impact and economic considerations using a particular DT platform [44].

10.2.3.2 Multi-level filtering criteria

Unlike the *multi-level filtering criteria* approach, the researchers have come up with multi-level filtering criteria to filter out the platforms based on their capabilities. According to the existing research done by Parle *et al.* and Gil *et al.* these filtering criteria are provided when selecting an open-source and proprietary DT platform to build a DT service. Parle *et al.* [3] described three-level filtering criteria that filter out platforms that do not meet the data integration requirements, analytics capabilities and visualisation capabilities. This approach aims to integrate the physical entities, generate insights for making decisions, aid in optimising the process and simulate scenarios. The review identified Microsoft Azure, Babylon.js, Siemens Xcelerator and Bentley iTwin.js platforms. Gil *et al.* [45] applied multi-level filtering criteria, including communication, storage, analytics, compositional, physical interventions, scalability, standardisation, reproducibility, interoperability and community support. The survey resulted in selecting Eclipse Ditto, Equinox, AASX Package Explorer, PYI40AAS, SAP I4.0 AAS and Eclipse Basyx platforms.

10.2.3.3 SWOT analysis

The *SWOT analysis* is an approach to identify the DT platform according to the strengths, weaknesses, opportunities and threats. Saari *et al.* provided a joint offering framework to assess the DT platforms based on SWOT analysis [46].

10.2.3.4 Cost–benefit analysis

The *cost–benefit analysis* measures the benefits and costs of applying different DT platform for the problem statement. Rubini *et al.* used this approach to identify and evaluate the disruption scenarios and potential benefits and costs of integrating a DT to improve the pharmaceutical manufacturing process, product quality, regulatory compliance and efficiency of the Lyophilisation process [47].

10.2.3.5 Benchmarking

The *benchmarking* involves comparing the results of the DT implementation with related different platforms. Kamath *et al.* [48] explored a benchmarking approach in his paper with five open-source platforms used in digital twinning such as Eclipse Hono, Eclipse Ditto, Apache Kafka, Influx DB and Grafana for the IoT operations, DT capabilities, virtual entity representation, analytics and visualisation using open data by Microsoft to benchmark scaling performance capacity suing testing tools such as Apache JMeter.

10.2.3.6 Pilot testing

The *pilot testing* approach or proof-of-concept (PoC) projects using a DT platform to prove the key features such as reusability, modularity and scalability in use cases. Aziz *et al.* [49] proposed a paradigm that explores a distributed architecture to enable software-centricity, compatibility and flexibility for purpose-oriented digital twinning. Rajesh *et al.* [50] have developed a PoC design of a brake system for predictive maintenance using the ThingWorx IoT platform.

10.2.3.7 Vendor evaluation

The *vendor evaluation* approach is a process of measuring existing supplier relationships. This is a comprehensive assessment method that includes evaluating the vendor's resources, recognising their roadmap and assessing their support and flexibility.

10.2.3.8 User feedback and case studies

The *user feedback* approach uses stakeholder engagement and collaboration about DT platforms. The *case study* approach involves reviewing existing case studies associated with the domain area used by targeted DT platforms.

10.2.4 Types of digital twin platforms

Parle *et al.* categorised DT platforms into three categories as open source, commercial and custom. The commercial DT platforms are offered by companies for subscription or licensed service. These platforms provide more robust customer support with comprehensive features and integration capabilities such as analytics, real-time monitoring, visualisation tools, scalability and regular over-the-air updates. The main drawback with commercial platforms is the high upfront costs regarding staffing and development for such projects. However, open-source involves public collaboration, engagement and learning for inspecting, utilisation and enhancing the repositories. The advantages of using open-source DT platforms are royalty-free, lower development time and costs, community support and scalability [3].

The open-source DT platforms are used by academic due to easy access, free and flexibility. But industry more often make the decision based on how organisational requirements are reflected upon their DT service.

10.2.4.1 Open source platforms

According to Parle *et al.*, an open-source DT platform is offered by organisations for open-source or license-free service. These platforms are based on community support for continuous development. The main advantage is that these platforms are free and flexible to use due to their open-source licensing. Also, these platforms offer customisation, allowing organisations to tailor the platform according to their needs without any costs. The main drawbacks of using open-source DT platforms are the requirement for technical expertise and resources to enable development and maintenance of such DT platforms [3].

Eclipse Ditto by Eclipse

The Eclipse Foundation manages a wide range of projects to provide open-source alternatives for building IoT products for the industry [6]. These open-source projects are licensed under the Eclipse Distribution License 1.0 (BSD) and the Eclipse Public License 2.0. In this section, we discuss how to design a DT architecture using the Eclipse Hono,[1] Eclipse Mosquitto[2] and Eclipse Ditto[3] projects.

[1]https://projects.eclipse.org/projects/iot.hono
[2]https://mosquitto.org/
[3]https://projects.eclipse.org/projects/iot.ditto

The Eclipse Hono project provides remote service interfaces for IoT devices and supports interaction regardless of the device communication protocols. It offers IoT device connectivity, data ingestion and device control using technologies such as Advanced Message Queuing Protocol (AMQP), Message Queue Telemetry Transport (MQTT),[4] HTTP and Apache Kafka.[5] The Eclipse Hono project aims to build a more generic, cloud-based IoT architecture to support the development of IoT platforms. Eclipse Hono supports a bidirectional flow of data, allowing devices to upload their sensory data (telemetry) and invoke functions or services (command and control) using the Eclipse Hono platform. Telemetry typically involves one-way data flow from IoT devices to business applications, with sensory readings such as temperature, humidity or illuminance, and property values like device manufacturer, model name or machine status. IoT devices do not expect messages from the Eclipse Hono platform when they send telemetry events. Command and control primarily represent the functionalities or services provided by IoT devices such as updates, querying telemetry events or setting configuration parameters. Unlike telemetry events, Eclipse Hono usually expects a response from the IoT device regarding the requested functionality or service. As with any other IoT platform, it is assumed that the number of telemetry events is larger than the number of command-and-control events. In conclusion, Eclipse Hono provides interfaces for managing and authorising IoT devices, sending telemetry events and handling command and control while ensuring secure message dispatching and supporting various message exchange patterns [1,39,45].

The Eclipse Mosquitto project provides a server implementation of the MQTT protocol, which developers can use as an alternative to Eclipse Hono, along with the Eclipse Streamsheets[6] project, which offers a real-time, spreadsheet-like interface to gather device data from MQTT, Open Platform Communications – Unified Architecture (OPC-UA), REST and other protocols. Moreover, the Eclipse Ditto project provides the DT pattern for IoT devices, enabling interactions and mirroring these connected devices as digital representations in the platform while offering features such as access control, search twin data and push notifications. It also provides various APIs to interact with IoT devices such as HTTP and WebSockets. With the same configuration, developers can extend the capability to integrate the Eclipse Ditto platform with Apache Kafka or VMware's RabbitMQ using AMQP, MQTT and Apache Kafka protocols. The functionality and services provided by Eclipse Ditto can be categorised into device-as-a-service (DaaS), state management of DTs and organisation of DTs [39,45]. DaaS in Eclipse Ditto turns IoT devices into services by exposing a hosted, unified, resource-based API capable of interacting with connected devices while abstracting the complexity of device types, protocols and communication patterns. State management of DTs means Eclipse Ditto represents each connected device as a digital representation with the help of telemetry events, such as sensory data or configuration properties, limited to

[4]https://mqtt.org/
[5]https://kafka.apache.org/
[6]https://projects.eclipse.org/projects/iot.streamsheets

different perspectives: the last reported values based on the last transmission, desired targeted property values and a real-time perspective reflecting events occurring at the current point in time.

Eclipse Ditto allows developers to organise DTs when interacting with a large number of connected devices, automatically indexing not only state data but also metadata such as model information, geolocations, serial numbers or software-based versioning. Briefly, Eclipse Ditto provides a unified, resource-based HTTP JSON API, WebSocket Application API, AMQP, MQTT and Apache Kafka end-points to manage metadata, manage states (live, reported and desired), represent connected devices to enable command and event-based interactions and integrate with Eclipse Hono for communication with devices using various communication protocols [39]. To interface with Eclipse Hono, we need to implement a custom application as an IoT app to manage the device, such as getting telemetry events, handling commands and response payloads and Eclipse Hono connectivity. To manage the device, we can use the documentation and guidelines provided by the manufacturer about interfacing using built-in servers, ports, socket communication, SDKs or driver applications.

To manage Eclipse Hono connectivity, the platform provides a series of APIs to perform device identity management, multitenancy, device provisioning, connecting devices, device notifications and command and control functions using a set of components and adapters based on different protocols such as Kafka, AMQP 1.0 or the experimental Google Pub/Sub, which is an alternative to Kafka. To access these functions through these protocols, you can use the AMQP Adapter Client for Java or a custom Hono HTTP Protocol Adapter. Moreover, to interface with Eclipse Ditto, we can use a frontend application that consumes WebSockets or HTTP based on a Nginx gateway, or an event-based backend application based on Apache Kafka or VMware's RabbitMQ, which consumes Kafka, HTTP and AMQP protocols. The event-based backend application requires some additional configuration of third-party applications to extend these functionalities.

Apart from that, Eclipse Ditto also uses MongoDB as a backing datastore and Docker or Kubernetes to run or deploy the Eclipse Ditto platform. Alternatively, we can use Amazon DocumentDB with MongoDB capabilities, with limitations, as a backing data store, and Docker Compose, Helm, k3s, Minikube or OpenShift to run or deploy the platform. The Eclipse Foundation has provided comprehensive documentation on how to install, run, operate and extend the Eclipse Ditto platform to build DT applications. It also uses service concepts such as connectivity, things, policies, thing-search and gateway to describe the external dependencies and provided/consumed API endpoints. Once we set up the platform, we can use the client SDK, which interfaces APIs for Java or JavaScript, to manage DTs using CRUD (create, read, update, delete), consume change notifications based on events, send or receive messages from devices connected to the DT, or use live channels to route commands or messages with a connected device. Additionally, you can use Python to create backend applications using Apache Kafka and VMware's RabbitMQ. Figure 10.1 shows a comprehensive architecture using Eclipse projects and third-party services. This does not include Google Pub/Sub since it is an experimental

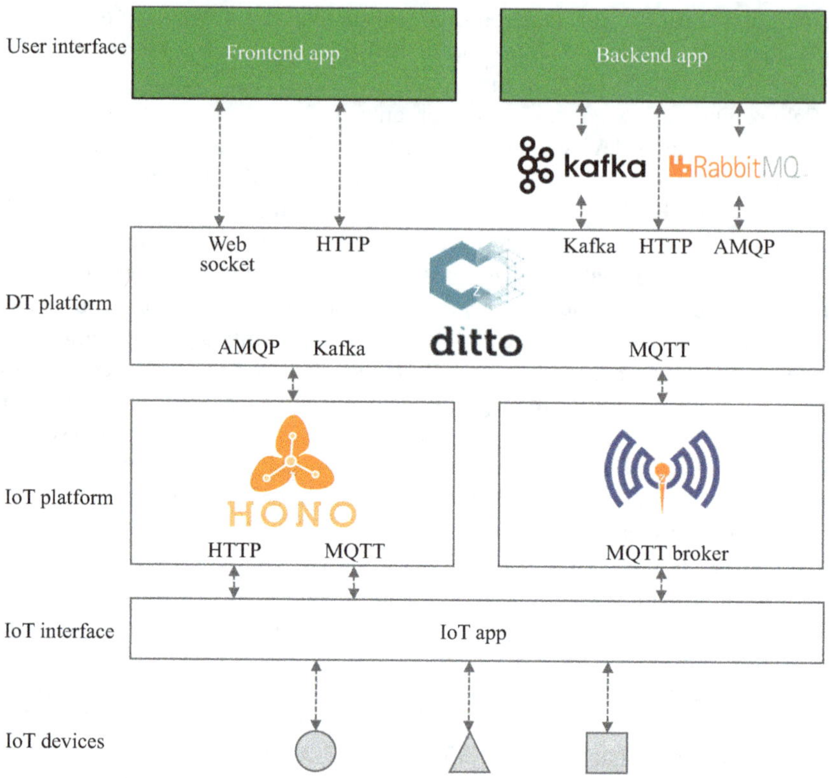

Figure 10.1 DT architecture designed using Eclipse, Apache and VMWare open-source products such as Eclipse Hono, Eclipse Ditto, Apache Kafka and VMWare RabbitMQ

setup with limitations. By using this architecture, we can develop frontend apps with user-friendly web, desktop or mobile applications, or backend apps that use email or messaging services to trigger the use of connected devices such as DaaS to improve the health and well-being of the staff members who operate these connected devices. This can be achieved by adding virtual safety parameters, increasing efficiency and productivity through automation and enhancing device health by estimating maintenance needs.

iTwin.js by Bentley

The iTwin Platform[7] is an open-source project by Bentley that consists of itwinjs-core and iTwinUI repositories to create, query, modify and visualise DT services.[8] This open-source platform is written in TypeScript. This platform provides administration, management, reality capture, report and insights, and review APIs

[7]https://www.itwinjs.org/
[8]https://github.com/iTwin

for the DT services [1]. This software suit can be used to create web applications using a standard web browser [6]. Parle *et al.* [3] provided SWOT analysis for iTwin.js and argued that the openly available APIs and backed by Bentley strengths, while the platform is not mature enough for industrial applications due to its weaknesses. But Parley *et al.* mentioned that cross collaboration could make this platform domain-specific as an opportunity, while a lack of features is a threat to using this open-source project.

DigitalLab by OpenCell
The DigitalLab by OpenCell[9] provides the plan and executes workflow, real-time prediction and monitors biological experiments in laboratory environments using Python programs executed in Arduino-based connected devices and the GCP to manage devices.[10]

Digital Twin IoT by Babylon.js
The Digital Twin IoT by Babylon.js[11] provides an open-source 3D render engine for web-based DT applications [3]. The platform provides the DT and data visualisation tools for IoT devices. The project is written in TypeScript and available on GitHub.[12] Parle *et al.* [3] provided a SWOT analysis for DT IoT platform. They argued open-source, cross-platform rendering engine as strengths, but licensing issues and not widely used in real-world applications as weaknesses. The wide community collaboration and the source code can be used to produce domain-specific solutions as opportunities, but uncertainty produces continuous updates, and security and privacy-related open-source repositories as weaknesses.

Kuzzle IoT by Kuzzle
The Kuzzle IoT by Kuzzle is an open-source, interoperable, scalable and extensible on-premises and platform-as-a-service software solution to perform remote and real-time inventory, information modelling, scenarios and predictions, geolocation and traceability to optimise performance and use of physical assets in the organisation.[13] The open-source projects associated with Kuzzle are available on GitHub.[14]

ThingsBoard IoT platform by ThingsBoard
The ThingsBoard by ThingsBoard is an open-source IoT platform for device management, data collection, processing and visualising by using Edge, IoT Gateway, MQTT Broker, Trendz Analytics and mobile application products based on community, cloud and professional licensing.[15] The platform has open-source thingsboard-edge, thingsboard-gateway, thingboard web-based and mobile user interfaces, repositories published in GitHub.[16]

[9]https://www.opencell.bio/digitallab
[10]https://opencell-community.github.io/
[11]https://www.babylonjs.com/digitalTwinIot/
[12]https://github.com/BabylonJS/Babylon.js
[13]https://kuzzle.io/kuzzle-iot-platform/digital-twins/
[14]https://github.com/kuzzleio
[15]https://thingsboard.io/
[16]https://github.com/thingsboard

10.2.4.2 Commercial platforms

According to Parle *et al.* [3], a commercial DT platform is a proprietary service offered by companies as a subscription model or licensed service. The companies provide extensive support, comprehensive features and capabilities for integration, real-time monitoring and analytics, and sophisticated visualisation tools. Ismail *et al.* mentioned that research associated with energy sector has proved DT has potential for anomaly detection, diagnostics and forecasting, optimisation and predictive maintenance making using historical temporal data generated by powerplants (such as photovoltaic power plants, hydropower plants, wind power plants, thermal power plants), transmission and distribution systems (such as T-Nexus) and other energy assets using commercial software such as Siemens PSS CAPE/ODMS, Nvidia Omniverse, Microsoft Azure Cloud and GE Predix [19].

Amazon Web Services by Amazon

Amazon Web Services (AWS) provides a whole set of tools such as AWS IoT Greengrass,[17] AWS IoT Sitewise,[18] AWS IoT TwinMaker,[19] AWS Compute[20] and Amazon Managed Grafana.[21] To develop a DT architecture based on AWS, we first need to set up an AWS account with an AWS Identity and Access Management (IAM) user with administrator permissions. Additionally, it will need a reliable internet connection to test, build or deploy, as the architecture is based on AWS, which is a cloud-based service. We will also need Python, GIT and the AWS Command Line Interface (AWS CLI) on the development computer to access AWS services. To implement the source code, we can use JetBrains PyCharm, Visual Studio Code or any other Python-supported Integrated Development Environment (IDE).

AWS IoT Greengrass is client software that runs on Windows or Ubuntu operating systems. This platform helps to program devices to act locally on the data they generate. We can also extend the functionality of edge devices by using pre-built software modules called components. To use AWS IoT Greengrass, we need to familiarise ourselves with concepts such as AWS IoT, Greengrass core device, Greengrass client device, Greengrass component and AWS IoT Greengrass Core software. The AWS IoT represents a specific device or logical entity, such as a PLC, Humidity Sensor or Factory. These are stored in the AWS IoT registry. The Greengrass core device, which is an AWS IoT, is a device that runs AWS IoT Greengrass Core software. AWS IoT Greengrass Core software includes all the required software on the Greengrass Core device. This comprises Nucleus, which is an essential component that provides minimum functions such as deployments, orchestration and lifecycle management, and optional components, which can be used to enable additional features such as streaming data or a CLI. The Greengrass client device is an AWS IoT thing that connects and communicates with the

[17]https://aws.amazon.com/greengrass/
[18]https://aws.amazon.com/iot-sitewise/
[19]https://aws.amazon.com/iot-twinmaker/
[20]https://aws.amazon.com/products/compute/
[21]https://aws.amazon.com/grafana/

Greengrass core device over the MQTT protocol. A Greengrass component is a pre-built public software module or custom module deployed and runs on the Greengrass core device to provide features and functionality. Once we have installed the Greengrass Development Kit CLI, we can build the component and then publish it to the AWS IoT Greengrass service and hence can use AWS IoT Greengrass to stream telemetry data to AWS IoT SiteWise.

The AWS IoT SiteWise collect asset models, properties, instances of asset models and asset hierarchy, which uses a time series data store to collect, store, organise and monitor data from enterprise systems. The asset models standardise the systems using names, descriptions, properties and definitions of the asset hierarchy. The asset property contains asset data, which can be either attributes, measurements, transforms or metrics. An attribute asset property is a static property such as a model name or manufacturer. The measurement asset property is a timestamped sensor data stream, such as Celsius or Fahrenheit values for temperature or lux values for illuminance. The transform asset property is transformed data points from one form to another such as converting Celsius values for temperature to Fahrenheit values. The metrics asset property is data that is aggregated over time such as an hourly average. Also, AWS SiteWise describes asset hierarchy, which shows the logical associations between asset models in the enterprise systems. AWS SiteWise provides CRUD operations for assets and models, monitoring data, querying data and the capability to interact with AWS services and other third-party services. As mentioned in the architecture, we can use the AWS IoT SiteWise Publish API to publish data using AWS Compute or the AWS IoT SiteWise Sync API for asset synchronisation with your AWS IoT SiteWise assets and models. Following this, the AWS IoT SiteWise Publish API can ingest timestamped data from enterprise systems to your assets using the *BatchPutAssetPropertyValue* method. Each request comprises *entryId*, *propertyAlias* and *propertyValues*. The *entry_Id* is a string, which is a unique entry ID that can be used to trace back if there is an error associated with the corresponding request. The *property_Alias* is a string, which is a data stream alias. The *property values* are a list of timestamp-quality-value structures that contain *value*, *timestamp* and optional *quality* fields. We can then use these values to process them using a custom application triggered by AWS Compute. The AWS IoT SiteWise Sync API can be used to sync existing AWS IoT SiteWise assets and models to AWS IoT TwinMaker entities, components and component types.

Besides the DT platform of AWS, AWS IoT has TwinMaker, which provides tools for modelling physical enterprise systems, connecting these models to their data sources, creating visualisations and making them available for end-users. The tools provided by AWS IoT TwinMaker include the entity-component system knowledge graph, scene composer, plug-ins for AWS services and third-party tools. The entity-component system knowledge graph provides tools for modelling the physical systems and organising and visualising the information contained within the AWS IoT TwinMaker workspaces. It also provides a single interface for querying based on the metadata about the system to generate visual graphs that show relationships between AWS IoT TwinMaker resources [6]. The scene composer tool is used to create 3D scenes optimised for web display using. gltf or .glb formats, converted based on previously built 3D/CAD models to create visual representations based on the data. We can also use the scene composer tool to overlay various attributes with visual elements to show changes in a user-friendly manner. The plug-ins for AWS services, such as Grafana and Amazon Managed Grafana, can be used to build dashboards for the end-users.

The third-party tools offered by Mendix provide AWS services like AWS IoT TwinMaker, Kinesis Video Streams and AWS IoT SiteWise. Lastly, the AWS IoT TwinMaker data connectors, such as the AWS IoT Twin-Maker data connector or the time series data connector and Athena tabular data connector, help to migrate data from data stores to AWS IoT TwinMaker. The requirements for such data connectors may vary based on where the data is stored. AWS IoT TwinMaker also provides APIs to connect and query data sources using its Unified Data Query interface. Besides, AWS provides visualisation and computing services to feature these DTs in a user-friendly manner. The Amazon Managed Grafana or Grafana Self-Managed services can be used to build dashboards for the end-users. Also, using programmable tools in AWS IoT TwinMaker, we can build frontend or backend applications to manipulate the physical devices.

Figure 10.2 shows the architecture designed using AWS. In this architecture, the lowest levels are IoT things, which are connected devices that generate sensory data or perform functions in an enterprise system. The AWS IoT Greengrass act as an edge computing service and interface between IoT things and the AWS cloud. The IoT things use an OPC UA endpoint to stream telemetry data to AWS IoT SiteWise. AWS IoT SiteWise contains assets to organise and store time series data of the enterprise system. AWS IoT TwinMaker Asset Synchronisation is a built-in service with AWS IoT SiteWise to reflect changes in AWS IoT SiteWise on the AWS IoT TwinMaker service. At the topmost level, we can develop frontend applications such as custom web applications using React or dashboards using Amazon Managed Grafana services, or backend applications using AWS Compute to access DT. We can use this architecture to increase efficiency and productivity by monitoring the enterprise system for predictive maintenance, remote monitoring and real-time production optimisation based on data generated by enterprise systems.

Azure Cloud by Microsoft

The Azure cloud is Microsoft's proprietary cloud platform. It provides platform as a service (PaaS) with a whole set of tools such as Azure IoT Hub,[22] Digital Twins,[23] App Service,[24] Event Grid,[25] Storage[26] and Analytics.[27] Along with Microsoft's reputation of innovation, quality and long product life spans, many companies use the Azure cloud [19]. The Azure Digital Twins (ADT) can be used to construct a DT of the physical entities to improve existing products, workflows

[22]https://azure.microsoft.com/en-gb/products/iot-hub
[23]https://azure.microsoft.com/en-us/products/digital-twins
[24]https://azure.microsoft.com/en-gb/products/app-service
[25]https://azure.microsoft.com/en-gb/products/event-grid
[26]https://azure.microsoft.com/en-us/products/storage
[27]https://azure.microsoft.com/en-us/products/category/analytics

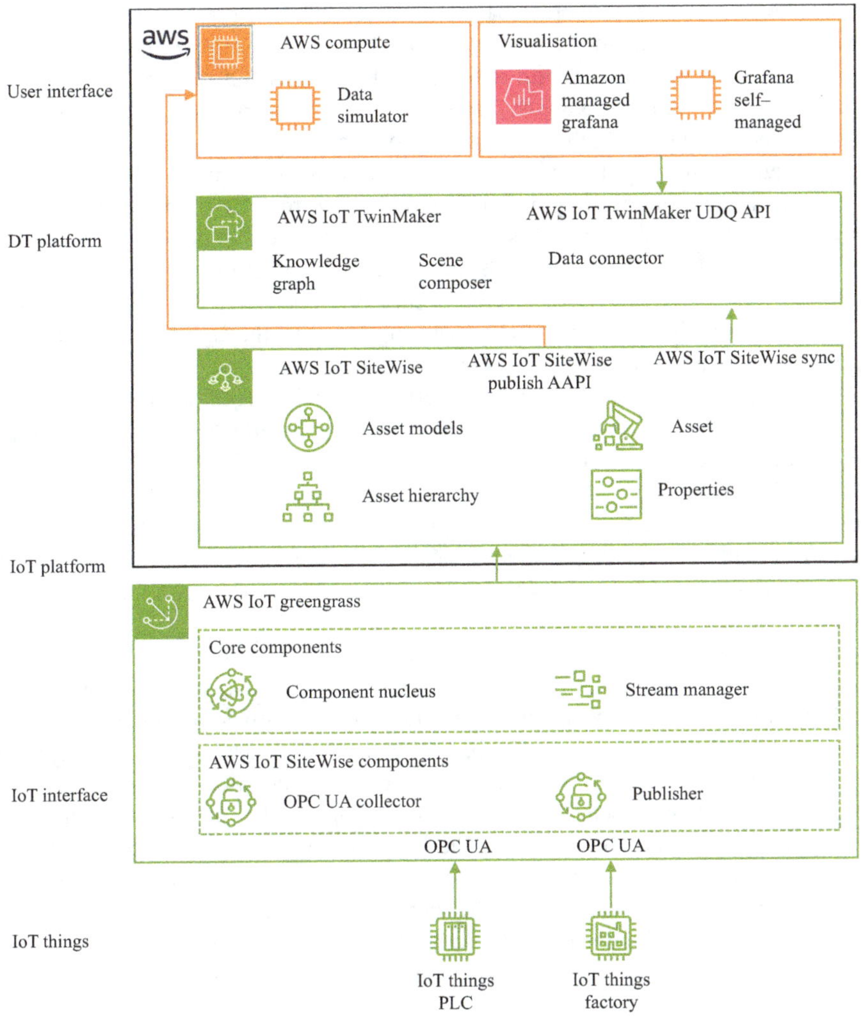

Figure 10.2 DT architecture designed using AWS's PaaS products such as AWS IoT Greengrass, AWS IoT SiteWise, AWS IoT TwinMaker, AWS Compute and AWS Managed Grafana

[6]. Parle *et al.* [3] mentioned scalability and interoperability of the Azure cloud as a strength, while the insufficient documentation and tutorials, the requirement of extensive knowledge about the Azure cloud, make it difficult to train employees, and PaaS requires connectivity, unlike a standalone application. But they have mentioned being able to represent various ontologies in DTs and being able to design custom adapters to connect to other services, regarded as an opportunity, while the stability of the platforms is regarded as a threat.

To develop a DT architecture based on Azure, we first need to set up an Azure account using a Microsoft Account with an Azure IAM user with administrator permissions. The Azure platform automatically assigns the required Azure role-based access control (Azure RBAC) rules when we sign up for the Azure account. Additionally, we need a reliable internet connection to test, build or deploy to access Azure cloud-based services. We also need a programming language (C#, Python, Java, JavaScript or Go), GIT and the Azure CLI on the development computer to access Azure services. To implement the source code, we can use an IDE such as JetBrains IDE, Visual Studio 2022, Visual Studio Code or any other supported tool. Next, we need develop a custom application which is client software running on Windows or Ubuntu operating systems, through any CLI, Desktop Application (such as WinUI, WPF, QT, Tkinter or any other native or cross-platform), Background Services, to interface the Azure IoT Hub with the connected devices. Once we program the application to extract telemetry events at intervals and execute device command requests and response payloads, we can then connect to Azure IoT Hub. According to Azure documentation, the Azure IoT Hub is a managed service in the Azure cloud that provides messaging patterns such as device-to-cloud messages, uploading files from devices and request-reply methods to establish two-way communication between the IoT application and connected devices [39].

We can also use other monitoring tools such as creation, connection and failure events. When designing DT platforms, we can use this two-way communication capability to update DT by updating the state in DT, requesting telemetry events and executing commands using Azure IoT Hub. The Azure Device Provisioning Service (DPS) is a helper service used for device management, such as provisioning and accessibility of connected devices. We can simply link our Azure IoT Hub with our Azure DPS instance by assigning the IoT Hub owner access policy. Then, we can provision a connected device using symmetric key attestation, X.509 certificate or TPM device mechanisms for authentication. Once we establish connectivity between the connected device and the Azure IoT Hub using Azure DPS, we can test device provisioning and elementary events using the Azure IoT Explorer tool locally.

ADT is a PaaS that helps to model physical environments, connect physical assets and query live execution environments using twin graphs, build visualisations using 3D assets and query historical data to analyse, predict and integrate with other Azure services. Additionally, Microsoft provides the Azure DT Explorer tool, which is a Graphical User Interface (GUI) to interact with the Azure DT graph. Apart from that, we can use SDKs such as the Azure Resource Manager SDK (ARM SDK) to manage ADT instances or resources, and the Azure IoT DT client library to manage twins, models and relationships. We can also use the Azure CLI to manage your ADT instance using Windows PowerShell or command-line applications. ADT uses Digital Twin Definition Language (DTDL) models to describe the DT of the connected devices. Based on the business requirements, we can define these models by adding data fields to capture or store data points of the connected device and relationships between each model in the physical space.

These DTDL models are JSON-LD files, which we can later upload into the ADT instance and manage using the GUI, SDK or CLI tools. Once we upload these DTDL models, we can then create DT based on those models. The DT are instances of the DTDL model types with which users directly interact in the ADT instance. For example, we can define a robot in a factory using DTDL, and then DT defines the actual robots used in the factory. The 'Getting Started' section of the DTDL subsection describes various metamodels and schemas used in a DTDL model [1]. We then use these DTs to develop applications based on the data stored in the ADT instance or triggers generated by ADT events.

In contrast to AWS, which has asset synchronisation between AWS IoT TwinMaker and AWS IoT SiteWise, Azure does not provide a direct link between those two instances. To do this, we need to subscribe to Microsoft.Devices.x event types using Event Grid, such as DeviceCreated, DeviceDeleted, DeviceConnected, Device Disconnected and DeviceTelemetry, in the Azure IoT Hub. To ingest telemetry events, we need to capture the Microsoft.Devices. DeviceTelemetry event type using a Function App. The Function App helps to execute system logic using readily available blocks of code to ingest each data point described in the IoT event into the associated DT in the ADT instance. We can use other IoT events to create, delete or update the state of the DT. Besides, we can implement this logic by using an Event Grid trigger function app within the Visual Studio IDE. Since this function app triggers using system events, we need to assign the identity as System Managed and allocate the necessary Azure RBAC to give the Function App access to the ADT instance. Once we implement the scenario, we can test whether data points from the connected devices are being sent to the DT in the ADT instance.

Following this, we can implement accessibility of the ADT instance using APIs, events or connectors. To implement the API, we need to create the logic based on how we intend to use the DT in our API. For example, we can use an HTTP trigger function app with the necessary Azure RBAC controls to access the DT in the ADT instance. This method can only be used to read data from the backing storage. For instance, we can read the content of a property class in the DT. We can read the data if the element is telemetry, as telemetry does not hold any backing storage other than events. To capture telemetry, we should use the second method, which involves using an Event Grid subscription. If we are implementing the ability to read property content in DT, we will need to incorporate authentication mechanisms to secure the ADT instance if it is accessible from an API.

Additionally, we can create an Event Grid Topic to capture DT lifecycle notifications, DT relationship changes notifications and DT telemetry messages event types from Event Routes of the ADT instance. To do this, we can connect these outputs using the endpoint of the ADT instance. For example, to capture Twin Update events, we can use Microsoft.DigitalTwins.Twin.Update to filter out other events. By filtering out irrelevant changes, we can reduce resource usage costs. Once we have the Event Route, we can connect it to the Function App using an Event Grid Subscription. In this case, we need an Event Grid Trigger function app with the necessary Azure RBAC permissions. Also, ADT provides connectors to integrate with other Azure platforms like Power Apps and Azure Logic Apps. By using these connectors, you can stream DT events into these platforms without requiring any source code for visualisation.

Figure 10.3 shows the Azure architecture for an end-to-end DT solution. This architecture shows that we can access the ADT instance using Azure DT Explorer as a GUI alternative. Additionally, we can implement a second flow to execute commands by adding flags to DT. Currently, Azure DT does not support execution logic, but we can use Azure IoT Hub to establish two-way communication between the platform and the connected device. We can listen to update events and add logic to identify command flags and execute request-reply methods via the Function App. we need to ensure the necessary Azure RBAC controls to execute these methods through the Function App.

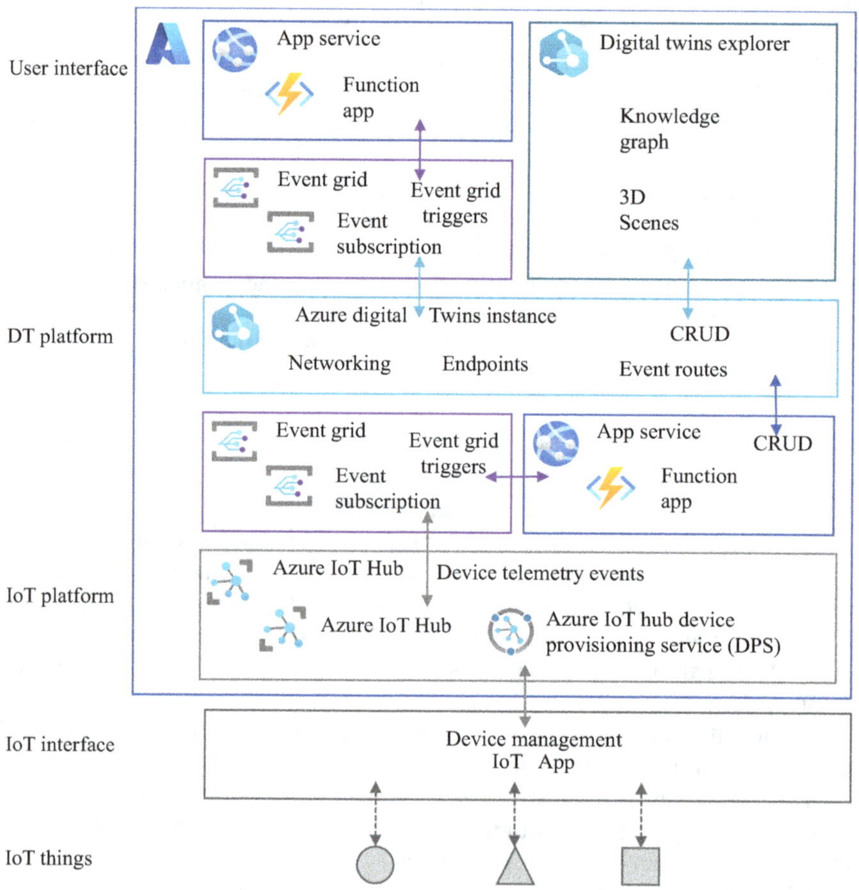

Figure 10.3 DT architecture designed using Azure's PaaS products such as Azure IoT Hub, Azure DT, Azure Event Grid and App Service.

Twinn by Royal Haskoning DHV

The Twinn[28] is a commercial proprietary software suit by Royal Haskoning DHV to connect physical and virtual assets for to manage risks, improve strategic and operational decisions in energy, financial services, industry, maritime and logistics, and water utilities sectors. The company provides the Aqua Suite, Climate Intelligence Suite and predictive simulation suite to power the DTs.

ThingWorx by PTC

The ThingWorx IIoT Platform[29] by PTC provides Industrial IoT capabilities to connect, build, analyse and manage industrial devices with standardised, repeatable and configurable framework [51]. Rajesh *et al.* described a PoC DT of a brake system for an automobile using ThingWorx to measure brake pressure at different vehicle speeds [50].

Bosch IoT Suite by Bosch

The Bosch IoT Suite[30] by Bosch provides a digital win framework for manufacturing companies. It provides features such as an open data model to enable the digital representation of the physical devices, avoid vendor lock-in and integration with other cloud platforms such as AWS. The framework is based on Eclipse IoT projects and MQTT and AMQP protocols [1].

Xcelerator by Siemens

The Siemens Xcelerator[31] by Siemens provides various products and services for adaptability, additive manufacturing, AI and asset management. Many existing research studies have mentioned industrial use cases; American Electric Power, FinGrid, Siemens Energy and OKB Gidropress have used Siemens Xcelerator to create DT models of power plants, transmission lines asset management for data collection and verification, and support predictive maintenance [19]. Parle *et al.* [3] performed a SWOT analysis for Siemens Xcelerator and identified strengths such as interoperability, scalability and continuous product improvements, and opportunities as possible collaboration between other companies and domains. They have mentioned less demand, lack of awareness and cost as threats. Parle also suggested Xcelerator is a good alternative for other big tech companies.

Maximo by IBM

The Maximo[32] by IBM is an application suite for integrated asset lifecycle management to increase reliability, longevity, efficiency and visibility of the business workflow. Shotz and Birdsall [52] mentioned that the Dubai Roads and Transport Authority used the Maximo framework to improve metro stations using the rule-based notification system.

[28]https://www.royalhaskoningdhv.com/en/twinn

[29]https://www.ptc.com/en/products/thingworx

[30]https://bosch-iot-suite.com/

[31]https://xcelerator.siemens.com/global/en.html

[32]https://www.ibm.com/products/maximo

Unity Industry by Unity 3D

The Unity Industry[33] by Unity provides various tools for interactive applications to measure results, enhance efficiency and improve visualisation. The platform enables real-time 3D, optimises efficiency and lowers costs, and communicates with stakeholders by integrating various data sources originating from the organisation. Unity provides various products to visualise data in virtual entities. Xiang *et al.* [53] proposed a novel approach to develop a DT platform for manufacturing systems using Unity 3D.

Omniverse by NVIDIA

The Omniverse[34] by NVIDIA is a platform to build metaverse applications to accelerate workflows in a production environment. Companies use the Omniverse for synthetic data generation, autonomous vehicle simulation, configurator development, reinforcement learning and virtual facility integration using the OpenUSD ecosystem [1]. Deutsche Bahn [54] developed a DT for an entire railway network using Siemens Xceletrator and Omniverse to simulate the railway network using datasets. This has helped for continuous improvements in the network, optimise the deployments [54].

10.2.4.3 Custom platforms

According to Parle *et al.*, the custom DT platforms are developed in-house to cater unique requirements of the domain. These platforms are highly flexible and designed to integrate with existing systems in the domain [3]. Parle *et al.* mentioned 5D-DT concept, SPHERE, uDiT, makeTwin and imseStudio as custom DT frameworks. First, the 5D-DT concept, Tao and Zhang expand the Grieves' three dimensions into five dimensions, adding DT data and DT services dimensions [55]. Second SPEHERE, which is the acronym for Service Platform to Host and SharE REsidential data) Elagiri *et al.* [56] aim to improve and optimise the construction process. Third uDiT platform, Yun *et al.* [57] propose a large-scale DT platform for driver assistance emphasising DT corporation, flexible data-centric communication and DT application. Fourth, makeTwin, Tao *et al.* [58] propose a software architecture for enterprise users for application management for configuration and migration in various application scenarios, functions and modes and validated using a fibre textile shop floor. Last imseStudio, Liu *et al.* [59] propose a blockchain-based five-layered architecture for small and medium enterprises in the manufacturing domain and verified using a 3D printing scenario to verify the effectiveness and efficiency.

10.3 Discussion and conclusion

The DT technology is an emerging technology to establish two-way communication to simulate attributes and behaviours between physical and virtual entities. The ability to synchronise state in real time, define physical entities using ontologies,

[33]https://unity.com/products/unity-industry
[34]https://www.nvidia.com/en-gb/omniverse/

widespread use of the cloud, AI, combined with high-speed internet connectivity, fuelled the recent growth in researching proof of concept digital twinning in multiple domains such as manufacturing, construction, logistics, medicine and agriculture. Regardless of the domain, the DT architecture follows key components (network, physical entity, physical environment, physical process, virtual entity, virtual environment, virtual process, synchronisation, synchronisation rate, state, fidelity and data), data requirements (time series data, master data and transactional data), modelling (physics-based models, analytics-based models, visual models and DES models) and technologies (IoT, cloud computing, AI, XR) to determine the type of architecture to be used in a case study.

Much research has suggested that the DT architecture follows a layered architecture with each layer assigned to perform acquisition, synchronisation, modelling and visualisation of the physical and virtual entities. This study focuses on two main architecture types, which achieve two-way communication: edge architecture and distributed architecture. The edge architecture uses standalone software deployed at the edge, and the distributed architecture uses cloud-based services geographically distributed to support the digital twinning process. The digital twinning process faces multiple challenges such as security and vulnerability, privacy, ethics, scalability and complexities, real-time communication issues, interoperability limitations, modelling complexities, data coherence and data quality.

The DT platforms, such as Microsoft Azure cloud, Amazon's AWS, Google's GCP and Eclipse's Ditto, are designed to overcome the challenges caused by the digital twinning process. These platforms can be divided into three types as open source, commercial and custom platforms based on the availability of the source code of core services, acceptable use policies and licensing by the vendors. The open-source platforms such as Eclipse, OpenCell and ThingBoard usually provide customisable, free-to-use source code with open-source licensing for the consumers. The commercial platforms, such as Azure cloud, Amazon AWS and Nvidia Omniverse, are closed-source, proprietary, licensed and distributed services. The custom platforms are designed by various organisations to cater to specific requirements that could not be achieved by any open-source or commercial platform in the market.

Even though the DT platforms solve many challenges, they have unique limitations and advantages. When designing a DT service, it is necessary to choose the architecture based on decision-making using MCDM, multilevel filtering criteria, SWOT analysis, cost–benefit analysis, benchmarking, pilot testing, vendor evaluation and use feedback and case studies related to the operational requirements of the organisation. In the digital twinning process, this chapter will provide important factors regarding the DT architecture and DT platforms and methodology for selecting the right combination based on the operational requirements.

References

[1] A. Hakiri, A. Gokhale, S. Ben Yahia, and N. Mellouli, 'A comprehensive survey on digital twin for future networks and emerging Internet of Things

industry', *Computer Networks*, vol. 244, p. 110350, 2024, doi:10.1016/j.comnet.2024.110350.
[2] G. Shao, S. Frechette, and V. Srinivasan, 'An Analysis of the New ISO 23247 Series of Standards on Digital Twin Framework for Manufacturing', in *Proceedings of ASME 2023 18th International Manufacturing Science and Engineering Conference, MSEC 2023*, 2023. doi:10.1115/msec2023-101127.
[3] D. Parle, G. Sharma, N. Anand, N. Padgaonkar, D. Stoddart, and D. J. Malley, 'A comparative analysis for harnessing digital twin platforms for net-zero manufacturing', *IEEE Access*, vol. 12, pp. 180175–180197, 2024, doi:10.1109/ACCESS.2024.3447475.
[4] Y. Wu, K. Zhang, and Y. Zhang, 'Digital twin networks: A survey', *IEEE Internet Things Journal*, vol. 8, no. 18, pp. 13789–13804, 2021, doi:10.1109/JIOT.2021.3079510.
[5] B. Björnsson, C. Borrebaeck, N. Elander, *et al.*, 'Digital twins to personalize medicine', *Genome Medicine*, vol. 12, no. 1, p. 4, 2020, doi:10.1186/s13073-019-0701-3.
[6] S. R. Jeremiah, A. El Azzaoui, N. N. Xiong, and J. H. Park, 'A comprehensive survey of digital twins: Applications, technologies and security challenges', *Journal of Systems Architecture*, vol. 151, p. 103120, 2024, doi:10.1016/j.sysarc.2024.103120.
[7] B. Tekinerdogan and C. Verdouw, 'Systems architecture design pattern catalog for developing digital twins', *Sensors*, vol. 20, no. 18, p. 5103, 2020, doi:10.3390/s20185103.
[8] B. Schleich, N. Anwer, L. Mathieu, and S. Wartzack, 'Shaping the digital twin for design and production engineering', *CIRP Annals*, vol. 66, no. 1, pp. 141–144, 2017, doi:10.1016/j.cirp.2017.04.040.
[9] T. Moshood, G. Nawanir, S. Sorooshian, and O. Okfalisa, 'Digital twins driven supply chain visibility within logistics: A new paradigm for future logistics', *Applied System Innovation*, vol. 4, no. 2, p. 29, 2021, doi:10.3390/asi4020029.
[10] R. van Dinter, B. Tekinerdogan, and C. Catal, 'Predictive maintenance using digital twins: A systematic literature review', *Information and Software Technology*, vol. 151, p. 107008, 2022, doi:10.1016/j.infsof.2022.107008.
[11] C. Verdouw, B. Tekinerdogan, A. Beulens, and S. Wolfert, 'Digital twins in smart farming', *Agricultural Systems*, vol. 189, p. 103046, 2021, doi:10.1016/j.agsy.2020.103046.
[12] I. Hasan and M. Habib, 'Blockchain technology to ensure traceability of agriculture supply chain management', *International Supply Chain Technology Journal*, vol. 8, no. 9, pp. 73295–73305, 2022, doi:10.20545/isctj.v08.i09.01.
[13] A. De Benedictis, N. Mazzocca, A. Somma, and C. Strigaro, 'Digital twins in healthcare: An architectural proposal and its application in a social distancing case study', *IEEE Journal of Biomedical and Health Informatics*, vol. 27, no. 10, pp. 5143–5154, 2023, doi:10.1109/JBHI.2022.3205506.
[14] P. Armeni, I. Polat, L. M. De Rossi, L. Diaferia, S. Meregalli, and A. Gatti, 'Digital twins in healthcare: Is it the beginning of a new era of evidence-

based medicine? A critical review', *Journal of Personalized Medicine*, vol. 12, no. 8, p. 1255, 2022, doi:10.3390/jpm12081255.

[15] S. Gahlot, S. R. N. Reddy, and D. Kumar, 'Review of smart health monitoring approaches with survey analysis and proposed framework', *IEEE Internet Things Journal*, vol. 6, no. 2, pp. 2116–2127, 2019, doi:10.1109/JIOT.2018.2872389.

[16] G. Bhatti, H. Mohan, and R. Raja Singh, 'Towards the future of smart electric vehicles: Digital twin technology', *Renewable and Sustainable Energy Reviews*, vol. 141, p. 110801, 2021, doi:10.1016/j.rser.2021.110801.

[17] D.-G. J. Opoku, S. Perera, R. Osei-Kyei, and M. Rashidi, 'Digital twin application in the construction industry: A literature review', *Journal of Building Engineering*, vol. 40, p. 102726, 2021, doi:10.1016/j.jobe.2021.102726.

[18] H. Bai and Y. Wang, 'Digital power grid based on digital twin: Definition, structure and key technologies', *Energy Reports*, vol. 8, pp. 390–397, 2022, doi:10.1016/j.egyr.2022.10.328.

[19] F. B. Ismail, H. Al-Faiz, H. Hasini, A. Al-Bazi, and H. A. Kazem, 'A comprehensive review of the dynamic applications of the digital twin technology across diverse energy sectors', *Energy Strategy Reviews*, vol. 52, p. 101334, 2024. doi:10.1016/j.esr.2024.101334.

[20] B. Koirala, H. Cai, F. Khayatian, *et al.*, 'Digitalization of urban multi-energy systems – Advances in digital twin applications across life-cycle phases', *Advances in Applied Energy*, vol. 16, p. 100196, *Energy Strategy Reviews*, vol. 52, p. 101334, 2024, doi:10.1016/j.adapen.2024.100196.

[21] A. Hazrathosseini and A. Moradi Afrapoli, 'The advent of digital twins in surface mining: Its time has finally arrived', *Resources Policy*, vol. 80, p. 103155, 2023, doi:10.1016/j.resourpol.2022.103155.

[22] Z. U. Rizqi, S.-Y. Chou, and W. N. Cahyo, 'A simulation-based digital twin for smart warehouse: Towards standardization', *Decision Analytics Journal*, vol. 12, p. 100509, 2024, doi:10.1016/j.dajour.2024.100509.

[23] G. Yu, X. Ye, X. Xia, and Y. Chen, 'Digital twin enabled transition towards the smart electric vehicle charging infrastructure: A review', *Sustain Cities and Society*, vol. 108, p. 105479, 2024, doi:10.1016/j.scs.2024.105479.

[24] H. Li, R. Zhang, S. Zheng, Y. Shen, C. Fu, and H. Zhao, 'Digital twin-driven intelligent operation and maintenance platform for large-scale hydro-steel structures', *Advanced Engineering Informatics*, vol. 62, p. 102661, 2024, doi:10.1016/j.aei.2024.102661.

[25] R. Brahmi, N. Boujnah, and R. Ejbali, 'Elaboration of innovative digital twin models for healthcare monitoring with 6G functionalities', *IEEE Access*, vol. 12, pp. 109608–109624, 2024, doi:10.1109/ACCESS.2024.3439269.

[26] L. Jin, X Zhai, K. Wang, *et al.*, 'Big data, machine learning, and digital twin assisted additive manufacturing: A review', *Materials & Design*, vol. 244, p. 113086, 2024, doi:10.1016/j.matdes.2024.113086.

[27] M. Grieves, '*Digital Twin: Manufacturing Excellence through Virtual Factory Replication*', *White Paper*, March 2014.

[28] Y. Liu, L. Zhang, Y. Yang, *et al.*, 'A novel cloud-based framework for the elderly healthcare services using digital twin', *IEEE Access*, vol. 7, pp. 49088–49101, 2019, doi:10.1109/ACCESS.2019.2909828.

[29] W. Hu, Y. He, Z. Liu, J. Tan, M. Yang, and J. Chen, 'Toward a digital twin: Time series prediction based on a hybrid ensemble empirical mode decomposition and BO-LSTM neural networks', *Journal of Mechanical Design*, vol. 143, no. 5, pp. 1–21, 2021, doi:10.1115/1.4048414.

[30] T. G. Ritto and F. A. Rochinha, 'Digital twin, physics-based model, and machine learning applied to damage detection in structures', *Mechanical Systems and Signal Processing*, vol. 155, p. 107614, 2021, doi:10.1016/j.ymssp.2021.107614.

[31] V. Kharchenko, O. Illiashenko, O. Morozova, and S. Sokolov, 'Combination of Digital Twin and Artificial Intelligence in Manufacturing Using Industrial IoT', in *2020 IEEE 11th International Conference on Dependable Systems, Services and Technologies (DESSERT)*, IEEE, 2020, pp. 196–201. doi:10.1109/DESSERT50317.2020.9125038.

[32] Y. Han, D. Niyato, C. Leung, *et al.*, 'A dynamic hierarchical framework for IoT-assisted digital twin synchronization in the metaverse', *IEEE Internet Things Journal*, vol. 10, no. 1, pp. 268–284, 2023, doi:10.1109/JIOT.2022.3201082.

[33] L. Morabito, M. Ippolito, E. Pastore, A. Alfieri, and F. Montagna, 'A discrete event simulation based approach for digital twin implementation', *IFAC-PapersOnLine*, vol. 54, no. 1, pp. 414–419, 2021, doi:10.1016/j.ifacol.2021.08.164.

[34] M. Attaran and B. G. Celik, 'Digital twin: Benefits, use cases, challenges, and opportunities', *Decision Analytics Journal*, vol. 6, p. 100165, 2023, doi:10.1016/j.dajour.2023.100165.

[35] International Organization for Standardization, 'ISO/IEC 30173:2023', Edition 1, 2023. Accessed: Jan. 12 2025. [Online]. Available: https://www.iso.org/standard/81442.html

[36] A. Wentzel, S. Attia, X. Zhang, G. Canahuate, C. D. Fuller, and G. E. Marai, 'DITTO: A visual digital twin for interventions and temporal treatment outcomes in head and neck cancer', *IEEE Transactions on Visualization and Computer Graphics*, vol. 31, no. 1, pp. 65–75, 2025, doi:10.1109/TVCG.2024.3456160.

[37] R. Kumahia, U. Demir, S. Pradhan, B. Salehihikouei, K. Chowdhury, and S. Ioannidis, 'DITTO: DIgital Twins for Testing and Optimizing Wireless Decisions', in *2024 IEEE International Conference on Metaverse Computing, Networking, and Applications (MetaCom)*, IEEE, 2024, pp. 121–128. doi:10.1109/MetaCom62920.2024.00031.

[38] Y. Lim, Y. K. Lee, J. Yoo, and D. Yoon, 'An Open Source-based Digital Twin Broker Interface for Interaction between Real and Virtual Assets', in *2022 13th International Conference on Information and Communication Technology Convergence (ICTC)*, IEEE, 2022, pp. 1657–1659. doi:10.1109/ICTC55196.2022.9952499.

[39] M. Picone, M. Mamei, and F. Zambonelli, 'A flexible and modular architecture for edge digital twin: Implementation and evaluation', *ACM Transactions on Internet of Things*, vol. 4, no. 1, pp. 1–32, 2023, doi:10.1145/3573206.

[40] B. Bolat-Akça and E. Bozkaya-Aras, 'Digital twin-assisted intelligent anomaly detection system for Internet of Things', *Ad Hoc Networks*, vol. 158, p. 103484, 2024, doi:10.1016/j.adhoc.2024.103484.

[41] P. Bellavista, N. Bicocchi, M. Fogli, C. Giannelli, M. Mamei, and M. Picone, 'Exploiting microservices and serverless for digital twins in the cloud-to-edge continuum', *Future Generation Computer Systems*, vol. 157, pp. 275–287, 2024, doi:10.1016/j.future.2024.03.052.

[42] C. Meijer, H.-W. Uh, and S. el Bouhaddani, 'Digital twins in healthcare: Methodological challenges and opportunities', *Journal of Personalized Medicine*, vol. 13, no. 10, p. 1522, 2023, doi:10.3390/jpm13101522.

[43] Y. Zheng, R. Lu, Y. Guan, S. Zhang, and J. Shao, 'Towards Private Similarity Query based Healthcare Monitoring over Digital Twin Cloud Platform', in *2021 IEEE/ACM 29th International Symposium on Quality of Service, IWQOS 2021*, 2021. doi:10.1109/IWQOS52092.2021.9521351.

[44] Z. Maserrat, A. A. Alesheikh, A. Jafari, N. K. Charandabi, and J. Shahidinejad, 'A Dempster–Shafer enhanced framework for urban road panning using a model-based digital twin and MCDM techniques', *ISPRS International Journal of Geo-information*, vol. 13, no. 9, p. 302, 2024, doi:10.3390/ijgi13090302.

[45] S. Gil, P. H. Mikkelsen, C. Gomes, and P. G. Larsen, 'Survey on open-source digital twin frameworks – A case study approach', *Software – Practice and Experience*, vol. 54, no. 6, pp. 929–960, 2024, doi:10.1002/spe.3305.

[46] L. Saari, M. Räikkönen, E. Hytönen, and K. Valkokari, 'Joint offering evaluation framework for assessing the feasibility and business value of a digital twin use case', *Systems Engineering*, vol. 27, no. 1, pp. 140–158, 2024, doi:10.1002/sys.21713.

[47] R. Rubini, R. Cassandro, C. Semeraro, Z. S. Li, and M. Dassisti, 'Cost-benefit evaluation of digital twin implementation for pharmaceutical lyophilization plant', *Communications in Computer and Information Science*, vol. 1886, pp. 398–407, 2023. doi:10.1007/978-3-031-49339-3_25.

[48] V. Kamath, J. Morgan, and M. I. Ali, 'Industrial IoT and Digital Twins for a Smart Factory: An Open Source Toolkit for Application Design and Benchmarking', in *2020 Global Internet of Things Summit (GIoTS)*, IEEE, 2020, pp. 1–6. doi:10.1109/GIOTS49054.2020.9119497.

[49] A. Aziz, S. S. Chouhan, O. Schelén, and U. Bodin, 'Distributed digital twins as proxies-unlocking composability and flexibility for purpose-oriented digital twins', *IEEE Access*, vol. 11, pp. 137577–137593, 2023, doi:10.1109/ACCESS.2023.3340132.

[50] P. K. Rajesh, N. Manikandan, C. S. Ramshankar, T. Vishwanathan, and C. Sathishkumar, 'Digital twin of an automotive brake pad for predictive maintenance', *Procedia Computer Science*, vol. 165, pp. 18–24, 2019, doi:10.1016/j.procs.2020.01.061.

[51] B. Cline, D. Kessler, J. MacKenzie, and J. Rydalch, 'An IoT Platform Delivers Expectations for a Standardized PHM System Framework', in 2024 *IEEE International Conference on Prognostics and Health Management (ICPHM)*, IEEE, 2024, pp. 239–242. doi:10.1109/ICPHM61352.2024.10627258.

[52] H. Shotz and J. Birdsall, 'A glimpse into the near future – digital twins and the Internet of Things', in *Advances in Road Infrastructure and Mobility*, 2022, pp. 425–438. doi:10.1007/978-3-030-79801-7_31.

[53] T. Xiang, B. Li, X. Pan, and Q. Zhang, 'Development of a Simple and Novel Digital Twin Framework for Industrial Robots in Intelligent Robotics Manufacturing', in *2024 IEEE 20th International Conference on Automation Science and Engineering (CASE)*, IEEE, 2024, pp. 4187–4193. doi:10.1109/CASE59546.2024.10711459.

[54] M. Geyer, 'On Track: Digitale Schiene Deutschland Building Digital Twin of Rail Network in NVIDIA Omniverse', NVIDIA. 2022, Accessed Jan. 09 2025. [Online]. Available: https://blogs.nvidia.com/blog/deutsche-bahn-railway-system-digital-twin/.

[55] F. Tao and M. Zhang, 'Digital twin shop-floor: A new shop-floor paradigm towards smart manufacturing', *IEEE Access*, vol. 5, pp. 20418–20427, 2017, doi:10.1109/ACCESS.2017.2756069.

[56] M. Elagiry, A. Dugue, A. Costa, and R. Decorme, 'Digitalization Tools for Energy-Efficient Renovations', in *The 8th Annual International Sustainable Places Conference (SP2020) Proceedings*, Basel Switzerland: MDPI, 2020, p. 9. doi:10.3390/proceedings2020065009.

[57] S. Yun, J.-H. Park, and W.-T. Kim, 'Data-centric middleware based digital twin platform for dependable cyber-physical systems', in *2017 Ninth International Conference on Ubiquitous and Future Networks (ICUFN)*, IEEE, 2017, pp. 922–926. doi:10.1109/ICUFN.2017.7993933.

[58] F. Tao, X. Sun, J. Cheng, *et al.*, 'makeTwin: A reference architecture for digital twin software platform', *Chinese Journal of Aeronautics*, vol. 37, no. 1, pp. 1–18, 2024, doi:10.1016/j.cja.2023.05.002.

[59] X. Liu, Y. Jiang, Z. Wang, R. Y. Zhong, H. H. Cheung, and G. Q. Huang, 'imseStudio: Blockchain-enabled secure digital twin platform for service manufacturing', *International Journal of Production Research*, vol. 61, no. 12, pp. 3984–4003, 2023, doi:10.1080/00207543.2021.2003462.

Chapter 11

Digital twins services implementation: Azure cloud

Gayan Dihantha Kuruppu Kuruppu Appuhamilage[1], *Maqbool Hussain*[1], *Wajahat Ali Khan*[1] *and Asad Masood Khattak*[2]

Abstract

Many platforms are designed to overcome the challenges associated with the digital twin infrastructure. These software platforms can be categorised into commercial, open-source or custom platforms based on the code availability for core services, acceptable use and licensing provided by the vendor. The commercial vendors provide subscription or license-based software packages, or cloud services, and are increasingly popular among organisations due to integrated features, security, availability and customer support. The Azure cloud by Microsoft stands out from other commercial digital twin platform vendors such as Amazon Web Services. The existing research suggested low-latency and highly scalable configurations, and integrated tools such as access, transmission, storage, analysis and visualisation have provided reduced risks when modelling, connecting, visualising and analysing the digital twins in real time for domains such as healthcare, aerospace and consumer electronics. The Azure Internet of Things, Azure Digital Twins (ADT), Function Apps, Microsoft Entra, Storage Accounts, No-SQL Databases and App Services are a few services associated with building digital twin services using the Azure cloud. The Azure cloud provided Digital Twin Definition Language (DTDL) based on JavaScript Object Notation for Linked Data (JSON-LD) to model physical entities and various interfaces such as Azure portal (Graphical User Interface (GUI)), Azure Command-Line Interface (CLI), Azure Application Programming Interface (REST API) and Azure SDK to manage Azure resources and manipulate the data and structures associated with the instances. In the digital twin models, this chapter presents the *schemas* such as *Primary*, *Complex*, *Geospatial* schemas, and *meta-classes* such as *Interface*, *Property*, *Telemetry*, *Relationship*, *Component* meta-models associated with DTDL with example code. In the Azure services section, the authors will discuss control plane APIs and data plane APIs by using *dotnet* Framework in *c-sharp* programming language. The control plane

[1]School of Computing, College of Science and Engineering, University of Derby, UK
[2]College of Technological Innovation, Zayed University, Dubai, UAE

APIs section discusses the creation and retrieval of instances of Azure resources using the Azure Resource Manager SDK. The data plane APIs section discusses retrieving a digital twin instance, managing models, manipulating twins and relationships and querying the digital twins instance using the ADT Core SDK. In summary, this chapter introduces concepts of building digital twin services using the Azure SDK.

Keywords: Azure Digital Twins; Azure IoT Hub; Azure Control Plane APIs; Azure Data Plane APIs; Azure Service Plane APIs; Digital Twin Definition Language.

11.1 Overview

This section will discuss the existing literature associated with building digital twin services using the Azure cloud. As a commercial platform by Microsoft, it has attracted a significant number of researchers and organisations to build proof of concept digital twin services based on Azure cloud services. The aims and goals and architectures of these case studies are different from each other, but there are significant similarities on how the common purposes such as using Azure Internet of Things (IoTs) to establish two-way communication between physical entity and cloud service, Azure Digital Twins (ADT) to as modelling tool or Function Apps to execute custom made scripts. Höfgen *et al.* stated ADT has provided more flexibility over Amazon Web Services of Digital Twins Modelling Language to model physical entities and the Azure Software Development Kit (Azure SDK) to develop tailor-made client apps in their research on the integration of digital twins with socket-based communication architecture [1].

Pfeiffe *et al.* compared the capabilities of modelling physical entities in Azure cloud, AWS and Eclipse Digital Twins and attempted to follow a standardised methodology with Object Oriented Unified Modelling Language to support interoperability and migration between platforms. The research used the Digital Twin Modelling Language JSON-LD format for Azure cloud, Vortolang textual modelling language for Eclipse and IoT TwinMaker to test their DTUML modelling language to standardise the modelling language for portability [2]. Zhong *et al.* [3] mentioned that the low latency and high availability of the Azure cloud provided an interactive Virtual reality-based novel digital twin framework based on stream sensor readings. This made their research accessible to external users due to cloud infrastructure. Zhang *et al.* [4] used Azure cloud services for device access, data transmission, storage, analysis and visualisation in their research on digital twins of energy equipment. Weckx *et al.* [5] presented a cloud-based digital twin framework for an adaptive clamping mechanism for composite manufacturing based on Azure services such as Azure IoT, ADTs and Function Apps. Ni *et al.* [6] presented a reference implementation using Azure cloud to solve challenges such as large datasets in the reinvention process in preserving historic buildings, and aimed at implementing the digital twin services as software-as-a-service for delivery and transferring the process to other historic buildings.

In this chapter, each subsection provides a step-by-step guide for authorising the programmable interface using token-based authentication, allocating resource groups and managing digital twins in their respective instances with control plane APIs by using Azure Resource Manager (ARM) library and manage the data and the structure in the digital twin instance with data plane APIs using ADTs Core library. Due to the limited comprehensive documentation on handling resources through control plane APIs using ARM SDK, interest groups face challenges in implementing dynamic resource allocation without accessing the Azure portal, Azure Command Line Interface (Azure CLI) or Azure REST APIs for real-world scenarios. The ARM enables the development of automated console, desktop, mobile and web applications to manage cloud resources without giving users direct access to the subscriptions. In addition to the ARM, this chapter discusses data plane APIs of the ADTs to manage models, twins, relationships and query the digital twin instance. In addition, this chapter places a greater emphasis on the ARM and ADTs Core SDK, enabling readers to identify patterns for creating programmable interfaces to manage the digital twin frameworks.

11.2 Development environment

To manage subscription resources, the developers will need either an Azure free subscription or a pay-as-you-go subscription in their Azure account. To follow the steps using the control plane APIs and data plane APIs, you must set up Visual.

11.2.1 The Azure subscription Studio 2022 on your personal computer

Azure offers two subscriptions: the *Azure Free Account* subscription and the *Pay-As-You-Go* subscription. The *Azure Free Account* subscription is available only to new Azure customers. It is ideal for proof of concept and exploring the full catalogue of services, including services with monthly free usage for 12 months, as well as free monthly allowances and other pay-as-you-go services until the credit limit is reached. This option also provides spending protection and can be upgraded to a Pay-As-You-Go subscription after 30 days or once the credit is fully utilised.

The *Pay-As-You-Go* subscription is available to existing customers for building workloads. Like the Azure Free Account option, it allows access to a wide range of free services, but you must pay for services once the free usage limits are exceeded. In this chapter, the authors recommend using *Azure Free Services* to explore basic Azure features and later on upgrading to the *Pay-As-You-Go* subscription for accessing standard or premium Azure services.

Please follow the steps given below.

1. Visit the Microsoft Azure product page[1] and click the **Get started with Azure** button located on the centre left of the page or use the **Get started with Azure** link in the top-right navigation bar.
2. Click the **Try Azure for free** button located in the centre left of the page. This action will redirect you to the Pick an account page[2] where you can select the

[1]https://azure.microsoft.com/en-gb
[2]https://login.microsoftonline.com/

existing account option or **use a different account** option if your desired account is not displayed.
3. After logging in with a new account or an existing one, you will be redirected to the Azure sign-up page. Here, you must enter your name, email, phone number and region. Once Azure verifies your details, you will be prompted to provide your payment information. After completing these steps, click the **Sign-up** button to finalise the creation of your Azure account.

11.2.2 Sign in to Azure from Visual Studio

To run or debug an Azure application in Visual Studio 2022, you will need to sign in to your Azure account from Visual Studio 2022. Follow the steps below to sign in using Visual Studio 2022:

1. Open your solution using Visual Studio 2022.
2. Go to the top right corner of the window, click on the *Sign In* button and choose the *Add another account* option. Then select *Microsoft*, which you can use to log in to your Azure subscription, whether it is a work, school or personal account.
3. In the Sign In to your account pop-up window, you can select the existing account or choose the Use another account option to select your Azure account.
4. You might then be asked for a password or two-factor authentication, depending on the security configuration of your Azure account.
5. Once you are signed in to your Azure account, you can access your Azure services from Visual Studio.

11.3 Digital twin models

This section will discuss the meta model classes such as Interface, Telemetry, Property, Relationship and Schemas such as primitive and complex schemas in the DTDL. The definitions are used to define the digital twin models and relationships to describe physical entities. The DTDL is based on (JSON-LD to encode linked data using JavaScript Object Notation (JSON). The main advantage is programming-language independent and able to represent physical entities in Plug and Play IoT services in the ADT instance. Currently, ADT support both DTDL version 2 and limited capabilities for DTDL version 3 in Azure D Explorer. The existing Azure DT Explorer can be used to upload or show DTDL version 3 models in the Model Graph panel. The Azure documentation recommends using DTDL version 3 due to its expanded capabilities over its predecessor, which are DTMI version relaxation, Array support for Property, increased limits for model inheritance and feature extensions such as the ability to decorate custom Interface schemas with semantic types. Since ADT Explorer fully supports DTDL version 2, this chapter uses DTDL version 2 to describe digital twin models and relationships.

A digital twin model created in DTDL is made up of meta-model classes such as *Interface*, *Command*, *Component*, *Property*, *Telemetry* and *Relationship* to describe the data, behaviour and organisation of the physical entities [7]. The data generated by these physical entities is gathered from various sources and then described as either *primitive* or *complex* schema types in those meta-model classes. The data types such as *Internationalised Resource Identifier* (IRI) and *Digital Twin Model Identifier* (DTMI) are used in DTDL. The IRI is a JSON-LD IRI to identify the nodes and properties, which can be relative or absolute to refer to DTDL elements or model-defined elements such as schemas. The DTMI is a case-sensitive identifier with scheme, path and version components as a string with a varying length of characters to identify *Interface*, *Property*, *Telemetry*, *Command*, *Relationship*, *Component* and *Complex* schema objects. If an element in a DTDL model does not include DTMI in the *@id* property, then Azure will assign *@id* property automatically by *Automatic Identifier Assignment*. When designing DTDL models, developers do not need to assign an individual *@id* property for each element in the DTDL model. To interact with digital twin models and twins, Microsoft has provided interactive tools such as the GUI (ADT Explorer[3]), Azure CLI[4], Azure REST API[5] and Software Development Kits (control plane APIs and data plane APIs[6]). The Azure services section of this chapter will further discuss how to interact with the digital twin instance using a programmable interface.

11.3.1 Schemas

The *Schema* is used to describe the on-the-wire or serialised format of a data point of a digital twin. The DTDL schema defines primary schema type such as *boolean*, *date*, *dateTime*, *double*, *duration*, *float*, *integer*, *long*, *string* and *time*, and complex schema types such as *Array*, *Enum*, *Map* and *Object* along with *Geospatial* schema to describe *GeoJson* geometry types such as line and multiline strings, point and multi-point, and polygons and multi-polygons. Also, it is compatible with serialising these schemas using *JSON*, *Avro* and *Protobuf*.

11.3.1.1 Primitive schema

Table 11.1 shows the names, descriptions and examples of each primitive schema type used in the DTDL.

11.3.1.2 Complex schema

The *complex schema* is a recursive schema made up of primitive schemas or any data type as described in the complex schema to describe the data points, which denotes them using *JSON object* or *JSON number* data types. The complex schemas are *Array*, *Enum*, *Map* and *Object*.

Array

The *Array* schema describes an indexable data type where each element is a primitive or complex schema. The ADTs service does not store Array-like schemas.

[3]https://learn.microsoft.com/en-us/azure/digital-twins/concepts-azure-digital-twins-explorer
[4]https://learn.microsoft.com/en-us/cli/azure/
[5]https://learn.microsoft.com/en-us/rest/api/azure/
[6]https://learn.microsoft.com/en-us/azure/digital-twins/concepts-apis-sdks

Table 11.1 List of primitive schema types used in the digital twin definition language

Primitive schema type	JSON data type	Description	Example
boolean	boolean	The *boolean* schema type is a *boolean* value that can be either *JSON value true (5)* or *JSON value false (6)*	*True/False*
date	string	The *date* schema type is a *date* value in ISO 8601 format is a *JSON string*	*2025-01-20*
dateTime	string	The *dateTime* schema type is a *date and time* value in ISO 8601 format is a *JSON string*	*2025-01-20T12:20:35*
double	number	The *double* schema type is a *finite numeric* value in IEEE 754 double-precision floating point format is a *JSON number*	*0.9972139932961029*
duration	string	The *duration* schema type is a *duration* value in ISO 8601 format is a *JSON string*	*P1Y6M13DT20H29M13S*
float	number	The *float* schema type is a *finite numeric* value in IEEE 754 single-precision floating point format is a *JSON number*	*0.1078036*
integer	number	The *integer* schema type is a *signed integral numeric* value in expressible in a 4-byte format and is a *JSON number*	*2107262543*
long	number	The *long* schema type is a *signed integral numeric* value in expressible in an 8-byte format and is a *JSON number*	*791678673*
string	string	The *string* schema type is a string value within the UTF8 format is a *JSON string*. The given example is a combination of Latin, Greek and Hebrew alphanumeric characters.	*לחBbsXזF1כGzטיצpפhקW2חZX ט7בCrz6צq99IאYk4C שמעלתנדסרקדגה6*
time	string	The *time* schema type is a time value in ISO 8601 format is a *JSON string*	*12:05:44*

When defining a data point using the *Array* schema, the Azure documentation suggests using the *Telemetry* element and extracting the Array data using the Event Grid service. If the data point is described using the *Property* element the Microsoft Azure will return an error message. The *Array* schema contains properties such as

Table 11.2 List of properties describes an Array schema

Property	Required	Data type	Limit	Description
@type	Required	Internationalised Resource Identifier	No limits	The *@type* property describes the schema type. The default value for the Array schema is *Array*.
@id	Optional	Digital Twin Model Identifier	2048 chars	The *@id* property is used to identify the *Array* schema. If there is no *@id* value, Azure will automatically assign this value.
comment	Optional	string	512 chars	The *comment* property describes the *Interface* for model authors.
description	Optional	localisable string	512 chars	The *description* property is used to display the description.
displayName	Optional	localisable string	512 chars	The *displayName* property is used to display the name of the Interface.
elementSchema	Required	A primary schema type or complex schema object	5 levels	The *schema* property is used to refer to a set of primary schema types such as *boolean*, *date*, *dateTime*, *double*, *duration*, *float*, *integer*, *long*, *string* and *time*, or complex schema objects such as *Array*, *Enum*, *Map* and *Object*.

@type, *@id*, *comment*, *description*, *displayName* and *elementSchema*. The *@type* and *elementSchema* are required, and others are optional. Table 11.2 shows the property names, requirements, data types, max limits and descriptions of each property associated with the *Array* schema. Figure 11.1 shows the JSON-LD definition of a *Telemetry* element with an *Array* schema in a DTDL model.

Enum

The *Enum* schema describes a set of constant string labels and associated values in integer or string. The *Enum* schema is different from the *Map* schema, where the values are constants. Also, Azure DT Explorer provides a drop-down UI component to select *Enum* values. The *Enum* schema contains properties such as *@type*, *@id*, *comment*, *description*, *displayName*, *enumValues* and *valueSchema*. The *@type* and *valueSchema* are required, and others are optional. Table 11.3 shows the property names, requirements, data types, max limits and descriptions of each property associated with the *Enum* schema. Figure 11.2 shows the JSON-LD definition of a *Property* element with an *Enum* schema in a DTDL model.

```
{
        "@type": "Telemetry",
        "@id": "dtmi:dtdl:context:complexModel:ArrayTelemetry;1",
        "comment": "an Array format with primitive schema types",
        "description": "to store a Array value",
        "displayName": "Array telemetry",
        "name": "ArrayTelemetry",
        "schema": {
          "@type": "Array",
          "elementSchema": "boolean"
        }
}
```

Figure 11.1 Telemetry element with an Array schema in a DTDL model

Table 11.3 List of properties describes an Enum schema

Property	Required	Data type	Limit	Description
@type	Required	Internationalised Resource Identifier	No limits	The *@type* property describes the schema type. The default value for the Enum schema is *Enum*.
@id	Optional	Digital Twin Model Identifier	2048 chars	The *@id* property is used to identify the *Enum* schema. If there is no *@id* value, Azure will automatically assign this value.
comment	Optional	string	512 chars	The *comment* property describes the *Interface* for model authors.
description	Optional	localisable string	512 chars	The *description* property is used to display the description.
displayName	Optional	localisable string	512 chars	The *displayName* property is used to display the name of the Interface.
enumValues	Optional	A set of *EnumValue* elements	No limits	The *enumValues* property describes a set of name/value mappings using *EnumValue* elements.
elementSchema	Required	A primary schema type	5 levels	The *schema* property is used to refer to a primary schema type such as *boolean*, *date*, *dateTime*, *double*, *duration*, *float*, *integer*, *long*, *string* and *time*.

EnumValue

The *EnumValue* element describes a mapping element of an Enum schema. The *EnumValue* element contains properties such as *@type*, *@id*, *comment*, *description*, *displayName*, *enumValue* and *name*. The *enumValue* and *name* are required, and others are optional. Table 11.4 shows the property names, requirements, data types, max limits and descriptions of each property associated with the *EnumValue* element. Figure 11.2 shows the JSON-LD definition of *EnumValue* elements with the *Enum* schema in a DTDL model.

```
{
      "@type": "Property",
      "@id": "dtmi:dtdl:context:complexModel:EnumProperty;1",
      "name": "EnumProperty",
      "schema": {
        "@type": "Enum",
        "@id": "dtmi:dtdl:context:complexModel:EnumProperty:Enum;1",
        "valueSchema": "integer",
        "enumValues": [
          {
            "@type": "EnumValue",
            "@id":
"dtmi:dtdl:context:complexModel:EnumProperty:Enum:EnumValue1;1",
            "name": "enumA",
            "enumValue": 1
          }
        ]
      }
}
```

Figure 11.2 Property element with an Enum schema in a DTDL model

Table 11.4 List of properties describes an Enum schema

Property	Required	Data type	Limit	Description
@type	Required	Internationalised Resource Identifier	No limits	The *@type* property describes the element. The default value for the EnumValue schema is *EnumValue.*
@id	Optional	Digital Twin Model Identifier	2048 chars	The *@id* property is used to identify the *EnumValue element.* If there is no *@id* value, Azure will automatically assign this value.
comment	Optional	string	512 chars	The *comment* property describes the *Interface* for model authors.

(Continues)

Table 11.4 (*Continued*)

Property	Required	Data type	Limit	Description
description	Optional	localisable string	512 chars	The *description* property is used to display the description.
displayName	Optional	localisable string	512 chars	The *displayName* property is used to display the name of the *EnumValue* element.
enumValue	Optional	literal	No limits	The *enumValue* property describes an integer or string value in the mapping.
name	Required	string	512 chars	The *name* property is a unique, alphanumeric string with underscores starting with a letter and the programming name of the *EnumValue* element.

Map

The *Map* schema describes a data type of key-value pairs sharing the same primitive or complex schema with all members in the *Map* schema. The *Map* schema is different from the *Enum* schema in that it can change values in the *mapKey* and *mapValue* elements. The ADTs Explorer provides separate text boxes for both key and value for each mapping element. The *Map* schema contains properties such as *@type, @id, comment, description, displayName, mapKey* and *mapValue*. The *@type, mapKey* and *mapValue* are required, and others are optional. Table 11.5 shows the property names, requirements, data types, max limits and descriptions of each property associated with the *Map* schema. Figure 11.3 shows the JSON-LD definition of the *Property* element with *Map* schema in a DTDL model.

MapKey

The *MapKey* element describes a key of the *Map* schema. The *MapKey* element contains properties such as *@type, @id, comment, description, displayName, name* and *schema*. The *name* and *schema* are required, and others are optional. Table 11.6 shows the property names, requirements, data types, max limits and descriptions of each property associated with the *MapKey* element. Figure 11.3 shows the JSON-LD definition of *MapKey* element with *Map* schema in a DTDL model.

MapValue

The *MapValue* describes a value of the *Map* schema. The *MapValue* element contains properties such as *@type, @id, comment, description, displayName, name* and *schema*. The *name* and *schema* are required, and others are optional. Table 11.7 shows the property names, requirements, data types, max limits and descriptions of each property associated with the *MapValue* element. Figure 11.3 shows the JSON-LD definition of the *MapValue* element with the *Map* schema in a DTDL model.

Table 11.5 List of properties describes the Map schema

Property	Required	Data type	Limit	Description
@type	Required	Internationalised Resource Identifier	No limits	The *@type* property describes the schema. The default value for the Map schema is *Map*.
@id	Optional	Digital Twin Model Identifier	2048 chars	The *@id* property is used to identify the *Map* schema. If there is no *@id* value, Azure will automatically assign this value.
comment	Optional	string	512 chars	The *comment* property describes the *Map* for model authors.
description	Optional	localisable string	512 chars	The *description* property is used to display the description.
displayName	Optional	localisable string	512 chars	The *displayName* property is used to display the name of the *EnumValue* element.
mapKey	Required	*MapKey* element	No limits	The *mapKey* property describes the keys in the mapping.
mapValue	Required	*MapValue* element	No limits	The *mapValue* property describes the value in the mapping.

```
{
        "@type": "Property",
        "@id": "dtmi:dtdl:context:complexModel:MapProperty;1",
        "name": "MapProperty",
        "writable": true,
        "schema": {
          "@type": "Map",
          "@id": "dtmi:dtdl:context:complexModel:MapProperty:Map;1",
          "displayName": "Map",
          "mapKey": {
            "@type": "MapKey",
            "name": "MapKey",
            "schema": "string"
          },
          "mapValue": {
            "@type": "MapValue",
            "name": "MapValue",
            "schema": "string"
          }
        }
}
```

Figure 11.3 Property element with Map schema in a DTDL model

Table 11.6 List of properties describes MapKey element

Property	Required	Data type	Limit	Description
@type	Optional	Internationalised Resource Identifier	No limits	The *@type* property describes the element. The default value for *MapKey* element is *MapKey*.
@id	Optional	Digital Twin Model Identifier	2048 chars	The *@id* property is used to identify the *MapKey* element. If there is no *@id* value, Azure will automatically assign this value.
comment	Optional	string	512 chars	The *comment* property describes the *MapKey* element for model authors.
description	Optional	localisable string	512 chars	The *description* property is used to display the description.
displayName	Optional	localisable string	512 chars	The *displayName* property is used to display the name of the *MapKey* element.
name	Required	string	No limits	The *name* property is a unique, alphanumeric with underscores starting with a letter and programming name of the *MapKey* element.
schema	Required	*string Primitive* schema	No limits	The *schema* property describes the data type of the value in the *MapKey* element.

Table 11.7 List of properties describes the MapValue element

Property	Required	Data type	Limit	Description
@type	Optional	Internationalised Resource Identifier	No limits	The *@type* property describes the element. The default value for the *MapValue* element is *MapValue*.
@id	Optional	Digital Twin Model Identifier	2048 chars	The *@id* property is used to identify the *MapValue* element. If there is no *@id* value, Azure will automatically assign this value.
comment	Optional	string	512 chars	The *comment* property describes the *MapValue* element for model authors.
description	Optional	localisable string	512 chars	The *description* property is used to display the description.

(Continues)

Table 11.7 (*Continued*)

Property	Required	Data type	Limit	Description
displayName	Optional	localisable string	512 chars	The *displayName* property is used to display the name of the *MapValue* element.
name	Required	string	No limits	The *name* property is a unique, alphanumeric with underscores starting with a letter and programming name of the *MapValue* element.
schema	Required	*A Primitive or complex* schema	5 levels	The *schema* property describes the data type of the element in the *MapValue* element.

Table 11.8 *List of properties describes Object schema*

Property	Required	Data type	Limit	Description
@type	Optional	Internationalised Resource Identifier	No limits	The *@type* property describes the schema. The default value for *Object* schema is *Object.*
@id	Optional	Digital Twin Model Identifier	2048 chars	The *@id* property is used to identify the *Object* schema. If there is no *@id* value, Azure will automatically assign this value.
comment	Optional	string	512 chars	The *comment* property describes the *Object* schema for model authors.
description	Optional	localisable string	512 chars	The *description* property is used to display the description.
displayName	Optional	localisable string	512 chars	The *displayName* property is used to display the name of the *Object* schema.
fields	Optional	A set of *Field* elements	No limits	The *fields* property describes the field descriptions using the *Field* elements.

Object

The *Object* schema describes a data type made up of named fields, like in struct in programming, with a primitive or complex schema. The *Object* schema helps to define data in classes using *Field* elements. The Azure DT Explorer provides separate text boxes for the value of each field. The *Object* schema contains properties such as contains *@type*, *@id*, *comment*, *description*, *displayName* and *fields*. The *@type* is required, and others are optional. Table 11.8 shows the property

```
{
       "@type": "Property",
       "@id": "dtmi:dtdl:context:complexModel:ObjectProperty;1",
       "displayName": "Object Property",
       "name": "ObjectProperty",
       "writable": true,
       "schema": {
         "@type": "Object",
         "@id": "dtmi:dtdl:context:complexModel:ObjectProperty:Object;1",
         "fields": [
           {
             "@type": "Field",
             "name": "Field1",
             "displayName": "Field 1",
             "schema": "double"
           },
           {
             "@type": "Field",
             "name": "Field2",
             "displayName": "Field 2",
             "schema": "double"
           }
         ]
       }
}
```

Figure 11.4 Property element with Object schema in a DTDL model

names, requirements, data types, max limits and descriptions of each property associated with the *Object* schema. Figure 11.4 shows the JSON-LD definition of *Property* element with an *Object* schema in a DTDL model.

Field
The *Field* element describes a field in an *Object* schema. The *Field* element contains properties such as contains contains *@type*, *@id*, *comment*, *description*, *displayName*, *name* and *schema*. The *name* and *schema* are required, and others are optional. Table 11.9 shows the property names, requirements, data types, max limits and descriptions of each property associated with the *Field* element. Figure 11.4 shows the JSON-LD definition of the *Field* element in an *Object* schema in a DTDL model.

11.3.1.3 Geospatial schema

The *Geospatial* schema is used to model geographic data structures. These are a set of geospatial schemas based on *Geo-JSON* geometry types such as *line*, *multi-line strings*, *point*, *multi-point*, *polygons* and *multi-polygons* data structures. The *lineString* schema term is a Geo-JSON LineString geometry type and schema IRI is *dtmi:standard:schema:geospacetial:lineString;3*. The *multiLineString* schema term is a Geo-JSON MultiLineString geometry type and schema IRI is *dtmi:standard: schema:geospatial:multiLineString;3*. The *multiPoint* schema term is a Geo-JSON MultiPoint geometry type and schema IRI is *dtmi:standard: schema:geospatial:*

Table 11.9 List of properties describes the Field element

Property	Required	Data type	Limit	Description
@type	Optional	Internationalised Resource Identifier	No limits	The *@type* property describes the schema. The default value for the *Field* element is *Field.*
@id	Optional	Digital Twin Model Identifier	2048 chars	The *@id* property is used to identify the *Field* element. If there is no *@id* value, Azure will automatically assign this value.
comment	Optional	string	512 chars	The *comment* property describes the *Field* element for model authors.
description	Optional	localisable string	512 chars	The *description* property is used to display the description.
displayName	Optional	localisable string	512 chars	The *displayName* property is used to display the name of the *Field* element.
name	Required	string	No limits	The *name* property is a unique, alphanumeric string with underscores starting with a letter and the programming name of the *Field* element.
schema	Required	*Primitive* or *Complex* schema	5 levels	The *schema property* describes the data type of the *Field* element.

```
{
        "@type": "Telemetry",
        "@id": "dtmi:dtdl:context:complexModel:GeospatialTelemetry;1",
        "displayName": "Geospatial Telemetry",
        "name": "GeospatialTelemetry",
        "schema": "point"
}
```

Figure 11.5 Telemetry element with a Geospatial schema in a DTDL model

multiPoint;3. The *multiPolygon* schema term is a Geo-JSON MultiPolygon geometry type and schema IRI is *dtmi:standard:schema:geospatial:multiPolygon;2*. The *point* schema term is a Geo-JSON Point geometry type and schema IRI is *dtmi:standard:schema:geospatial:point;2*. The *polygon* schema term is a Geo-JSON Polygon geometry type and schema IRI is *dtmi:standard:schema:geospatial:polygon;2*. The ADT service does not store geospatial schemas since the values are denoted in an *Array* schema. To read these values, developers must use *Telemetry* elements and the Azure Event Grid service. Figure 11.5 shows the JSON-LD definition of the *Telemetry* element with *Geospatial* schema in a DTDL model.

11.3.2 Meta classes

11.3.2.1 Interface

The *Interface* is a reusable meta-model class to describe the *Command, Component, Relationship* and *Telemetry* contents of a digital twin, which is limited to 1 MiByte. The size is inclusive of the curly braces of its definition and not limited to the text of the extended Interfaces component schema. The *Interface* contains properties such as *@context, @type, @id, comment, contents, description, displayName, extends* and *schemas*. The *@context, @type* and *@id* are required, and others are optional. Table 11.10 shows the property names, requirements, data types, max limits and descriptions of each property associated with the *Interface* meta-class. Figure 11.6 shows the JSON-LD definition of the *Interface* meta-class of a digital twin.

Table 11.10 List of properties used to describe the Interface meta-class

Property	Required	Data type	Limit	Description
@context	Required	Internationalised Resource Identifier	2048 chars	The *@context* property describes the context used when processing the *Interface* meta-class. The value of the *@context* for the DTDL v2 is *dtmi: dtdl:context;2*, and for the DTDL v3 is *dtmi: dtdl:context;2*. The default value for the *@context* property is *dtmi:dtdl:context;2* is used in this chapter.
@type	Required	Internationalised Resource Identifier	No limits	The *@type* property describes the type used when processing the *Interface* meta-class. The default value of the *@type* is *Interface.*
@id	Required	Digital Twin Model Identifier	128 chars	The *@id* property is used to identify the *Interface*. In this chapter, *dtmi:dtdl: context: Factory;1* and *dtmi:dtdl:context: Robot;1* are used to identify the *Factory* digital twin and *Robot* digital twin.

(Continues)

Table 11.10 (*Continued*)

Property	Required	Data type	Limit	Description
comment	Optional	string	512 chars	The *comment* property describes the *Interface* for model authors.
contents	Optional	A set of elements	100,000 elements	The *contents* property describes a set of *Commands*, *Components*, *Properties*, *Relationships* and *Telemetries* elements.
description	Optional	localisable string	512 chars	The *description* property is used to display the description.
displayName	Optional	localisable string	512 chars	The *displayName* property is used to display the name of the Interface.
extends	Optional	A set of *Interfaces*	1024 *Interfaces,* 10 levels	The *extends* property is used to refer set of *Interfaces* to inherit the contents.
schemas	Optional	A set of complex schema objects	No limits	The *schema* property is used to refer a set of complex schema objects such as *Arrays*, *Enums*, *Maps* or *Objects*.

```
{
        "@context": "dtmi:dtdl:context;2",
        "@type": "Interface",
        "@id": "dtmi:dtdl:context:primitiveModel;1",
        "comment":  "has primitive schema types ",
        "description":  "to create a digital twin with primitive schema",
        "displayName": "Primitive Model",
        "contents": [ ]
}
```

Figure 11.6 The Interface meta-model class in a DTDL model

11.3.2.2 Property

The *Property* element describes the state and synchronisation of that state between components, like in a distributed system. The *Property* element can be used to store various states, which can be static, such as Model ID or Manufacturer Name or dynamic data points generated, such as Temperature or Illuminance, by the physical system in its backing storage. This synchronisation can only be achieved by programmatically ingesting by mapping the data point from the IoT device with the *Property* element of the DTDL model associated with the particular device. The *Property* element contains properties such as *@type*, *@id*, *comment*, *description*, *displayName*, *name*, *schema* and *writable*. The *@type* property, *name* property, and *schema* property are required, and others are optional. Table 11.11 shows the property names, requirements, data types, max limits and descriptions of each property associated with the *Property* element. Figure 11.7 shows the JSON-LD definition of the *Property* element of a digital twin.

Table 11.11 List of properties used to describe the Property element

Property	Required	Data type	Limit	Description
@type	Required	Internationalised Resource Identifier	No limits	The *@type* property describes the type used when processing the *Property* element. The default value of the *@type* is *Property*.
@id	Optional	Digital Twin Model Identifier	2048 chars	The *@id* property is used to identify the *Property* element. If there is no *@id* value, Azure will automatically assign this value.
comment	Optional	string	512 chars	The *comment* property describes the *Property* for model authors.
description	Optional	localisable string	512 chars	The *description* property is used to display the description.
displayName	Optional	localisable string	512 chars	The *displayName* property is used to display the name.
name	Required	string	*512 chars*	The *name* property is a unique, alphanumeric with underscores starting with a letter and programming name of the *Property* element.
schema	Optional	A primary schema object	No limits	The *schema* property is used to refer a set of primary schema objects such as *boolean*, *date*, *dateTime*, *double*, *duration*, *float*, *integer*, *long*, *string* and *time* or complex schema objects such as *Enum*, *Map* and *Object*. The *Array* data type does not support by DTDL version 2 for *Property* elements.
writable	Optional	boolean	No limits	The *writable* property indicates whether the *Property* element is writable or not. The default value is false.

```
{
        "@type": "Property",
        "@id": "dtmi:dtdl:context:primitiveModel:booleanProperty;1",
        "comment": "a primitive boolean format",
        "description": "to store a boolean value",
        "displayName": "boolean property",
        "name": "booleanProperty",
        "schema": "boolean",
        "writable": true
}
```

Figure 11.7 The Property element class in a DTDL model

11.3.2.3 Telemetry

The *Telemetry* element describes the non-static data emitted such as sensory inputs, stream of data, alerts or information messages by connected devices. For example, temperature from a thermostat or orientation or angular velocity from a gyroscope sensor, which are streams of data which can be used to measure based on time-stamps. The data, unlike in the *Property* element, does not save a backing store. The data can only be accessed through telemetry events from the Azure Event Grid service. The *Telemetry* element contains properties such as *@type*, *@id*, *comment*, *description*, *displayName*, *name* and *schema*. The *@type* property and *name* property are required, and others are optional. Table 11.12 shows the property names, requirements, data types, max limits and descriptions of each property associated with the *Telemetry* element. Figure 11.8 shows the JSON-LD definition of the *Telemetry* element of a digital twin.

11.3.2.4 Relationship

The *Relationship* element describes an outgoing link to another model. The *Relationship* element can be used to store various states, which can be static or dynamic data points generated by the physical system in its backing storage. The *Relationship* contains properties such as *@type*, *@id*, *comment*, *description*, *displayName*, *maxMultiplicity*, *minMulitplicity*, *name*, *properties*, *target* and *writable*. The *@type* property and *name* property are required, and others are optional. Table 11.13 shows the property names, requirements, data types, max limits and descriptions of each property associated with the *Relationship* element. Figure 11.9 shows the JSON-LD definition of the *Relationship* element of a digital twin.

11.3.2.5 Component

The *Component* element describes the inclusion of *Interfaces* by value. The difference between *Component* elements and *Relationship* elements are *Component* is a part of the *Interface*, whereas a *Relationship* is a link to an *Interface*. According to DTDL version 3, the *Component* element cannot contain other *Component* elements. The *Component* element contains properties such as *@type*, *@id*, *comment*, *description*, *displayName*, *name* and *schema*. The *@type* property and *name*

Table 11.12 List of properties used to describe the Telemetry element

Property	Required	Data type	Limit	Description
@type	Required	Internationalised Resource Identifier	No limits	The *@type* property describes the type used when processing the *Telemetry* element. The default value of the *@type* is *Telemetry*.
@id	Optional	Digital Twin Model Identifier	2048 chars	The *@id* property is used to identify the *Telemetry* element. If there is no *@id* value, Azure will automatically assign this value.
comment	Optional	string	512 chars	The *comment* property describes the *Telemetry* for model authors.
description	Optional	localisable string	512 chars	The *description* property is used to display the description.
displayName	Optional	localisable string	512 chars	The *displayName* property is used to display the name.
name	Required	string	*512 chars*	The *name* property is a unique, alphanumeric string with underscores starting with a letter and the programming name of the *Telemetry* element.
schema	Optional	A primary or complex schema object	No limits	The *schema* property is used to refer a set of primary schema objects, such as *boolean*, *date*, *dateTime*, *double*, *duration*, *float*, *integer*, *long*, *string* and *time*, or complex schema objects such as *Array*, *Enum*, *Map* and *Object*. The *Array* data type only supports *Telemetry* elements.
writable	Optional	boolean	No limits	The *writable* property indicates whether the *Property* element is writable or not. The default value is false.

```
{
    "@type": "Telemetry",
    "@id": "dtmi:dtdl:context:complexModel:GeospatialTelemetry;1",
    "comment": "an Geospatial schema",
    "description": "to store a Geospatial schema",
    "displayName": "Geospatial Telemetry",
    "name": "GeospatialTelemetry",
    "schema": "point"
}
```

Figure 11.8 The Telemetry element class in a DTDL model

Table 11.13 List of properties used to describe the Relationship element

Property	Required	Data type	Limit	Description
@type	Required	Internationalized Resource Identifier	No limits	The *@type* property describes the type used when processing the *Relationship* element. The default value of the *@type* is *Relationship.*
@id	Optional	Digital Twin Model Identifier	2048 chars	The *@id* property is used to identify the *Relationship* element. If there is no *@id* value, Azure will automatically assign this value.
comment	Optional	string	512 chars	The *comment* property describes the *Telemetry* for model authors.
description	Optional	localisable string	512 chars	The *description* property is used to display the description.
displayName	Optional	localisable string	512 chars	The *displayName* property is used to display the name.
maxMultiplicity	Optional	integer	value >= 1	The *maxMultiplicity* property describes the maximum multiplicity of the target *Relationship*.
minMultiplicity	Optional	integer	value = 0	The *minMultiplicity* property describes the minimum multiplicity of the target *Relationship*.
name	Required	string	*512 chars*	The *name* property is a unique, alphanumeric with underscores starting with a letter and programming name of the *Relationship* element.
properties	Optional	A set of *Property* elements	No limits	The *properties* property describes *Relationship* specific properties.
target	Optional	Digital Twin Model Identifier	2048 chars	The *target* property sets the *@id* of the target model. If the value is empty, the target instance can be any model.
writable	Optional	boolean	No limits	The *writable* property indicates whether the *Relationship* element is writable or not. The default value is false.

```
{
        "@type": "Relationship",
        "name": "has_robot",
        "target": "dtmi:dtdl:context:Robot;1"
}
```

Figure 11.9 The Relationship element class in a DTDL model.

Table 11.14 List of properties used to describe the Component element

Property	Required	Data type	Limit	Description
@type	Required	Internationalised Resource Identifier	No limits	The *@type* property describes the type used when processing the *Component* element. The default value of the *@type* is *Component.*
@id	Optional	Digital Twin Model Identifier	2048 chars	The *@id* property is used to identify the *Component* element. If there is no *@id* value, Azure will automatically assign this value.
comment	Optional	string	512 chars	The *comment* property describes the *Component* for model authors.
description	Optional	localisable string	512 chars	The *description* property is used to display the description.
displayName	Optional	localisable string	512 chars	The *displayName* property is used to display the name.
name	Required	string	*512 chars*	The *name* property is a unique, alphanumeric string with underscores starting with a letter and the programming name of the *Component* element.
schema	Required	Interface	No limits	The *schema* property describes the *Interface* of a target model without nested *Component* elements.

```
{
        "@type": "Component",
        "name": "hasTool",
        "schema": "dtmi:dtdl:context:Robot:Tool;1"
}
```

Figure 11.10 The Component element class in a DTDL model

property are required, and others are optional. Table 11.14 shows the property names, requirements, data types, max limits and descriptions of each property associated with the *Component* element. Figure 11.10 shows the JSON-LD definition of the *Component* element of a digital twin.

Currently, ADTs service does not support commands. Although Azure supports commands in its modelling, but cannot be used to develop programmable interfaces. So, this tutorial will not discuss the *Command* element, and the data types such as *CommandRequest* and *CommandResponse* elements.

11.3.3 JSON-LD DTDL models

In this tutorial authors use DTDL to define models. The following are five types of DTDL models used in this chapter.

11.3.3.1 ComplexModel.json

This model defines complex schemas such as the *Array*, *Enum*, *Map*, *Object* and *Geospatial* schema types. The *Array* and *Geospatial* schema types were mentioned under *Telemetry* elements, and others were in *Property* elements due to ADT service limitations on handling array data types. This model is mentioned in the *ComplexModel.json* file in the *DTDLModels* folder of the *DigitalTwinServices* repository.[7]

11.3.3.2 PrimitiveModel.json

This model defines primitive schemas such as the *boolean*, *date*, *dateTime*, *double*, *duration*, *float*, *integer*, *long*, *string* and *time* schema types in *Property* elements. This model is mentioned in the *PrimitiveModel.json* file in the *DTDLModels* folder of the *DigitalTwinServices* repository.[8]

11.3.3.3 FactoryModel.json

This model defines a *Relationship* element with the Robot Model. This model is mentioned in the *FactoryModel.json* file in the *DTDLModels* folder of the *DigitalTwinServices* repository.[9]

11.3.3.4 RobotModel.json

This model defines a primitive schema and a *Component* element. This model is mentioned in the *RobotModel.json* file in the *DTDLModels* folder of the *DigitalTwinServices* repository.[10]

11.4 Azure services

This chapter will discuss manipulating ADTs with primitive and complex schema data and performing digital twin life cycle operations using the C # programming language in a .net version 8 environment. In this chapter, we use ARM for control plane APIs and ADT for data plane APIs using SDK to manipulate ADT instances, DTDL models, digital twins and relationship instances.

[7]https://github.com/gayanvoice/DigitalTwinServices/blob/master/DTDLModels/ComplexModel.json
[8]https://github.com/gayanvoice/DigitalTwinServices/blob/master/DTDLModels/PrimitiveModel.json
[9]https://github.com/gayanvoice/DigitalTwinServices/blob/master/DTDLModels/FactoryModel.json
[10]https://github.com/gayanvoice/DigitalTwinServices/blob/master/DTDLModels/RobotModel.json

11.4.1 Control plane APIs

The control plane APIs are used to manage the Azure services from a programmable interface. The NuGet library to manage control plane APIs for ADTs is the Microsoft ADTs management client library.[11] This section will discuss basic authentication, managing resource groups and managing the ADT instance by using ARM.

11.4.1.1 Default Azure Credential

To use control plane APIs using the ARM SDK, it is required to authenticate the application with the Azure cloud by using an Azure account during runtime. The developers can use different identity credential authentication mechanisms for their console, desktop and web applications. Table 11.15 shows Identity Credential classes provided by Azure. Each Identity Credential class provides unique ways to

Table 11.15 List of Identity Credential classes

Class	Description
EnvironmentCredential class	The *EnvironmentCredential* class uses *service principal with secret, service principal with certificate* or *username and password* methods in authentication process.
WorkloadIdentityCredential class	The *WorkloadIdentityCredential* class uses Microsoft Entra Workload ID to authenticate in host services supporting workload identity such as Kubernetes.
ManagedIdentityCredential class	The *ManagedIdentityCredential* class uses the managed identity associated with the service.
SharedTokenCacheCredential class	The *SharedTokenCacheCredential* class is a legacy class replaced by the *VisualStudioCredential* class, which uses tokens provided to Visual Studio that are stored in the local cache file.
VisualStudioCredential class	The *VisualStudioCredential* class shares the same mechanism as the *SharedTokenCacheCredential* class, using data from Visual Studio 2017 or later.
VisualStudioCodeCredential class	The *VisualStudioCodeCredential* class uses the Azure Account extension in Visual Studio Code to authenticate.
AzureCliCredential class *AzurePowerShellCredential* class	The *AzureCliCredential* class uses an access token generated by the Azure CLI. The *AzurePowerShellCredential* class uses an access token generated by the Azure PowerShell.
AzureDeveloperCliCredential class	The *AzureDeveloperCliCredential* class uses an access token generated by Azure Developer CLI.
InteractiveBrowserCredential class	The *InteractiveBrowserCredential* class uses the default browser to interactively authenticate the user.

[11] https://www.nuget.org/packages/Azure.ResourceManager.DigitalTwins

authenticate the Azure account. If the application requires automatic authentication or System Assigned Identity in its life cycle, it is not recommended to request authentication manually from the end-user for each API request using an interactive browser, username or password, or any symmetric key-based mechanism. For CLI, background service applications or Function Apps, it is recommended to use the *DefaultAzureCredential* class because it combines the Azure hosting environment. In this method, the application will take credential information from the Azure CLI in the local environment.[12]

In this implementation, the *DefaultAzureCredential* class is used to authenticate the application to access Azure ARM APIs. Due to an authentication error of not identifying the subscription, authors used the *DefaultAzureCredentialOptions* class to manually set the *Tenant ID* to get the subscription associated with the Azure account. The *ArmClient* class uses the *TokenCredential* class in its constructor to create the entry point for ARM clients. The developers can set the instance of the *DefaultAzureCredential* class in its constructor. The *ArmClient.GetDefaultSubscription* method is used to get the default subscription from the Azure account. The developers can also use *ArmClient.GetSubscriptionResource* method to get an individual subscription or an *ArmClient.GetSubscriptions* method to get the collection of subscriptions associated with the Azure account. Figure 11.11 shows code for requesting the default subscription using the *DefaultAzureCredential* class.

11.4.1.2 Resource group

The *resource group* is a container for categorising Azure services in an Azure subscription. This categorisation helps businesses manage and organise resources based on their business requirements. By using control plane APIs through the ARM SDK can dynamically allocate resource groups via a programmable interface. The *Azure Identity client* library for token authentication based on Microsoft Entra ID and *Azure Resource Manager* library to enables create, get, update, delete and list resources and resource groups using ARM. Figure 11.12 shows .NET CLI commands to install libraries and Figure 11.13 shows the namespaces used in the source code, to manage resource groups using ARM.

The rest of this section discusses on creating resource groups and retrieving the resource groups by name using ARM.

```
DefaultAzureCredential defaultAzureCredential = new DefaultAzureCredential(
    new DefaultAzureCredentialOptions() { TenantId = tenentId });
ArmClient armClient = new ArmClient(defaultAzureCredential);
SubscriptionResource subscriptionResource =
       await armClient.GetDefaultSubscriptionAsync();
```

Figure 11.11 Requesting the default subscription associated with the Azure account using DefaultAzureCredential class

[12]https://learn.microsoft.com/en-us/dotnet/api/azure.identity.defaultazurecredential

```
dotnet add package Azure.Identity
dotnet add package Azure.ResourceManager
```

Figure 11.12 The .NET CLI commands to install Azure Identity and Azure Resource Manager packages

```
using Azure.Identity;
using Azure.ResourceManager.Resources;
using Azure.ResourceManager;
using Azure;
```

Figure 11.13 The Azure Identity and Azure Resource Manager namespaces

```
ResourceGroupCollection resourceGroupCollection =
       subscriptionResource.GetResourceGroups();
ResourceGroupData resourceGroupData =
       new ResourceGroupData(location: Azure.Core.AzureLocation.UKSouth);
ArmOperation<ResourceGroupResource> resourceGroupResourceArmOperation =
    await resourceGroupCollection.CreateOrUpdateAsync(
        waitUntil: WaitUntil.Completed,
        resourceGroupName: resourceGroupName,
        data: resourceGroupData);
ResourceGroupResource resourceGroupResource =
       resourceGroupResourceArmOperation.Value;
```

Figure 11.14 Creating a new resource group using Azure Resource Manager

Create

The resource group is a container that holds resources associated with a solution. For example, developers can create digital twin instances, function apps, storage accounts and event grid resources in the same resource group to manage the accessibility for a department in the organisation. This process is flexible and can be done according to the requirements of the organisation. The perquisite for creating a resource group is an instance of *SubscriptionResource* class. The *GetResourceGroups* method will return an instance of *ResourceGroupCollection* class representing operations associated with resource groups. To create a new resource group, developers need an instance of *ResourceGroupData* class to represent resource group information and an unique name to identify the resource group. The constructor of the *ResourceGroupData* class requires *AzureLocation* struct to represent the Azure geography in the *location* parameter. Then *CreateOrUpdateAsync* method in the *ResourceGroupCollection* class can be used create or update a resource group. The method requires *WaitUntil* enum in its *waitUntil* parameter to indicate whether the method should return once it started or completed operation, the name of the resource group to *resourceGroupName* parameter and the instance of the *ResourceGroupData* class to *data* parameter. The *Value* property in the *ArmOperation* class will return the *ResourceGroupResource* type once the operation completed. Figure 11.14 shows how to create a resource group using *CreateOrUpdateAsync* method of the *ResourceGroupCollection* class.

To check resource groups in Azure portal, users can click on the *Resource groups* menu in the *Settings* menu group of the *Subscription* service in the Azure portal, to check the newly created resource group in the Azure portal. The list of resource groups created are shown in a table in the working pane of the *Subscription* service.

Get

The prerequisites for getting a resource group is an instance of *SubscriptionResource* class. As mentioned earlier, *GetResourceGroups* method will return an instance of *ResourceGroupCollection* class to handle operations associate with resource groups. The *GetAsync* method has the *resourceGroupName* parameter to specify the name of the resource group and it will return the instance of *ResourceGroupResource* class. Figure 11.15 shows the source code associated with requesting a resource group by name using ARM. To check the resource group in detail using Azure portal, users can click on the resource group name from the table in the working plane of the *Subscription* service.

11.4.1.3 Managing the Azure Digital Twin resource

The *Azure Digital Twin* is a platform provides tools for organisations to manage digital representations of physical entities to collect insights, optimise existing products and services. By using the control plane APIs organisations can interact with ADT resource programmatically using custom interfaces. The *Azure Identity client* library for token-based authentication based on *Microsoft Entra ID* and *Azure Digital Twins management client* library to enable create, get, update, delete and list digital twin instances using ARM. Figure 11.16 shows .NET CLI commands to install libraries and Figure 11.17 shows the namespaces used in the source code, to manage ADT instances using ARM.

The rest of this section discuss on creating and retrieving an ADT instances using ARM.

Create

The prerequisite for creating a digital twin is an instance of *ResourceGroupResource* class. The *GetDigitalTwinsDescriptions* method will return an instance of *DigitalTwins*

```
ResourceGroupCollection resourceGroupCollection =
      subscriptionResource.GetResourceGroups();
ResourceGroupResource resourceGroupResource =
      await resourceGroupCollection.GetAsync(resourceGroupName);
```

Figure 11.15 Getting a resource group by name using Azure Resource Manager

```
dotnet add package Azure.Identity
dotnet add package Azure.ResourceManager
dotnet add package Azure.ResourceManager.DigitalTwins
```

Figure 11.16 The .NET CLI commands to install Azure Identity and Azure Digital Twins management client packages

```
using Azure.Identity;
using Azure.ResourceManager.DigitalTwins;
using Azure.ResourceManager.DigitalTwins.Models;
using Azure.ResourceManager.Resources;
using Azure.ResourceManager;
using Azure;
```

Figure 11.17 The Azure Identity and Azure Digital Twin management client namespaces

```
DigitalTwinsDescriptionCollection digitalTwinsDescriptionCollection =
    resourceGroupResource.GetDigitalTwinsDescriptions();
DigitalTwinsDescriptionData digitalTwinsDescriptionData =
       new DigitalTwinsDescriptionData(AzureLocation.UKSouth);
digitalTwinsDescriptionData.PublicNetworkAccess =
       DigitalTwinsPublicNetworkAccess.Enabled;
ArmOperation<DigitalTwinsDescriptionResource> armOperation =
    await digitalTwinsDescriptionCollection.CreateOrUpdateAsync(
        waitUntil: WaitUntil.Completed,
        resourceName: resourceName,
        data: digitalTwinsDescriptionData);
DigitalTwinsDescriptionResource digitalTwinsDescriptionResource =
       armOperation.Value;
```

Figure 11.18 Creating a new digital twin instance using Azure Resource Manager

DescriptionCollection class which represents a collection of digital twin resources and operations associating with managing digital twin instances. To create a new digital twin instance, developers need an instance of *DigitalTwinsDescriptionData* class to represent digital twin description data and a unique name to identify the digital twin instance. The constructor of the *DigitalTwinsDescriptionData* class which requires *AzureLocation* struct to represent the Azure geography in the *location* parameter. The *DigitalTwinsPublicNetworkAccess* struct is used to determine whether the digital twin instance is available as public or private in *PublicNetworkAccess* property of the instance of the *DigitalTwinsDescriptionData* class. The *CreateOrUpdateAsync* method in the collection requires *WaitUntil* enum to specify when to return either in its start or wait until operation is completed in *waitUntil* parameter, the name of the digital twin instance in *resourceName* parameter and the instance of *DigitalTwinDescriptionData* class in *data* parameter. If the Arm Operation waits until operation is completed, then developers can return the newly created digital twin instance by *Value* property. Figure 11.18 shows the source code for creating a digital twin instance using ARM.

Get

The prerequisite for getting a digital twin instance is an instance of *ResourceGroupResource* class. The *GetDigitalTwinsDescriptionAsync* method will return an instance of *DigitalTwinsDescriptionResource* class of the digital twin instance. The method has the *resourceName* parameter to specify the name of the digital twin instance. Figure 11.19 shows the source code associated with requesting a digital twin instance by name using ARM. An individual instance can be chosen from the ADT portal or in the resources working pane of the resource group of the Azure portal.

11.4.2 Data plane APIs

The data plane APIs provides capabilities provided by the instance of the resource type by using a programmable interface. Unlike the control plane APIs where it has the capability to manage Azure resources, the data plane provides endpoints to manage data and governance of the instance. The NuGet library associated with the data plane APIs for ADT is Azure IoT Digital Twins client library.[13] This section will discuss initialising client endpoint for data plane APIs, managing models, managing twins, managing relationships and query the instance using ADT Core library.

The *Azure Digital Twins core client* library provides tools to manage the models, twins, relationships and query in the ADT instance. To use the client library, developers require the *Azure Identity client* library for token-based authentication based on Microsoft Entra ID and the *hostname* of the ADT instance. Figure 11.20 shows the . NET CLI commands to install libraries and Figure 11.21 shows the namespaces used in the source code to manage the ADT instance.

11.4.2.1 Getting an Azure Digital Twin instance

The Digital Twins Service Client provides methods to manipulate the data in an ADT instance. The prerequisites for this class are the ADT instance hosting URI in the *endpoint* parameter and the token credential in the *credential* parameter. The hosting URI can be copied from the *Host name* field in the *Essentials* group in the working

```
DigitalTwinsDescriptionResource digitalTwinsDescriptionResource =
        Await resourceGroupResource.GetDigitalTwinsDescriptionAsync(
                resourceName: resourceName);
```

Figure 11.19 Retrieving a digital twin instance by name using Azure Resource Manager

```
dotnet add package Azure.Identity
dotnet add package Azure.ResourceManager
dotnet add package Azure.ResourceManager.DigitalTwins
dotnet add package Azure.DigitalTwins.Core
```

Figure 11.20 The .NET CLI commands to install Azure Identity, Azure Digital Twins management client and Azure IoT Digital Twins client libraries

[13]https://learn.microsoft.com/en-us/dotnet/api/overview/azure/digitaltwins.core-readme

```
using Azure.DigitalTwins.Core;
using Azure.Identity;
using Azure.ResourceManager.DigitalTwins;
using Azure.ResourceManager.DigitalTwins.Models;
using Azure.ResourceManager.Resources;
using Azure.ResourceManager;
using Azure;
```

Figure 11.21 The Azure Identity, Azure Resource Manager and Azure Digital Twins client namespaces

```
Uri digitalTwinsUri = new UriBuilder(Uri.UriSchemeHttps,
        digitalTwinsDescriptionResource.Data.HostName).Uri;
DigitalTwinsClient digitalTwinsClient = new DigitalTwinsClient(
    new Uri(digitalTwinsUri.ToString()), defaultAzureCredential);
```

Figure 11.22 Initialising the Digital Twins Service Client using the DefaultAzureCredential class and Azure Resource Manager

pane of the ADT instance. The programmable way to extract the hostname is by using ARM. The developers can define the *HostName* property of the Data object in the instance of the *DigitalTwinsDescriptionResource* class in the *hostName* parameter, and *UriSchemeHTTPS* for the *schemeName* parameter in the *UriBuilder* class to return the URI of the hostname for the *endpoint* parameter of the constructor. As mentioned earlier, in token-based authentication methods, the instance of the *DefaultAzureCredential* class is used in the *credential* parameter of the constructor. As shown in Figure 11.22, a developer can retrieve the Digital Twin Service Client by using Azure Identity and ARM. The *DigitalTwinsDescriptionResource* class provides methods to manipulate models, twins, relationships and query the digital twin instance.

11.4.2.2 Managing DTDL models

This section will discuss managing models defined in the DTDL in the ADT instance using data plane APIs. The process of uploading models into the instance, retrieving uploaded models, decommissioning the existing models and deleting models from the instance will be discussed by using data plane APIs. The alternative to manage models is ADT Explorer. The *Azure IoT Digital Twins client* library enables *create, get, decommission* and *delete* methods to handle model operations.

Upload

The prerequisite for uploading a model is an instance of the *DigitalTwinsClient* class and a DTDL model initialised in a *string* variable. The *CreateModelsAsync* method creates one or more models asynchronously. The result of this method will return newly created models in an array. Each instance of the *DigitalTwinsModelData* class contains the model definition and metadata. Figure 11.23 shows the code creates one model and returns its model definition and metadata from the ADT instance.

```
Response<DigitalTwinsModelData[]> digitalTwinsModelDataArrayResponse =
    await digitalTwinsClient.CreateModelsAsync(new[] { dtdlModelFile });
DigitalTwinsModelData[] digitalTwinsModelDataArray =
       digitalTwinsModelDataArrayResponse.Value;
DigitalTwinsModelData digitalTwinsModelData =
       digitalTwinsModelDataArray.First();
```

Figure 11.23 Creating and retrieving the definition and metadata of a single model from an Azure Digital Twins instance

```
Response<DigitalTwinsModelData> digitalTwinsModelDataResponse =
    await digitalTwinsClient.GetModelAsync(modelId);
DigitalTwinsModelData digitalTwinsModelData =
       digitalTwinsModelDataResponse.Value;
```

Figure 11.24 Get the definition and metadata of a model from the Azure Digital Twins instance

```
Response response = await digitalTwinsClient.DecommissionModelAsync(modelId);
```

Figure 11.25 Decommission a model from the Azure Digital Twins instance

Get

The prerequisite for getting a model from an instance of the *DigitalTwinsClient* class and model ID is to initialise a *string* variable. The *GetModelAsync* method retrieves the model by *modelId* string parameter asynchronously. The model ID is described in the *@id* property in an *Interface* meta class of a model, for example *dtmi:dtdl:context:primitiveModel;1*. The result of this method will return a model in an instance of the *DigitalTwinsModelData* class, which contains the model definition and metadata in application/JSON format. Figure 11.24 shows how to retrieve the model by its model ID from the ADT instance.

Decommission

The prerequisite for decommissioning a model in an instance of the *DigitalTwinsClient* class and model ID is to initialise it in a *string* variable. This method can be used if any model is no longer in use or a newer version of the model is created in the instance. By decommissioning a model, it will disable the use of the model ID from creating new instances of the decommissioned model. The *DecommissionModelAsync* method decommissions a model by the *modelId* parameter of *String* type asynchronously. The model ID is described in the *@id* property in an *Interface* meta class of a model, for example *dtmi:dtdl:context: primitiveModel;1*. The result of this method will return an instance of the *Response* class. The model's decommissioning status is described in the *ModelData* record of the *DigitalTwinsModelData class.* Figure 11.25 decommissions a model by its model ID from the ADT instance.

```
Response response = await digitalTwinsClient.DeleteModelAsync(modelId);
```

Figure 11.26 Delete a model from the Azure Digital Twins instance

Delete

The prerequisite for deleting a model from an instance of the *DigitalTwinsClient* class and model ID is to initialise it in a variable with the *String* data type. This method can be used to remove the model from the instance. Unlike the decommissioning method, the delete method will remove the model from the instance. The *DeleteModelAsync* method removes a model by the *modelId* parameter of *String* type asynchronously. The model ID is described in the *@id* property in an *Interface* meta class of a model, for example *dtmi:dtdl:context:primitiveModel;1*. The result of this method will return an instance of the *Response* class. Figure 11.26 shows how to delete a model by its model ID from the ADT instance.

11.4.2.3 Managing digital twins

This section will discuss managing digital twins in the ADT instance using data plane APIs. The process of creating or replacing, retrieving, updating properties, publishing telemetry and deleting digital twins from the instance will be discussed by using data plane APIs. The alternative to manage digital twins is ADT Explorer. The *Azure IoT Digital Twins client* library enables *create or replace*, *get*, *publish telemetry*, *update* and *delete* methods to handle digital twin operations.

Create or replace

The prerequisite for creating or replacing a digital twin is defining the property values of the elements, instances of the *BasicDigitalTwin* class and *DigitalTwinsClient* class. When defining values for each property, it requires considering the schema types of the JSON that are compatible in the programming language. For example, Figure 11.27 shows how the compatible data types of each schema type are initialised in variables. The primary schema types, such as *date*, *dateTime*, *duration* and *time* schemas, convert the values to the String data type with the supporting string patterns of the JSON. The complex schemas, such as *object* and *map* schemas, used instances of the *Object* and *Dictionary* classes. The structure and data type for each complex schema must be defined according to the JSON for each element defined in the DTDL. Figure 11.28 shows the methods to generate the string pattern for the *duration* schema and randomised alphanumeric string using English, Hebrew and Greek for the *string* schema in UTF-8 format.

To define a digital twin in an ADT instance, it is required to initialise a *BasicDigitalTwin* class with *Id*, *MetaData* and *Content* properties. The model ID, for example *dtmi:dtdl:context:primitiveModel;1*, is defined in the *ModelId* property of a *DigitalTwinMetadata* class. The twin ID must be a unique identification in a *String* value, such as *Primitive_TDT*, for each digital twin in the ADT instance must be defined in the *Id* property of the *BasicDigitalTwin* class. The *Content* property in the *BasicDigitalTwin* class is used to describe each property element in

```
bool booleanValue = true;
string dateValue = DateTime.Now.ToString("yyyy-MM-dd");
string dateTimeValue = DateTime.Now.ToString("yyyy-MM-ddThh:mm:ss");
double doubleValue = new Random().NextDouble();
string durationValue = GenerateRandomISO8601Duration();
float floatValue = (float)new Random().NextDouble();
int integerValue = new Random().Next();
long longValue = (long)new Random().Next();
string stringValue = GenerateRandomUTF8String(256);
string timeValue = DateTime.Now.ToString("hh:mm:ss");
int enumValue = 2;
object objectValue = new {
        Field1 = new Random().NextDouble(),
        Field2 = new Random().NextDouble()
    };
Dictionary<string, string> mapValue = new Dictionary<string, string>
{
    { "Priority", GenerateRandomUTF8String(8) }
};
```

Figure 11.27 Defining the data types and patterns associated with JSON-LD with c-sharp programming language

```
private string GenerateRandomISO8601Duration()
{
    Random random = new Random();
    int years = random.Next(0, 5);
    int months = random.Next(0, 12);
    int days = random.Next(0, 31);
    int hours = random.Next(0, 24);
    int minutes = random.Next(0, 60);
    int seconds = random.Next(0, 60);
    return $"P{years}Y{months}M{days}DT{hours}H{minutes}M{seconds}S";
}

private static string GenerateRandomUTF8String(int length)
{
    const string chars =
"ABCDEFGHIJKLMNOPQRSTUVWXYZabcdefghijklmnopqrstuvwxyz0123456789אבגדהוזחטיכלמנסעפצקרשתαβγδεζ
ηθικλμνξοπρστυφχψωΑΒΓΔΕΖΗΘΙΚΛΜΝΞΟΠΡΣΤΥΦΧΨΩ\r\n";
    StringBuilder stringBuilder = new StringBuilder(length);
    Random random = new Random();
    for (int i = 0; i < length; i++)
      stringBuilder.Append(chars[random.Next(chars.Length)]);
    return stringBuilder.ToString();
}
```

Figure 11.28 Generating random ISO8601 durations and alphanumeric strings with English, Hebrew and Greek languages

```
BasicDigitalTwin basicDigitalTwin = new BasicDigitalTwin
{
    Id = twinId,
    Metadata = { ModelId = modelId },
    Contents =
        {
            { "booleanProperty", booleanValue },
            { "dateProperty", dateValue },
            { "dateTimeProperty", dateTimeValue },
            { "doubleProperty",  doubleValue },
            { "durationProperty", durationValue },
            { "floatProperty",  floatValue },
            { "integerProperty",  integerValue },
            { "longProperty",  longValue },
            { "stringProperty",  stringValue },
            { "timeProperty",  timeValue },
            { "EnumProperty", enumValue },
            { "ObjectProperty", objectValue },
            { "MapProperty", mapValue },
        },
};
```

Primary schema

Complex schema

Figure 11.29 Initialising an instance of the BasicDigitalTwin class with model Id, twin Id and contents properties

```
Response<BasicDigitalTwin> basicDigitalTwinResponse =
await digitalTwinsClient.CreateOrReplaceDigitalTwinAsync<BasicDigitalTwin>(
       basicDigitalTwin.Id, basicDigitalTwin);
BasicDigitalTwin basicDigitalTwin = basicDigitalTwinResponse.Value;
```

Figure 11.30 Creating or replacing a digital twin in the Azure Digital Twins instance

a *Dictionary* class with *string* and *object* data types in its key-value pairs. Figure 11.29 shows an instance of the *BasicDigitalTwin* class with values.

The *CreateOrReplaceDigitalTwinAsync* method will return an instance of the newly created digital twin asynchronously. To create an instance, the *twin Id* and the instance of the *BasicDigitalTwin* class are required. The result of this method will return the *BasicDigitalTwin* class of the digital twin, which is an optional helper class for deserialising the digital twin. Figure 11.30 shows how to create or replace digital twins in the ADT instance.

Get

The prerequisites for getting a digital twin are an instance of the *DigitalTwinsClient* class and the twin ID in a *String* variable. The *GetDigitalTwinAsync* method can be used to get the digital twin using the twin Id parameter asynchronously. The result of this method will return an instance of the *BasicDigitalTwin* class. Digital Figure 11.31 shows how to retrieve a digital twin from the ADT instance.

The resulting *BasicDigitalTwin* class shows individual property values stored in the digital twin as bytes rather than in a readable format. As shown in

```
Response<BasicDigitalTwin> basicDigitalTwinResponse =
    await digitalTwinsClient.GetDigitalTwinAsync<BasicDigitalTwin>(twinId);
BasicDigitalTwin basicDigitalTwin = basicDigitalTwinResponse.Value;
```

Figure 11.31 Retrieving a digital twin from an Azure Digital Twins instance

```
Dictionary<string, object> contentDictionary =
        new Dictionary<string, object>();
ICollection<string> keyCollection = basicDigitalTwin.Contents.Keys;
if (keyCollection.Count() > 0)
{
    foreach (string key in keyCollection)
    {
        object value = basicDigitalTwin.Contents[key];
        contentDictionary.Add(key, value);
    }
}
```

Figure 11.32 Extracting values from properties in a digital twin

```
JsonPatchDocument jsonPatchDocument = new JsonPatchDocument();
jsonPatchDocument.AppendAdd("/booleanProperty", booleanValue);
jsonPatchDocument.AppendAdd("/dateProperty", dateValue);
jsonPatchDocument.AppendAdd("/dateTimeProperty", dateTimeValue);
jsonPatchDocument.AppendAdd("/doubleProperty", doubleValue);
jsonPatchDocument.AppendAdd("/durationProperty", durationValue);
jsonPatchDocument.AppendAdd("/floatProperty", floatValue);
jsonPatchDocument.AppendAdd("/integerProperty", integerValue);
jsonPatchDocument.AppendAdd("/longProperty", longValue);
jsonPatchDocument.AppendAdd("/stringProperty", stringValue);
jsonPatchDocument.AppendAdd("/timeProperty", timeValue);
```

Primary schema

```
jsonPatchDocument.AppendAdd("/EnumProperty", enumValue);
jsonPatchDocument.AppendAdd("/ObjectProperty", objectValue);
jsonPatchDocument.AppendAdd("/MapProperty", mapValue);
```

Complex schema

Figure 11.33 Initialising the JsonPatchDocument class with the Property element name and values

Figure 11.32, individual property key-value pairs can be extracted from the *Contents* property using a foreach loop on the key collection and adding them into a *Dictionary* with *String* and *object* data types.

Update properties

The prerequisites for updating properties in a digital twin are instances of the *JsonPatchDocument* class and the *DigitalTwinsClient* class, and the twin ID in a *String* variable. The *JsonPatchDocument* class, described in updating properties, belonged to the *Azure* namespace. Sometimes this class conflicts with the *Newtonsoft.Json* namespace. Developers can select which property elements they require to change the state by the *AppendAdd* method in which takes the *name* of the property and the *value* object. Figure 11.33 shows an instance of the *JsonPatchDocument* class with values assigned to each property element.

```
Response response = await digitalTwinsClient
        .UpdateDigitalTwinAsync(twinId, jsonPatchDocument);
```

Figure 11.34 Updating Property elements in a digital twin by using an Azure Digital Twin instance

```
double[] doubelArray = new double[10];
Random random = new Random();
for (int i = 0; i < 10; i++)
{
    doubelArray[i] = random.NextDouble();
}
Dictionary<string, double> geopartialSchema = new Dictionary<string, double>
{
    { "latitude", new Random().NextDouble() },
    { "longitude", new Random().NextDouble() * -1 }
};
object payloadObject = new
{
    ArrayTelemetry = doubelArray,
    GeospatialTelemetry = geopartialSchema
};
```

Figure 11.35 Initialising array and geospatial schema types in a payload object

Then *UpdateDigitalTwinAsync* method can be used to update the state of the digital twin. This method requires the twin Id and an instance *JsonPatchDocument* class. Figure 11.34 shows the *UpdateDigitalTwinAsync* method to update *Property* elements of a digital twin.

Publish telemetry

The perquisites for publishing telemetry in a digital twin are an instance of the *DigitalTwinsClient* class, a *payload* object describing the *Array* schema values and the twin ID in a *String* variable. In c-sharp programming language, the *Array* schema type can be easily initialised based on the data type of the *Array* telemetry element. The example given below the *Array* schema type is a *Boolean* schema. In the *Geospatial* schema, the data can only be represented in a *Dictionary* class with *String* and *double* data types. Then, an *Object* class is used to create a *payload* object. As shown in Figure 11.35, a payload object is created to publish the *Array* schema and *Geospatial* schema. The *PublishTelemetryAsync* method can be used to publish the telemetry using twin ID, a unique Globally Unique Identifier (GUID) and a serialised payload object asynchronously. The result of this method will return an instance of the *Response* class. Figure 11.36 shows how to publish telemetry to a digital twin.

Delete

The prerequisites for deleting a digital twin are an instance of the *DigitalTwinsClient* class and the twin ID in a *String* variable. The *DeleteDigitalTwinAsync* method can

```
Response response =
    await digitalTwinsClient.PublishTelemetryAsync(
        digitalTwinId: twinId,
        messageId: Guid.NewGuid().ToString(),
        payload: JsonConvert.SerializeObject(payloadObject));
```

Figure 11.36 Publishing payload object using twin ID, GUID and serialised payload object

```
Response response = await digitalTwinsClient.DeleteDigitalTwinAsync(twinId);
```

Figure 11.37 Deleting a digital twin from the Azure Digital Twin instance

```
BasicRelationship basicRelationship = new BasicRelationship();
basicRelationship.TargetId = targetId;
basicRelationship.Name = name;
string relationshipId = $"{sourceId}-{name}-{targetId}";
```

Figure 11.38 Initialising BasicRelationship class and relationshipId variables

be used to delete a digital twin using the twin ID parameter asynchronously. The result of this method will return an instance of the *Response* class. Figure 11.37 shows how to delete a digital twin.

11.4.2.4 Managing relationships

This section will discuss managing relationships between digital twins in the ADT instance using data plane APIs. The process of creating or replacing, retrieving and deleting relationships from the instance will be discussed by using data plane APIs. The alternative to manage digital twins is ADT Explorer. The Azure IoT Digital Twins client library enables create or replace, get, get incoming, get relationships and delete methods to handle relationships between digital twins.

Create or replace

The perquisites for creating or replacing relationships between digital twins are an instance of the *DigitalTwinsClient* class and the source twin ID, target twin ID and name of the relationship in *String* variables. The *BasicRelationship* class defines the target ID and name of the relationship between two digital twins. The *name* of the relationship is described in the definition of the source digital twin. The relationship ID must be a unique identifier in the instance. Figure 11.38 shows the initialisations of the *BasicRelationship* class and *relationshipId* variables. The *CreateOrReplaceRelationshipAsync* method is used to create or replace a relationship between digital twins asynchronously. The result of this method will return an instance of the *BasicRelationship* class of the newly created relationship. Figure 11.39 shows how to create or replace a digital twin.

```
Response<BasicRelationship> basicRelationshipResponse =
        await digitalTwinsClient.CreateOrReplaceRelationshipAsync<BasicRelationship>(
                digitalTwinId: sourceId,
                relationshipId: relationshipId,
                relationship: basicRelationship);
BasicRelationship basicRelationship2 = basicRelationshipResponse.Value;
```

Figure 11.39 Create or replace a relationship in the Azure Digital Twin instance

```
Response<BasicRelationship> basicRelationshipResponse =
        await digitalTwinsClient.GetRelationshipAsync<BasicRelationship>(
                digitalTwinId: sourceId,
                relationshipId: relationshipId);
BasicRelationship basicRelationship = basicRelationshipResponse.Value;
```

Figure 11.40 Retrieving the outgoing relationship of a source digital twin

```
AsyncPageable<IncomingRelationship> incomingRelationshipAsyncPageable =
        digitalTwinsClient.GetIncomingRelationshipsAsync(digitalTwinId: targetId);
List<IncomingRelationship> incomingRelationshipList =
        new List<IncomingRelationship>();
await foreach (IncomingRelationship incomingRelationship
        in incomingRelationshipAsyncPageable)
{
        incomingRelationshipList.Add(incomingRelationship);
}
```

Figure 11.41 Retrieving the list of incoming relationships of the target digital twin

Get a basic relationship

The prerequisites to get an outgoing relationship by its relationship ID are an instance of the *DigitalTwinsClient* class, the source *twin ID* and the *relationship ID* of the relationship in *String* variables. The *GetRelationshipAsync* method is used to get an outgoing relationship between digital twins asynchronously. The result of this method will return an instance of the *BasicRelationship* class of the requested relationship. Figure 11.40 shows how to get an outgoing relationship in a *BasicRelationship* class.

Get incoming relationships

The prerequisites to get the list of incoming relationships are an instance of the *DigitalTwinsClient* class, *target twin ID* in a *String* variable. The *GetIncomingRelationshipsAsync* method is used to get the list of incoming relationships asynchronously. The result of this method will return an instance of the *AsyncPageable* class with the *BasicRelationship* type. By using *await*, *foreach* and iterator, developers can extract *IncomingRelationship* classes. Figure 11.41 shows how to retrieve a list of incoming relationships using an iterator and then add it to a *List* class.

```
AsyncPageable<BasicRelationship> basicRelationshipAsyncPageable =
        digitalTwinsClient.GetRelationshipsAsync<BasicRelationship>(
                digitalTwinId: sourceId);
List<BasicRelationship> basicRelationshipList = new List<BasicRelationship>();
await foreach (BasicRelationship basicRelationship in basicRelationshipAsyncPageable)
{
    basicRelationshipList.Add(basicRelationship);
}
```

Figure 11.42 Retrieving the list of outgoing relationships of the source digital twin

```
Response response = await digitalTwinsClient.DeleteRelationshipAsync(
        digitalTwinId: sourceId,
        relationshipId: relationshipId);
```

Figure 11.43 Deleting a digital twin relationship from the source digital twin

Get outgoing relationships

The prerequisites to get the list of outgoing relationships are an instance of the *DigitalTwinsClient* class and the *source twin ID* in a *String* variable. The *GetRelationshipsAsync* method is used to get the list of outgoing relationships asynchronously. The result of this method will return an instance of the *AsyncPageable* class with the *BasicRelationship* type. By using *await, foreach* and iterator, developers can extract *BasicRelationship* classes. Figure 11.42 shows how to retrieve a list of outgoing relationships using an iterator and then add them to a *List* class.

Delete

The prerequisites to delete a relationship are an instance of the *DigitalTwinsClient* class, the *source twin ID*, *relationship ID* in a *String* variable. The *DeleteRelationshipAsync* method is used to delete a relationship asynchronously. The result of this method will return an instance of the *Response* class. Figure 11.43 shows how to delete a relationship from a source digital twin.

11.4.2.5 Query

This section will discuss custom database query language and capabilities for querying digital twins and relationships in the digital twin graph to extract information on data and structures using the ADT query language in an ADT instance. The query language allows developers to extract data and structures based on data and definitions, model information, incoming and outgoing relationships, properties and tag properties. The query language supports various clauses, such as *SELECT*, *FROM*, *MATCH*, *JOIN* and *WHERE*, as well as functions, operators and reserved keywords. The query operations are case sensitive for names defined in the DTDL. Also, it requires escaping the single quotation mark using a backslash. Otherwise, the query will result in an empty response with no errors. There are two main limitations in querying the twin graph are the latency of the current state and the fact that it only shows the current state of the physical system. First, the query result takes around 10 s of latency to reflect the changes made to the digital twins and relationships. If the digital twin service requires an immediate result, developers have to choose the Azure SDK as discussed earlier in the retrieving and reading contents of digital twins and relationships using data plane APIs. Second, the property field in digital twins only stores the current state of the physical system. To include historical data, the ADT instance must connect to an Azure Data Explorer cluster or any custom Function Apps that store data in a database.

The following are a few SQL queries supported, as examples.

Select all

Fetches all digital twins and associated incoming and outgoing relationships. The sample query given below is the default SQL query in the ADT Explorer.

*SELECT * FROM DIGITALTWINS*

Query by function

Fetch digital twins by property and metadata. Developers can use functions such as *ARRAY_CONTAINS*, *CONTAINS*, *ENDSWITH*, *IS_BOOL*, *IS_DEFINED*, *IS_NULL*, *IS_NUMBER*, *IS_OBJECT*, *IS_OF_MODEL*, *IS_PRIMITIVE*, *IS_STRING* and *STARTSWITH*.

The sample query given below the twin graph will show Robot digital twins with the temperature property defined with any value.

*SELECT * FROM DIGITALTWINS WHERE IS_DEFINED (temperature)*
*SELECT * FROM DIGITALTWINS T WHERE IS_NUMBER (T. temperature)*
*SELECT * FROM DIGITALTWINS WHERE IS_OF_MODEL ('dtmi:dtdl:context: Robot;1')*

Query by operator

The following operators can be used to query the twin graph. The source given below demonstrates a query by operator.

1. Comparison operators (such as equality expressions (=, !=), ordered comparison of expressions (<, >) or both ordered comparison operators and equality expressions (<=, >=)).
2. Contains operators (such as IN or NIN operators)
3. Logical operators (such as AND, OR, NOT operators)

*SELECT * FROM DIGITALTWINS T WHERE T. temperature > 0.3*
*SELECT * FROM DIGITALTWINS T WHERE T. MapProperty.Priority = 'Z k'*

Reserved Keywords

Like any other programming language, there are reserved keywords in ADT to define its core functions. Developers can use these keywords to build the query strings to fetch the digital twins and associated relationships. These keywords are 1. *ALL* 2. *AND* 3. *AS* 4. *ASC* 5. *AVG* 6. *BY* 7. *COUNT* 8. *DESC* 9. *DEVICES_JOBS*

```
AsyncPageable<BasicDigitalTwin> basicDigitalTwinAsyncPageable =
    digitalTwinsClient.QueryAsync<BasicDigitalTwin>(query);
List<BasicDigitalTwin> basicDigitalTwinList = new List<BasicDigitalTwin>();
await foreach (BasicDigitalTwin basicDigitalTwin
       in basicDigitalTwinAsyncPageable)
{
    basicDigitalTwinList.Add(basicDigitalTwin);
}
```

Figure 11.44 Querying digital twins using the Azure Digital Twins instance

10. *DEVICES_MODULES* 11. *DEVICES* 12. *ENDS_WITH* 13. *FALSE* 14. *FROM* 15. *GROUP* 16. *IN* 17. *IS_BOOL* 18. *IS_DEFINED* 19. *IS_NULL* 20. *IS_NUMBER* 21. *IS_OBJECT* 22. *IS_PRIMITIVE* 23. *IS_STRING* 24. *MAX* 25. *MIN* 26. *NOT* 27. *NOT_IN* 28. *NULL* 29. *OR* 30. *ORDER* 31. *SELECT* 32. *STARTS_WITH* 33. *SUM* 34. *TOP* 35. *TRUE* 36. *WHERE* 37. *IS_OF_MODEL.*

To query the twin graph, developers need to create a few query strings using the ADT query language. Make sure that the property values exist in the digital twins and relationships; otherwise, the twin graph will return an empty set of results or an error message if the query string is incorrect and cannot identify the properties. Then edit the query field of the twin graph and click on the *Run Query* button to fetch the result. The prerequisites for querying a digital twin are an instance of the *DigitalTwinsClient* class and a *query* in a String variable. The *QueryAsync* method can be used to query digital twins or relationships asynchronously. The result of this method will return an instance of the *AsyncPageable* class with *BasicDigitalTwin* or *BasicRelationship* types. Figure 11.44 shows how to query a digital twin instance.

11.5 Discussion and conclusion

The digital twin platforms are designed to solve challenges such as security, scalability, standardisation and cross-platform integration to provide the real-time synchronisation of states and two-way communication between physical entities and their virtual counterparts. These software platforms are available as commercial, open-source and custom, based on the code availability for core services, acceptable use and licensing provided by the vendors. The Azure cloud by Microsoft is one of the significant commercial Platform-as-a-Service platforms that provide digital twin services. The Azure cloud provides free and pay-as-you-go subscriptions and guidelines for acceptable use based on licencing to enable organisations to use Azure services based on hourly or monthly reserved rates for their basic, standard and premium pricing scales. Existing literature has suggested that Azure cloud provides low-latency and highly scalable configurations and integrated tools for accessing, transmitting, storing, analysing and visualising the digital twin services in real time for domains such as healthcare, aerospace and consumer electronics. The researchers frequently used Azure IoT to establish two-way communication between the physical entity and cloud services, Function Apps to execute specialised custom source code, Event Grid to publish and subscribe events, Storage Accounts to store structured and unstructured data objects, Azure Database services to handle SQL and No-SQL database operations, and ADT to manage models, twins and relationships in the proof-of-concept digital twin service architectures. The ADT service provides the digital twin modelling language, which is a programming language-neutral JSON-LD to create standardised models based on physical attributes, behaviours and relationships in physical entities. The Azure cloud provides the ARM and ADT core software development kits to manage Azure resources and data, and structures in each instance by using programming interfaces. The book chapter explains a step-by-step process on how to set up the development environment, model the physical entities using digital twin modelling language, manage the Azure services by using control plane and data plane programmable interfaces to develop digital twin services using the Azure cloud.

References

[1] J. Höfgen, B. Vogel-Heuser, F. Bi, *et al.*, 'Architecture of a Versatile Digital Twin with Socket-Based Communication and Azure DT', in *2023 IEEE 19th International Conference on Automation Science and Engineering (CASE)*, IEEE, 2023, pp. 1–8. doi:10.1109/CASE56687.2023.10260340.

[2] J. Pfeiffe, D. Lehner, A. Wortmann, and M. Wimmer, 'Modeling capabilities of digital twin platforms – old wine in new bottles?', *The Journal of Object Technology*, vol. 21, no. 3, p. 3:1, 2022, doi:10.5381/jot.2022.21.3.a10.

[3] Y. Zhong, B. Marteau, A. Hornback, *et al.*, 'IDTVR: A Novel Cloud Framework for an Interactive Digital Twin in Virtual Reality', in *2022 IEEE 2nd International Conference on Intelligent Reality (ICIR)*, IEEE, 2022, pp. 21–26. doi:10.1109/ICIR55739.2022.00020.

[4] Z. Zhang, J. Jiang, and X. Cheng, 'Research on Digital Twin Model of Energy Equipment', in *2022 IEEE 2nd International Conference on Power, Electronics and Computer Applications (ICPECA)*, IEEE, 2022, pp. 264–268. doi:10.1109/ICPECA53709.2022.9718834.

[5] S. Weckx, B. Meyers, J. Jordens, *et al.*, 'Development and deployment of a digital twin for monitoring of an adaptive clamping mechanism, used for high performance composite machining', *IET Collaborative Intelligent Manufacturing*, vol. 4, no. 2, pp. 112–122, 2022, doi:10.1049/cim2.12052.

[6] Z. Ni, Y. Liu, M. Karlsson, and S. Gong, 'Enabling preventive conservation of historic buildings through cloud-based digital twins: A case study in the City Theatre, Norrköping', *IEEE Access*, vol. 10, pp. 90924–90939, 2022, doi:10.1109/ACCESS.2022.3202181.

[7] T. Bilen, E. Ak, B. Bal, and B. Canberk, 'A proof of concept on digital twin-controlled WiFi core network selection for in-flight connectivity', *IEEE Communications Standards Magazine*, vol. 6, no. 3, pp. 60–68, 2022, doi:10.1109/MCOMSTD.0001.2100103.

Conclusion: the future of digital twins and their transformative impact

Digital twins (DTs) have appeared as an evolutionary and fundamental technology in the modern digital era. The DTs technologies are revolutionising operational efficiency, predictive analysis and real-time monitoring and bridging the gap between the physical and digital worlds by creating dynamic, data-driven virtual counterparts of physical systems, enabling comprehensive simulations and optimised decision-making. Across multiple sectors, including urban planning, healthcare, manufacturing and industrial operations, the adoption of DTs has enhanced efficiency, sustainability and innovation because of its ability to analyse large amounts of data, forecast future events and provide real-time insights. In other words, DTs have significantly improved competence and adaptability in complex systems in different domains. Beyond conceptualisation, evaluating the maturity levels of DTs' technologies ensures successful implementation across different domains. The development of structured DT maturity models helps organisations and industries to assess their readiness for adoption, optimise their technological investments and integrate cybersecurity safeguards. Despite DTs' advanced capabilities, they seemed a selective alternative rather than a perfect replication of physical objects and systems, particularly in high-risk sectors. Therefore, it is also crucial to recognise their inherent limitations, challenges and future opportunities. Alternatively, DTs offer immense potential; their implementation presents challenges that must be addressed to unlock their full capabilities. Covering all these aspects, the following are the conclusive key points of discussion in this book.

C.1 Digital twin maturity and implementation frameworks

Beyond conceptualisation, a key feature of DT adoption is assessing their maturity levels across different domains and applications. The development of DT maturity models is the need to have a structured framework for evaluating DT technology readiness and optimising deployment strategies. The nine-dimensional maturity model explores key architectural components such as business models, system security, data models, networks and connectivity, deployment strategies and artificial intelligence (AI) integration and provides a comprehensive framework for organisations to refine their DT strategies. By defining maturity levels and operational criteria within these parameters, organisations can systematically assess their DT capabilities and ensure alignment with industry standards. A critical insight that can be summarised is that DT maturity and implementation framework is not exclusively a technological challenge, but it also demands strategic planning, leadership, regulatory bodies and cross-functional collaboration. The success of DT adoption depends on organisations' ability to define operational strategies, align business models and prioritise security and governance frameworks that minimise risks and maximise technological benefits.

C.2 Understanding digital twin limitations and challenges

While DTs offer innovative possibilities across multiple domains, they also present fundamental limitations and challenges that must be recognised to ensure their effective deployment. One major challenge of DTs is the potential misinterpretation and misrepresentation of digital models of their real-world physical objects and systems. Despite the advanced nature of DT technology, these digital counterparts remain with limited and approximate representations rather than precise replications, occasionally overlooking specific attributes and interactions within the real-world environment. This issue becomes particularly problematic in high-risk sectors such as healthcare, where inaccuracies in predictive DT models may lead to incorrect diagnoses or ineffective treatment plans. Similarly, in smart city planning, excessive reliance on DT models can cause policymakers to misinterpret urban dynamics, leading to inefficient resource allocation. Additionally, privacy and cybersecurity concerns continue to be critical obstacles. The implementation of DTs requires wide-ranging data collection, especially in complex and sensitive systems and applications such as healthcare systems, raising concerns about surveillance and data protection. Cyber threats with DTs implementation, ranging from unauthorised access to complex data breaches. Therefore, DT's system should come up with robust security frameworks, encryption mechanisms and AI-driven cybersecurity measures to safeguard sensitive information. Furthermore, DTs rely on interoperability among different platforms and systems; therefore, achieving continuous integration across heterogeneous digital infrastructures remains a complex challenge. The cost of implementation, data accuracy requirements and continuous system updates are also among the challenges of DTs, particularly for smaller organisations and industries with limited technical capacities. Categorically, limitations of DTs implementation can be listed as:

1. **Over-reliance on virtual models**: The assumption that DTs can perfectly replicate physical models can lead to inaccuracies, overlooked flaws and potential failures in real-world applications.
2. **Data privacy and security risks**: In sectors like urban planning and healthcare, DTs require extensive data collection, raising concerns regarding privacy breaches, surveillance and cybersecurity vulnerabilities.
3. **Interoperability and standardisation**: The complexity of integrating DTs across different platforms, technologies and industries remains a critical challenge, necessitating standardised protocols for smooth communication.
4. **High implementation costs and resource requirements**: The adoption of DTs involves significant computational power, skilled personnel and financial investment, posing barriers for smaller entities.

5. **Simulation limitations**: While simulations play a key role in DT implementation, their adaptability remains constrained, particularly in dynamic and unpredictable environments.

These challenges emphasise the need for continuous collaboration between academia, industry and government to develop regulatory frameworks, address ethical concerns and ensure safe and effective DT integration.

C.3 Advancements in DT security and emerging technologies

As DTs become more interconnected, they present unprecedented security weaknesses, particularly in critical high-risk sectors such as healthcare and industrial operations. Cyber threats such as unauthorised access, system intrusions and data breaches emphasise the need for robust security solutions. Addressing cybersecurity risks requires implementing advanced technologies comparable to quantum cryptography, blockchain-enhanced security models and AI-driven anomaly detection systems. Quantum cryptography, as recommended by the National Institute of Standards and Technology (NIST), offers highly secure encryption frameworks that could redefine security protocols in DT applications across healthcare and industrial operations. Blockchain technology is an increasingly valuable asset in DT-based cybersecurity, reinforcing data integrity, identity authentication and transaction security. Integration of quantum encryption with blockchain technology can provide unparalleled security, ensuring that DT-based infrastructures remain resilient to hacking attempts. Additionally, deploying zero-trust security models, where each access request undergoes continuous authentication, reduces vulnerabilities in distributed DT systems. In addition, automated regulatory compliance tools can be implemented to facilitate adherence to policies like GDPR. Future research directions are in the direction of quantum-enabled blockchain architectures to combat emerging cyber threats and prevent unauthorised system intrusions. The decentralisation of DT ecosystems demands sophisticated Edge AI solutions capable of processing massive volumes of real-time data. Deploying zero-trust security models within DT infrastructures ensures that every access request undergoes continuous authentication, reducing security vulnerabilities in distributed systems. Addressing the security concerns is essential for building trust in DT applications and mitigating external risks.

C.4 The role of digital twins in future technological advancements

As the world progresses into the era of Industry 5.0, the role of DTs in technological advancements becomes increasingly significant. The ongoing evolution of Industry emphasises human-centric, AI-assisted manufacturing ecosystems, where DT technology plays a critical role in enhancing efficiency, customisation and sustainable production. As businesses transition towards adaptive cyber-physical systems, DTs facilitate intelligent automation, predictive maintenance and optimised resource management. Organisations deploying DTs can leverage predictive analytics, AI-powered automation and real-time data monitoring to enhance productivity and adapt to market changeability. Advanced communication technologies, including 5G, IoT-driven predictive analytics and quantum computing, will further elevate the capabilities of DTs in decision-making and real-time intelligence generation. By harnessing AI-assisted analytics, businesses can move beyond traditional automation toward collaborative AI-human workflows, where DT-driven data insights foster innovation, enhance productivity and ensure long-term sustainability.

Furthermore, DTs have become helpful in smart city planning, helping decision-makers to optimise transportation, enhance infrastructure resilience and reduce environmental impact. By integrating DT models with real-time monitoring systems, cities can forecast traffic congestion accurately, manage energy consumption efficiently and develop sustainable urban landscapes that align with global climate concerns. Moreover, advanced technologies such as blockchain integration within DT-assisted smart cities offer efficient, transparent, decentralised governance models, enabling citizens to engage in urban decision-making while ensuring data privacy and security. However, in urban planning, decision-makers over-relying on DTs may misinterpret city dynamics, leading to inefficient resource distribution. Therefore, a human-in-loop system is needed to support DT implementation more effectively. However, to fully leverage DTs in smart cities, challenges like data standardisation, cross-domain security and regulatory compliance must be addressed. Future innovations in edge computing and AI-driven optimisation will further empower public administrators to create liveable, smart cities that adapt dynamically to evolving societal needs. In addition, integration of DTs with cloud-based solutions will also make scalable implementations more accessible.

C.5 The future of digital twins: research, policy and industry collaboration

As future research directions in the DTs domain, governments, researchers and industry leaders must collaborate to refine interoperability frameworks, enhance computational efficiencies and develop standardised implementation protocols that enable seamless DT integration across diverse sectors. As DT adoption accelerates, global regulations and standardisation frameworks must evolve to ensure ethical implementation and prevent misuse. Addressing concerns about data ownership, regulatory compliance and AI governance is pivotal for fostering trustworthy DT ecosystems. While DT technology is widely incorporated in manufacturing, healthcare and smart cities, its adaptability in unconventional sectors, including agriculture, retail, environmental conservation and urban resilience strategies, highlights its broad transformative potential.

Moving forward, the widespread adoption of DTs depends on regulatory compliance, ethical implementation and standardisation efforts across industries.

Governments, researchers and business leaders must collaborate to establish interoperability frameworks, refine computational efficiencies and develop unified DT security protocols. Expanding DT applications beyond traditional sectors into agriculture, retail and environmental conservation highlights their adaptability and long-term viability. As technological advancements in AI, IoT, blockchain and quantum computing continue to evolve, DTs will shape a more connected and intelligent future. Their ability to drive digital transformation will enable organisations to optimise processes, mitigate risks and foster sustainable development across global industries. The future success of DTs hinges on their ability to evolve alongside emerging technologies such as artificial general intelligence, quantum computing, blockchain and edge computing.

In conclusion, DTs represent one of the most revolutionary technological innovations of the modern era, bridging the gap between physical and digital worlds. While challenges remain, including cybersecurity vulnerabilities, ethical concerns and integration complexities, ongoing research and interdisciplinary collaboration will boost DTs into new dimensions of human-centric innovation. As governments and organisations embrace the potential of DTs, their impact on efficiency, sustainability and technological evolution will grow exponentially, unlocking new possibilities for intelligent, data-driven ecosystems. In other words, to ensure long-term success, organisations and industries must prioritise ethical AI integration, security, interoperability and regulatory compliance. The continued evolution of DT technology, coupled with advancements in quantum computing, AI-driven simulations and blockchain security, will shape the next wave of digital transformation. By fostering collaboration between government, industry and academia, DTs can become a cornerstone for advancing human-centric innovation and digital intelligence in the years ahead.

Index

accessibility 226
accountability 143
accuracy 5–6, 26
acquisition layer 174
adaptive infrastructure management 118
additive manufacturing 214
Advanced Message Queuing Protocol (AMQP) 254–5
advanced supply chain management 226–7
agriculture 9
AI-assisted manufacturing ecosystems 317
AI-enhanced decision-making 159
Amazon Web Services (AWS) 69, 258, 260
analytical algorithms 12
analytics-based models 242
Apache Kafka 252, 254, 255
application layer 158
application programming interface (API) 4
Array schema 277–9
artificial general intelligence (AGI) 65
artificial intelligence (AI) 26, 62, 70–1, 112, 134, 144–5, 172, 181–3, 184, 190, 214, 216, 224–5, 243, 315
Arts & Humanities Research Council (AHRC) 94–5
augmented reality (AR) 72–3, 135, 214, 217, 242
automated validation of internet security protocols and applications (AVISPA) 180
automatic network guardian for electrical systems (ANGEL) 182
automobile safety 10
automotive industry 9
autonomous robots 214
AWS Command Line Interface (AWS CLI) 258
Azure cloud 260, 274
  development environment 275
    Azure from Visual Studio 276
    Azure subscription Studio 2022 275–6
  digital twin models 276
    JSON-LD DTDL models 295
    meta classes 288–95
    schemas 276–87
Azure Command Line Interface (Azure CLI)
Azure Digital Twins (ADT) 260, 274
Azure Resource Manager (ARM) library 275
Azure Resource Manager SDK (ARM SDK) 262
Azure services 295
  control plane APIs 296
    Azure Digital Twin resource 299–301
    Default Azure Credential 296–7

resource group 297–9
data plane APIs 301
Digital Twin instance 301–2
digital twins 304–9
DTDL models 302–4
query 311–13
relationships 309–11
Azure Software Development Kit (Azure SDK) 274

behaviour manager 245
benchmarking 252
big data analytics 62, 214, 217
big data technologies 68–9
big digital twin data (BDTD) sharing 180
Bitcoin 137, 155
BlackEnergy 175
blockchain 129, 161, 177–81, 184–5, 190, 217–18
digital twins and smart city 133–6
empowering smart city 132–3
infrastructure 144
layers 158
potential of digital twin technologies in smart city development 131–2
role of digital twins in creating people-centred smart city 131
smart city 137
enhanced traceability and transparency 137–8
foundation for secure and efficient smart city operations 138–9
global urbanisation trend 130
improved connectivity and efficient service management 138
overview 137
Bluetooth 29
Bosch IoT Suite 265
botnet 178
Burrows–Abadi–Needham (BAN) logic 179
business models 24, 41–2

capability 6
Capital Expenditures (CapEx) 69
ChatGPT 191
circular economy (CE) 214–15
citizen-centric services 110, 143, 159
citizen engagement 91, 146–7, 156
data-driven decision-making 95–7
foundations for virtual Bradford 92–5
city managers 172
civic engagement 162
client engagement 10
cloud computing 69, 144, 190, 217, 243
communication and protocol manager (CPM) 245
communication systems 140
complexity 229, 248
ComplexModel.json 295
composition manager 245
comprehensive analysis 172
conceptualisation 5
condition monitoring 120
connections 194
consensus mechanisms 139
conservatives 33
control charts 200
control plane APIs 296
Azure Digital Twin resource 299–301
Default Azure Credential 296–7
resource group 297–9
cost–benefit analysis 252
counterpart 4

cross-domain security 185
cultural capability 34
cultural transformation 11
customisable deployment 159
customisation, personalisation and circularity 221–2
custom platforms 266
cyberattacks 14, 175–6, 177
cyber-physical systems 214, 216
cyber physical systems (CPS) 191
cybersecurity
  enhancements 225–6, 228
  measures 145
cyber threats 317

data 241
data breaches 14, 174–5
data capture 152
data coherence 249
data collection 11–12, 62
  drones 66–7
  Internet of Things 64–5
  robotics 65–6
data-driven decision-making 95–7
data fusion 110–11
data integration 24, 110–11
data integrity 140, 143, 155
data links 4
data management 174
data manager 245
data models 26, 43–4
data plane APIs 301
  Azure Digital Twin instance 301–2
  managing digital twins 304–9
  managing DTDL models 302–4
  managing relationships 309–11
  query 311–13
data platforms 216
data preparation 44–5
data presentation 63, 72
  extended reality 72–5
  holographic communications 75–6
data privacy 31, 121–2, 141, 228
data processing 63
  artificial intelligence 70–1
  big data technologies 68–9
  cloud providers 69–70
data quality 249
data representation 44–5
data security 121–2, 141, 143, 155, 228
data sources 4
data sovereignty 162
data storage 24, 29, 45
decentralised applications (dApps) 138
decentralised autonomous organisations (DAOs) 181
decentralised decision-making 197
decentralised governance 162
decentralised identity (DID) management 158, 159
decision-making process 8, 65, 177
decision support and optimization 112
DeepLabV3 172
deployment 42–3
device-as-a-service (DaaS) 254
Device Provisioning Service (DPS) 262
digital methods 131
digital thread 218
digital transformation 11, 215
digital twin database (DTD) 193, 194
Digital Twin Definition Language (DTDL) models 262
digital twin environment (DTE) 193
Digital Twin Model Identifier (DTMI) 277

digital twinning 24
digital twins (DTs) 2, 23, 61, 107, 133, 161, 171, 214–16, 238, 315
applications in smart cities 110
efficient energy management and longevity 118–20
flood monitoring and emergency response services 117–18
intelligent infrastructure and asset maintenance 120–1
public epidemic services 115–17
smart cities management brain 110–12
transportation and traffic management 112–15
architecture 239
data requirements 241–3
key components 239–41
case studies and industry examples 223
challenges 13–14, 247
data coherence 249
data quality 249
ethics 248
interoperability 249
modelling complexities 249
privacy 248
real-time communication 248
scalability and complexity 248
security and vulnerability 248
challenges and opportunities 121, 228–30
data security and privacy 121–2
integration of variety of systems and technologies 122
intelligent infrastructure and asset maintenance 122–3
characteristics 7–8
concept 133–4
conceptualisation 25
conceptual maturity model 41–7
connection of quality control, Industry 4.0 and 198
existing quality control studies 202
quality measures 200–1
real-time monitoring framework 198–200
data collection 64–7
data presentation 72–7
data processing 68–71
defined 11–13
different architectures 243
distributed architecture 245–7
edge architecture 244–5
levels 243–4
evolution of digital twin technology 224–6
fundamental characteristic 26
historical journey 2–3
innovation 80
integration with Industry 5.0 technologies 226–8
layer 157
lifestyle 80–1
limitations and challenges 316–17
maturity and implementation frameworks 315–16
models 276
JSON-LD DTDL models 295
meta classes 288–95
schemas 276–87
platforms 249
advantages 250–1
benchmarking 252
cost–benefit analysis 252
limitations 249–50
multi-criteria decision-making 251
multi-level filtering criteria 252

- pilot testing 252
- SWOT analysis 252
- user feedback and case studies 253
- vendor evaluation 253

quantum encryption 183–4
reference architecture 27–8
research, policy and industry collaboration 318–19
security and emerging technologies 317
security by design 77–9
security threats 173
- cyberattacks 175–6
- data breaches 174–5
- other security threats 176–7

services 238–9
situational control and connected metaverse 135
sustainability 79–80
synchronisation 196
system architecture 173
taxonomy 3
- accuracy 5–6
- capability 6
- counterpart 4
- data sources and data links 4
- fidelity 6
- interface 5
- life cycle 7
- synchronisation 5
- time of creation 6–7

technological infrastructure 144–5
types of digital twin platforms 253
- commercial platforms 258–66
- custom platforms 266
- open source platforms 253–7
- virtual simulations and result prediction 134–5

digital virtualisation 195
discrete event simulation (DES) models 242
distributed architecture 245–7
distributed denial of services (DDoS) attacks 175–6
distributed ledger technology (DLT) 132
Dragonfly attack 175
drones 66–7
dynamic DTs 7–8
dynamic policy simulation 160
dynamic resource optimization 109

early warning systems 117
Eclipse Ditto 252
Eclipse Hono platform 252, 254
Eclipse Mosquitto project 254
edge AI 185
edge architecture 244–5
edge computing 144, 217
edge security 185
electric vehicles (EVs) 156
electronic health records (EHR) 239
emergency services 146
empowering patients 152
energy consumption 146
energy efficiency 219, 225, 229
energy optimization 119
energy systems 10
engineering 9
enhanced predictive maintenance 225, 227
Enum schema 279–80
EnumValue element 281–2
environmental monitoring 147, 156, 219
3Es (Environment, Economy and Experience) 79
ethics 248
Everything-as-a-Service (XaaS) 194

extended reality (XR) 72, 172, 243
  augmented reality 72–3
  mixed reality 74–5
  virtual reality 73–4

FactoryModel.json 295
Fashionistas 33
feature selection 182
federated digital twin 196
federated learning 181
feedback-driven urban planning 108–9
fidelity 6, 241
field element 286
5G networks 144, 217
fog computing 191
fostering medical research 152
fourth industrial revolution 214

gender equality 100
General Data Protection Regulation (GDPR) 141, 174
Generative AI (GenAI) 65
Geographic Information Systems (GIS) 91
geospatial schema 286–7
global collaboration layer 158
global–local inconsistency detection 182
global positioning system (GPS) 66
Google Cloud Platform (GCP) 69, 245
Google Earth 92
governance 146–7, 156
governance capability 35
government-backed initiatives 97–9
Grafana 252
grey literature 35

hash function 180
healthcare 9, 23, 26, 146, 156
  innovations 227
  planning 116
Higher Education Innovation Fund (HEIF) 97
hologram 75
human-centric and sustainable approach 220–1
human-centric manufacturing 226
humanities-led place-based research 99–101
human-machine interactions 191
Hyper Text Transfer Protocol (HTTP) 246

Identity and Access Management (IAM) 258
implementation pathway 161
Industrial Internet of Things (IIoT) 178, 214
Industry 4.0 65, 171, 181, 190–1, 214, 216
  applications and use cases 218–19
  benefits and challenges 219–20
  key components and technologies 216–18
Industry 5.0 214, 317
Influx DB 252
information exfiltration 176
information transparency 197
infrastructure longevity 119
Integrated Development Environment (IDE) 258
integration modeling 113
intelligence and awareness 197
intelligent digital twin services 196–7
intelligent infrastructure and asset maintenance 120–1, 122–3
intelligent manufacturing systems (IMS) 190

digital transformation products 191–2
digital twin and its five dimensions 192
connections 194
digital twin database 194
physical objects 193
service 194
virtual models 193
digital twin implementation layers 195
digital twin synchronisation 196
digital virtualisation 195
federated digital twin 196
intelligent digital twin services 196–7
modelling and simulation 196
information required for digital twin development 194
interconnection/connectivity 197
interface 5
Internationalised Resource Identifier (IRI) 277
Internet of Medical Things (IoMT) 172
Internet of Things (IoT) 64–5, 108, 132, 144, 172, 190, 214, 216, 238, 243
Internet of Vehicles (IoV) 180
interoperability 65, 141, 143, 156, 158, 197, 249
interplanetary file system (IPFS) 179
iTwin platform 256–7

JSON-LD DTDL models 295
ComplexModel.json 295
FactoryModel.json 295
PrimitiveModel.json 295
RobotModel.json 295

key exchange rate (KER) 183
knowledge 197

large language model (LLM) 174
last-mile delivery 67
layered blockchain infrastructure 159
leadership capability 34
lifecycle management 7, 120
lifestyle 80–1
LockerGoga 175
logistics 10

machine learning (ML) 24, 62, 112, 134, 144–5, 172, 195, 216, 224–5
magnetic resonance imaging (MRI) 66
Man-in-the-middle (MitM) attacks 176
manufacturing engineering 10
MapKey element 282
Map schema 282
MapValue element 282–5
market capability 34
master data 242
maturity models 32–5, 41–7
Maximo 265
measurement model 47–53
Message Queue Telemetry Transport (MQTT) 254–5
meta classes 288
component 291–5
interface 288–9
property 289–91
relationship 291
telemetry 291
metaverse 135
metric & logs manager 245
microservices 30
Microsoft's Azure 69, 245
MIRACL library 152
mixed reality (MR) 74–5, 172
model development 12–13
modelling complexities 249

modular digital twin ecosystem 158
MongoDB 255
multi-criteria decision-making approach (MCDM) 251
multi-level filtering criteria approach 252
multivocal literature review 35

National Aeronautical Space Administration (NASA) 3
National Institute of Standards and Technology (NIST) 317
network 240
network digital twin (NDT) system 177
networking protocols 243
network issues 250
Next-G Alliance (NGA) 82
non-fungible tokens (NFTs) 181

objectives setting 11
Object schema 285–6
Omniverse 266
online learning 182
ontologies 29
Open Platform Communications – Unified Architecture (OPC-UA) 254
open-source methods 93
open source platforms 253–7
Operating Expenses (OpEx) 69
operational capability 34
optimal utilisation 230
optimising resources 152

packet auditor 178
participatory governance 160
peer-to-peer trading 160
personalised healthcare for waste reduction 230
personalised medicine 24
physical entity 24, 240
physical environment 240
physical layer 157
physical objects (POs) 193
physical process 240
physical twin 27
physics-based models 242
pilot testing approach 252
platform as a service (PaaS) 260
platform dependence 250
PowerGrid operators 132, 175
predictive analytics 202
predictive maintenance 8, 113, 119, 120, 134
predictive modeling 111–12
PrimitiveModel.json 295
PRISMA technique 202
privacy 248
product lifecycle management and closed-loop systems 218–19
Product Security and Telecommunications Infrastructure (PSTI) Act 77
Programmable Logic Controllers (PLCs) 175
proof of authority (PoA) 181
proof-of-concept (PoC) 252
Proof of Stake (PoS) 144
property technology (PropTech) 98–9
proposed conceptual model 157
  application layer 158
  benefits 160–1
  blockchain layers 158
  digital twin layer 157
  global collaboration layer 158
  implementation pathway 161
  key features 158–60
  physical layer 157

user interface layer 158
public acceptance 142
public communication 116
public epidemic services 115–17
public transport systems 132
Python code 113–14

Qassim region 152
quality control 198, 202
quality education 100
quality measures 200–1
quantum bit error rate (qBER) 183
quantum computing 184–5
quantum cryptography 184
quantum key distribution (QKD) 183

ransomware attacks 175
Real-or-Random (ROR) model 179
real-time analytics 143
real-time communication 248
real-time data 225
real-time flood monitoring 117
real-time monitoring 111
real-time monitoring framework 198–200
Reference Architectural Model Industry 4.0 (RAMI 4.0) 31
regulatory compliance 185
remote patient monitoring 172
resilience 109–10
resource allocation 116
resource manager 245
resource networks 160
resource optimisation 141, 143, 146, 218
REvil 176
risk assessment 117–18, 120–1
risk management 10, 109–10
robotics 65–6
robotic surgery 172
RobotModel.json 295
Rogue devices 176
Royal Haskoning DHV 265

scalability 141, 160, 229, 248
schema 277
complex schema 277–86
geospatial schema 286–7
primitive schema 277
security 248
security by design 77–9
self-evolving 8
sensors 216
6G networks 217
smart agriculture 227
smart cities 228
smart cities management brain 110
applications and advantages 112
key features and functions 110–11
smart city 23, 26, 67, 130
enhanced traceability and transparency 137–8
features 109
implications for future smart city development 162–3
integrating blockchain and DT 139–42
key characteristics of a blockchain-enabled smart city 142–3
lessons learned from real-world deployments 155–6
potential for scaling and expanding model 156–7
smart contracts 132, 178, 179
smart manufacturing 25
smartness 61
digital twin 64

triquetra inside context triangle 63
software development kits (SDKs) 243, 246
software layer 172
special skillset 250
stacked sparse autoencoders (SSAE) 182
state 241
strategic capability 34
Stuxnet attack 175
Supervisory Control and Data Acquisition (SCADA) 175
supply chain 10
management 191, 238
transparency and optimisation 219
sustainability 9, 79–80, 143, 147, 156, 160, 162–3, 225, 229
Sustainable Development Goals (SDGs) 79, 92, 99–101
sustainable energy management 227
SWOT analysis 252
synchronisation 5, 240–1
layer 174
rate 241
systematic literature review (SLR) 25, 27
system integration 218
system security 42

taxonomy 3
accuracy 5–6
capability 6
counterpart 4
data sources and data links 4
fidelity 6
interface 5
life cycle 7
synchronisation 5
time of creation 6–7
technical assistance 197
technology capability 35
ThingWorx 265
3D modelling 12, 217
three-dimensional (3D) ultrasound 66
time of creation 6–7
time series data 241–2
tiny machine learning (TinyML) 185
traffic management 112–15, 145–6, 156
transactional data 242
transparency 143, 160
transportation management 112–15, 145–6
transportation systems 140, 172
transport management 156

Unity Industry 266
urban management 123–4
urban planning 9, 123–4, 172, 228
user engagement 153
user feedback approach 253
user-friendly interfaces 226
user interface layer 158
user interfaces 145
user training 13

vendor evaluation approach 253
Vinici system 66
virtual entity 24, 240
virtual environment 240
virtual models (VMs) 172, 193
virtual object 243
virtual process 240
virtual reality (VR) 73–4, 135, 172, 217, 242
Virtual Singapore project 154
virtual twins 24
visualisation tools 145

visual models 242
VMware's RabbitMQ 255
vulnerability 248

Wasserstein distance-based generative adversarial network (WaGAN) 180
waste reduction 218
white literature 35
Wi-Fi 29

Xcelerator 265

zero trust architecture 185
zero-trust security models 317
ZigBee 29
zombies 175

www.ingramcontent.com/pod-product-compliance
Lightning Source LLC
La Vergne TN
LVHW011843200926
848484LV00002B/394